Houghton
Mifflin
Harcourt

TEXAS
SCIENCE
fusion

fusion [FYOO • zhuhn] a combination of two
or more things that releases energy

This Write-In Student Edition belongs to

Raquel Emiliano

Teacher/Room

Mrs. Wood

Consulting Authors

Michael A. DiSpezio
Global Educator
North Falmouth, Massachusetts

Marjorie Frank
*Science Writer and Content-Area Reading
    Specialist*
Brooklyn, New York

Michael Heithaus
*Executive Director, School of Environment, Arts, and
    Society*
*Associate Professor, Department of Biological
    Sciences*
Florida International University
North Miami, Florida

Donna Ogle
Professor of Reading and Language
National-Louis University
Chicago, Illinois

Front Cover: *stingray* ©Jeffrey L. Rotman/Corbis; *moth* ©Millard H. Sharp/Photo Researchers, Inc.; *astronaut* ©NASA; *thermometer* ©StockImages/Alamy; *gear* ©Garry Gay/The Image Bank/Getty Images.

Back Cover: *geyser* ©Frans Lanting/Corbis; *frog* ©DLILLC/Corbis; *flask* ©Gregor Schuster/Getty Images; *rowers* ©Stockbyte/Getty Images.

Printed in the U.S.A.

ISBN   978-0-544-02550-9

3 4 5 6 7 8 9 10   0868   21 20 19 18 17 16 15 14

4500472266   BCDEFG

Texas

PROGRAM AUTHORS

Dr. Candy Dawson Boyd
Professor, School of Education
Director of Reading Programs
St. Mary's College
Moraga, California

Dr. Geneva Gay
Professor of Education
University of Washington
Seattle, Washington

Rita Geiger
Director of Social Studies and
Foreign Languages
Norman Public Schools
Norman, Oklahoma

Dr. James B. Kracht
Associate Dean for Undergraduate
Programs and Teacher Education
College of Education
Texas A&M University
College Station, Texas

Dr. Valerie Ooka Pang
Professor of Teacher Education
San Diego State University
San Diego, California

Dr. C. Frederick Risinger
Director, Professional Development
and Social Studies Education
Indiana University
Bloomington, Indiana

Sara Miranda Sanchez
Elementary and Early Childhood
Curriculum Coordinator
Albuquerque Public Schools
Albuquerque, New Mexico

CONTRIBUTING AUTHORS

Dr. Carol Berkin
Professor of History
Baruch College and the Graduate
    Center
The City University of New York
New York, New York

Lee A. Chase
Staff Development Specialist
Chesterfield County Public Schools
Chesterfield County, Virginia

Dr. Jim Cummins
Professor of Curriculum
Ontario Institute for Studies in
    Education
University of Toronto
Toronto, Canada

Dr. Allen D. Glenn
Professor and Dean Emeritus
Curriculum and Instruction
College of Education
University of Washington
Seattle, Washington

Dr. Carole L. Hahn
Professor, Educational Studies
Emory University
Atlanta, Georgia

Dr. M. Gail Hickey
Professor of Education
Indiana University-Purdue
    University
Fort Wayne, Indiana

Dr. Bonnie Meszaros
Associate Director
Center for Economic Education and
    Entrepreneurship
University of Delaware
Newark, Delaware

Editorial Offices: Glenview, Illinois • Parsippany, New Jersey • New York, New York
Sales Offices: Parsippany, New Jersey • Duluth, Georgia • Glenview, Illinois •
    Coppell, Texas • Ontario, California

www.sfsocialstudies.com

CONTENT CONSULTANTS

Catherine Deans-Barrett
World History Specialist
Northbrook, Illinois

Dr. Michael Frassetto
Studies in Religions
Independent Scholar
Chicago, Illinois

Dr. Gerald Greenfield
Hispanic-Latino Studies
History Department
University of Wisconsin, Parkside
Kenosha, Wisconsin

Dr. Jacquelyn Harrison
Texas History
The Bob Bullock Texas State History
    Museum
Austin, Texas

Dr. Frederick Hoxie
Native American Studies
University of Illinois
Champaign, Illinois

Dr. Cheryl Johnson-Odim
Dean of Liberal Arts and Sciences and
    Professor of History
African American
    History Specialist
Columbia College
Chicago, Illinois

Dr. Michael Khodarkovsky
Eastern European Studies
University of Chicago
Chicago, Illinois

Robert Moffet
U.S. History Specialist
Northbrook, Illinois

Dr. Ralph Nichols
East Asian History
University of Chicago
Chicago, Illinois

Dr. Thad Sitton
Texas History
St. Edward's University
Austin, Texas

CLASSROOM REVIEWERS

Diana Vicknair Ard
Woodlake Elementary School
St. Tammany Parish
Mandeville, Louisiana

Dr. Charlotte R. Bennett
St. John School
Newburgh, Indiana

Sharon Berenson
Freehold Learning Center
Freehold, New Jersey

Betsy Blandford
Pocahontas Elementary School
Powhatan, Virginia

Gloria Cantatore
Public School #5
West New York, New Jersey

LuAnn Curran
Westgate Elementary School
St. Petersburg, Florida

Louis De Angelo
Office of Catholic Education
Archdiocese of Philadelphia
Philadelphia, Pennsylvania

Dr. Trish Dolasinski
Paradise Valley School District
Arrowhead Elementary School
Glendale, Arizona

Dr. John R. Doyle
Director of Social Studies Curriculum
Miami-Dade County Schools
Miami, Florida

Dr. Roceal Duke
District of Columbia Public Schools
Washington, D.C.

Peggy Flanagan
Roosevelt Elementary School
Community Consolidated School
    District #64
Park Ridge, Illinois

Mary Flynn
Arrowhead Elementary School
Glendale, Arizona

Sue Gendron
Spring Branch ISD
Houston, Texas

Su Hickenbottom
Totem Falls Elementary School
Snohomish School District
Snohomish, Washington

Sally Hunter
Highland Park Elementary School
Austin ISD
Austin, Texas

Allan Jones
North Branch Public Schools
North Branch, Minnesota

Brandy Bowers Kerbow
Bettye Haun Elementary School
Plano ISD
Plano, Texas

Sandra López
PSJA Service Center
San Juan, Texas

Martha Sutton Maple
Shreve Island School
Shreveport, Louisiana

Lyn Metzger
Carpenter Elementary School
Community Consolidated School
    District #64
Park Ridge, Illinois

Marsha Munsey
Riverbend Elementary School
West Monroe, Louisiana

Christine Nixon
Warrington Elementary School
Escambia County School District
Pensacola, Florida

Liz Salinas
Supervisor
Edgewood ISD
San Antonio, Texas

Beverly Scaling
Desert Hills Elementary
Las Cruces, New Mexico

Madeleine Schmitt
St. Louis Public Schools
St. Louis, Missouri

Barbara Schwartz
Central Square Intermediate School
Central Square, New York

Ronald Snapp
North Lawrence Community Schools
Bedford, Indiana

Lesley Ann Stahl
West Side Catholic Consolidated
    School
Evansville, Indiana

Carolyn Moss Woodall
Loudoun County of Virginia Public
    Schools
Leesburg, Virginia

Suzanne Zaremba
J. B. Fisher Model School
Richmond Public Schools
Richmond, Virginia

ISBN: 0-328-01786-8

Contents

Social Studies Handbook

Let the Discovery Begin   H2

Building Citizenship Skills   H4

Building Geography Skills   H6

Building Research Skills   H16

Unit 1   A Land Called Texas

Begin with a Primary Source   2
Meet the People   4
Reading Social Studies   *Main Idea and Details*   6

Chapter 1 • The Geography of the Lone Star State 8

Lesson 1 • Texas Today   **10**
Map Adventure   *Touring Texas*   14
Map and Globe Skills   *Use an Elevation Map*   18

Lesson 2 • Don't Mess with Texas   **20**
Fact File   *You can make your home greener!*   25
BIOGRAPHY *"Lady Bird" Johnson*   27

Lesson 3 • Weather and Climate   **28**
DK Dorling Kindersley   *Extreme Weather*   34

Lesson 4 • Plants and Animals   **36**
Fact File   *Plants as Texas Symbols*   40
Literature and Social Studies   *Texas Alphabet*   41
Map Adventure   *A Journey South*   42
Fact File   *Animals Are Texas Symbols*   43
BIOGRAPHY *Isamu Taniguchi*   45
Citizen Heroes   *Solving Problems*   46
Chapter 1 Review   48

"The richness of the soil, healthfulness of climate, [nearness] to the sea, [promise] a reward which few spots on the globe could furnish."

—Stephen F. Austin
1821

Unit 1 Continued

Chapter 2 • The Natural Regions of Texas — 50

Lesson 1 • The Central Plains Region — **52**
Then and Now   Living History — 54

Lesson 2 • The Great Plains Region — **56**

Lesson 3 • The Mountains and Basins Region — **60**

Lesson 4 • The Coastal Plains Region — **64**
BIOGRAPHY John Biggers — 69
Here and There in the Western Hemisphere
     Houston and Vancouver — 70
Thinking Skills   Make Generalizations — 72
Chapter 2 Review — 74

End with a Legend   The Legend of the Bluebonnet — **76**
Unit 1 Review — **78**
Discovery Channel School   Unit 1 Project — **80**

Unit 2 Texas Long Ago

Begin with a Primary Source — 82
Meet the People — 84
Reading Social Studies   Compare and Contrast — 86

Chapter 3 • The First Texans — 88

Lesson 1 • The Earliest Texans — **90**
Research and Writing Skills   Use Reference Sources — 94

Lesson 2 • The People of the Coastal Plains — **96**
Fact File   Other Native Americans of the Coastal Plains — 99
Smithsonian Institution   Native American Artifacts — 101

Lesson 3 • People of the Mountains and Plains — **102**
Fact File   Other Native Americans of the Plains,
     Mountains, and Basins — 105
BIOGRAPHY Patrisia Gonzales — 107

Lesson 4 • Civilizations of the Western Hemisphere — **108**
Chapter 3 Review — 112

"The country . . . is as good in every respect as a man could wish for."
—Stephen F. Austin

Unit 2 Continued

Chapter 4 • Europeans Come to Texas   114

Lesson 1 • Exploration Leads to Texas   **116**
Literature and Social Studies   *Cabeza de Vaca*   119
Map Adventure   *Follow Coronado*   121
Fact File   *More Explorers in Texas*   122
BIOGRAPHY Francisco Vásquez de Coronado   124
Here and There in the Western Hemisphere
    California Exploration   125

Lesson 2 • Spaniards Settle in Texas   **126**
Map and Globe Skills   *Find Latitude and Longitude*   132
Chapter 4 Review   134

Chapter 5 • Texas Colonies and Conflicts   136

Lesson 1 • Colonists Come to Texas   **138**
Then and Now   *Mexican Independence Day*   139
Fact File   *Empresarios*   144
Citizen Heroes   *A Decision for Democracy*   146

Lesson 2 • Trouble Brews in Texas   **148**
BIOGRAPHY Stephen F. Austin   151
Chart and Graph Skills   *Compare Line and Bar Graphs*   152
Chapter 5 Review   154

End with Diary Entries   *The Diary of Mary Austin Holley*   **156**
Unit 2 Review   **158**
Discovery Channel School   *Unit 2 Project*   **160**

Unit 3 Independence and Statehood

"*Texas must be defended and liberty maintained.*"

—Sam Houston

Begin with a Primary Source   162
Meet the People   164
Reading Social Studies   *Cause and Effect*   166

Chapter 6 • The Republic of Texas   168

Lesson 1 • The Revolution Begins   **170**
BIOGRAPHY Juan Seguín   177
Research and Writing Skills
Identify Primary and Secondary Sources   178

Lesson 2 • The Battle of the Alamo   **180**
Fact File   *Leaders Inside the Alamo, 1836*   182
BIOGRAPHY Susanna Dickinson   185
Chart and Graph Skills   *Read a Time Line*   186

Lesson 3 • Victory at San Jacinto   **188**
Literature and Social Studies
    Noah Smithwick's Recollections   189
Map Adventure   *Mapping Battle Sites*   190
Then and Now   *The Lone Star Flag*   193
Fact File   *Presidents of the Republic of Texas*   194
Citizen Heroes   *Bringing Texans Together*   196
Here and There in the Western Hemisphere
    Bolivia and Independence   198
Chapter 6 Review   200

Chapter 7 • The Lone Star State   202

Lesson 1 • The Rise of the Lone Star State   **204**
BIOGRAPHY Sam Houston   211
Issues and Viewpoints   *Should Texas Become a State?*   212
Smithsonian Institution   *American Life in 1845*   214

Lesson 2 • The United States and Mexico at War   **216**
Map and Globe Skills   *Use an Inset Map*   220
Chapter 7 Review   222

End with Historical Fiction   *Angel of the Alamo*   **224**
Unit 3 Review   **226**
Discovery Channel School   *Unit 3 Project*   **228**

Unit 4 A Changing State

Begin with a Primary Source   230
Meet the People   232
Reading Social Studies   *Sequence*   234

Chapter 8 • New Challenges for Texas   236

Lesson 1 • Life on the Texas Frontier   **238**
Then and Now   *The Texas State Fair*   240

Lesson 2 • Texans and the Civil War   **242**
Thinking Skills   *Recognize Point of View*   248

Lesson 3 • War and Slavery Come to an End   **250**
Then and Now   *Juneteenth*   251
Chapter 8 Review   254

Chapter 9 • The Close of a Century   256

Lesson 1 • The Indian Wars   **258**
BIOGRAPHY *Quanah Parker*   265

Lesson 2 • The Texas Cattle Kingdom   **266**
Map Adventure   *Inspecting Texas Brands, 1879*   268
BIOGRAPHY *Charles Goodnight*   270
Here and There in the Western Hemisphere
   Cattle Ranching in Texas and Argentina   271
Citizen Heroes   *Going Beyond the Call of Duty*   272

Lesson 3 • Cattle Drives on Texas Trails   **274**
Literature and Social Studies
   I'm Going to Leave Old Texas Now   277
BIOGRAPHY *Johanna July*   279
DK Dorling Kindersley   *Cowboys and Cowgirls*   280

Lesson 4 • Railroads Reach Texas   **282**
Map and Globe Skills   *Use Map Scale*   288
Chapter 9 Review   290

End with a Poem   *Cowboy Poetry*   **292**
Unit 4 Review   **294**
Discovery Channel School   *Unit 4 Project*   **296**

"I rode the range, when it was new . . . and many a pleasant memory is mine as I hark back to the cow camps, long before barbed wire fence days."

—trail driver J. E. Pettus

Unit 5 Texas Enters the Twentieth Century

"I came to the conclusion that this . . . was the greatest place on earth for oil and gas."

—Pattillo Higgins

Begin with a Primary Source 298
Meet the People 300
Reading Social Studies   Summarize 302

Chapter 10 • The Gate Opens to Industry 304

Lesson 1 • Changes and Growth **306**
Fact File   Population Growth in Texas, 1860–1920 307
Then and Now   Children at Work 308
DK Dorling Kindersley   Inventions in the Home 310
BIOGRAPHY Elisabet Ney 311
Thinking Skills   Identify Fact and Opinion 312

Lesson 2 • Texas Gold! **314**
Map Adventure   On the News Trail 316
Chart and Graph Skills   Read a Cross Section Diagram 318
Chapter 10 Review 320

Chapter 11 • Texans at Home and Abroad 322

Lesson 1 • Troubles in Texas and Overseas **324**
BIOGRAPHY Katherine Stinson 329

Lesson 2 • The Roaring Twenties **330**
Here and There in the Western Hemisphere
    Deep Ellum and Harlem 334
Research and Writing Skills   Research on the Internet 336

Lesson 3 • Hard Times in Texas **338**
Literature and Social Studies   Dust Bowl Refugee 340
Fact File   Some Texas Heroes of World War II 342
Fact File   Texans with Tales, Tunes, and in the Visual Arts 345
BIOGRAPHY Samuel Taliaferro Rayburn 347
Citizen Heroes   Courage Under Fire 348
Map and Globe Skills   Read a Road Map 350
Chapter 11 Review 352

End with an Oral History   W. Silas Vance **354**
Unit 5 Review **356**
Discovery Channel School   Unit 5 Project **358**

Unit 6 Texas, Our Texas

Begin with a Primary Source   360
Meet the People   362
Reading Social Studies   *Draw Conclusions*   364

Chapter 12 • Modern Times in Texas   366

Lesson 1 • Moving Forward   **368**
Then and Now   *Working for Civil Rights*   369
Fact File   *Other Changing Industries in Texas*   371
Map Adventure   *Space Center Houston*   372
BIOGRAPHY Lyndon Baines Johnson   375
Smithsonian Institution   *Americans in Space*   376
Map and Globe Skills   *Read a Time Zone Map*   378

Lesson 2 • Cultural Expressions   **380**
Fact File   *Sports Stars*   384
BIOGRAPHY Lance Armstrong   387
Issues and Viewpoints   *Trade Across Borders*   388
Research and Writing Skills   *Read a Newspaper*   390
Chapter 12 Review   392

Chapter 13 • Government in Texas   394

Lesson 1 • Government for Texans   **396**
Here and There in the Western Hemisphere
   Austin and Saltillo — Sister Cities   404

Lesson 2 • Texas Citizens and Leaders   **406**
Fact File   *How to Contact Your Local and State Leaders*   408
BIOGRAPHY Barbara Jordan   411
Citizen Heroes   *Known for Honesty*   412
Research and Writing Skills   *Write Notes and Outlines*   414
Chapter 13 Review   416

End with a Song   *Texas, Our Texas*   **418**
Unit 6 Review   **420**
Discovery Channel School   *Unit 6 Project*   **422**

"The more each of us knows and understands, the better our chances are for . . . building a . . . democracy. . . ."
—Bill Moyers

Reference Guide

Atlas: World and United States   R2
Geography Terms   R16
Facts About Our Fifty States   R18
United States Documents: The Declaration of Independence   R22
Atlas: Texas   R26
Texas Governors   R31
Texas Time Line   R32
Texas Missions   R36
Flag Etiquette   R38
Texas Symbols   R40
Gazetteer   R41
Biographical Dictionary   R45
Glossary   R51
Index   R57
Credits   R71

★ BIOGRAPHY ★

"Lady Bird" Johnson   27   Quanah Parker   265
Isamu Taniguchi   45   Charles Goodnight   270
John Biggers   69   Johanna July   279
Patrisia Gonzales   107   Elisabet Ney   311
Francisco Vásquez de Coronado   124   Katherine Stinson   329
Stephen F. Austin   151   Samuel Taliaferro Rayburn   347
Juan Seguín   177   Lyndon Baines Johnson   375
Susanna Dickinson   185   Lance Armstrong   387
Sam Houston   211   Barbara Jordan   411

Maps

Locating Places 9, 51, 89, 115, 137, 169, 203, 237, 257, 305, 323, 367, 395

Texas Today 10
Texas in the Western Hemisphere 11
Texas and Its Neighbors 13
Types of Landforms 15
Texas Elevations 18
Ingleside, Texas 20
Texas Panhandle, Galveston, Leander 28
Average July Temperatures 32
Average Yearly Precipitation 32
Tyler, Monterrey 36
Central Plains Region 52
The Central Plains Region of Texas 53
Great Plains Region 56
The Great Plains Region of Texas 57
The Great Plains Region of the U.S. and Its Neighbors 57
Mountains and Basins Region 60
The Mountains and Basins Region of Texas 61
The Rocky Mountains Region of the U.S. and Its Neighbors 61
Coastal Plains Region 64
The Gulf Coastal Plains Region of the U.S. and Its Neighbors 65
The Coastal Plains Region of Texas 65
The Port City of Houston 70
The Port City of Vancouver 71
Alibates Flint Quarries National Monument 90
Routes from Beringia 91
Caddoan Mounds, Livingston 96
Native Americans in Texas 98
Ysleta, Eagle Pass 102
Native Americans: Plains, Mountains, and Basins 105
Tikal, Tenochtitlan, and Cuzco 108
Empires of the Western Hemisphere 110
Palo Duro Canyon, Galveston Island, Garcitas Creek 116
Routes of Spanish Explorers 117
California Exploration 125
Ysleta, San Antonio 126
Missions, Presidios, and Villas in Texas 128
Lines of Latitude 132
Lines of Longitude 132

Latitude and Longitude in Texas 133
San Felipe de Austin; Victoria; Dolores, Mexico 138
Location of Austin Colony 140
San Felipe de Austin; Saltillo and Mexico City, Mexico 148
Cities of the Texas Revolution 170
Early Texas Battles, 1835 171
San Antonio, Laredo 180
Texas Cities, 1836–1839 188
The Battle of San Jacinto 191
Texas and Bolivia 199
Texas Cities, 1836–1846 204
The Republic of Texas, 1836–1845 205
Ethnic Settlements, 1850 209
Guadalupe Hidalgo, Palo Alto 216
Texas in the United States in 1846 217
Palo Alto National Battlefield 220
The Battle of Palo Alto 220
New Braunfels 238
Immigration into Texas, 1865 239
Texas Cities, 1860–1865 242
Union and Confederate States, 1861–1865 245
Major Battles in Texas During the Civil War 246
Austin 250
Indian Territory 258
West Texas Indian Wars of the 1870s 261
South Texas, King Ranch 266
Texas and Argentina 271
Cattle Drive Cities 274
Texas Trailherders 276
Ft. Worth, Marshall, Childress, Clarendon 282
Railroads in Texas, 1870–1900 283
Major Railroads in Texas 288
Major Railroads Around Dallas 288
Dallas, Fort Worth, Lufkin 306
Beaumont 314
Oil Discoveries, 1918 315
Laredo, San Antonio 324
Major Allied and Central Powers, 1917 326
Dallas 330
Texas Panhandle, Hawaii 338
Road Map, Eastern Texas 351
Houston, Dallas, Austin 368
Major Oil and Natural Gas Fields, 1975 370
Time Zones of North America 378

San Antonio, Austin, Art 380
Texas Festivals 382
Austin; Washington, D.C. 396
Austin, Saltillo 405
Houston 406

Skills

Reading Social Studies
Main Idea and Details 6
Compare and Contrast 86
Cause and Effect 166
Sequence 234
Summarize 302
Draw Conclusions 364

Map and Globe Skills
Use an Elevation Map 18
Find Latitude and Longitude 132
Use an Inset Map 220
Use Map Scale 288
Read a Road Map 350
Read a Time Zone Map 378

Thinking Skills
Make Generalizations 72
Recognize Point of View 248
Identify Fact and Opinion 312

Research and Writing Skills
Use Reference Sources 94
Identify Primary and Secondary Sources 178

Research on the Internet 336
Read a Newspaper 390
Write Notes and Outlines 414

Chart and Graph Skills

Compare Line and Bar Graphs 152
Read a Time Line 186
Read a Cross Section Diagram 318

Fact File

You can make your home greener! 25
Plants as Texas Symbols 40
Animals Are Texas Symbols 43
Other Native Americans of the
    Coastal Plains 99
Other Native Americans of the Plains,
    Mountains, and Basins 105
More Explorers in Texas 122
Empresarios 144
Leaders Inside the Alamo, 1836 182
Presidents of the Republic
    of Texas 194
Population Growth in Texas,
    1860–1920 307
Some Texas Heroes of World War II 342
Texans with Tales, Tunes, and in
    the Visual Arts 345
Other Changing Industries
    in Texas 371
Sports Stars 384
How to Contact Your Local and
    State Leaders 408

Citizen Heroes

Solving Problems 46
A Decision for Democracy 146
Bringing Texans Together 196
Going Beyond the Call of Duty 272
Courage Under Fire 348
Known for Honesty 412

Issues and Viewpoints

Should Texas Become a State? 212
Trade Across Borders 388

Then and Now

Living History 54
Mexican Independence Day 139
The Lone Star Flag 193
The Texas State Fair 240
Juneteenth 251
Children at Work 308
Working for Civil Rights 369

Here and There

Houston and Vancouver 70
California Exploration 125
Bolivia and Independence 198
Cattle Ranching in Texas
    and Argentina 271
Deep Ellum and Harlem 334
Austin and Saltillo—Sister Cities 404

Literature and Social Studies

Texas Alphabet 41
Cabeza de Vaca 119
Noah Smithwick's Recollections 189
I'm Going to Leave Old Texas Now 277
"Dust Bowl Refugee" 340

Map Adventure

Touring Texas 14
A Journey South 42
Follow Coronado 121
Mapping Battle Sites 190
Inspecting Texas Brands, 1879 268
On the News Trail 316
Space Center Houston 372

Graphic Organizers

Reading Social Studies
    Main Idea and Details 6
Main Idea and Details 17
Main Idea and Details 26
Main Idea and Details 33
Main Idea and Details 44
Chapter 1 Summary 48
Main Idea and Details 55
Main Idea and Details 59
Draw Conclusions 63
Summarize 68
Chapter 2 Summary 74
Reading Social Studies
    Compare and Contrast 86
Compare and Contrast 93
Compare and Contrast 100
Compare and Contrast 106
Compare and Contrast 111
Chapter 3 Summary 112
Compare and Contrast 123
Compare and Contrast 131
Chapter 4 Summary 134
Summarize 145
Compare and Contrast 150
Chapter 5 Summary 154
Reading Social Studies
    Cause and Effect 166
Cause and Effect 176
Cause and Effect 184
Cause and Effect 195
Chapter 6 Summary 200
Cause and Effect 210
Cause and Effect 219
Chapter 7 Summary 222
Reading Social Studies
    Sequence 234
Sequence 241
Sequence 247
Sequence 253
Chapter 8 Summary 254
Sequence 264
Sequence 269
Sequence 278
Sequence 287
Chapter 9 Summary 290
Reading Social Studies
    Summarize 302
Summarize 309
Summarize 317
Chapter 10 Summary 320
Summarize 328
Summarize 333
Summarize 346
Chapter 11 Summary 352
Reading Social Studies
    Draw Conclusions 364
Draw Conclusions 374
Draw Conclusions 386
Chapter 12 Summary 392

Draw Conclusions 403
Draw Conclusions 410
Chapter 13 Summary 416

Charts, Graphs, Diagrams, Tables, Time Lines

Meet the People Time Lines 4, 84, 164, 232, 300, 362

Chart: Four Natural Regions of Texas 72

Unit 2 Time Line 82

Chapter 3, Lesson 4 Time Line 108

Chapter 4, Lesson 1 Time Line 116, 123

Chapter 4, Lesson 2 Time Line 126, 131

Diagram: Bahia 128

Diagram: A Texas Mission 130

Chapter 4 Review Time Line 134

Chapter 5, Lesson 1 Time Line 138, 145

Chapter 5, Lesson 2 Time Line 148, 150

Line Graph: Population of Texas, 1850–2000 152

Bar Graph: Population of Texas, 1850–2000 152

Bar Graph: Populations of Texas and Louisiana, 1850–1900 153

Chapter 5 Review Time Line 154

Unit 3 Time Line 162

Chapter 6, Lesson 1 Time Line 170, 176

Chapter 6, Lesson 2 Time Line 180, 184

Time Line: The Alamo, 1836 186

Chapter 6, Lesson 3 Time Line 188, 195

Chapter 6 Review Time Line 200

Chapter 7, Lesson 1 Time Line 204, 210

Chapter 7, Lesson 2 Time Line 216, 219

Chapter 7 Review Time Line 222

Unit 4 Time Line 230

Chapter 8, Lesson 1 Time Line 238, 241

Chapter 8, Lesson 2 Time Line 242, 247

Pie Charts: Percentage of Texans Enslaved 243

Chapter 8, Lesson 3 Time Line 250, 253

Chapter 8 Review Time Line 254

Chapter 9, Lesson 1 Time Line 258, 264

Chapter 9, Lesson 2 Time Line 266, 269

Chapter 9, Lesson 3 Time Line 274, 278

Chapter 9, Lesson 4 Time Line 282, 287

Bar Graph: Six Leading Texas Industries by 1900 285

Line Graph: Population Changes in Six Texas Cities 286

Bar Graph: Texas Railroad Mileage 287

Chapter 9 Review Time Line 290

Unit 5 Time Line 298

Chapter 10, Lesson 1 Time Line 306, 309

Line Graph: Population Growth in Texas, 1860–1920 307

Chapter 10, Lesson 2 Time Line 314, 317

Diagram: Beam Pumping Unit 319

Chapter 10 Review Time Line 320

Chapter 11, Lesson 1 Time Line 324, 328

Chapter 11, Lesson 2 Time Line 330, 333

Chapter 11, Lesson 3 Time Line 338, 346

Chapter 11 Review Time Line 352

Unit 6 Time Line 360

Chapter 12, Lesson 1 Time Line 368, 374

Time Line: Space and Technology 373

Chapter 12, Lesson 2 Time Line 380, 386

Bar Graph: Ethnic Groups of Children in Texas, 2000 381

Chapter 12 Review Time Line 392

Chapter 13, Lesson 1 Time Line 396, 403

Chart: Municipal Government 398

Chart: Texas State Government 400

Chart: How a Bill Becomes a Law 402

Chapter 13 Review Time Line 416

Let the Discovery Begin

Your world can turn upside down on a roller coaster—like this one at Six Flags® Magic Mountain that has six loops and rolls. Many people experience thrills and chills every year on hundreds of roller coasters in the United States.

Make an exciting discovery of your own: Find a cool coaster in your state. The Titan is a favorite ride at Six Flags Over Texas amusement park. Towering 225 feet high, the steel coaster has an 85-mile-an-hour drop and a 120-foot dark tunnel. Let's go!

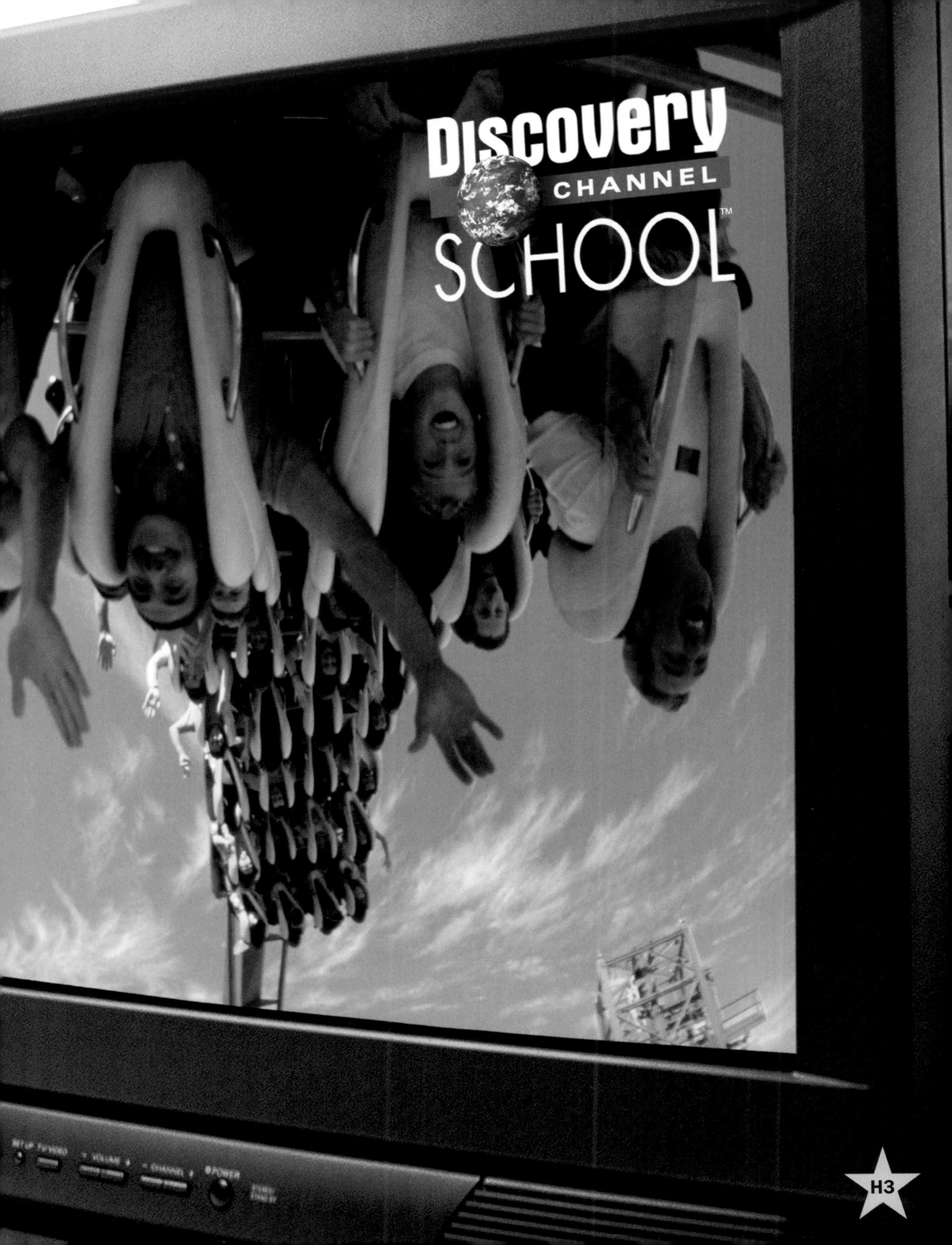
Discovery
CHANNEL
SCHOOL

Building Citizenship Skills

There are six ways to show good citizenship: through respect, fairness, caring, responsibility, courage, and honesty. In your textbook, you will learn about people who used these ways to help their community, state, and country.

Respect
Treat others as you would want to be treated. Welcome differences among people.

Fairness
Take turns and follow the rules. Listen to what other people have to say.

Caring
Think about what someone else needs.

Responsibility
Do what you are supposed to do and think before you act.

Courage
Do what is right even when the task is hard.

Honesty
Tell the truth and do what you say you will do.

★ Citizenship in Action ★

Good citizens make careful decisions. They solve problems in a logical way.
How will these students handle each situation as good citizens?

Decision Making

The students are choosing a pet for their classroom. The following steps will help them make a decision.

1. **Tell what decision you need to make.**
2. **Gather information.**
3. **List your choices.**
4. **Tell what might happen with each choice.**
5. **Act according to your decision.**

Problem Solving

Sometimes students argue at recess over whose turn it is to use a ball. The fourth graders above can use the following steps to help them solve the problem.

1. **Name the problem.**
2. **Find out more about the problem.**
3. **List ways to solve the problem.**
4. **Talk about the best way to solve the problem.**
5. **Solve the problem.**
6. **Then figure out how well the problem was solved.**

Building Geography Skills
Five Themes of Geography

Geography is the study of Earth. This study can be divided into five themes that help you understand why Earth has such a wide variety of places. Each theme reveals something different about a place, as the example of Big Bend National Park shows.

Location

Where can something be found?
Big Bend National Park is located at about 29°N, 103°W.

Place

How is this area different from others?
Big Bend has mountains, desert, and the largest river in Texas.

Human/Environment Interaction

How have people changed this place?
Sometimes the haze of air pollution keeps you from seeing long distances in the park.

Movement

How has movement changed the region? Native Americans and Spanish explorers left a rich history as they passed through.

Region

What is special about Big Bend's region? The park is in an area of Texas where the Rio Grande "bends" around dry lands.

Building Geography Skills
Map and Globe Skills Review

What Does a Globe Show?

This is an image of Earth. It lets you clearly see some of Earth's large landforms (continents) and bodies of water (oceans).

The image below shows Earth as it actually is.

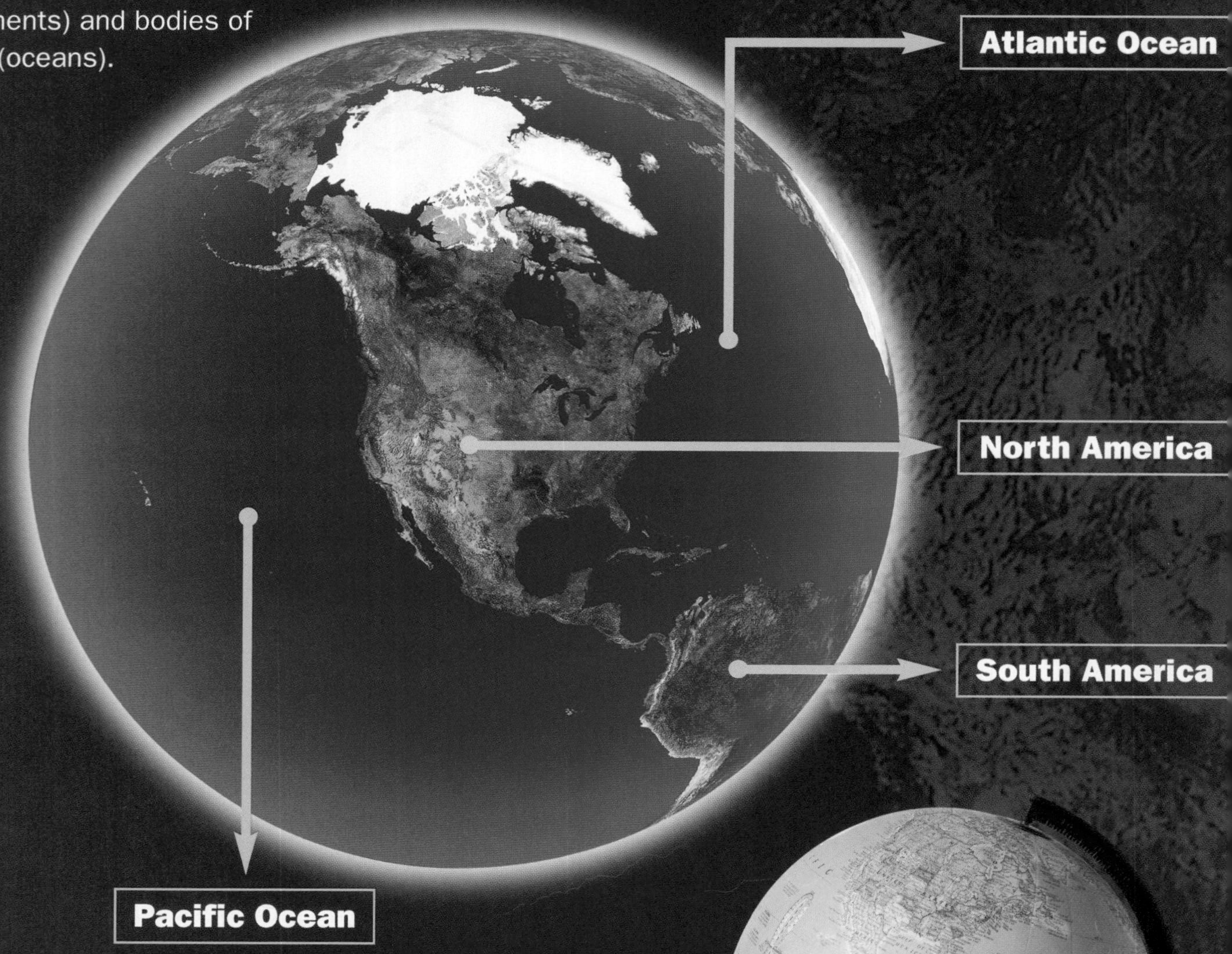
Atlantic Ocean
North America
South America
Pacific Ocean

NORTH
ATLANTIC
OCEAN

At the right is a **globe,** a small copy of Earth you can hold in your hands. It has drawings of Earth's seven continents and four oceans. Can you name the continents and oceans not shown here?

A globe also shows the two imaginary lines that divide Earth into halves—the **equator** and the **prime meridian.**

Hemispheres: Northern and Southern

As with any kind of a ball, you can see only half of Earth and a globe at a time. Half views of Earth have names—**hemispheres**—and the illustration at left below shows Earth separated into these views at the equator line. The **Northern Hemisphere** is the half north of the equator, which circles Earth halfway between the poles. However, there is only one way to see the Northern Hemisphere all at once. You have to turn a globe until you are looking down directly at the North Pole. The picture below shows that view. What are the only continents not found, at least in part, in the Northern Hemisphere?

The **Southern Hemisphere** is the half of Earth south of the equator. The picture below turns the globe until you are looking down directly at the South Pole. You see all of the Southern Hemisphere. Which hemisphere—Northern or Southern—contains more land?

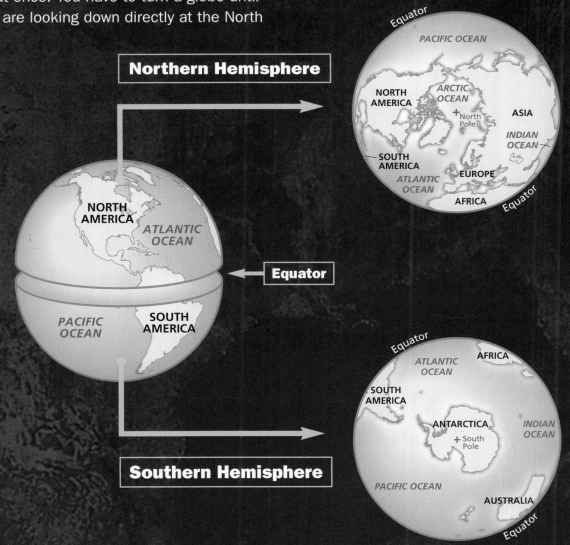

Northern Hemisphere

Equator
PACIFIC OCEAN
NORTH AMERICA
ARCTIC OCEAN
+ North Pole
ASIA
INDIAN OCEAN
SOUTH AMERICA
ATLANTIC OCEAN
EUROPE
AFRICA
Equator

NORTH AMERICA
ATLANTIC OCEAN

Equator

PACIFIC OCEAN
SOUTH AMERICA

Southern Hemisphere

Equator
ATLANTIC OCEAN
AFRICA
SOUTH AMERICA
ANTARCTICA
+ South Pole
INDIAN OCEAN
PACIFIC OCEAN
AUSTRALIA
Equator

Building Geography Skills
Map and Globe Skills Review

Hemispheres: Western and Eastern

Earth has two other hemispheres. They are formed by dividing Earth into halves a different way, along the prime meridian. The prime meridian is an imaginary line that runs from the North Pole to the South Pole. It passes through Greenwich, England, an area of London. The **Eastern Hemisphere** is the half east of the prime meridian. The prime meridian passes through which continents?

The **Western Hemisphere** is the half of Earth west of the prime meridian. Which two continents are found entirely within this hemisphere? Which of the four oceans is not found in this hemisphere? In which two hemispheres is the United States found?

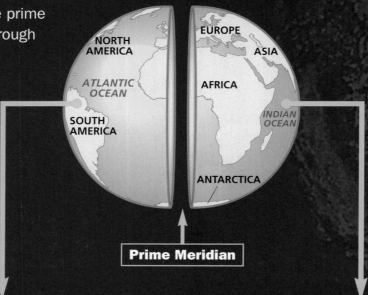

Prime Meridian

Western Hemisphere

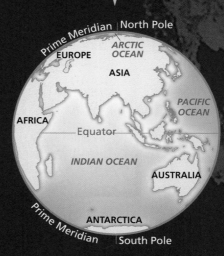

Eastern Hemisphere

Understand Latitude and Longitude

Mapmakers created a system for noting the exact location of places on Earth. The system uses two sets of imaginary circles crossing Earth. They are numbered in units called **degrees.**

Lines of **latitude** are the set of circles that go east and west. The equator is 0 degrees (0°) latitude. From there, the parallel circles go north and south. They get smaller and smaller until they end in dots at the North Pole (90°N) and the South Pole (90°S). The globe below at the left is tilted to show latitude lines 15° apart up to the North Pole. Most of the United States falls between which degrees of latitude?

Lines of **longitude** are the set of circles that go north and south. They are all the same size. The prime meridian is 0° longitude. However, from there, the degrees fan out between the North and South poles. They are not parallel and go east and west for 180°, not just 90°. The globe below at the right shows longitude lines 15° apart. They meet at 180° on the other side of Earth directly behind the prime meridian. Most of Africa falls between which degrees of longitude?

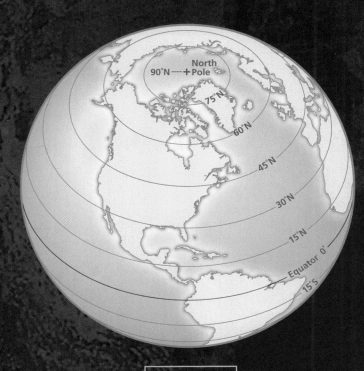

Latitude

Longitude

Use Map Features to Help Read Maps

A **title** tells what a map is about. What is the title of the map below?

A **political map** shows the location of cities, states, and countries. A **physical map** adds landforms and water such as mountains and rivers. What kind of map is on this page?

A **compass rose** is a decorative pointer that shows the four major directions, or **cardinal directions.** On the compass roses in this textbook, **north** is straight up and is marked with an N. **East** is to the right, **south** is straight down, and **west** is to the left. This compass rose also shows **intermediate directions,** which are

pointers halfway between cardinal directions. Intermediate directions are **northeast, southeast, southwest,** and **northwest.** What city is northeast of Corpus Christi?

Many maps have **symbols** in a **key** or legend. A symbol is a mark, a drawing, or color that stands for something else. What mark below shows cities with more than 1 million people?

Some maps have a **locator,** a small globe or map found in a corner. It shows where the main map is located within a larger area of Earth. Describe what you see in the locator.

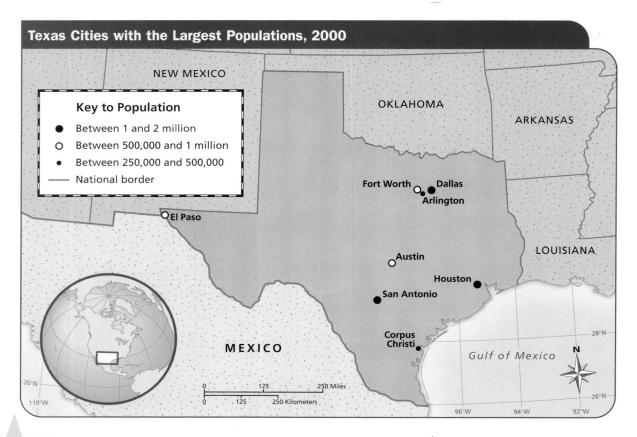

Texas Cities with the Largest Populations, 2000

Key to Population
- ● Between 1 and 2 million
- ○ Between 500,000 and 1 million
- • Between 250,000 and 500,000
- — National border

Use a Map Scale

A **scale** will help you figure out how far it is in real miles or kilometers from one point on a map to another. It can be found in a nearly empty spot to make it easier to read. Starting at 0, a scale marks off tens, hundreds, or even thousands of miles. The measurement chosen depends on the size of the area shown. One way to use the scale is to hold the edge of a scrap of paper under the scale and copy the scale onto it. Then you can place your copy directly on the map and measure the distance between two points. Use the scale on the map below to help you find out about how far it is in miles from Columbia to Harrisburg and from Victoria to Groce's Ferry.

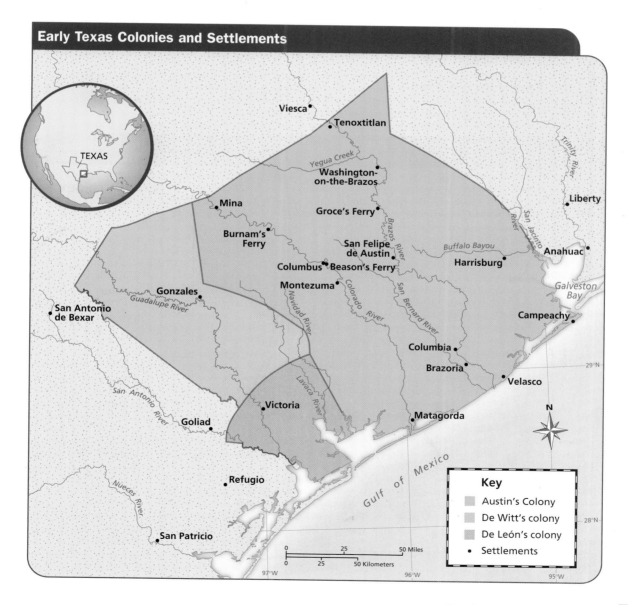

Early Texas Colonies and Settlements

Key
- Austin's Colony
- De Witt's colony
- De León's colony
- • Settlements

Building Geography Skills
Map and Globe Skills Review

Use a Grid

A city map shows the streets of a city. It might also show some points of interest to visitors or natural features such as rivers and lakes. What natural features do you see on the map of downtown San Antonio below? Point to and name a street.

This map also has a **grid.** A grid is a system of rows of imaginary squares on the map. The rows of squares are numbered and lettered along the edges of the map. You can find places where rows of numbers and letters cross. All you need is an index.

An **index** is an alphabetical listing of places you are likely to be searching for. The letter-number combination attached to each then tells you where the two rows cross. In this square, you can find the place you are looking for.

Suppose you want to find where the Tower of the Americas is. Look for "Tower of the Americas" in the Index. You'll see that it is located in D4. Find the "D" row on the map and move your finger to where the "4" row crosses it. Now find the Alamo the same way.

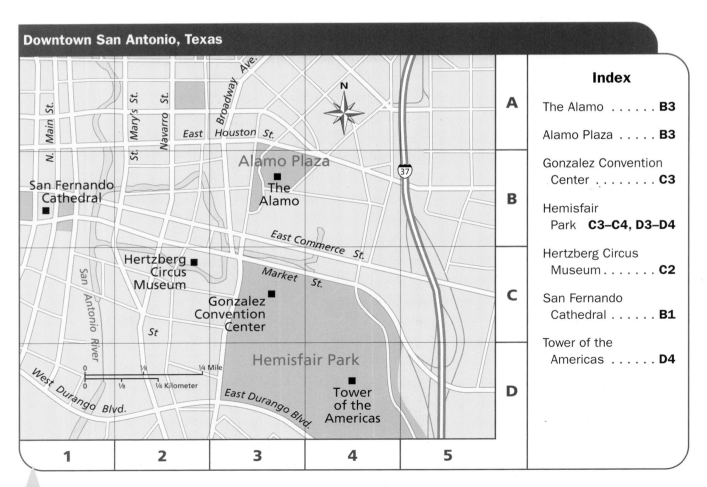

Downtown San Antonio, Texas

Index

The Alamo	**B3**
Alamo Plaza	**B3**
Gonzalez Convention Center	**C3**
Hemisfair Park	**C3–C4, D3–D4**
Hertzberg Circus Museum	**C2**
San Fernando Cathedral	**B1**
Tower of the Americas	**D4**

Use Latitude and Longitude for Exact Location

Lines of latitude and longitude are a lot like city-map grid rows. Think of latitude as the east-west rows of letters on the grid map on the opposite page. Think of longitude as the north-south rows of numbers. The point where latitude and longitude cross is an exact location. If a city or place is found at or nearly at where latitude and longitude lines cross, the city or place takes those two numbers as its exact location.

Look at the map of Texas below. The exact location of Palo Alto Battlefield is almost 26°N, 98°W. Lake Meredith National Recreation Area is almost exactly at 36°N, 102°W. What is almost exactly at 32°N, 106°W?

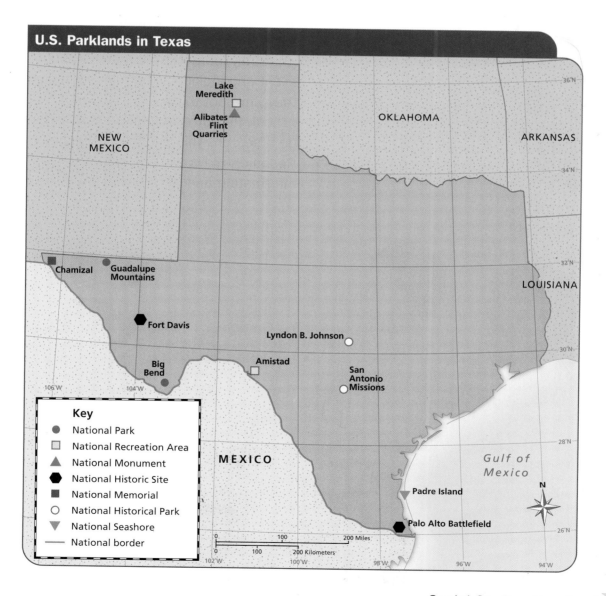

U.S. Parklands in Texas

Key
- National Park
- National Recreation Area
- National Monument
- National Historic Site
- National Memorial
- National Historical Park
- National Seashore
- National border

When you need to find information for a report or a project, you can use three main resources:

Technology Resources

Print Resources

Community Resources

The information you find can be from either primary or secondary sources. **Primary sources** are documents that were written by people who were at an event and saw it or who lived at that time. Journals, diaries, letters, and photographs are all primary sources. When you write an entry in your journal, you are creating a primary source. Items such as a concert program or a store receipt are also primary sources.

Secondary sources are descriptions of an event written by people who have researched the event. These people tell what they learned from reading about the event and looking at primary sources, but they were not there.

Look for both kinds of sources when you do research. This section of Building Research Skills will help you find information and report what you have found.

Technology Resources

There are many kinds of technology resources that you can use when you look for information. You can use the Internet, CD-ROMs, other software (such as databases), television programs, and radio programs.

The Internet is a system of linked computers that can store information for others to find and use. The World Wide Web, which is part of the Internet, has a great deal of information.

It is important to know who put the information on the Web. Check the information by finding at least three reliable sources that give similar information.

You can mark the Web sites you want to look at again. Click Bookmarks or Favorites at the top of your screen.

Search Engines

Before you turn on your computer, you need to plan your research. If you want to do research on the Rio Grande, write down some words that you can use to search the World Wide Web. The name of the river would be a good search term. The name of a town through which it passes might also be a good search term. If you have not used a search engine before, ask a friend, librarian, teacher, or parent for help.

Search by Subject To find search engines, click on SEARCH or NET SEARCH at the top of your screen. Type your key words into the search engine field. Then click SEARCH or GO.

If you can't find what you need, try a different search engine. It might be connected to a different set of information.

Search by Address World Wide Web sites have Uniform Resource Locators, or URLs. A URL is like an address. If you already know the address of a site that might have the information you need, type it in the LOCATION/GO TO box in the upper left corner of the screen. Here is an example of a URL: *http://www.sfsocialstudies.com*

Print Resources

There are many reference tools that you can use to find information. A reference tool is any source of information.

Books are reference tools. Libraries often have reference shelves with books such as atlases and almanacs, as well as dictionaries and encyclopedias. Usually, reference materials in a library cannot be checked out, but you can use them to look up information while you are at the library.

Encyclopedia

An encyclopedia is a collection of articles, listed alphabetically, on various topics. When you need information quickly, an encyclopedia is a good choice. Electronic encyclopedias, available on the Internet or CD-ROM, often have sound and video clips in addition to words.

Dictionary

A dictionary is a collection of words, their spellings, their meanings, and their pronunciations. Words in a dictionary are arranged in alphabetical order. If you hear or read a word you don't understand, you can look it up in a dictionary. Many dictionaries also include abbreviations, names, and descriptions of well-known people and places.

Atlas

An atlas is a collection of maps. Some atlases have one particular kind of map. Others have a variety of maps showing elevation, crops, population, natural resources, languages spoken, or historical developments. Teachers and librarians can help you find the type of atlas that would be best for your search.

Almanac

An almanac is a book or computer resource that lists many facts about a variety of topics. Almanacs are usually organized in sections by topic. Much information is given in charts, tables, and lists. Almanacs are usually updated every year, so they have the latest statistics on population, sports records, political events, weather, and other interesting topics.

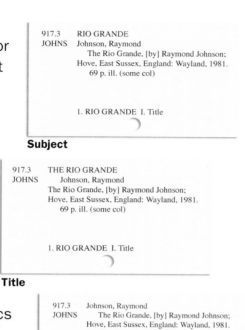

917.3 RIO GRANDE
JOHNS Johnson, Raymond
    The Rio Grande, [by] Raymond Johnson;
    Hove, East Sussex, England: Wayland, 1981.
    69 p. ill. (some col)

1. RIO GRANDE I. Title

Subject

917.3 THE RIO GRANDE
JOHNS   Johnson, Raymond
    The Rio Grande, [by] Raymond Johnson;
    Hove, East Sussex, England: Wayland, 1981.
    69 p. ill. (some col)

1. RIO GRANDE I. Title

Title

917.3 Johnson, Raymond
JOHNS   The Rio Grande, [by] Raymond Johnson;
    Hove, East Sussex, England: Wayland, 1981.
    69 p. ill. (some col)

1. RIO GRANDE I. Title

Author

Nonfiction Books

A nonfiction book is a book on a particular topic that was researched and written by someone who knows about that topic. Nonfiction books can be a valuable reference tool.

In a library, all nonfiction books are numbered and placed in order on the shelves. Books on the same subject are grouped together. Whether your library has a computer catalog or a card catalog, you can search for a book by title, subject, or author.

Once you find information on a book that looks interesting, look for the call number of the book. That number will guide you to the area of the library where you will find the book. A librarian can help you.

Periodicals

A periodical, such as a newspaper or a magazine, is published on a regular basis, usually daily, weekly, or monthly. Most libraries have a special periodical section. Many magazines and newspapers also have their own Web sites where you can read all or part of the publication on-line.

Libraries have guides that list magazine articles by subject. The *Children's Magazine Guide* and the *Readers' Guide to Periodical Literature* are the most frequently used guides. These guides list information by title, subject, and author. Each entry in the guide lists the title of the article or story, the author, the name and date of the magazine, and the page number on which the article appears. If your library has the magazine, you can find it and read the article.

Community Resources

In addition to the Internet and print resources, the people in your community are good sources of information. If you are studying the birds at Big Bend National Park, you can talk to people at government agencies, such as the Division of Wildlife Resources. Or try a local college, university, or natural history museum for information. Perhaps you know someone who has visited the park often for many years. You might want to interview that person for more information.

Interviews

An interview is a good way to find out what people in your community know. This means asking them questions about the topic you are studying. Follow these steps:

Plan ahead

- List the people you want to interview.
- Call or write to ask if you can interview them. Let the person know who you are and why you need information.
- Agree on a time and place for the interview.
- Find out about the topic that you want to discuss.
- Write down questions that you want to ask at the interview.

Ask/Listen/Record

- Ask questions clearly.
- Listen carefully. Be polite. Do not interrupt.
- Write notes so that you will remember what was said. Write down the person's actual words. If possible, use a tape recorder to help you remember.

Wrap-up

- Thank the person when you are finished with the interview.
- Send a thank-you note.

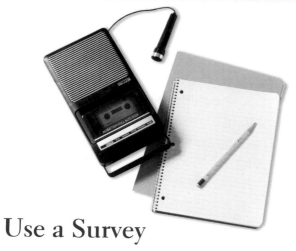

Use a Survey

Another way to find information in your community is to conduct a survey. A survey is a list of questions that you ask people, recording everyone's answers. This gives you an idea about what the people in your community know, think, or feel about a subject. You can use yes/no questions or short-answer questions. To record the things you find out, you will want to make a tally sheet with a column for each question. If you were doing research about a river that is near your town, your survey sheet might look this this:

The following steps will help you plan a survey:

- Write down a list of questions.
- Decide where you want to conduct the survey. How many people do you want to ask?
- Use a tally sheet when conducting the survey so that you can record people's answers.
- After the survey, look through the responses and summarize what you found out.

Write for Information

Another way to get information from people or organizations in your community is to e-mail or write a letter asking for information. Use these steps:

- Plan what you want to say before you write.
- Be neat and careful about spelling and punctuation.
- Tell who you are and why you are writing.
- Thank the person.

Our River

	How long have you lived in our community?	How often do you visit the river?	How has the river changed since you have been coming here?	What do you like about the river?
Person 1	30 years	Not very often— I haven't been there for years.	It seems dirtier. I hear that there are fewer fish because it's so polluted.	It's peaceful there.
Person 2	Two years	Every day	There used to be more ducks and a few geese. Now there are more geese.	I like fishing. I throw everything back, but it's relaxing to fish.

Writing a Research Report

Prewrite

- Decide on a topic for your report. Your teacher may tell you what kind of report to research and write and how long it should be.
- Write down questions that you want to find out about the topic.
- Use different sources to find information and answer your questions. Be sure to write down all your sources. This list of sources is called a **bibliography**.
- Take notes from your sources.
- Review the notes you have taken from all your sources.
- Write down the main ideas that you want to write about. Two or three ideas are enough for most reports.
- Make an outline, listing each main idea and some details about each main idea.

Write a First Draft

- Using your outline, write what you have learned, using sentences and paragraphs. Each paragraph should be about a new idea.
- When you use exact words from your sources, put them in quotation marks and write down the source from which you got the information. This list will become part of your bibliography.

Revise

- Read over your rough draft. Does it make sense? Do you need more information about any main idea?
- Change any sentences or paragraphs that do not make sense. Add anything that will make your ideas clear.
- Check your quotations to make sure they are accurate.

Edit

- Proofread your report. Correct any errors in spelling, grammar, capitalization, sentence structure, and punctuation.

Publish

- Add pictures, maps, or other graphics that will help make your report interesting.
- Write or type a final copy as neatly as possible.

A Land Called TEXAS

What is special about people and places in Texas?

"The richness of the soil, healthfulness of climate, [nearness] to the sea, [promise] a reward which few spots on the globe could furnish."

—Stephen F. Austin, 1821

Julian Onderdonk's 1912 painting, ***Bluebonnet Field,*** shows the beauty of Texas during the springtime.

Stephen Fuller Austin

1793–1836

Birthplace: southwestern Virginia

Leader of Texas settlement

- Established the first colony of United States settlers in Texas in 1821
- Founded San Felipe de Austin in 1824
- Became known as the "Father of Texas"

Roy Bedichek

1878–1959

Birthplace: Cass County, Illinois

Writer, environmentalist

- Wrote *Adventures with a Texas Naturalist* about his experiences with nature in Texas
- Encouraged responsible use of natural resources in Texas
- Director of the University Interscholastic League (UIL)

Isamu Taniguchi

1897–1992

Birthplace: Osaka, Japan

Landscape architect

- Designed and built Japanese Garden at Zilker Park in Austin as a gift to the city and to symbolize world peace
- Named Austin's Most Worthy Citizen of 1985
- Taught young students, called "Sprout Scouts," about organic gardening in Austin

Ila Loetscher

1905–2000

Birthplace: Calendar, Iowa

Turtle preservationist

- Known as the "Turtle Lady"
- Worked to bring turtle eggs from Mexico to nesting sites on South Padre Island
- Founded Sea Turtle, Inc. to protect the sea turtles and educate the public

| 1780 | 1800 | 1820 | 1840 | 1860 | 1880 |

1793 • Stephen Fuller Austin 1836

1878

For more information, go online to *Meet the People* at **www.sfsocialstudies.com**.

Claudia Taylor "Lady Bird" Johnson

1912–
Birthplace: Karnack, Texas
Conservationist
- First Lady of the United States, wife of President Lyndon B. Johnson
- Urged Congress to pass the Highway Beautification Act
- Founded the Lady Bird Johnson Wildflower Center in Austin

John Biggers

1924–2001
Birthplace: Gastonia, North Carolina
Artist, art educator in Texas
- Founded the art department at Texas Southern University in Houston in 1949
- Created murals reflecting his African American heritage
- Honored after his death with a Texas Medal of the Arts Award in 2001

Sally Kristen Ride

1951–
Birthplace: Encino, California
Astronaut
- Selected in 1978 by NASA in Houston to be a mission specialist on its space shuttle flights
- Became the first American woman on a space mission
- Member of the President's Committee of Advisors on Science and Technology

1900	1920	1940	1960	1980	2000

- Roy Bedichek — 1959
- 1897 • Isamu Taniguchi — 1992
- 1905 • Ila Loetscher — 2000
- 1912 • Claudia Taylor "Lady Bird" Johnson
- 1924 • John Biggers — 2001
- 1951 • Sally Kristen Ride

A Land Called Texas

Main Idea and Details

Knowing how to recognize main ideas will help you understand what you read.

> **A main idea is the most important thought in a paragraph or passage.**

Supporting Detail	Supporting Detail	Supporting Detail

- A main idea can be stated or unstated.
- When it is unstated, the reader must use the important details to figure out the main idea.
- The supporting details give more information about the main idea.

Read the following paragraph. The **main idea** and **details** have been highlighted.

In Chapter 1, you will read about the land called Texas. What a huge state it is! It is large enough to have many types of landforms and waterways. Mountains, deserts, and beaches all are part of Texas. The state of Texas covers more than 266,000 square miles. Of the fifty states, only Alaska is larger. Texas is almost twice the size of the country of Japan.

A Large and Varied Land

How would you describe Texas to someone who knows nothing about the state? You might begin by saying that Texas is a large and varied land. The state has hills and mountains, forests and deserts. It has plateaus and plains, caves and canyons.

Texas has four main natural regions. Each region has special qualities that make it different from the other regions. For example, some regions of Texas have level prairies and rolling hills. Other Texas regions have mountains and desert areas.

Many natural resources can be found within the four regions of Texas. These include lush forests and rich soil. Texas also has valuable minerals such as oil and natural gas.

One of the state's most important natural resources is water. In fact, water is one of the most important natural resources in the world. Most of the rivers flow above the ground, but some flow below it. Water from Texas's major rivers and streams flows into the Gulf of Mexico.

Apply it!

Use the reading strategy of finding the main idea and details to answer these questions.

1. What sentence states the main idea of the passage?

2. What details from the passage support the following main idea? *Many natural resources can be found within the four regions of Texas.*

3. What is the main idea of the last paragraph?

CHAPTER 1

The Geography of the Lone Star State

Lesson 1

Austin
People in Austin enjoy Barton Springs pool.

1

Lesson 2

Ingleside
Volunteers in Ingleside help beautify Texas.

2

Lesson 3

Texas Panhandle
Texas weather can be sizzling hot or freezing cold.

3

Lesson 4

Rio Grande Valley
Citrus fruits are grown in this part of Texas.

4

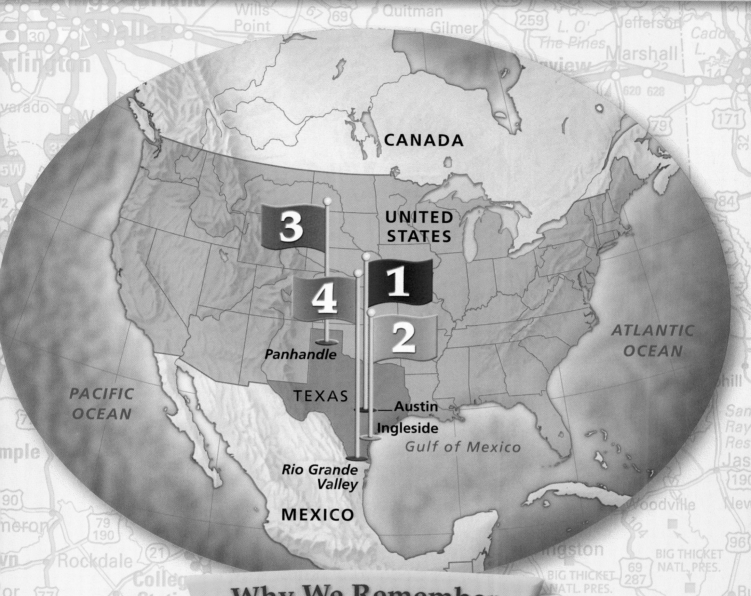

CANADA

UNITED STATES

3

4 1

2

Panhandle

PACIFIC OCEAN

TEXAS

Austin

Ingleside

ATLANTIC OCEAN

Gulf of Mexico

Rio Grande Valley

MEXICO

Why We Remember

People around the world often recognize the shape of Texas. But who can tell you about the land and its people? Texans take pride in telling about the spirit of their state. They write songs about its rivers, poems about its mountains, and stories about its wide-open spaces. They joke about the many types of Texas weather. They even have sayings about protecting its natural environment. As a Texan, you may already know a lot about your state. Soon you will read even more. This will help you understand Texas today.

TEXAS
• Austin

MEXICO

Gulf of
Mexico

PREVIEW

Focus on the Main Idea
Located on the North American continent in the Western Hemisphere, Texas has many landforms and waterways.

PLACES

Western Hemisphere
North America
Mexico
Canada
Gulf of Mexico
Guadalupe Peak
Austin

PEOPLE

Sally Ride

VOCABULARY

trade
landform
geography
escarpment
plateau
plain
waterway
aquifer
spring

Texas Today

You Are There
Get ready for a Texas adventure! You are going to learn about Texas's place in the world and what makes Texas special. Texans have a lot to brag about!

Texas is so big. What would Texas look like from a satellite 22,300 miles above Earth? You might be able to see the Texas beaches along the coast. If the satellite camera zooms in closer to Earth, you might see the mountains in western Texas, the forests, and the dry desert. There is so much to see!

Soon you'll know why Texans say, "The sun has risen. The sun has set. We still aren't out of Texas yet!"

Main Idea and Details
As you read, look for main ideas and details that tell you about Texas.

Texas in the Western Hemisphere

You live in Texas. You know that it is a big state. If you were an astronaut or a space explorer, in orbit around Earth, Texas would appear tiny from above. Astronaut Sally Ride, who has lived in Texas, orbited Earth for six days in 1983. She was a crew member aboard the space shuttle *Challenger*. Ride had this to say about her work:

"Our future lies with today's kids and tomorrow's space exploration."

▶ Sally Ride was the first American woman astronaut to fly in space.

Ride saw the entire Western Hemisphere from far above Earth. The Western Hemisphere is the western half of Earth. It contains two continents, North America and South America. North America is the continent where Texas is located. North America is also located in the Northern Hemisphere, which is the northern half of Earth.

Look at the map of the Western Hemisphere. Texas may not look very big on this map, but it is larger than all but the three largest countries in North America. It is also larger than some countries in South America. In fact, Texas is larger than more than 100 of the world's countries!

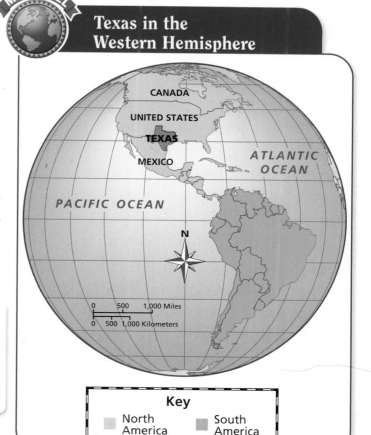

Key
North America   South America

▶ In North America, besides the United States, only Canada and Mexico are larger than Texas.

MAP SKILL Location *On what continent is Texas located?*

Notice that Texas is part of the United States. It shares a border with Mexico. It also borders the Gulf of Mexico, which is connected to the Atlantic Ocean. The location of Texas is fine for trade, the buying and selling of goods. Goods from Texas and other places in the world can be moved in and out of Texas on trains, planes, ships, or trucks.

REVIEW Name the two hemispheres in which Texas is located. ◑ **Main Idea and Details**

Texas in North America

You have read that North America is the continent where Texas is located. Look at the map on page 13. Notice that the countries that border the United States are **Mexico** and **Canada.** These neighbors have a special relationship with the United States and Texas.

Next find the states that border Texas on the map. They are Louisiana, Arkansas, Oklahoma, and New Mexico. Each of these states shares land features or waterways with Texas.

Now find a large body of water near Texas. It is the **Gulf of Mexico.** Louisiana and Texas share its waters for fishing and tourism. In fact, you will read more about a favorite vacation spot for Texans. It is an island near the Texas coast called Padre Island National Seashore. Notice that Mexico is near this island too. On the map, find areas of Mexico that border the Gulf of Mexico. Tourists from Mexico, Texas, and other places in the world visit the beaches of Mexico.

Louisiana and Arkansas border the eastern part of Texas. These state borders are heavily wooded areas. In Texas, the Big Thicket National Preserve is a dense forest near the Louisiana border. Alligators live there! These alligators are protected by national laws that limit the hunting of alligators.

North of Texas, the state of Oklahoma has rolling grasslands. Find Oklahoma on the map. Like nearby areas in Texas, Oklahoma has many farms and cattle ranches. What river separates much of Oklahoma from Texas?

Rugged mountains rise from the western part of Texas. As in other parts of Texas, you can see ranchers and horses on the range. Across the border from this area of mountains and deserts is the state of New Mexico. You will read more about how the mountains of both Texas and New Mexico extend through other parts of North America.

▶ Padre Island is one of Texas's national parklands.

▶ About 350 types of birds live in or visit the Big Thicket National Preserve each year.

▶ In West Texas, ranchers and cowhands ride the range where valleys meet mountains.

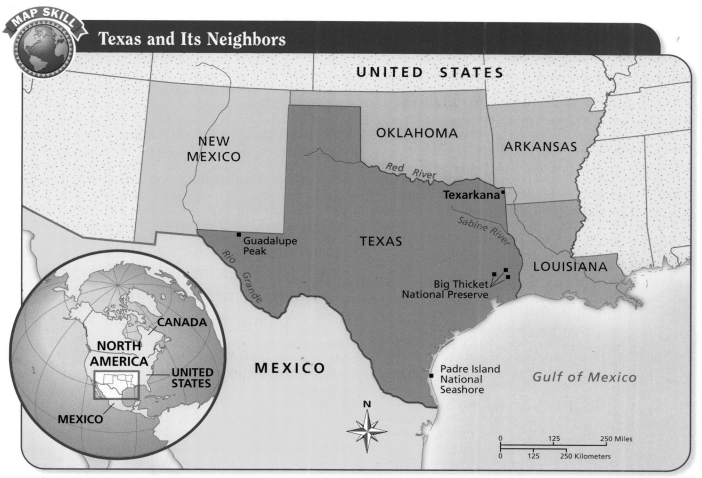

MAP SKILL

Texas and Its Neighbors

UNITED STATES

NEW MEXICO

OKLAHOMA

ARKANSAS

Red River

Texarkana

Sabine River

TEXAS

Guadalupe Peak

LOUISIANA

Big Thicket National Preserve

Rio Grande

CANADA

NORTH AMERICA

UNITED STATES

MEXICO

MEXICO

Padre Island National Seashore

Gulf of Mexico

N

0   125   250 Miles

0   125   250 Kilometers

▶ **Four states and Mexico border Texas.**

MAP SKILL Use Intermediate Directions *What direction is Arkansas from Texas?*

The tallest mountain in Texas rises above the rocky earth in the western part of Texas. It is called **Guadalupe** (gwah dul OOP ay) **Peak.** This high spot in the Texas landscape is near the New Mexico border.

Look at the map to see which river is a natural border between Texas and Mexico. It is the Rio Grande. In Units 2 and 3, you will read about a time when Texas was a part of Mexico. The Rio Grande was not a national border then.

REVIEW Name four U.S. states that border Texas. ⟳ **Main Idea and Details**

▶ **When you look out from the mountaintops in Big Bend National Park in Texas, you can see the mountains and deserts of Mexico.**

The Shape of Texas

Crunch! Have you ever nibbled a tortilla chip to make it the shape of Texas? People around the world know the shape of Texas. In fact, many people in Texas buy objects such as earrings, belt buckles, and serving bowls—all in the shape of Texas. What is so special about the shape of a state?

To begin, consider what the shape of Texas looks like to you. Does it resemble a boot topped by a cowboy hat? Perhaps you see a skillet with a "Panhandle." You might even see a spinning Texas tornado!

Next, look closely at the shape of Texas on the map below. Use your hand to measure the state from west to east. Now measure it from north to south. You might say that Texas is about as tall as it is wide.

Finally, look at the outline of Texas. Find the straight lines of the Panhandle. These lines show where people made borders with other states. Other lines in the outline are formed by natural features. For example, notice that rivers form wavy borders. Bays in the Gulf of Mexico create jagged borders.

REVIEW In what ways is the shape of Texas special? Main Idea and Details

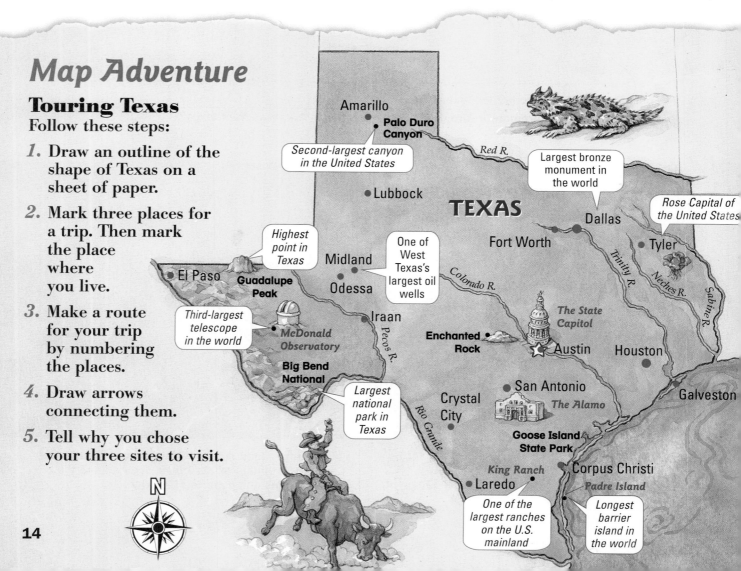

Map Adventure

Touring Texas
Follow these steps:

1. Draw an outline of the shape of Texas on a sheet of paper.

2. Mark three places for a trip. Then mark the place where you live.

3. Make a route for your trip by numbering the places.

4. Draw arrows connecting them.

5. Tell why you chose your three sites to visit.

Amarillo
Palo Duro Canyon
Second-largest canyon in the United States
Red R.
Largest bronze monument in the world
Rose Capital of the United States
Lubbock
TEXAS
Dallas
Fort Worth
Tyler
Highest point in Texas
El Paso
Guadalupe Peak
Midland
One of West Texas's largest oil wells
Odessa
Colorado R.
Trinity R.
Neches R.
Sabine R.
Third-largest telescope in the world
McDonald Observatory
Iraan
Pecos R.
Enchanted Rock
The State Capitol
Austin
Houston
Big Bend National
Largest national park in Texas
Rio Grande
Crystal City
San Antonio
The Alamo
Galveston
Goose Island State Park
King Ranch
Corpus Christi
Padre Island
Laredo
One of the largest ranches on the U.S. mainland
Longest barrier island in the world

N

14

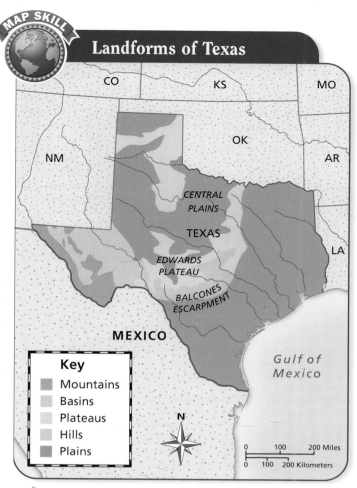

MAP SKILL

Landforms of Texas

CO   KS   MO

NM   OK   AR

CENTRAL
PLAINS

TEXAS   LA

EDWARDS
PLATEAU

BALCONES
ESCARPMENT

MEXICO

Gulf of
Mexico

Key

- ▢ Mountains
- ▢ Basins
- ▢ Plateaus
- ▢ Hills
- ▢ Plains

N

0   100   200 Miles
0   100   200 Kilometers

▶ Plains are the most common landform in Texas.

MAP SKILL Use a Landform Map *What
landform separates the Edwards Plateau from the
plains to the south?*

Landforms

Look at the map on this page. It
shows features of Earth's surface,
such as hills, mountains, and basins.
Each one is a type of **landform.** The
study of Earth's land and how people
use it is called **geography.**

You will read more about the landforms
of Texas, such as the Balcones
Escarpment. An **escarpment** is a line
of steep slopes or cliffs. You will also
read about plateaus and plains, such
as the Edwards Plateau and the Central
Plains. A **plateau** is a high, level stretch
of land. A **plain** is a large area of flat
land with gently rolling hills and few trees.

Now look at the drawing on this
page. It shows another view of types
of landforms. What types of landforms
are in your area of Texas?

REVIEW What is a landform?
⟳ **Main Idea and Details**

▶ Compare the landforms below to
their locations on the map above.

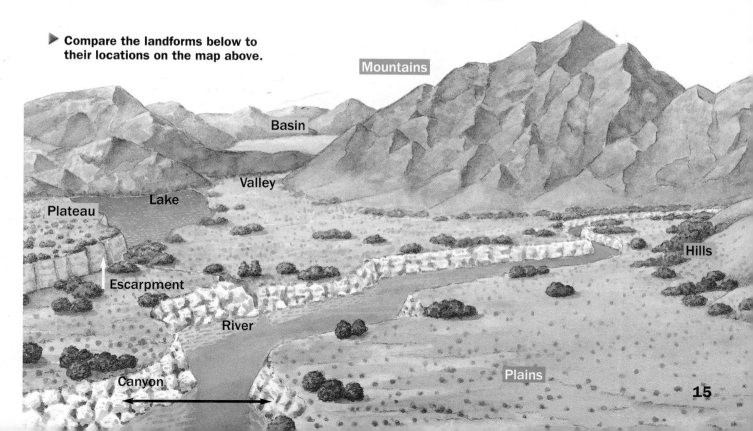

Mountains

Basin

Valley

Lake

Plateau

Hills

Escarpment

River

Canyon

Plains

15

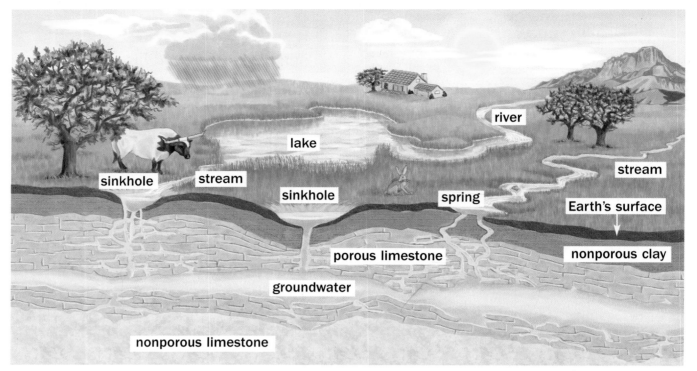

labels on diagram: river, lake, stream, sinkhole, stream, sinkhole, spring, Earth's surface, porous limestone, nonporous clay, groundwater, nonporous limestone

▶ **Porous rock, or rock through which water passes easily, surrounds the groundwater of the aquifer. Nonporous rock does not allow water to pass through easily.**

DIAGRAM SKILL *What does the diagram show beneath Earth's surface?*

Water

Like landforms, waterways form part of Earth's surface. A **waterway** is a body of water, such as a river, lake, or gulf. People often live near waterways. Homes and businesses depend on water. Waterways are also used for transportation.

Water from major Texas rivers flows into the Gulf of Mexico. Some rivers, such as the Brazos River and the Sabine River, flow directly into the Gulf. Others, such as the Red River, flow into the Mississippi River before traveling to the Gulf.

Some water in Texas is underground. Layers of rock lie under the soil in parts of Texas. In some places, this rock is limestone. In other places, it is sandstone. Streams that sink into the ground can pass through this soft rock. The water stays in the rock to form an aquifer. An **aquifer** is an underground layer of spongy rock that holds water. Sometimes this groundwater leaks out of the rocks and flows underground through openings in the rock. Find the aquifer and sources of underground water in the diagram above.

Water supplies for Texans come from a variety of sources. Some communities pump water out of aquifers for their daily use. Other people harvest, or gather, water from natural springs to drink. A **spring** is a place where underground water comes to the surface. Find an example of spring water in the diagram above.

▶ Barton Springs is a natural swimming pool in Austin. For hundreds of years, its waters have been a welcome relief in the summer heat.

Some natural springs in Texas form sparkling pools. These "swimming holes" provide an escape from hot summer temperatures. In **Austin**, for example, Barton Springs is a popular pool. Texans swim in its 68°F waters year-round.

REVIEW What is an aquifer?
⟳ **Main Idea and Details**

Summarize the Lesson

• Texas is located in the Western Hemisphere.

• Texas is located on the continent of North America.

• Texas has a relationship with Canada and Mexico, as well as with states that border Texas.

• Texas has many kinds of landforms and waterways.

★ LESSON 1   REVIEW

Check Facts and Main Ideas

1. ⟳ **Main Idea and Details** On a separate sheet of paper, complete the following Main Idea and Details chart.

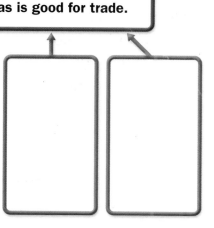

Main Idea: The location of Texas is good for trade.

Goods can easily move into and out of the state on trains, planes, ships, or trucks.

2. Describe some of the landforms and waterways in Texas.

3. How do people get water from aquifers?

4. Why do people build cities near waterways?

5. **Critical Thinking:** *Analyze Information* Why are aquifers important to Texans?

Link to 〜∞〜 Art

Draw a Special Place Think about a landform near your community. Draw a picture of you and your family there. Use a tour book or search the Internet to find more information about the place you choose.

17

Map and Globe Skills

Use an Elevation Map

What? Elevation (el uh VAY shun) is the height of land above sea level. People usually measure elevation in feet or meters. At sea level, elevation is 0 feet.

An elevation map shows the heights of land areas. Elevation maps usually can be found in atlases. The elevation map shown on this page will help you understand the geography of Texas.

You have read that Texas has a variety of landforms — mountains, basins, plateaus, hills, and plains. On the map below, the colors on the map key are used to show the ranges of height of these various landforms.

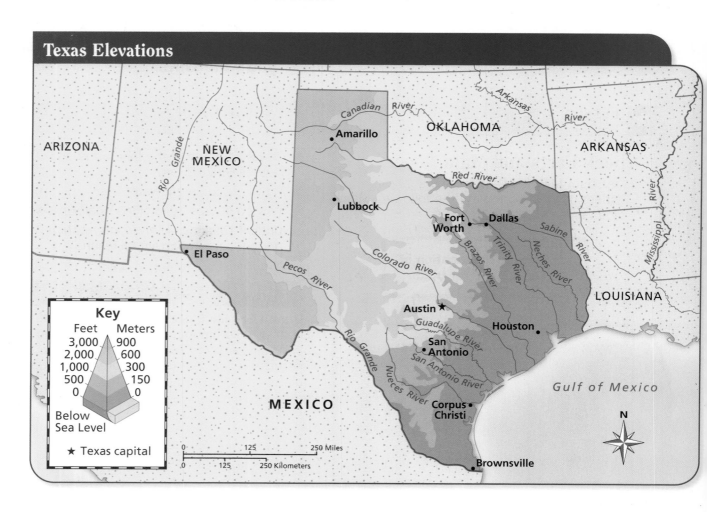

Texas Elevations

Key

Feet	Meters
3,000	900
2,000	600
1,000	300
500	150
0	0

Below Sea Level

★ Texas capital

0   125   250 Miles

0   125   250 Kilometers

Why? An elevation map helps you see the different heights of landforms. It can also show other information, such as the course of rivers. If you know that rivers flow from higher elevations to lower elevations, you can use an elevation map to determine the direction in which a river flows.

How? To use an elevation map, first scan the map. Then read the map key. Finally, compare the information in the key with the areas shown on the map.

Look at the map on page 18. Study the areas on the map. Notice how the colors change as your eyes move across the map.

Now look at the map key. Notice that the key shows elevations as blocks of color. To see what part of Texas is at sea level, first find the block of color for 0 to 500 feet elevation on the map key. You can see that the dark green color is used to show areas that are between sea level and 500 feet above sea level.

Now trace a river in Texas from its highest to its lowest elevation.

Remember that water flows downhill. Find the Colorado River on the map. The area where the Colorado River begins is orange. On the map key, this represents an elevation of more than 2,000 feet. The Colorado River begins at an elevation of more than 2,000 feet above sea level. It flows through areas of lower elevation until it reaches the Gulf of Mexico, which is at sea level.

Think and Apply

1. What is the elevation range of the light green areas of Texas?

2. What is the elevation range of Houston?

3. At what elevation range does the Pecos River enter Texas?

4. Why might you want to read an elevation map while planning a trip through the mountains of Texas?

For more information, go online to the *Atlas* at **www.sfsocialstudies.com**.

TEXAS
• Ingleside

PREVIEW

Focus on the Main Idea
Texans must work together to learn about and take care of the state's natural resources.

PLACES
Ingleside

PEOPLE
Lady Bird Johnson

VOCABULARY
environment
resource
natural resource
renewable resource
nonrenewable resource
drought
conserve
pollution
recycle

Don't Mess with Texas

You Are There You spot an old shoe partly buried in the sand. You pry the shoe loose and drop it into a large trash bag. You and your classmates are cleaning up Surfside Beach. You've joined hundreds of other volunteers who have gathered as part of the Adopt-a-Beach program.

At the end of the day, you and the other volunteers will have collected more than 16,400 pounds of trash! You're proud to help keep your state beautiful.

That evening, you and your grandmother go outside. Together, you put a bumper sticker on her car. It says "Don't mess with Texas."

Don't mess with Texas.

Main Idea and Details
As you read, look for details that support the main ideas about taking care of Texas.

▶ **If you live near the mountains of West Texas, what kinds of activities might you enjoy?**

Natural Resources

Bumper stickers, billboards, television announcements—even official state highway signs say "Don't mess with Texas." Why? It is important to take care of the environment of Texas. The word **environment** means the surroundings of living things.

People make changes to their environment. They clear land, build roads, and place dams across rivers. Yet people are also affected by their environment. It often brings enjoyment. For example, you may sail boats if you live near the Gulf of Mexico. You may climb mountains if you live in the western part of the state.

People use materials from their environment. You probably use water from a nearby source or eat plants from nearby fields and gardens. Materials that help people meet their needs are called **resources.**

Resources that come from the earth are called **natural resources.** Trees, water, minerals, and soil are examples of natural resources. How do you think these natural resources help people live?

On the next few pages, you will read more about natural resources in Texas. What can you do to protect them? Think about ways you can help.

REVIEW What do the words "Don't mess with Texas" mean to you? **Draw Conclusions**

Renewable Resources

Some natural resources can be renewed, or replaced, after they are used. These are called **renewable resources.** For example, workers may cut down trees to provide wood for building houses. They can also replace the trees by planting new ones.

Anyone who has planted a tree knows that it takes a long time for new trees to grow. People in the lumber industry most often plant new trees to replace the trees they cut down. In this way, they help protect this valuable renewable resource.

The rich soil found in parts of Texas is another renewable resource. Soil can be lost when wind and water sweep it away. Soil can be harmed when farmers plant the same crops in it year after year. This happens because each type of plant takes in certain kinds of nutrients from the soil. Nutrients are materials plants and animals need to live and grow. Over time, the plants use up the nutrients.

Most farmers know how to take special care of the soil. They may add nutrients back into the soil through fertilizers. They may also plant different types of crops on their land at different times. This helps the nutrients in the soil build up. Even so, soil renews itself very slowly.

REVIEW What causes soil to lose its nutrients? **Cause and Effect**

▶ **Even though trees grow slowly, the lumber industry works to replace trees that are harvested.**

▶ Fossil fuels cannot be replaced. Using fossil fuel resources carefully can help them last much longer.

Nonrenewable Resources

Nonrenewable resources are resources that cannot be replaced. Minerals are nonrenewable resources. Most minerals are substances that form in the ground. Texas businesses mine useful minerals, such as sulfur, uranium, and gypsum. Each of these minerals is helpful to people in some way. For example, gypsum is used to make materials for buildings. Sulfur is used to make some shampoos.

Other nonrenewable resources are fossil fuels. They come from remains of animals or plants that lived long ago. It takes millions of years for fossil fuels to form deep underground. Fossil fuels include oil, natural gas, and coal.

Fossil fuels are a source of energy that can be used to heat your home, your school, and other buildings. The gasoline used in buses, trucks, and cars is made from petroleum, a kind of fossil fuel.

Someday people may run out of fossil fuels! Where will they find power for their homes, businesses, and cars? Scientists and other experts are exploring ways to use other energy resources.

Solar energy is energy that comes from the sun. Solar energy can be used to provide power for homes, businesses, and cars. Other ways to generate power come from wind and water. How might these energy sources help with energy needs in the future?

REVIEW Why are some fuels called nonrenewable resources?

☼ **Main Idea and Details**

▶ The Rio Grande's name means "Great River." How does pollution affect the people and animals that drink its water?

Water

Water is one of the most important natural resources in the world. Texans get almost all of their water from two sources—aquifers and reservoirs. A reservoir is a place where water is collected for drinking, farming, and other uses. Most lakes in Texas are reservoirs.

Texans face many problems with their water supply. For example, people are using the water in aquifers faster than it is being replaced by rainfall. Scientists fear that some Texas aquifers may run dry.

Another problem is caused by long periods with no rain. These periods, called **droughts,** cause the water level in aquifers and reservoirs to drop. During a drought, local governments ask people to **conserve** water, or to limit its use. Families may be asked not to water lawns or wash cars.

Yet another problem, **pollution,** occurs when harmful substances enter the environment. Rain washes oil and toxins, or poisons, into rivers. People sometimes dump wastes from factories into rivers and over aquifers. This can threaten the wildlife and people that depend on the water. How do you think it affects people who drink the water?

Large cleanup projects can help with these problems. The goal of one such project is to clean up Texas's largest river, the Rio Grande. This river has become very polluted. It provides water for citizens in the United States and Mexico. People in both countries are planning together to clean up the river.

REVIEW What threatens our water resources? **Cause and Effect**

Texans Help Conserve

What do you do to conserve natural resources? Perhaps you turn off the water as you brush your teeth. Perhaps you recycle glass, plastic, cans, or paper. To **recycle** something is to use it more than once.

Recycling helps the environment in many ways. It prevents waste and saves space in landfills, or places where trash is buried. Recycling also saves energy that would be needed to produce new objects. In fact, recycling one glass bottle saves enough energy to operate a 100-watt light bulb for four hours!

Some people design "green buildings" with the environment in mind. If you could visit a "green" home, you might notice windows that catch cool breezes. You might be served a dinner cooked with solar power. Your host might water the plants with the same water used to rinse the dishes!

REVIEW How does recycling help the environment? **Summarize**

FACT FILE

You can make your home greener!

1. Don't waste water.
2. Turn off lights.
3. Buy recycled products.
4. Reuse and recycle.
5. Don't throw away broken objects. Try to fix them.
6. Use your bike or public transportation.

Texans Help Beautify

Some people, like Frances Sawyer, help keep their communities beautiful. For years, Sawyer has organized volunteers in **Ingleside.** The volunteers plant bushes and vines at the town's library.

Other citizens help keep the state's highways beautiful. Many volunteer groups have "adopted" a section of a Texas highway. They pick up wrappers, drinking cups, and cans along the roadside. Their efforts have helped clean up about 9,000 miles of Texas roads!

Lady Bird Johnson led the movement to beautify the highways of Texas and the United States. You will read about her in the biography feature on page 27.

REVIEW Name some ways in which people help keep Texas beautiful.
↪ **Main Idea and Details**

Summarize the Lesson

- **Natural resources are resources that come from the earth.**
- **Renewable resources, such as trees, can be replaced.**
- **Nonrenewable resources, such as fossil fuels, cannot be replaced.**
- **Texans face many challenges with their water supply.**

★ **LESSON 2** **REVIEW**

Check Facts and Main Ideas

1. ↪ **Main Idea and Details:** On a separate sheet of paper, complete the following Main Idea and Details chart.

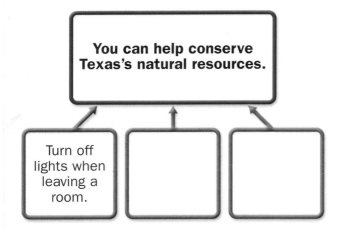

You can help conserve Texas's natural resources.

Turn off lights when leaving a room.

2. Name two renewable and two nonrenewable resources. Tell how people use them to meet basic needs.

3. What do local governments sometimes ask people to do during droughts? Explain why they do this.

4. What effect does pollution have on Texas waterways?

5. **Critical Thinking:** *Analysis* Give two examples of how people make changes to their environment. Explain why they make these changes.

Link to 🔗 **Writing**

Write a Speech Persuade students at your school to recycle materials such as paper, cans, and plastic. Read your speech aloud to a group of friends.

CLAUDIA ALTA TAYLOR
"Lady Bird" JOHNSON

1912–present

When Claudia Alta Taylor was a small child, she was nicknamed "Lady Bird." A family nurse said she was "as pretty as a lady bird."

Lady Bird learned to love nature at an early age in her hometown of Karnack. In the East Texas countryside, she searched for wild blossoms and enjoyed the crush of pine needles under her feet. She roamed the edges of Caddo Lake.

Lady Bird later married Lyndon Baines Johnson. He was our nation's 36th President. As First Lady of the United States, Mrs. Johnson drew upon her love of nature. She developed many programs to protect the beauty of the nation's roadsides and parks. She has written,

Mrs. Johnson chose a wildflower pattern for the china dishes in the White House.

"My special cause . . . is to preserve the wildflowers and native plants that define the regions of our land. . . ."

The Lady Bird Johnson Wildflower Center is located in Austin, Texas. It is a national research center.

Learn from Biographies

How do you think Lady Bird Johnson's childhood experiences helped her as First Lady?

For more information, go online to *Meet the People* at **www.sfsocialstudies.com**.

LESSON 3

TEXAS PANHANDLE

TEXAS

Leander •

Galveston

Weather and Climate

PREVIEW

Focus on the Main Idea
Texas has many types of weather, including rain, snow, tornadoes, and hurricanes.

PLACES

Galveston
Leander
Texas Panhandle

VOCABULARY

hurricane
weather
tornado
norther
blizzard
climate
temperature
precipitation

You Are There

The year is 1900. This is a true story about a terrible storm:

On a rainy, gray day in Galveston, Louise Bristol plays outside. When she sees water rising in the street, Louise scurries into her house. She does not know that a powerful hurricane is coming.

Inside, Louise sees her mother busily preparing for the storm. As the water from the hurricane rises to floor level, Louise watches in horror as her mother swings an ax into the air! *Bam!* Her mother slams the ax into the beautifully polished wood floors of their home. *Bam* again! This will prevent the house from being carried away by the flood. Soon water rushes under the front door and through the holes Mrs. Bristol has made.

Main Idea and Details
As you read, look for main ideas in each paragraph.

The Galveston Hurricane

The true story you have just read is about a fierce hurricane that struck **Galveston** in 1900. A **hurricane** is a violent storm with high winds and heavy rains. Hurricanes develop over a body of water such as an ocean or gulf. The same hurricane that hits Texas may also hit coastal towns in other states and in Mexico.

The Galveston hurricane destroyed the city and killed more than 6,000 people. More than a hundred years later, it is still considered one of the worst natural disasters in United States history.

Would such a storm cause as much damage today? It is hoped that it would not. A 17-foot-high seawall was built to help protect Galveston's houses and buildings from hurricanes.

In 1900 many people did not know to leave Galveston before the storm hit. How could this be? They did not have the communication tools of today. Nor did they have some other kinds of technology. With today's radar and other equipment, scientists can now track storms and warn about them long before they hit the coast.

A hurricane is one type of weather. **Weather** describes the air at a certain time and place. Most Texans wake up to fair weather each day. However, severe weather is always a possibility.

REVIEW Why is the 1900 Galveston hurricane considered one of the worst natural disasters in U.S. history?
🔁 **Main Idea and Details**

▶ **In 1900 the Galveston hurricane left the city in shambles.**

Severe Weather

You read that hurricanes sometimes wreck the Gulf Coast. A part of the Great Plains including west-central Texas is known as Tornado Alley. A **tornado** is a fierce and swirling funnel of wind. It is filled with rain, dust, and often hail. It may form inside thunderstorm clouds.

The winds in a tornado can lift cars off the road or blow houses off their lots. In 2000 a tornado passed through **Leander.** One resident saw parts of roofs swirling around and around in the air. She later said the tornado "sounded like a train."

During the fall and winter, other types of storms from Canada blow through northern and western parts of Texas. A **norther** is a powerful mass of cold air. These freezing blasts turn the sky a bluish-black color. Is it any wonder that Texans call them "blue northers"? They can make the temperature drop 50 degrees in just two hours!

"Blue northers" sometimes bring blizzards. A **blizzard** is a storm with high winds, snow, and ice. A severe blizzard in 1886–1887 nearly ruined the cattle industry in Texas. Many cattle froze to death.

REVIEW How are a tornado and a hurricane alike? **Compare and Contrast**

▶ West Texas tornadoes, such as this one, can leave a path of destruction.

▶ Winter in the Panhandle of Texas brings frost and ice and sometimes snow.

Climate

Texas weather does not have to be severe to change quickly. As the saying goes, "If you don't like the weather, just wait a minute."

The **climate** of an area describes weather patterns there over a long period of time. Legendary Texas writer J. Frank Dobie wrote in 1928, "A traveler who came to Texas in the 1840s described the climate as 'tropical between northers.'"

An area's location on Earth affects its climate. For example, some areas in the world are near the equator, an invisible line across the middle of the globe. These areas are among the hottest places on Earth. Countries such as Colombia and Brazil in South America and Kenya in Africa are on the equator.

Texas is not on the equator. However, Texas is closer to the equator than to the very cold areas of the Arctic and Antarctica. In general, Texas has a warm climate because it is fairly close to the equator.

The climate in Texas differs from place to place. For example, winters in the **Texas Panhandle** are colder than those in southern Texas. Which of these areas is closer to the equator?

REVIEW How does distance from the equator affect climate? **Summarize**

Temperature

Temperature is a measurement telling how hot or cold something is. What affects temperatures in Texas?

First, Texas lies fairly close to the equator, as you have read. Temperatures at the equator are the highest ones on Earth.

Second, differences among elevations cause different temperatures. You have read that elevation is the height of land above sea level.

Look at the map showing Texas temperatures below. The highest temperatures occur near lower elevations. The lowest temperatures occur in higher areas.

Third, bodies of water affect temperature. Breezes blow from the Gulf of Mexico across Texas. During the spring and summer, these breezes keep coastal areas cooler than inland areas. During the winter, however, Gulf breezes keep coastal areas warmer than inland areas. What do you think causes this to happen?

REVIEW Name three things that can affect temperature.
⟳ **Main Idea and Details**

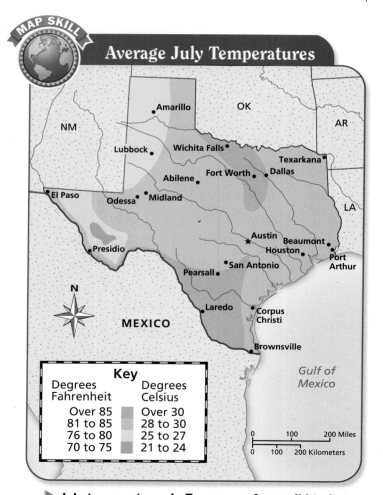

MAP SKILL Average July Temperatures

Key

Degrees Fahrenheit	Degrees Celsius
Over 85	Over 30
81 to 85	28 to 30
76 to 80	25 to 27
70 to 75	21 to 24

▶ July temperatures in Texas vary from mild to hot.

MAP SKILL Use a Map Key *Which city is hotter in July—Laredo or Lubbock?*

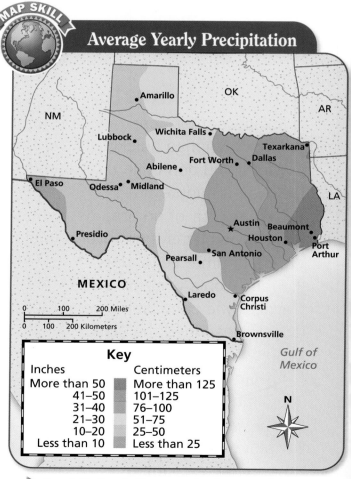

MAP SKILL Average Yearly Precipitation

Key

Inches	Centimeters
More than 50	More than 125
41–50	101–125
31–40	76–100
21–30	51–75
10–20	25–50
Less than 10	Less than 25

▶ Precipitation in Texas varies from west to east.

MAP SKILL Understand Cardinal Directions *From Dallas, would you travel east or west to find a dry climate?*

Precipitation

Too wet to plow.

That was a real gully washer.

Both are old-time sayings about precipitation. **Precipitation** is the moisture that falls to the ground. It can be in the form of rain, hail, sleet, and snow. Precipitation occurs in different amounts throughout the state.

Look at the precipitation map on page 32. It shows that, in general, the amount of precipitation increases as you go from west to east. For example, El Paso receives about 8 inches on average but Port Arthur receives about 57 inches of rainfall per year.

REVIEW What forms of precipitation fall on Texas? 🔁 **Main Idea and Details**

Summarize the Lesson

- **Texas has severe weather such as tornadoes, hurricanes, floods, and blizzards.**
- **The word *climate* refers to an area's weather patterns over a long period of time.**
- **Temperatures in Texas are affected by elevation, distance north or south, and the Gulf of Mexico.**
- **Precipitation in Texas increases from west to east.**

★ **LESSON 3**   **REVIEW**

Check Facts and Main Ideas

1. 🔁 **Main Idea and Details** On a separate sheet of paper, complete the following Main Idea and Details chart.

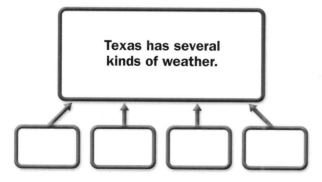

Texas has several kinds of weather.

2. How do scientists track storms along the coast today?

3. How does the climate of Texas compare with that of countries that lie along the equator?

4. How do temperature and precipitation differ in Wichita Falls and Port Arthur?

5. Critical Thinking: *Evaluate* Do you think that money should be spent on equipment to track storms, such as the hurricane in Galveston? Why do you think as you do?

Link to 🔗 **Science**

Read About Storms Choose a type of storm that interests you. Research the topic in the library or on the Internet. Draw a picture of the storm and write a paragraph to describe it.

Extreme Weather

We Texans know just how changeable the weather in our state can be. Sometimes Texas weather can be dangerous as well! Heavy Texas thunderstorms sometimes can produce balls of ice called hailstones. Hail is made when air currents in a thundercloud force lumps of ice up and down within the cloud. Each time a hailstone is forced upward, it collects another layer of ice. When the hailstones become too heavy, they fall to Earth. Even small hailstones can cause much damage. A hailstone the size of a grapefruit can be very dangerous. Hailstones 4.5 inches across have fallen in Arlington, Temple, College Station, and other parts of Texas!

Cross section of a hailstone

Ice Pack
Hailstones are made up of layers of ice. The hailstone picks up layers of ice as it travels upward through the cloud. This hailstone is one of the largest ever recorded. It is 7.5 inches across!

Corn crop destroyed by a severe hailstorm

Heavy Storm
Hailstones can be dangerous even if they are not very large. Most hailstones are the size of peas. A road covered with small hailstones can be very slippery. Large hailstones can damage property and crops. A severe hailstorm that hit central Texas and part of Mexico in May 1995 caused more than $1 billion in damage.

Hail Alley
A belt of land stretching from Texas to Montana is known as "Hail Alley." This region often has severe thunderstorms and hail. Farmers here take out insurance in case their crops are destroyed by hail.

Dangerous Driving

It can be unsafe to drive through a hailstorm. The road becomes very slick. Wind and heavy hail can also cause damage to cars and trucks. The hailstone that hit this windshield was about the size of a grapefruit and fell at a speed of more than 100 miles per hour.

Windshield shattered by a hailstone during a storm near Burlington, Colorado, in 1990

This hailstone is the size of a grapefruit.

Big Chill

Severe thunderstorms can produce huge hailstones such as this one. It is 4 inches across. In 2000, Texas had six reports of hail 4.5 inches across or larger.

Drivers park their vehicles at the side of the road as they wait for the danger to pass.

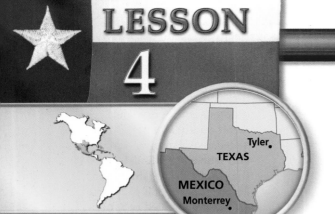

TEXAS
Tyler
MEXICO
Monterrey

PREVIEW

Focus on the Main Idea
Many different plants and animals live in Texas.

PLACES

Rio Grande Valley
Tyler
Monterrey, Mexico

PEOPLE

Roy Bedichek
Isamu Taniguchi

VOCABULARY

vegetation
natural vegetation
cultivated vegetation
sorghum
irrigation
orchard
citrus fruit
endangered
threatened

Plants and Animals

You Are There When you visit Texas places with your grandfather, you like to learn about nature. On a summer evening in Beaumont, you see a tall tree covered with large, white flowers and shiny, dark green leaves. It is a magnolia tree. The following week at your home in Goliad, you sit on the limb of a mighty oak tree. A few months later, during October, you stand beneath a tall, leafless tree near a river in Johnson City. You reach down to pick up a plump pecan. "The pecan tree is a Texas state symbol," your grandfather explains.

Then he invites you to learn about other plants of Texas. You hope he says you can eat some of them and that they taste as good as this pecan you just cracked open!

Main Idea and Details As you read, notice how the headings describe main ideas of each section.

Natural Vegetation

Dark green vines adorn white sand dunes along the beach. Pine needles glisten in a thick forest in eastern Texas. Fresh blossoms gush from spiky yucca plants in the desert of western Texas.

Many types of plants and trees, or **vegetation,** grow in Texas. Where they grow depends on climate and soil. Natural vegetation includes trees, grasses, flowers, and plants that grow without having people plant or care for them.

You have read that eastern Texas has the wettest climate in the state. This climate supports dense forests with tall trees and thick brush. In contrast, the drier western part of Texas has smaller trees and grasses that need little water. Some types of desert plants, such as cacti, grow well there.

Temperature also affects natural vegetation. You may have seen photographs of palm trees growing in warm places such as Hawaii or parts of Mexico. Palm trees also grow well in the warmer parts of Texas. You can see them waving in the breezes along the south Texas coast. They also grow along parts of the Rio Grande. But farther north, palm trees cannot survive freezing winter temperatures.

▶ Yucca blooms in the drier parts of Texas.

REVIEW How does climate affect the plants that grow in eastern Texas? in western Texas?
⟳ **Main Idea and Details**

▶ These coastal flowering vines grow along sand dunes near the Gulf of Mexico.

37

Vegetation Helps People

Roy Bedichek, a Texas naturalist, loved nature. He encouraged people to learn from nature. Like most nature lovers, Bedichek observed his surroundings. Once the sight of an old oak tree caused him to wonder:

"For how many hundreds of years [has] this shadow fallen upon that same slope at sunrise...?"

The next time you are outdoors, ask yourself questions about what you see: "What animals does this tree shelter? What kind of plant is this? Where else in the world does it grow?"

Some workers have a job that helps people enjoy vegetation. They are called landscape designers. These artists design outdoor spaces. They decide where to plant flowers and trees. In Austin, Isamu Taniguchi (ih sah moo tah nuh GOO chee) planned and built a Japanese garden. It was a gift to the people of Texas.

REVIEW How does asking questions about their surroundings help people learn about nature? **Draw Conclusions**

▶ Isamu Taniguchi's garden in Austin is open to the public.

Texas Crops

Parts of the breakfast you ate this morning may have been grown in Texas. Your toast may have been made from grain grown in the northern part of the state. Your orange juice may have come from oranges grown in the Rio Grande Valley. Crops such as these are examples of cultivated vegetation, or plants that people grow from seeds or other plant parts.

Texas has more than 205,000 farms. The major crops in Texas are cotton, wheat, corn, and grain sorghum. Sorghum is a kind of grass and grain raised as food for animals. More cotton is grown in Texas than in any other state.

▶ Cotton, a major crop in Texas, is often shipped to factories for making cloth.

▶ The Rio Grande Valley produces citrus fruits, which are then shipped to places across the country.

You may wonder how farmers grow crops in the drier parts of Texas. Farmers there have learned to give nature a helping hand. This help comes in the form of irrigation. When farmers irrigate their land, they create a system of ditches, pipes, or streams. This system transports water to their crops. The water comes from aquifers, rivers, and lakes.

Some crops come from trees. For example, the pecans in your family's favorite pecan pie may come from trees grown in Texas orchards. An orchard is a place where fruit and nut trees are grown.

Peaches grow in orchards. The Texas Hill Country is known for its delicious peaches. People travel many miles to buy peaches picked fresh from these trees.

Citrus fruits, such as grapefruit and oranges, grow on trees in the Rio Grande Valley. These popular fruits are shipped to many states. In Texas, the Texas Ruby Red grapefruit is the official state fruit.

Other produce from Texas includes peanuts, watermelons, cantaloupes, carrots, and onions. Some Texas farmers even grow flowers! Tyler is known as the Rose Capital of America. Growers there produce more than 400 varieties of roses.

REVIEW Name three crops grown in Texas. ⟳ Main Idea and Details

FACT FILE

Plants As Texas Symbols

Plants are important natural resources in Texas. Read about plants that have become symbols of our state.

State Flower

State Fruit

▶ The Texas red grapefruit was first developed by Texas citrus growers in 1929. Its bright red fruit is sweet and juicy.

▶ The bluebonnet gets its name from its blue blossoms, which look like sunbonnets.

State Tree

State Pepper

▶ Jalapeño peppers are hot in Texas! Texas ranks third in pepper production in the United States.

▶ The pecan tree earned its title of Texas State Tree in 1919. People enjoy pecans in pies, candy, and stuffing.

State Vegetable

▶ The Texas sweet onion, also called the 1015, was created by Texas growers.

Sideoats grama
Bouteloua curtipendula
Grass Family
(Poaceae)

Blooms: June–November

Range: Throughout U.S. except extreme s.e. & n.w. portions

Habitat: Prairies, grasslands & forest openings

State Grass

▶ The prickly pear cactus displays yellow, red, or purple flowers in spring and summer.

State Plant

▶ Sideoats grama provides a healthful meal for livestock. It also helps control erosion.

Mammals, Reptiles, and Birds

Texas animals come in all shapes and sizes. In the western part of the state, large mountain lions prowl on mountain ridges. Bighorn sheep graze on tender grass while horned toads scoot along the desert floor. Golden eagles soar overhead. At night, the haunting howl of a coyote breaks the silence.

Scenes such as these occur all over the state. But the mammals, reptiles, and birds vary across the regions.

In eastern Texas forests, small squirrels bury acorns in the forest floor. Deer nibble blackberries. Farther south and west, wild pigs known as javelinas gulp cacti, thorns and all. Rattlesnakes and lizards sun on rocks. On the plains, prairie dogs busily burrow in the dirt.

Texas has more types of birds— about 600—than any other state in the country. You can see white-faced ibises in swamps along the Gulf. Perhaps you have heard the call of a screech owl in your own neighborhood.

Some birds from eastern and western parts of the United States fly through Texas when migrating. It is no wonder that bird watchers come from around the world to visit Texas.

REVIEW Name one large and one small Texas animal.

Compare and Contrast

Literature and Social Studies

Many books have been written about Texas. The page below is from *Texas Alphabet,* by Laurie Parker. How many of these "m" words do you know?

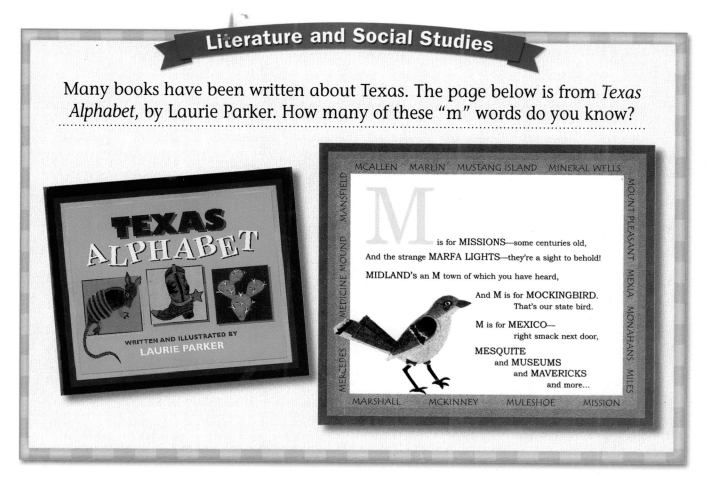

TEXAS ALPHABET
WRITTEN AND ILLUSTRATED BY LAURIE PARKER

MCALLEN   MARLIN   MUSTANG ISLAND   MINERAL WELLS

MANSFIELD
MEDICINE MOUND
MERCEDES

MOUNT PLEASANT
MEXIA
MONAHANS
MILES

M is for MISSIONS—some centuries old, And the strange MARFA LIGHTS—they're a sight to behold! MIDLAND's an M town of which you have heard,

And M is for MOCKINGBIRD. That's our state bird.

M is for MEXICO— right smack next door,

MESQUITE and MUSEUMS and MAVERICKS and more...

MARSHALL   MCKINNEY   MULESHOE   MISSION

The Monarch Migration

The monarch butterfly is the state insect. Each fall, tens of millions of adult monarchs migrate from their homes in the United States. As they journey southward toward Mexico, they flock through Texas in great numbers. Once in Monterrey, Mexico, they settle in a mountain forest to pass the winter. There the butterflies sometimes cover whole trees. These trees become shimmering sculptures of orange and black! In the spring the butterflies begin the long journey back north. Along the way, females lay eggs on milkweed plants and then die. Their offspring complete the journey. They return to the same places their parents left. Then the cycle begins again.

REVIEW At what time of year do the monarchs arrive in Mexico?
Sequence

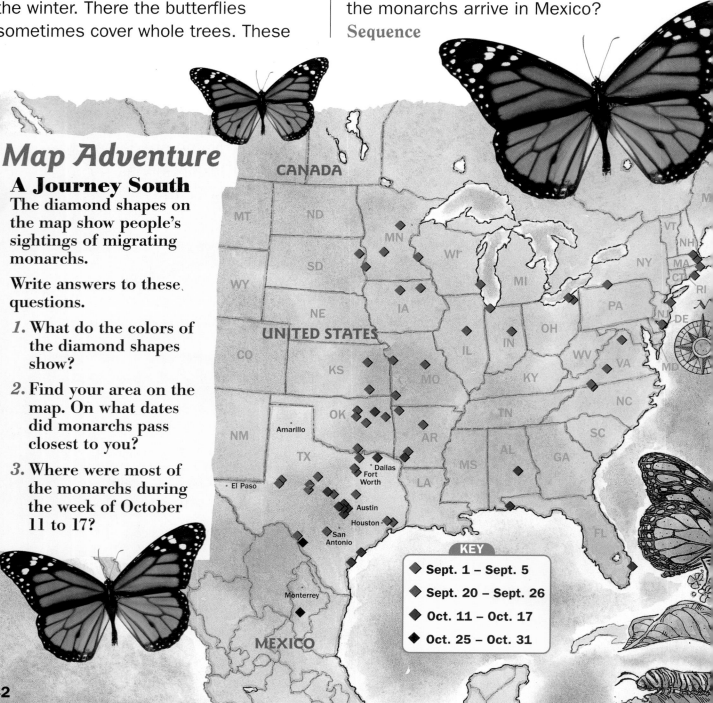

Map Adventure

A Journey South

The diamond shapes on the map show people's sightings of migrating monarchs.

Write answers to these questions.

1. What do the colors of the diamond shapes show?

2. Find your area on the map. On what dates did monarchs pass closest to you?

3. Where were most of the monarchs during the week of October 11 to 17?

KEY
- ◆ Sept. 1 – Sept. 5
- ◆ Sept. 20 – Sept. 26
- ◆ Oct. 11 – Oct. 17
- ◆ Oct. 25 – Oct. 31

FACT FILE

Animals Are Texas Symbols

Which of these animals live in your area?

▶ **Longhorns** are named for their long horns. In 1927, a herd of official state longhorns was formed to preserve the breed.

State Large Mammal

▶ **Mockingbirds** imitate the calls of other birds. They can even imitate the sounds of whistles and sirens!

▶ **Armadillos** are about the size of large cats. They use their keen sense of smell to find food.

State Small Mammal

State Bird

▶ **Horned lizards,** or horny toads, can flatten their bodies and freeze in place when a predator is near.

State Reptile

State Flying Mammal

▶ **Mexican free-tailed bats** keep pests from bugging *you!* Bats in the colony at Bracken Cave eat almost 250 tons of insects per night!

Endangered Species of Texas

In 1999, 46 species of Texas animals and 28 of the state's plants were considered endangered. A plant or animal that is **endangered** is one that is in danger of dying out completely. Endangered Texas animal species include Kemp's Ridley sea turtles and whooping cranes. The star cactus, the Texas snowbell, and the Texas prairie dawn are among the state's endangered plants. Some other Texas plants and animals are said to be **threatened.** This means that they are likely to become endangered. Federal and state laws protect both endangered and threatened plants and animals.

REVIEW Why do people have laws to protect endangered plants and animals? **Draw Conclusions**

How You Can Help

What can you do to help endangered and threatened plants and animals in Texas? First, learn as much as you can! Most zoos in Texas offer programs about endangered animals. Also, many wildlife refuges give tours. They give visitors a chance to see plants and animals in their natural habitats. Habitats are the places in nature where the plants and animals live.

One danger to different plants and animals is the loss of their habitat. You can make choices to help protect the environment. For example, you can choose not to litter. You can select bug sprays that do not harm nearby plants or animals. Some Texans are even buying ranch land to help protect the plants and animals on it.

REVIEW Name two ways in which you can help protect threatened and endangered plants and animals.
⊙ **Main Idea and Details**

Summarize the Lesson

- **Types of vegetation include natural vegetation and cultivated vegetation.**
- **Major crops in Texas include cotton, wheat, corn, and grain sorghum.**
- **Some Texas crops, such as pecans, peaches, and citrus fruits, grow on trees.**
- **Many types of mammals, birds, and reptiles live in Texas.**

★ **LESSON 4** **REVIEW**

Check Facts and Main Ideas

1. ⊙ **Main Idea and Details** On a separate sheet of paper, complete the following Main Idea and Details chart.

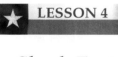

> Texas has a variety of animals.

> Western Texas:

> Eastern Texas:

> Southern Texas:

2. Describe the vegetation that grows in the eastern part of the state.

3. Think about the foods you have eaten this week. Which foods may have come from a Texas crop?

4. Why do plants, trees, and animals vary from region to region?

5. **Critical Thinking: *Point of View*** Do you think that protecting endangered and threatened plants and animals is important? Why or why not?

Link to ⟠ Science

Make a Display Learn about one endangered or threatened animal that lives in or near your area. Draw a picture of the animal and write a description of it. With your classmates, create a display of your work.

ISAMU TANIGUCHI
1897–1992

Isamu Taniguchi was seventeen when he came to the United States from his home in Japan. He farmed in northern California for many years.

After moving to Austin, Texas, Taniguchi designed and built a Japanese garden in Zilker Park. Working without pay, Taniguchi changed three acres of rugged, hilly land into a garden with graceful waterfalls and lotus ponds.

Taniguchi wanted the garden to be a symbol of world peace. In 1969, after the garden was finished, Taniguchi said,

"We are all so much in a hurry that we never take the time to look and see the beauty around us."

BIOFACT

As he created his garden, Taniguchi was inspired by the presence of a large cedar tree that he named "Mother Tree."

During the 1980s, Taniguchi worked with children called "Sprout Scouts." He showed them how a small seed could become a large plant. He showed them how the tools, seeds, and soil of his garden work together.

Learn from Biographies

Why do you think Isamu Taniguchi worked without pay to create a garden for the citizens of Austin?

For more information, go online to *Meet the People* at **www.sfsocialstudies.com.**

Solving Problems

▶ Ila Loetscher cared enough about turtles to give her time for their protection.

How do you get people to pay attention to a problem you care about? Ila Loetscher cared deeply about sea turtles. She was determined to teach the public about this endangered species—even if she looked silly while doing it!

Sea turtles face several dangers, most of them from humans. People build seawalls that keep mother turtles from finding nesting areas. Garbage that has been thrown into the ocean kills turtles. Fishing nets accidentally trap turtles, and they drown. Also, people eat turtles and make objects out of their shells.

When Loetscher moved to the Texas coast in the 1950s, many endangered turtles found a friend. Loetscher lived in a beach house on South Padre Island, just behind the dunes, or sand hills, that face the Gulf of Mexico. Soon she became involved in an effort to help turtles find nests in the dunes. When she was given some of the turtles to care for and to study, Loetscher realized how much she loved the creatures. From then on, she dedicated her life to their cause.

Loetscher created a stage behind her beach house. Twice a week she held "turtle talks" for children and adults. She taught her visitors all about the turtles—their history, habits, and habitats. She would even hug the turtles!

BUILDING CITIZENSHIP
Caring

Respect
Responsibility
Fairness
Honesty
Courage

"I found out that is the only way—by loving the turtles—that I can show the children that turtles are worth loving."

The turtle talks got people's attention. Loetscher taught tens of thousands of people that the fate of the sea turtle is a cause worth caring about.

Loetscher became well known as the "Turtle Lady." Stories about her appeared in newspapers, in magazines, and on television. In 1977, Loetscher founded Sea Turtle, Inc., an organization aimed at protecting turtles.

Although Loetscher died in 2000, Sea Turtle, Inc. carries on her work. In the coming chapters, you will read about other heroes whose actions have made a difference in Texas and in the nation.

Caring in Action

Link to Current Events Research other people or groups of people who care about threatened or endangered animals in Texas. In what ways do these people show that they care?

47

Chapter Summary

 Target Skill ## Main Idea and Details

On a separate sheet of paper, fill in the details that support the main idea stated in the chart.

> Texas is a land of great variety.

Vocabulary

Match each word with the correct definition or description.

1 plateau (p. 15)

2 resource (p. 21)

3 pollution (p. 24)

4 climate (p. 31)

5 endangered (p. 43)

a. weather patterns over time

b. result of harmful substances that threaten the environment

c. a material that people use

d. high, level stretch of land

e. in danger of dying out completely

People

Write at least three sentences explaining why each of the following people has been important in Texas. Give examples of specific ways in which each person has improved the state.

1 **Sally Ride** (p. 11)

2 **Lady Bird Johnson** (p. 27)

3 **Roy Bedichek** (p. 38)

4 **Isamu Taniguchi** (p. 38)

Facts and Main Ideas

1 On what continent is Texas located?

2 What are two renewable resources found in Texas?

3 Where do the highest temperatures occur in Texas?

4 What are four major Texas crops?

5 **Main Idea** What are three types of landforms found in Texas?

6 **Main Idea** How is water quality in Texas being improved?

7 **Main Idea** Name three state symbols.

8 **Main Idea** Name one mammal, one reptile, and one bird that live in Texas.

9 **Critical Thinking:** *Draw Conclusions* How might the leaders of Texas promote the conservation of fossil fuels?

Internet Activity

To get help with vocabulary, people, and terms, select the dictionary or encyclopedia from *Social Studies Library* at **www.sfsocialstudies.com**.

Write About Texas

1 **Write a letter to a friend** who has never visited Texas. Briefly describe the variety of landforms, waterways, and climates in the state.

2 **Write a poem** about one of the plants or animals of Texas. Begin by making a list of things to say about your subject. Then use your list to create a poem.

3 **Write a billboard message** urging citizens of Texas to conserve water. Make a poster using drawings, slogans, and other techniques to draw attention to your message.

Apply Skills

Use Elevation Maps

Look at the elevation map on page 18. Then answer the questions.

1 How do you know that this is an elevation map?

2 What two features of the map help you see the different elevations of places in Texas?

3 How does using an elevation map help you understand the geography of Texas?

CHAPTER 2

The Natural Regions of Texas

Lesson 1

The Central Plains
This region is home to cattle ranches and dinosaur tracks.

1

Lesson 2

The Great Plains
The Palo Duro Canyon is the site of a popular musical.

2

Lesson 3

The Mountains and Basins
El Paso is the largest city in this region.

3

Lesson 4

The Coastal Plains
This region has both coastal areas and inland areas.

4

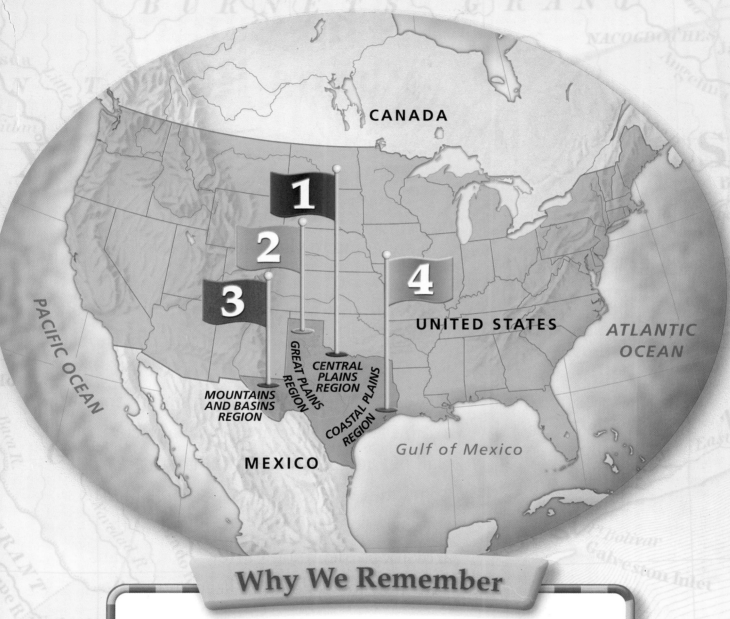

CANADA

PACIFIC OCEAN

UNITED STATES

ATLANTIC OCEAN

1

2

3

4

GREAT PLAINS REGION

CENTRAL PLAINS REGION

COASTAL PLAINS REGION

MOUNTAINS AND BASINS REGION

MEXICO

Gulf of Mexico

Why We Remember

Most Texans call their state by one name—Texas. However, Texans have always used different names for different parts of the state. Some names, such as East Texas, borrow words from the compass. Others refer to special places or landforms. For example, the Valley is a shortened term for *Rio Grande Valley*. Geographers, too, have given special names to the natural regions of Texas. These four regions share land features with other parts of North America.

CENTRAL
PLAINS
REGION

PREVIEW

Focus on the Main Idea
The Central Plains region of Texas is located in the north-central part of the state and is a part of a larger land area in North America.

PLACES

Central Plains region
Grand Prairie
Cross Timbers
Rolling Plains
Fort Worth
Abilene

VOCABULARY

region
livestock
landmark

The Central Plains Region

You Are There You have just been named the newest reporter of Texas Kids TV! For your first assignment, you are going to visit the four regions of Texas.

Your first stop is the Central Plains region. You want to do a great job as you report on Fort Worth, the city "where the West begins." The camera gets a close-up of some items on exhibit at the National Cowgirl Museum and Hall of Fame. You have to hurry to get to the Log Cabin Village to report on how pioneers lived. Do you have time to check out the artwork at the Amon Carter Art Museum? Your new job is going to keep you on the go!

Target Skill

Main Idea and Details As you read, look for details that help you understand what life is like in the different parts of the Central Plains region.

The Land

On the map below, find the **Central Plains region** of Texas. It is a physical, or natural, region. A natural **region** is a large area whose parts have something in common, such as natural resources or landforms.

The land in the Central Plains region of Texas rises from an elevation of about 750 feet above sea level in the east to about 2,000 feet in the west. Notice that the Central Plains region of Texas is broken into three smaller areas. They are the Grand Prairie, the Cross Timbers, and the Rolling Plains.

Now zoom out to the larger region of North America that connects to the Central Plains region of Texas. Find the Central Plains region of North America on the map below. It is a flat and rolling region that extends from Texas through parts of Canada. In this chapter, you will also read about other regions in Texas that extend to parts of the United States and other countries in North America. Before you leave the Central Plains region of Texas, however, take a close look at its three major areas and cities.

REVIEW What are two things that parts of a natural region may have in common? ⟳ **Main Idea and Details**

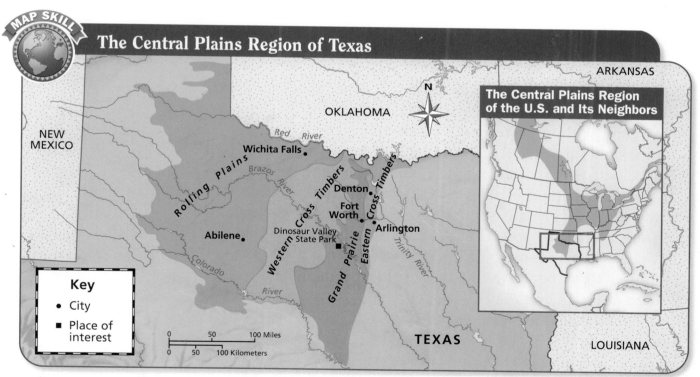

MAP SKILL

The Central Plains Region of Texas

ARKANSAS

OKLAHOMA

N

NEW MEXICO

Red River

Wichita Falls

Rolling Plains

Brazos River

Western Cross Timbers

Denton

Eastern Cross Timbers

Fort Worth

Arlington

Abilene

Dinosaur Valley State Park

Grand Prairie

Trinity River

Colorado River

The Central Plains Region of the U.S. and Its Neighbors

Key
- • City
- ■ Place of interest

0   50   100 Miles
0   50   100 Kilometers

TEXAS

LOUISIANA

▶ The Central Plains region of Texas is a part of the larger Central Plains region of North America.

MAP SKILL Use a Map Key and Symbols *What place of interest is located in the Grand Prairie?*

Major Areas and Cities

The **Grand Prairie** area of the Central Plains region of Texas is a grassy land. It is a place where people raise **livestock**, such as beef cattle, dairy cattle, sheep, goats, hogs, chickens, and turkeys. Farmers grow cotton, corn, and other grains. This area's resources also include limestone, sand, and gravel.

The **Cross Timbers** area gets its name from two thin strips of forest that cross the prairies. Some of the trees have been cut down. Now farmers in this area grow peaches, hay, peanuts, wheat, and sorghum. Area ranchers raise cattle, sheep, and goats. Oil, gas, clay, sand, stone, and gravel—these are some of the other resources found in the Cross Timbers area.

Ranches dot the **Rolling Plains** area. This area's rocky soil is better for ranching than for farming. Still, some farmers grow wheat, cotton, and sorghum. Rich oil fields are also in this area.

Early in its history, **Fort Worth** was the end of the trail. That is, it was the stopping point for long cattle drives. Today Fort Worth is not just a "Cowtown." It is home to many museums and several universities. It has thriving industries such as meatpacking and aircraft building.

Living History

Then and Now

Take a step back in time at Dinosaur Valley State Park near Glen Rose. Be careful, though. You might step into a dinosaur's footprint!

Scientists think that about 113 million years ago an ocean covered parts of Texas. Dinosaurs roamed across the shore. Over time, some dried-mud dinosaur tracks were covered by soil. They remained hidden for millions of years. Then, in more recent times, the flowing water of the Paluxy River began to uncover the footprints. It continues to uncover them today.

This special area is now protected as a state park. It will help preserve the dinosaur tracks for future generations.

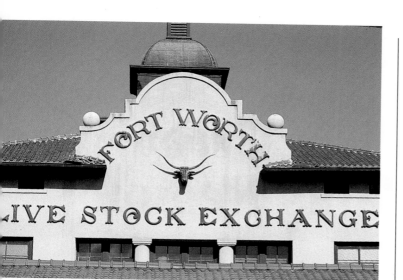
► The cattle industry in Fort Worth still thrives today.

Abilene was founded in 1881 near a newly built railroad. The city today is well known for its rich oil and gas fields. In fact, people demonstrating oil-drilling tools at a nearby fair in 1981 actually struck oil! Three universities are located in Abilene. Arlington, Denton, and Wichita Falls are some other cities in this region.

Landmarks stand out from the area around them. Some **landmarks,** such as a mountain with an interesting shape, are natural features. Some people think of the Cross Timbers in the Central Plains as a natural landmark.

Many of the trees in this area have been cleared. In some places, though, you can still see this natural landmark.

REVIEW Name one detail each about Fort Worth and Abilene today.
↻ Main Idea and Details

Summarize the Lesson

- The Central Plains region is made up of the Grand Prairie, the Cross Timbers, and the Rolling Plains.
- Fort Worth and Abilene are two major cities in the Central Plains region.
- The Cross Timbers is thought by some people to be a natural landmark in the Central Plains region.

★ LESSON 1
REVIEW

Check Facts and Main Ideas

1. ↻ **Main Idea and Details:** On a separate sheet of paper, complete the following Main Idea and Details chart.

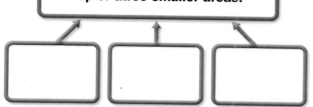

The Central Plains region is made up of three smaller areas.

2. What is a natural region?
3. How are the three areas of the Central Plains alike and different?
4. Describe the Central Plains region of Texas.
5. **Critical Thinking:** *Make Inferences* Why is there so much farming and ranching in the Central Plains region?

Link to ◦—◦◦—◦ Mathematics

Find the Age of Abilene You read that Abilene was founded in 1881. Subtract that number from the number of this year to figure out how old Abilene is today.

LESSON 2

GREAT PLAINS REGION

PREVIEW

Focus on the Main Idea
The natural resources of the Great Plains region make it a good place for farming, ranching, and oil production.

PLACES

Great Plains region
Caprock Escarpment
High Plains
Edwards Plateau
Llano Basin
Amarillo
Lubbock
Midland
Odessa
Palo Duro Canyon

VOCABULARY

mohair
helium
retail
wholesale

The Great Plains Region

You Are There

On the second stop of your reporting tour, you see a tall stone column rising out of the landscape. You learn that it is called the Lighthouse of Palo Duro Canyon. The colors on the sides of the canyon walls seem to change as the day goes on. You plan to tell your viewers that long ago this whole canyon was under water. The place you are standing was once the floor of the ocean!

You hope the cameras can help your viewers be as amazed by this place as you are.

Main Idea and Details As you read, pay attention to details that can help you understand the three areas of the Great Plains region.

Target Skill

The Land

The larger Great Plains region of North America stretches from Canada to Mexico. As a part of this larger region, the **Great Plains region** of Texas is a high, flat grassland.

On the map, find the **Caprock Escarpment** in Texas. This line of steep slopes or cliffs helps to separate the Great Plains and Central Plains regions of Texas. Notice that the Great Plains region has three areas.

The **High Plains** area is located mainly in the Panhandle. Petroleum, natural gas, and rich soils are some of the area's resources. Farmers use underground water supplies from aquifers to irrigate crops. Irrigation helps make this area the state's top producer of wheat, cotton, and sorghum. Cattle ranching is another important industry in this area.

The **Edwards Plateau** area lies just south of the High Plains. A plateau is a high, level stretch of land. However, some of the Edwards Plateau is hilly. In fact, it is called the Texas Hill Country. Almost half of the world's mohair comes from counties in or near this area. **Mohair** is the hair of angora goats. It is spun into fine yarn. Oil is produced in a part of the Edwards Plateau known as the Permian Basin.

The **Llano Basin** area is a rocky, bowl-shaped area on the eastern edge of the Edwards Plateau.

REVIEW What three areas make up the Great Plains region of Texas?
↻ **Main Idea and Details**

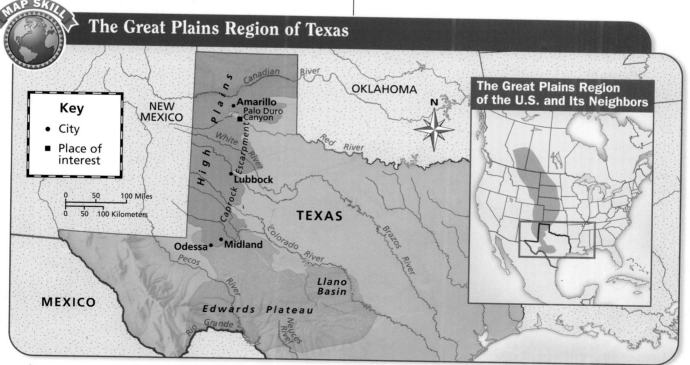

MAP SKILL

The Great Plains Region of Texas

Key
- ● City
- ■ Place of interest

0   50   100 Miles
0   50   100 Kilometers

NEW MEXICO

Canadian River

High Plains

● Amarillo
■ Palo Duro Canyon

White River

Caprock Escarpment

● Lubbock

OKLAHOMA

N

Red River

TEXAS

Colorado River

Brazos River

Odessa ● ● Midland

Pecos River

Llano Basin

MEXICO

Edwards Plateau

Rio Grande

Nueces River

The Great Plains Region of the U.S. and Its Neighbors

▶ Grain production and cattle ranching are important to the economy of the Great Plains throughout North America.

MAP SKILL Regions *How might the Great Plains in North America be similar to the Great Plains of Texas?*

Major Cities

In 1893, someone listed Amarillo's population as "between 500–600 humans and 50,000 head of cattle." **Amarillo** was founded in 1887 near the new railroad line. Soon it was home to a booming cattle market. The word *amarillo* means "yellow" in Spanish. No one knows for sure why that name was chosen. Maybe it was because of the pale yellow color of the area's soil. Or perhaps the town got its name from the yellow wildflowers that grow there. Most of the town's first houses were painted yellow in honor of the name.

Today tourists visiting the Amarillo area can see attractions such as the Palo Duro Canyon. Amarillo is also a center for the cattle, agriculture, health care, and natural gas industries.

Helium is one of the natural gases found in the area. It has no color or smell and is lighter than air. You might have seen party balloons filled with helium.

Lubbock, "the Hub of the Plains," was founded in 1890. It grew quickly after the Santa Fe railroad built a line through it in 1909. Today Lubbock is home to Texas Tech University. Many people in Lubbock work in education and health care. Others are manufacturers or farmers. Retail and wholesale industries there provide goods for buyers. **Retail** merchants sell to the public. **Wholesale** merchants sell to other businesses.

The sister cities of **Midland** and **Odessa** have large oil and gas industries. Area farmers and ranchers can shop and do business in Midland and Odessa.

REVIEW What are four major cities in the Great Plains region?

⟳ **Main Idea and Details**

▶ The popular musical *Texas* is performed each summer in a large outdoor theater in Palo Duro Canyon State Park near Amarillo.

A Natural Landmark

During a period of 90 million years, a river cut a path through the Caprock Escarpment. Today that path is called the **Palo Duro Canyon.** It is the second largest canyon in the United States. Only the Grand Canyon in Arizona is larger. The Palo Duro Canyon is more than 100 miles long and, in most places, more than six miles wide. It is up to 800 feet deep.

▶ The towering rock formation in the Palo Duro Canyon is called "The Lighthouse."

The words *palo duro* mean "hard wood" in Spanish. Many hardwood shrubs and trees grow in the canyon.

In 1933 a large part of the canyon became Palo Duro Canyon State Park. More than half a million people from around the world visit this park each year. Many come to see the popular musical *Texas.*

REVIEW Why do you think tourists from around the world like to see *Texas?* **Draw Conclusions**

Summarize the Lesson

- **The Great Plains region is made up of the High Plains, the Edwards Plateau, and the Llano Basin.**
- **Four major cities in the Great Plains region are Amarillo, Lubbock, Midland, and Odessa.**
- **Palo Duro Canyon is a major natural landmark in the region.**

★ LESSON 2   **REVIEW**

Check Facts and Main Ideas

1. ↻ **Main Idea and Details:** On a separate sheet of paper, complete the following Main Idea and Details chart.

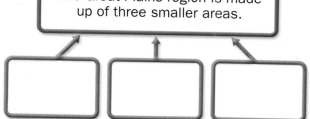

The Great Plains region is made up of three smaller areas.

2. What natural resources are found in the Great Plains region of Texas?

3. What does the Spanish word *amarillo* mean? What are some reasons why Amarillo might have been given that name?

4. Describe the Great Plains region of Texas.

5. **Critical Thinking:** *Draw Conclusions* Why would cities grow up around railroads?

Link to ⦻ **Science**

Learn About Helium Look in an encyclopedia for information about helium. Then answer these questions: What is helium? Where is it found? What are its uses?

MOUNTAINS AND BASINS REGION

The Mountains and Basins Region

You Are There

While planning your TV report on the Mountains and Basins region, you notice that there aren't many cities on the map. The largest city is El Paso. You make a list of some of the questions you want to answer in your report.

- What kinds of work do people do here?
- What kinds of crops grow here?
- The towns are so far apart. How long does it take for children to get to school?

One place you are planning to visit is the McDonald Observatory. You are going to interview some of the scientists studying the stars. You had better brush up on your astronomy before the interviews.

Draw Conclusions As you read, look for reasons why so few people live in the Mountains and Basins region.

The Land

Towering peaks, rocky canyons, flowering cacti—these are a few wonders you might see in the **Mountains and Basins region** of Texas. Find this region on the map. It is about the same size as the state of South Carolina! But it is only a small part of the larger Rocky Mountains region of North America.

Now find Guadalupe Peak on the map. It is the highest point in Texas. It reaches 8,749 feet above sea level.

The **basins** of this region are low, bowl-shaped landforms located between the mountains. The basins of Texas make up part of the Chihuahuan (chee WAH wun) Desert, a natural area Texas shares with Mexico. A **desert** is a dry area that receives fewer than 10 inches of rain per year.

The dry, rocky soil makes it hard for people to farm and ranch. The mountains create barriers between distant towns. But Big Bend National Park and Guadalupe Mountains National Park together attract about a half million visitors each year. If you visit these parks, you might see mountain lions, peregrine falcons, and rattlesnakes. You might also stop in at the McDonald Observatory in the heart of the Davis Mountains. As a visitor, you can view the universe from one of the most powerful telescopes in the world!

REVIEW What effect does the rugged landscape have on the economy of this region? *Cause and Effect*

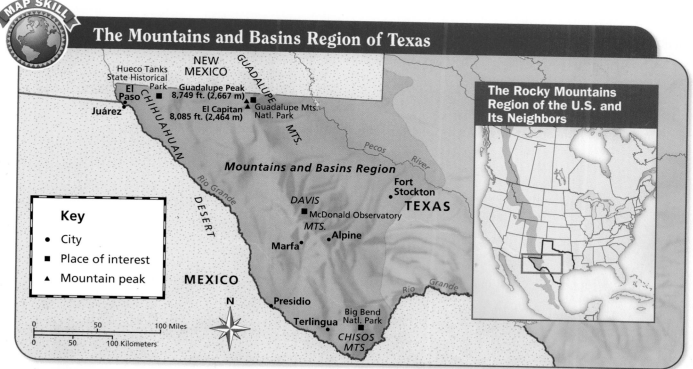

MAP SKILL

The Mountains and Basins Region of Texas

Hueco Tanks State Historical Park
NEW MEXICO
GUADALUPE
El Paso
Guadalupe Peak 8,749 ft. (2,667 m)
Juárez
CHIHUAHUAN
El Capitan 8,085 ft. (2,464 m)
Guadalupe Mts. Natl. Park
MTS.
Pecos River
Mountains and Basins Region
Fort Stockton
TEXAS
DAVIS
McDonald Observatory
MTS.
Rio Grande
DESERT
Alpine
Marfa

Key
- • City
- ■ Place of interest
- ▲ Mountain peak

MEXICO
N
Presidio
Terlingua
Big Bend Natl. Park
Rio Grande
CHISOS MTS.

0 50 100 Miles
0 50 100 Kilometers

The Rocky Mountains Region of the U.S. and Its Neighbors

▶ The mountains of Texas are a part of the Rocky Mountains region of North America.

MAP SKILL Human-Environment Interactions *What challenges do people face if they live in a mountainous region?*

Major Cities

El Paso is the only major Texas city in the Mountains and Basins region. It is so far away from other major cities in Texas that it is in a different **time zone.** A time zone is an area in which all the clocks are set to the same time. When it is 7:00 in most other parts of Texas, it is only 6:00 in El Paso.

El Paso is located on the **border,** or boundary line, that Texas shares with Mexico. This border follows the Rio Grande. Across the Rio Grande from El Paso is the Mexican city of **Juárez** (HWAHR es). More than one and one-half million people live in these two cities.

One popular tourist spot near El Paso is Hueco (WAY coe) Tanks State Historical Park. *Hueco* is a Spanish word used to describe hollows in rocks that hold rainwater. Long ago, water collected in these hollows provided drinking water for early Texans.

Small towns are widely scattered throughout the Mountains and Basins region. High school students in Terlingua (tur LING wah) used to travel 160 miles each day to attend school in Alpine! Are you surprised that the students did not like getting up at 5:00 A.M. to catch the school bus? In 1997 the people of Terlingua built a high school of their own.

REVIEW How is El Paso different from other major Texas cities? Name two ways. **Compare and Contrast**

▶ Hollows in rocks at Hueco Tanks State Historical Park form tanks that hold rainwater.

▶ El Paso is the fifth-largest city in Texas and the largest city in the Mountains and Basins region.

A Natural Landmark

El Capitan is a magnificent mountain in Guadalupe Mountains National Park. It stands out because of its size and shape. Some people say El Capitan

▶ **El Capitan rises from the mountains and basins in West Texas.**

looks like a giant ship. Others compare it to a huge sea creature. Early settlers used this mountain as a landmark. It helped them find their way through the Guadalupe Pass. Travelers still use the mountain as a landmark today.

REVIEW Why does El Capitan hold special meaning for so many people? **Draw Conclusions**

Summarize the Lesson

• **The Mountains and Basins region is a large area in West Texas.**

• **El Paso is the only major city in the Mountains and Basins region.**

• **The mountain named El Capitan is a natural landmark in this region.**

★ LESSON 3 **REVIEW**

Check Facts and Main Ideas

1. **Draw Conclusions** How does the environment in the Mountains and Basins region affect farming and ranching? On a separate sheet of paper, complete the following chart to show your answer.

Reasons

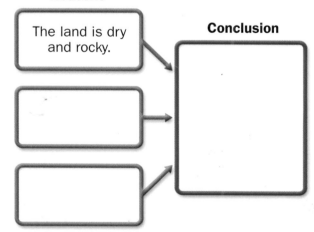

2. Where is the Mountains and Basins region located?

3. What is a major resource of the Mountains and Basins region?

4. Describe the Mountains and Basins region of Texas.

5. **Critical Thinking: *Draw Conclusions*** Why do tourists choose to visit the Mountains and Basins region?

Link to ⬥⬥ Language Arts

Write a Description Look again at the photographs in this lesson. Pick out the one you like best. Then describe the picture in words. Help readers see the picture you are describing. When you have finished, check your word picture for correct grammar and spelling. Did you use capital letters and punctuation correctly too?

COASTAL PLAINS REGION

PREVIEW

Focus on the Main Idea
The Coastal Plains region is home to the state's three largest cities and many land features.

PLACES

Coastal Plains region
Piney Woods
Gulf Coast Plain
South Texas Plain
Post Oak Belt
Blackland Prairie
Houston
San Antonio
Dallas
Austin
Padre Island

PEOPLE

John Biggers

VOCABULARY

inland
bayou
lignite
port
trading post
barrier island
mainland

The Coastal Plains Region

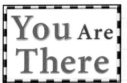

You Are There
You have saved the largest region of Texas, the Coastal Plains region, for your last broadcast. You plan a special report on John Biggers, the artist who created powerful artwork showing his neighborhood in Houston.

You also want your viewers to see the blue sky over the beaches of Corpus Christi and the sun shining on the dome of the state capitol in Austin. You really want to squeeze in some time to show people the Alamo in San Antonio. How can you fit it all in? There is just so much to see and do in Texas!

Summary As you read, look for details to help you write a summary about the Coastal Plains region.

The Land

Would you rather play in the snow or splash in the waves at the beach? Would you like to grow citrus fruits or pine trees? You can do all of these in the **Coastal Plains region.** It depends on how far north or south you go or on the time of the year.

Look at the Coastal Plains region of Texas on the map. It is the largest region in Texas, covering about one-third of the state. It runs along the edge of the Gulf of Mexico. This region of Texas is a part of the larger Gulf Coastal Plains region of North America.

On the map, see how the larger region extends from Florida through Mexico. The land areas in this larger region share some of the same kinds of plant life, climate, soil, and natural resources. Notice that many areas of this region border the Gulf of Mexico. What types of industries do you think these areas might have in common? How might weather patterns in these areas be similar?

The Coastal Plains region of Texas reaches **inland,** or away from the coast toward land, about 250 miles. This large region is made up of five smaller areas: the Piney Woods, the Gulf Coastal Plain, the South Texas Plain, the Post Oak Belt, and the Blackland Prairie. Find them on the map.

REVIEW Why do you suppose that parts of Florida and Texas's Rio Grande Valley grow similar crops?
Draw Conclusions

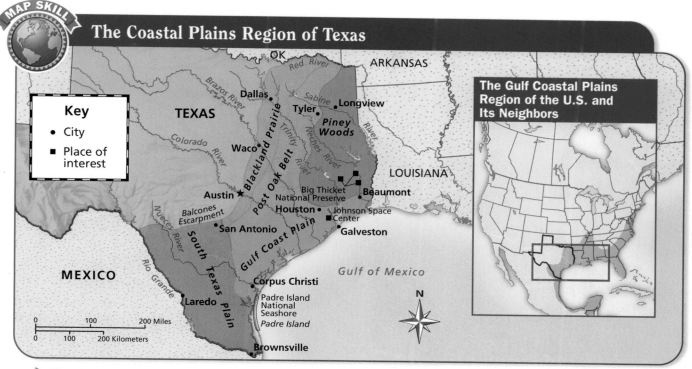

The Coastal Plains Region of Texas

Key
- • City
- ■ Place of interest

OK
Red River
ARKANSAS
TEXAS
Brazos River
Dallas
Sabine River
Longview
Tyler
Piney Woods
Colorado River
Waco
Blackland Prairie
Post Oak Belt
Trinity River
Neches River
LOUISIANA
Austin ★
Balcones Escarpment
Big Thicket National Preserve
Beaumont
Houston
Johnson Space Center
San Antonio
Gulf Coast Plain
Galveston
Nueces River
South Texas Plain
MEXICO
Rio Grande
Corpus Christi
Gulf of Mexico
Laredo
Padre Island National Seashore
Padre Island
N
Brownsville

0   100   200 Miles
0   100   200 Kilometers

The Gulf Coastal Plains Region of the U.S. and Its Neighbors

▶ The Coastal Plains region is the largest natural region in Texas.

MAP SKILL Use a Land and Water Map *What body of water borders the Coastal Plains region of Texas?*

Areas of the Region

The **Piney Woods** area of Texas is part of a large forest that stretches from the coast of the Atlantic Ocean to Texas. Many people in this area of Texas work in the lumber industry. Others grow fruits and vegetables. Some raise cattle in areas where trees have been cleared. Still others work in the oil industry.

Four national forests are in this area. In the national forests, tree cutting is controlled and trees are often replanted. A national preserve known as the Big Thicket has been set aside to protect the animals and plants that live there.

The **Gulf Coast Plain** area lies next to the Gulf of Mexico. It reaches from Port Arthur to Corpus Christi. This area is where most of Texas's major rivers empty into the Gulf. It has bays and slow-moving streams called **bayous.**

They cut into the low land of the coast. Farther inland the land is flat and fertile. It is good for ranching and for raising crops such as cotton and sorghum. Oil rigs on platforms rise out of the Gulf of Mexico. Oil wells dot the land in the area too. As you might guess, fishing is also an important industry.

The **South Texas Plain** area reaches from San Antonio to Brownsville and from the Rio Grande to the Gulf of Mexico. Much of this area is dry land covered with thorny brush. Oil wells are common sights here, but farming and ranching are the major industries. Many large cattle ranches, such as the King Ranch, are found in this area.

Farmers in the Rio Grande Valley enjoy rich soil and mild temperatures. They irrigate using water from the Rio Grande. It is no wonder that Texas is among the top five states in the production of fresh vegetables.

▶ Shrimp boats are common along parts of the Texas coast.

This area is also known for its orchards of citrus fruits, such as oranges and grapefruit.

The **Post Oak Belt** area stretches from San Antonio to the northeast corner of the state. This area is made up of rolling hills and prairie. Farmers grow cotton, corn, and sorghum. Oil, gas, and **lignite,** a kind of soft coal, are other area resources.

The **Blackland Prairie** area lies to the west of the Post Oak Belt. This area takes its name from its rich, dark soil. Farmers grow grains and cotton. The Blackland Prairie also yields oil, gas, and building materials such as limestone and gravel.

REVIEW How would you compare the landscape of the South Texas Plains to that of the Piney Woods?
Compare and Contrast

Major Cities

Houston, a port city, is located near the Gulf of Mexico. A **port** is a place where ships can dock to load or unload cargo. The Port of Houston is a major center for trade with foreign countries. Houston is also home to the Johnson Space Center, the Texas Medical Center, and many artists. You will read about **John Biggers,** an artist, on page 69.

In **San Antonio,** people from around the world visit the Institute of Texan Cultures to learn about Texas and its people. They also enjoy San Antonio's

▶ Many people in Dallas work in government, manufacturing, transportation, and trade.

famous Riverwalk and the Alamo. Many people who live in San Antonio work for the government or in medical research or the tourist industry.

Dallas is located in the Blackland Prairie. The city began in 1841 as a **trading post,** or small frontier store. People there traded products grown or made locally for food and other supplies. Today Dallas is a leading business center.

Austin, our state capital, is home to several colleges and universities. Many people in Austin hold government, education, or computer-industry jobs.

Some other large cities in the Coastal Plains region are Longview, Galveston, Brownsville, Laredo, Bryan/College Station, and Waco.

REVIEW Name one detail about each major city in the Coastal Plains region. **Main Idea and Details**

A Natural Landmark

Padre Island is a narrow strip of sandy land that runs along the south Texas coast. It is about 110 miles long and up to 3 miles wide. It is the longest sand beach in the United States!

Padre Island is a barrier island. Barrier islands are narrow islands between the ocean and the mainland, or the main part of a continent. They protect the mainland from the full force of hurricanes and tropical storms.

In 1962 the U.S. government set aside most of the island's beachfront to preserve the sand dunes, plants, and animals there. It is called the Padre Island National Seashore.

REVIEW Why are barrier islands important? Main Idea and Details

Summarize the Lesson

- **The Coastal Plains region makes up about one-third of Texas.**
- **Houston, Austin, San Antonio, and Dallas are major cities in the Coastal Plains region.**
- **Padre Island is a natural landmark in this region.**

★ LESSON 4 **REVIEW**

Check Facts and Main Ideas

1. Summary On a separate sheet of paper, complete the following chart.

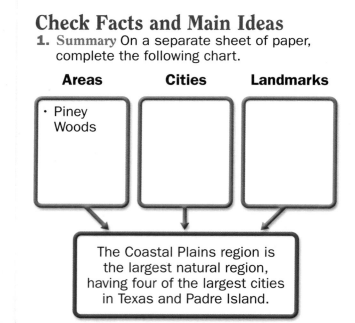

Areas	Cities	Landmarks
• Piney Woods		

The Coastal Plains region is the largest natural region, having four of the largest cities in Texas and Padre Island.

2. What are some ways that people in the Gulf Coast Plain area of Texas earn their living?

3. What is one way that people in the Coastal Plains region changed the land to make it better for farming?

4. Describe the Coastal Plains region of Texas.

5. Critical Thinking: *Draw Conclusions* Why do you suppose Texas's three largest cities are located in the Coastal Plains region?

Link to ⟷ **Science**

Learn About Hurricanes Read about hurricanes in an encyclopedia or in another reference source. How do hurricanes affect this region of Texas?

JOHN BIGGERS
1924–2001

John Biggers was a well-known artist and teacher who lived in Houston. He was the founder of the art department at Texas Southern University in Houston.

The artist was born in North Carolina into a large family. As children, John and his older brother often crawled under their house to listen to the trains go by. They used the soft, red clay to mold models of tiny buildings, houses, and wagons. Then they dug ditches for streams. As an adult, Dr. Biggers recalled the experience fondly:

> **BIOFACT** *As an artist and an art teacher, Dr. John Biggers was awarded a Texas Medal of Arts Award.*

"As I think of it now, this was my first real exercise in creativity."

John Biggers studied art in college. He created artworks that expressed his feelings about African American culture. He painted murals, or works of art painted on walls. They reflect the spirit of African American people. He also taught his students to look to their own heritage for ideas.

Learn from Biographies

How do you think John Biggers's childhood experiences helped him develop the skills he needed to become an artist?

For more information, go online to *Meet the People* at **www.sfsocialstudies.com**.

Houston

At the same time that a large cargo ship pulls into the Port of Houston today, an ocean liner will dock at the Port of Vancouver in

Canada. The booming cities of Houston and Vancouver are located in two different countries. However, they have much in common.

Houston is the fourth-largest city in the United States. More than 1.6 million people live in Houston. It is also one of the country's busiest ports. Ships from around the world dock there each day.

Vancouver, Canada's third-largest city, is one of that country's busiest ports. It is a major port for trade across

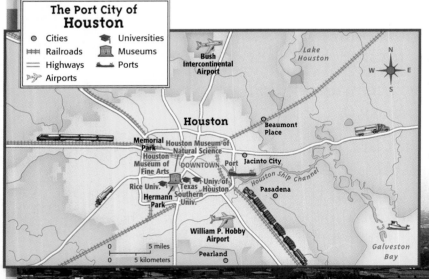

The Port City of Houston

- Cities
- Universities
- Railroads
- Museums
- Highways
- Ports
- Airports

Bush Intercontinental Airport

Lake Houston

Houston

Beaumont Place

Memorial Park

Houston Museum of Natural Science

Houston Museum of Fine Arts

DOWNTOWN

Port

Jacinto City

Houston Ship Channel

Rice Univ.

Texas Southern Univ.

Univ. of Houston

Pasadena

Hermann Park

William P. Hobby Airport

Galveston Bay

Pearland

0   5 miles

0   5 kilometers

and Vancouver

the Pacific Ocean. Its nickname, "Canada's Gateway to the Pacific," describes the city well.

Houston's port connects to the Houston Ship Channel. This deep canal stretches between the Port of Houston and the inland waters of Galveston Bay. Houston is a center for both ocean and rail transportation.

Vancouver is surrounded on three sides by water. Its harbor connects to the Pacific Ocean through an inlet, a narrow water passage. Ships pass through this inlet as they travel to and from the Vancouver Harbor. Railroads connect Vancouver with inland areas.

▶ **If you visit Houston or Vancouver today, you will find similar things to do:**
- **play at any of several large parks and visit university campuses**
- **tour museum exhibitions or window shop in the shadows of skyscrapers**
- **ride city buses and depart from a modern airport**

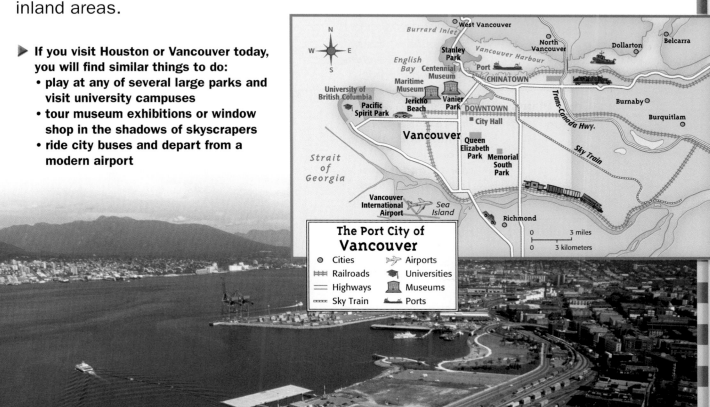

The Port City of Vancouver

⊙ Cities	✈ Airports
⊞⊞⊞ Railroads	🏛 Universities
═ Highways	🏛 Museums
⊏⊏⊏ Sky Train	⚓ Ports

Thinking Skills

Make Generalizations

What? A generalization is a broad statement or rule that applies to many examples. Clue words such as *all, most, many, some, sometimes, usually, seldom, few,* or *generally* often tell you that a generalization is being made.

An example of a generalization is *Most pizzas have cheese.* Readers can make generalizations based on main ideas, details, and their own knowledge as they read. A good generalization is supported by facts and examples. A poor generalization is not supported by facts and examples.

Four Natural Regions of Texas			
Region	**Some Features**	**Major Cities**	**Landmarks**
Central Plains Region	flat and rolling three smaller areas farming and ranching building materials	Fort Worth Abilene	The Cross Timbers
Great Plains Region	high, flat grasslands three smaller areas farming and ranching oil and gas mohair and topaz Texas, the musical Caprock Escarpment	Amarillo Lubbock Midland Odessa	Palo Duro Canyon
Mountains and Basins Region	rocky soil mountains and desert tourism and wildlife McDonald Observatory Guadalupe Mountains Big Bend National Park	El Paso	El Capitan
Coastal Plains Region	wet and dry land Gulf of Mexico five smaller areas farming and ranching forests oil and gas building materials	Houston San Antonio Dallas Austin	Padre Island

Why? In this chapter, you read about the natural regions of Texas. One way to understand the facts in the chapter is to make generalizations about them. Making generalizations helps you see similarities between ideas and facts that may appear different at first.

How? To make a generalization, you gather and compare information about a topic. Then you bring this information together to make a general statement. In some cases, you add your own knowledge to the information.

Suppose you wanted to make a generalization about the four regions of Texas. First, read the table on page 72. Then review and gather information about these four areas. In what ways are the regions similar? In what ways are they different? When you find similarities, you have the beginnings of a generalization. Before you make your generalization, be sure that you have enough facts or examples to support it. Otherwise, the generalization may be poor.

1. Name a feature shared by three of the four regions of Texas. Give your response in the form of a generalization.

2. What generalization can you make about the cities in the four regions?

3. Make a generalization about the landmarks of the four Texas regions.

4. Tell whether the following generalization is good or poor: *All Texas regions have gulf ports for shipping.* Explain your answer.

5. Look at the generalizations you made in items 1–3 above. Underline the clue word in each generalization.

Chapter Summary

Main Idea and Details

On a separate sheet of paper, fill in the details that support the main idea stated in the chart.

Texas has four main natural land regions.

Vocabulary

On a separate sheet of paper, use each vocabulary word in a sentence. Give clues about the meaning of the vocabulary word in the sentence.

1. **region** (p. 53)
2. **landmark** (p. 55)
3. **desert** (p. 61)
4. **border** (p. 62)
5. **bayou** (p. 66)
6. **mainland** (p. 68)
7. **inland** (p. 65)

People and Places

Write a sentence about each person or place listed below. Include at least one detail you learned from this chapter in each sentence.

1. **Cross Timbers** (p. 54)
2. **Amarillo** (p. 58)
3. **El Capitan** (p. 63)
4. **Padre Island** (p. 68)
5. **John Biggers** (p. 69)

Facts and Main Ideas

1. Why is the Rolling Plains area of the Central Plains region of Texas less suited to farming than other areas of this region?

2. What important resources come from the Edwards Plateau area? Name two.

3. What four large cities are located in the Coastal Plains region?

4. **Main Idea** How would you describe the Central Plains region of Texas?

5. **Main Idea** How would you describe the Great Plains region of Texas?

6. **Main Idea** Why do fewer people live in the Mountains and Basins region than in any other Texas region?

7. **Critical Thinking:** *Compare and Contrast* How are the landforms in the western part of Texas different from those in the eastern part of the state?

Write About Regions

1. **Write a description** of the land where you live. Then tell which region and area of Texas you live in.

2. **Write slogans** that sum up the best qualities of the four regions of Texas. Create one slogan for each region. The slogans should be brief.

3. **Write a paragraph** for a Texas tourism Web site in which you encourage people to visit the Mountains and Basins region of Texas.

Apply Skills

Make Generalizations

Look at the chart on page 72. Then answer the questions.

1. How can you use the information in the chart to make a generalization?

2. What is one way that all four regions are alike?

3. Finish these generalizations:
Most of the regions of Texas ____.
All of the regions of Texas have ____.

Internet Activity

To get help with vocabulary, people, and terms, select the dictionary or encyclopedia from *Social Studies Library* at **www.sfsocialstudies.com**.

THE LEGEND OF THE BLUEBONNET

An Old Tale of Texas
Retold and Illustrated
by Tomie dePaola

For many years, Texans have told stories about the origins of the bluebonnet. One such legend is retold, or told again, and illustrated by Tomie dePaola. A group of Native Americans known as Comanche believe they must burn something special so the rain will return after the drought. They must give the ashes to the Great Spirits. The following excerpt is about a young Comanche girl's sacrifice, or gift, to the Great Spirits. She hopes this deed will save her people.

. . . She ran to the place on the hill where the Great Spirits had spoken to the shaman. Stars filled the sky, but there was no moon. "O Great Spirits," She-Who-Is-Alone said, "here is my warrior doll. It is the only thing I have from my family who died in this famine. It is my most valued possession. Please accept it." . . . And before she could change her mind, she thrust the doll into the fire.

She watched until the flames died down and the ashes had grown cold. Then, scooping up a handful, She-Who-Is-Alone scattered the ashes to the Home of the Winds, the North and the East, the

South and the West. And there she fell asleep until the first light of the morning sun woke her.

She looked out over the hill, and stretching out from all sides, where the ashes had fallen, the ground was covered with flowers—beautiful flowers, as blue as the feathers in the hair of the doll, as blue as the feathers of the bird who cries "Jay-jay-jay."

. . . As the People sang and danced their thanks to the Great Spirits, a warm rain began to fall and the land began to live again. From that day on, the little girl was known by another name— "One-Who-Dearly-Loved-Her-People."

And every spring, the Great Spirits remember the sacrifice of a little girl and fill the hills and valleys of the land, now called Texas, with the beautiful blue flowers.

Even to this very day.

Unit Review

Main Ideas and Vocabulary

TEST PREP

Read the passage below and use it to answer the questions that follow.

Texas is a large state near the center of the Western Hemisphere, on the continent of North America. It has a variety of landforms and waterways.

Its renewable natural resources include forests, soil, and water. Nonrenewable Texas resources include natural gas and oil.

Texas has a variety of climates. Elevation, latitude, and the Gulf of Mexico affect its temperatures. The state sometimes has severe weather such as tornadoes, hurricanes, and floods.

Major Texas crops include cotton, wheat, and sorghum. Many types of mammals, birds, and reptiles are found in the state.

Texas has four natural regions. The Central Plains region is mostly flat. The Great Plains region is a high, flat grassland west of the Central Plains.

The Mountains and Basins region is a large, mostly dry area in far West Texas. El Paso is its only major city.

The Coastal Plains region stretches across south and east Texas. Padre Island, off the Texas coast, is a natural landmark.

1 In this passage, the word *landforms* means—
   A natural features of Earth's surface
   B continents
   C elevations
   D soils that are good for farming

2 According to the passage, which of these is an important Texas resource?
   A silver
   B coffee
   C oil
   D iron

3 In this passage, the word *sorghum* means a—
   A type of mineral
   B type of mammal
   C type of soil
   D type of crop

4 In what region is Padre Island?
   A Central Plains
   B Great Plains
   C Mountains and Basins
   D Coastal Plains

Vocabulary

Match each word to its definition.

1. **geography** (p. 15)

2. **natural resource** (p. 21)

3. **temperature** (p. 32)

4. **natural vegetation** (p. 37)

5. **basin** (p. 61)

a. plant life that grows without the help of people

b. low, bowl-shaped landform

c. study of Earth's land and how people use it

d. a measurement of hot or cold

e. resources that come from nature

Apply Skills

Use an Elevation Map to Describe a Journey
Ask classmates to review the elevation map of Texas on page 18. Then take turns describing at least three elevations that a driver would pass through when traveling a long distance across Texas.

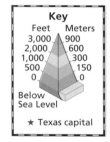

Key

Feet	Meters
3,000	900
2,000	600
1,000	300
500	150
0	0

Below Sea Level

★ Texas capital

Read on Your Own

Look for books like these in the library.

Write and Share

Write a Booklet Organize yourselves into eight groups according to the eight lessons in Unit 1. In your groups have everyone write and illustrate a paragraph about a favorite part of the lesson. Then combine each group's work and add it to a class booklet.

Eye on Our Region

Take visitors on a video tour of your region of Texas. Show what's great about it.

1 Form a group and choose an interesting topic about your region of Texas.

2 Make a map of your region.

3 Make a list of facts about your topic. Draw pictures that illustrate your facts. Write a sentence or two to describe each picture.

4 Put your group's pictures together. Put them in the sequence in which you will show them. Use your map as an introduction. This is your video tour to share with the class.

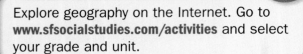

Internet Activity

Explore geography on the Internet. Go to **www.sfsocialstudies.com/activities** and select your grade and unit.

What might Texas have been like a long time ago?

1300   1400   1500

1325
Aztecs build
Tenochtitlan.

1492
Columbus reaches
the Americas.

1521
Spanish
defeat the
Aztecs.

1528
Cabeza
de Vaca
reaches
Texas.

1540
Coronado
begins
his search
for gold.

> ## "The country . . . is as good in every respect as a man could wish for."
>
> —Stephen F. Austin, in his journal entry of
> September 20, 1821, during his first trip to Texas

Ancient artists painted pictographs on the walls of Panther Cave. Panther Cave is located in Seminole Canyon State Historical Park in Val Verde County.

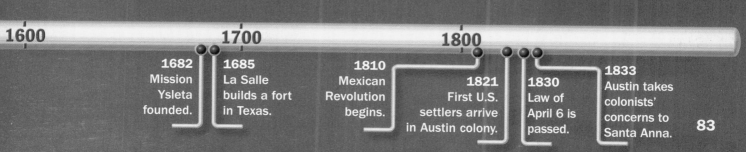

1600

1700

1800

1682
Mission Ysleta founded.

1685
La Salle builds a fort in Texas.

1810
Mexican Revolution begins.

1821
First U.S. settlers arrive in Austin colony.

1830
Law of April 6 is passed.

1833
Austin takes colonists' concerns to Santa Anna.

Alvar Núñez Cabeza de Vaca

c. 1490–c. 1556

Birthplace: Jerez de la Frontera, Spain

Spanish explorer

- Sailed to Americas from Spain in 1528 with Pánfilo de Narváez
- Landed on what was probably Galveston Island off the Texas coast
- Traveled on foot throughout the Southwest

Francisco Vásquez de Coronado

c. 1510–1554

Birthplace: Salamanca, Spain

Spanish explorer

- Led explorers in search of the Seven Cities of Cíbola
- Continued to lead this group into Texas in search of gold
- Was one of the first Europeans to see Palo Duro Canyon

René-Robert Cavelier, Sieur de La Salle

1643–1687

Birthplace: Rouen, France

French explorer

- Sailed the Mississippi River and claimed the surrounding land for France
- Landed in Texas with French colonists in 1684
- Helped establish Fort St. Louis in Texas in 1685

Mary Austin Holley

1784–1846

Birthplace: New Haven, Connecticut

Writer and teacher

- Cousin of Stephen F. Austin
- Published accounts of her travels and life in Texas
- Wrote *Texas*, the first history of Texas written in English

1390	1440	1490	1540	1590	1640	1690

c. 1490– c. 1556
Alvar Núñez Cabeza de Vaca

1510–1554
Francisco Vásquez de Coronado

1643–1687
René-Robert Cavelier, Sieur de La Salle

84

For more information, go online to *Meet the People* at **www.sfsocialstudies.com**.

Lorenzo de Zavala

1788–1836

Birthplace: Tecoh, Mexico

Political leader

- Supported democratic reforms in Mexico as a newspaper editor and politician
- Received a grant in 1829 to bring settlers to southeastern Texas
- Supported the Texas independence movement and became the first vice president of the Republic of Texas

Stephen Fuller Austin

1793–1836

Birthplace: southwestern Virginia

Leader of Texas settlement

- Established the first colony of United States settlers in Texas in 1821
- Founded San Felipe de Austin in 1824
- Became known as the "Father of Texas"

Jane Herbert Wilkinson Long

1798–1880

Birthplace: Charles County, Maryland

Farmer and businesswoman

- Spent the winter of 1821 with only her children and their servant, Kian, on Point Bolivar
- Operated a successful plantation near Richmond
- Became known as the "Mother of Texas"

Patrisia Gonzales

1959–

Birthplace: Fort Worth, Texas

Journalist, author, teacher

- Writes a newspaper column that appears in cities all over the United States
- Honored in El Paso's "Writers of the Pass Hall of Fame"
- Teaches college classes in journalism

1790	1840	1890	1940	1990	2040	2090

1784–1846
Mary Austin Holley

1788–1836
Lorenzo de Zavala

1793–1836
Stephen Fuller Austin

1798–1880
Jane Herbert Wilkinson Long

1959–
Patrisia Gonzales

Texas Long Ago

Target Skill

Compare and Contrast

Features that are alike	Features that are different

- To **compare** is to tell how two or more things are alike. To **contrast** is to tell how two or more things are different.
- Clue words such as *like, similar, as*, and *also* show comparisons.
- Clue words such as *unlike, different,* and *but* show contrasts.
- Sometimes authors do not use clue words. Readers must make comparisons for themselves.

Read the following paragraph. The sentences that **compare** and **contrast** have been highlighted.

In Unit 1, Chapter 2, you read about the natural regions of Texas. The Central Plains and Great Plains regions are alike in some ways. For example, both have some flat, grassy areas. The Mountains and Basins region and the Coastal Plains region are unlike each other. The Mountains and Basins region has dry, rocky soil, but the Coastal Plains region has rich soil that is good for growing crops.

Comparing the Lives of the Early Texans

The land we know as Texas has been home to many different people. The first of these people were hunters who lived here thousands of years ago. They moved on foot from place to place, following animal herds. As the largest animals died out, people began to change their way of life. Some settled down in villages. They learned to farm the land.

Many years later, Plains Indians, such as the Comanche, lived on this land. Like their earliest relatives, they were hunters who followed bison herds. They carried their homes made of poles and animal skins with them. These people were also traders. They exchanged horses and goods made from bison for food, tools, and other supplies.

People such as the Jumano, from the Mountains and Basins region, were mainly farmers. They lived in permanent homes made from bricks of dried mud and straw. Unlike the hunters, they did not have to follow animal herds. This gave them time to develop many kinds of art.

The Caddo, from the northern part of the Coastal Plains region, were farmers. Other people who lived on the coast were hunters and gatherers, such as the Karankawa. Most of their diet was seafood.

Use the reading strategy of comparing and contrasting to answer these questions.

1 In what way were the lives of the first people of Texas like the lives of the Comanche, who lived there later?

2 How were the homes of the Plains Indians different from those who lived in the Mountains and Basins region?

3 What clue words in the passage help you notice comparisons and contrasts?

CHAPTER 3

The First Texans

Lesson 1

Beringia
10,000–15,000 years ago
A land bridge opens
between continents.

1

Lesson 2

Caddoan Mounds
1,200 years ago
The Caddo build villages
in the Piney Woods.

2

Lesson 3

Ysleta
Today
The Tigua continue the
Pueblo tradition in Texas.

3

Lesson 4

Tenochtitlan
1325
The Aztecs build a grand
city on Lake Texcoco.

4

1
Beringia
Bering Strait

3

2

4

Ysleta

Caddoan Mounds

Tenochtitlan

PACIFIC OCEAN

ATLANTIC OCEAN

Why We Remember

Today we think of ourselves as Texans, but what did the first people who lived here call themselves? If you could go back in time about 15,000 years, you might find out. The first people in Texas did not leave a written record of their lives. We find clues about these people by studying objects they left behind. However, Europeans who came to Texas 500 years ago wrote about what they saw. These records help us piece together a rich story about the people who lived in Texas long ago.

89

Bering Strait

Alibates
Flint Quarries
National
Monument

PREVIEW

Focus on the Main Idea
The earliest Texans were hunters, but later some groups began to farm and settle in communities.

PLACES

Beringia
Bering Strait
Alibates Flint Quarries
  National Monument

VOCABULARY

descendant
artifact
archaeologist
atlatl
quarry
culture
agriculture

The Earliest Texans

You Are There

It is January 1983. You are one of several workers digging carefully at the site of an ancient camp north of Austin. The highway department found this site by Brushy Creek, near Leander. Some of the people working here think this camp could be more than 10,000 years old.

Suddenly, the worker next to you uncovers a bone—a human finger bone! You watch as workers slowly uncover a whole skeleton. It is the skeleton of a woman who lived, died, and was buried here more than 9,500 years ago. A grinding stone and a fossilized shark's tooth were buried with her.

Because they found the skeleton near Leander, the workers name it "Leanderthal Lady."

▶ **Fossilized shark's tooth**

Compare and Contrast As you read about some of the First Americans, look for ways in which their lives were different from your own.

Target Skill

The First Trail to Texas

People like the Leanderthal Lady lived on the Texas plains 10,000 years ago or more. They walked from place to place looking for food. They carried the few belongings they owned.

These people were descendants of the first people to live in North America. **Descendants** are a person's children, grandchildren, and so on. No one is sure when the first people arrived in North America. Some scholars say it may have been as many as 50,000 years ago.

How did they get here? There are several theories, or possible explanations. Some say the First Americans may have sailed from the Eastern Hemisphere or traveled across the North Atlantic from Europe. One strong theory is that the First Americans came over a land bridge called **Beringia.**

Find the **Bering Strait** on the map. Long ago this waterway did not exist. Instead, a grassy plain connected Asia and North America. This was Beringia. Hungry herds of huge animals—woolly mammoths and giant bison—grazed on the plain. The meat from one of these animals fed many people. From its hide, the hunters sewed clothing and shelters. Hunters may have followed the huge animals from Asia into North

Routes from Beringia

ARCTIC OCEAN

ASIA

Bering Strait

EUROPE

ALASKA

NORTH AMERICA

ATLANTIC OCEAN

TEXAS

Gulf of Mexico

Caribbean Sea

PACIFIC OCEAN

SOUTH AMERICA

0   1,000   2,000 Miles

0   1,000   2,000 Kilometers

N

▶ **The First Americans may have followed these routes**

MAP SKILL Understand Directions *Does the main route lie closer to the east coast or the west coast of both continents?*

America. Over time, the descendants of these hunters moved southward.

REVIEW What was the area around the Bering Strait like long ago? What is it like today? ↻ **Compare and Contrast**

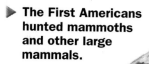

▶ **The First Americans hunted mammoths and other large mammals.**

91

▶ An archaeological dig at Alibates Flint Quarries National Monument

Learning About the Past

The people who lived in Texas 10,000 years ago left clues about their lives—bones, campfire ashes, broken pots, and other artifacts. An artifact is an object made by people. A scientist who finds and studies these clues is called an archaeologist.

These clues have given archaeologists an idea of what life was once like in the land we call Texas. Hunters stalked herds of huge animals. These hunters used throwing sticks, called atlatls (aht LAHT ulz), to make their spears fly far and fast. Atlatls have been found at sites throughout Texas.

▶ Flint spear point

Once a kill was made, the hunters and their families feasted on the animal. Leftover meat was cut into strips and dried so it could be eaten at a later time.

At the hunters' camp, the animal's hide, or skin, was used to make clothing and tents. The animal's bones were used to make tools, such as needles. When the animal herds moved on, the people followed them.

Some groups of people traded with each other. A place on the Texas Panhandle has given archaeologists clues about this trading. The place is called the Alibates Flint Quarries National Monument. A quarry is an open pit where people mine, or dig up, rocks. At least 10,000 years ago, people mined flint here. Flint is a hard rock, and it was used to make points for arrows and spears. Flint artifacts from this quarry have been found all over North America. By putting these clues together, archaeologists believe that early people traded Texas flint with others who lived throughout North America.

REVIEW How did the work of early hunters differ from the work that was done back at the camp?
◑ Compare and Contrast

Changes in Ways of Life

As time passed, the huge mammoths and giant bison began to die out. People continued to hunt elk, buffalo, bear, and other animals, but they also began to eat more nuts, berries, seeds, and roots.

About 2,000 years ago, the **culture,** or way of life, changed for the people of the Southwest. They began to practice **agriculture.** That means they planted seeds to grow their own food. At first, farmers grew mostly maize, or corn. Later, they added beans, squash, and tomatoes to their harvest.

It takes time for plants to grow, so people settled near their crops. They built villages. People wove baskets and made pottery to store crops they had dried for later use. Baskets, pottery, and dried foods became important trading goods.

The descendants of the First Americans lived in the Western Hemisphere when Europeans arrived. Today these descendants are sometimes called Native Americans or American Indians.

► **Artifacts from Alibates Flint Quarries**

REVIEW How were the lives of early Texas farmers different from the lives of the first people in Texas?
 Compare and Contrast

Summarize the Lesson

- **About 50,000 years ago** The first people may have arrived in North America.

- **10,000–15,000 years ago** The first people arrived in Texas.

- **2,000 years ago** People in Texas began to grow their own food.

★ **LESSON 1** **REVIEW**

Check Facts and Main Ideas

1. Compare and Contrast On a separate sheet of paper, fill in the chart below. The chart should show comparisons and contrasts between the lives of the first people in Texas and those of 2,000 years ago.

Alike	Different

2. How may the first people have come to North America?

3. Why did people follow herds of animals?

4. What goods might people have traded for flint from Alibates Flint Quarries?

5. **Critical Thinking:** *Make Generalizations* Suppose that you lived in your area of Texas 2,000 years ago. What might you have traded with distant groups?

Link to ⚭ **Writing**

Write a Letter Write a letter to a group of ten-year-olds who lived in Texas 10,000 years ago. Tell them about your life today. What type of home do you live in? How do you get food? What do you do for fun? Point out three differences between your time and theirs.

Research and Writing Skills

Use Reference Sources

What? Reference sources contain facts about subjects. Dictionaries and encyclopedias are reference sources. So are almanacs and atlases. All of these reference sources are available as CD-ROMs. The Internet can be a reference source as well.

Why? Reference sources provide facts that you can use to write reports and to do other projects. Do you want to learn more about the earliest people in Texas? The sources on these pages are a good place to begin.

▶ **The Internet has hundreds of reference sources. Using a key word or phrase, such as "First Americans," you can explore information about a topic. The World Wide Web is the pathway to resources on the Internet. See page 336 for a lesson on how to do research on the Internet.**

▶ **A dictionary gives the meanings of words. It also shows how to pronounce and spell each word. Dictionaries list words in alphabetical order. Some dictionaries explain word origins.**

▶ **An encyclopedia is a set of books that gives facts about people, places, things, and events. Topics in an encyclopedia are arranged in alphabetical order.**

▶ **An almanac has facts and figures on many subjects. Much of the information is in charts and tables. Most almanacs are updated every year.**

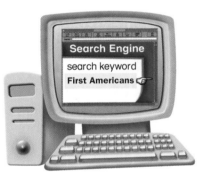

Recreational Visits to National Parks in Texas

This data on daily recreational visits to national park sites in Texas was provided by the National Park Service.

Name of Facility	1996	1997	1998	1999	2000
Alibates Flint Quarries National Monument	3,276	3,363	3,293	3,047	3,131
Amistad National Recreation Area	1,238,990	1,084,443	1,129,811	1,164,166	1,234,506
Big Bend National Park	279,454	305,882	338,442	327,649	262,320
Big Thicket National Preserve	111,626	77,633	56,283	63,997	62,009
Chamizal National Memorial	186,130	193,649	186,480	162,495	183,418
Fort Davis National Historic Site	64,560	62,191	64,846	60,419	54,988
Guadalupe Mountains National Park	223,584	231,980	227,924	219,591	198,728
Lake Meredith National Recreation Area	1,676,466	1,683,646	1,636,419	1,779,138	1,615,751
Lyndon B. Johnson National Historical Park	136,892	129,667	124,212	122,118	108,728
Padre Island National Seashore	840,236	677,492	707,999	630,562	759,596
Rio Grande Wild and Scenic River	498	489	462	678	909
San Antonio Missions National Historical Park	1,239,970	1,328,958	1,118,905	1,224,178	1,393,894
Total Recreational Visits	**6,001,682**	**5,779,393**	**5,595,076**	**5,758,036**	**5,877,978**

Alibates Flint Quarries National Monument is located within Lake Meredith National Recreation Area near Fritch, Texas. Alibates flint, distinctive for its varied coloration, occurs in dolomite outcrops atop Permian Aged Redbeds in the Canadian River valley. Early inhabitants left shallow its as evidence of quarry activity.

Amistad National Recreation Area is located near Del Rio, Texas. Situated on the United States-Mexico border, Amistad NRA is known primarily for excellent year-round, water-based recreation, including boating, fishing, swimming, scuba diving, and water-skiing. Amistad NRA also provides opportunities for picnicking, camping, and hunting. The reservoir, at the confluence of the Rio Grande, Devils, and Pecos rivers, was created by Amistad Dam in 1969.

Big Bend National Park is located on the "big bend" of the Rio Grande in Texas. Situated on the boundary with Mexico along the Rio Grande, Big Bend National Park is a place where countries and cultures meet. It is also a place that merges natural environments, from desert to mountains. The park covers 801,000 acres of west Texas in the place where the Rio Grande makes a sharp turn—

Chamizal National Monument is located in El Paso, Texas. Chamizal National Monument commemorates the 1963 Chamizal Treaty between the United States and Mexico—a treaty that ended a century-long border dispute. The monument celebrates and promotes cultural understanding and goodwill.

Fort Davis National Historic Site is located in Fort Davis, Texas. Soldiers from Fort Davis, a key post in West Texas, helped open the area to settlement and protected travelers and merchants along the San Antonio-El Paso Road from 1854 to 1891. Today the fort is regarded as the best preserved in the Southwest.

Guadalupe Mountains National Park is located in Salt Flat, Texas. Rising from the desert, this mountain mass contains portions of the world's most extensive and significant Permian limestone fossil reef. Also featured are a tremendous earth fault, lofty peaks, unusual flora and fauna, and a colorful record of the past. Guadalupe Peak, the highest point in Texas at 8,749 feet; El Capitan, a massive limestone formation; McKittrick Canyon; and the "Bowl" are significant park features.

---

mammoth | mango

mam·moth (mam'əth), **1** a large elephant with a hairy skin and long curved tusks. The last mammoth died thousands of years ago. **2** huge; gigantic: *Digging the Panama Canal was a mammoth undertaking.* **1** *noun,* **2** *adjective.* [Mammoths lived long ago in Europe or Northern Asia. The name for the animal comes from a Russian word.]

mammoth (definition 1)
about 10 feet (3 meters) high at the shoulder

man (man), **1** an adult male person. When a boy grows up, he becomes a man. **2** a human being; person: *No man can be certain of the future.* **3** the human race: *Man has existed for thousands of years.* **4** a male follower, servant, or employee: *Robin Hood and his merry men.* **5** a husband: *man and wife.* **6** one of the pieces that is moved about on a board in such games as chess and checkers. **7** to supply with a crew: *We can man ten ships.* **8** to serve or operate: *Man the guns.* **1–6** *noun, plural* **men; 7,8** *verb,* **mans, manned, man·ning.** [Man comes from an earlier English word meaning "a human being." Look at the word history for *woman,* another word from the same root.]

man·age (man'ij), **1** to control; handle; direct: *Good riders manage their horses well. They hired*

mandolin

man·do·lin (man'də lin'), a musical instrument with a pear-shaped body and four to six pairs of metal strings. *noun.*

mane (mān), the long, heavy hair on the back of the neck of a horse, or around the head of a lion. *noun.*

ma·neu·ver (mə nü'vər), **1** a planned movement of troops or warships: *Every year the army and navy hold maneuvers for practice.* **2** a skillful plan or movement; clever trick: *When we refused to sell his idea, he tried to force it on us by a series of maneuvers.* **3** to plan skillfully; use clever tricks; scheme: *Scheming people always maneuver to get what they want.* **4** to move or handle skillfully: *maneuvered the car through the heavy traffic with ease.* **1,2** *noun,* **3,4** *verb.*

man·ga·nese (mang'gə nēz'), a hard, brittle, grayish-white metal. Manganese is a chemical element, often used mixed with other metals. *noun.*

man·ger (mān'jər), a box or trough in which or other food can be placed for horses or cows to eat. *noun.*

man·gle (mang'gəl), **1** to cut or tear roughly; hurt badly when he caught it in moving machinery. **2** to do or play badly; ruin: *child mangled the music because it was too dif-*

Mammoth   529   **Mammoth Cave National Park**

In addition, mammals have been domesticated to do work for humans, and to keep humans company. However, many large, undomesticated mammals are now endangered.

Mammoth, an extinct group of mammals closely related to modern-day elephants. Mammoths are among the most well-understood of all extinct animals. This understanding comes through fossils, specimens preserved in ice, and from the art of prehistoric humans.

There were many species of mammoths, but they all shared several distinct features. They were about as large as the modern African elephant—from nine to eleven feet tall at the shoulder, and from four to six tons in weight. The Imperial Mammoth of North America stood 14 feet at the shoulder. Most mammoths had long, curved tusks, small ears, and tall, dome-like skulls. Some were covered in a coat of coarse hair up to 20 inches long.

Mammoths were living in Africa 4 million years ago. During the Pleistocene Epoch (from 2.5 million to 10,000 years ago), they spread to Europe, Asia, and North America. The best known and most widely understood species was the Wooly, or Siberian mammoth. Wooly mammoth have been found not only in Siberia, but across Northern Europe and North America. Some specimens have been found almost completely preserved.

Mammoths appear frequently in ice age cave

Another theory is that the changes in climate at the end of the ice age made life more difficult for the mammoth. Nearly every species of mammoth was extinct by about 10,000 years ago.

The last surviving mammoths were the dwarf mammoths of Wrangel Island. These mammoths stood about six feet tall at the shoulder. They survived until about 4,000 years ago, an age in which pyramids were being built in Egypt.

Mammoth Cave National Park, the Kentucky, U.S. park that encloses Mammoth Cave and the Flint Ridge System. The park itself covers an area of 52,419 acres. It was established in 1941. Up until that time Mammoth Cave had to compete with other caves for tourists. In the 1950s, links between these caves were discovered. Finally, in 1972, a passage was discovered linking Mammoth Cave to Flint Ridge. Combined, these two caves form the longest known cave system in

94

How? You can find many of these reference sources in a library. A librarian can help you explore each source.

Use a dictionary Look at a dictionary in your classroom. Read the dictionary entry for *mammoth*. Notice that guide words at the top of the page help you find the word. The pronunciation of *mammoth* is given after its spelling. The definition of *mammoth* follows. Finally, the dictionary gives the origin of the word.

Use an encyclopedia Like a dictionary, an encyclopedia contains guide words at the top of each page. Notice that the photograph adds meaning to the information about mammoths.

Use an atlas The maps in an atlas can help you find out where specific countries, cities, or physical features are located.

Use an almanac Subjects in an almanac are not listed in alphabetical order. You must use the almanac's index to find information about a topic. The chart in the almanac shown on page 94 gives more information about the Alibates Flint Quarries National Monument. It also tells about other national monuments in Texas.

Think and Apply

1. What reference source gives the origin of words?

2. What reference source is not arranged in alphabetical order?

3. What reference source would you use to find information for a report about mammoths?

4. What reference sources might you use to learn more about the First Americans?

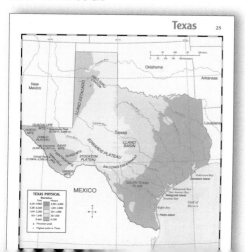

▶ An **atlas** is a book of maps and other related information. Some atlases have road maps. Others show the landforms in certain areas.

LESSON 2

Caddoan Mounds •
Livingston •

PREVIEW

Focus on the Main Idea
Many different groups of Native Americans have lived on the Coastal Plains of Texas.

PLACES
Caddoan Mounds
Livingston

VOCABULARY
migrate
confederacy
reservation
nomad
dugout canoe

The People of the Coastal Plains

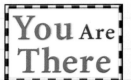
You Are There

Look at those huge mounds of earth! What are they? You strain to hear the guide. "Archaeologists believe these mounds were built more than 1,200 years ago. They were used as tombs and as bases for temples." You are standing in what was once a large city— one of many built throughout the Mississippi Valley by the Mound Builders. This city is now the Caddoan Mounds State Historical Park near Alto. It was once a busy place filled with farmers, builders, traders, and artists. The guide asks, "Would you like to see a reconstructed Caddoan house?" Everyone nods and says "Yes," and you realize that you can hardly wait to see it.

Compare and Contrast
As you read, note the similarities and differences in the ways the people of the Coastal Plains lived.

96

▶ **Reconstructed Caddoan house, Caddoan Mounds State Historical Park**

The Caddo

More than 1,200 years ago, Mound Builders **migrated,** or moved, south into the Piney Woods region to the site of **Caddoan Mounds.** The Mound Builders' culture began more than 3,000 years ago. It spread through the eastern and central parts of what is now the United States. The Caddo (KAD oh) are descendants of the Mound Builders.

The Caddo were farmers. During planting season, the Caddo gathered from neighboring villages and worked together to plant each field, day after day, until all the farmland was planted. In this way, the Caddo community worked together to make sure there was enough food for the next season. The Caddo also made fine pottery. If the Caddo needed something they could not make or grow, they traded food and pottery with other Native Americans to get it.

The Caddo lived in beehive-shaped houses that were pointed at the top and wide across the bottom. The houses were made of wood frames covered with mats of long, dried grasses. Often, several Caddo families lived in one house, so some houses were very large.

Caddo groups were organized into a confederacy. A **confederacy** is made up of groups of people who agree to work together for a common goal. The Caddo confederacy, for example, may have worked together to keep their villages safe from enemies.

By the mid-1800s, the United States had moved the Caddo from Texas to a reservation in Oklahoma. A **reservation** is an area of land set aside as a place for Native Americans to live. Today about 2,000 Caddo live near Binger, Oklahoma. Although they do not live in Texas anymore, the Caddo gave our state a great gift. The name *Texas* comes from a Caddo word that means "friend."

REVIEW What are two ways in which the Caddo used their environment to meet their needs? **Draw Conclusions**

The Karankawa

The Karankawa (kah ran KAH wah) lived south of the Caddo, along the coast of the Gulf of Mexico. They were nomads. A **nomad** is a person who does not have a permanent home but who moves from place to place within a certain area.

During the winter, the Karankawa lived along the shore and on islands off the coast. They caught fish and shellfish for food. They traveled the waterways in **dugout canoes**—canoes made by scooping out a long log. These canoes were large enough to carry a whole family. The Karankawa's winter villages were large, with enough wood-frame houses to shelter hundreds of people. Unlike the Caddo, who had a confederacy, the Karankawa had chiefs who each led a village.

In the summer, these villages broke into smaller bands of families, each with its own leader. These bands moved farther inland to hunt small animals and birds and to gather wild plants.

The Karankawa moved their houses with them from place to place. These houses had walls made of woven grasses and animal skins. In the summer, the Karankawa adjusted the wall coverings to allow breezes to pass through.

The Karankawa were often the first Native Americans that Europeans met when they arrived on the Texas coast. As Europeans moved into Texas, they moved onto the Karankawa's lands. By the mid-1800s, the Karankawa had died out from European diseases and from many battles with European groups.

REVIEW How did the Karankawa adapt to life in winter and life in summer? ⟳ **Compare and Contrast**

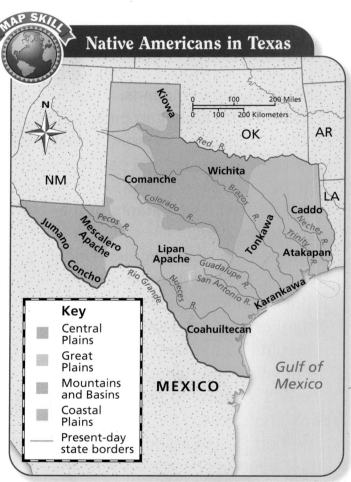

MAP SKILL

Native Americans in Texas

Key
- Central Plains
- Great Plains
- Mountains and Basins
- Coastal Plains
- Present-day state borders

▶ **Before Europeans came, many Native Americans lived in the land we call Texas.**

MAP SKILL Region *What Native Americans lived in each of the four regions of Texas?*

FACT FILE

Other Native Americans of the Coastal Plains

Name of Native American Group	Where They Lived	How They Lived	How Their Lives Have Changed
Wichita [WI chih taw]	North near Red River, beginning in the 1700s	Nomads and hunters in winter, farmers the rest of the year	The Wichita have a reservation near Andarko, Oklahoma.
Atakapan [uh TAK uh puhn]	Near modern-day Houston and east into Louisiana, beginning thousands of years ago	Nomad hunters and gatherers	The Atakapan died out by the late 1800s from European diseases.
Coahuiltecan [koh uh WEEL tek un] *The name "Coahuiltecan" describes many different groups that lived in the same area.*	All across southern Texas, beginning thousands of years ago	Nomads, hunters, and gatherers	Descendants live throughout South Texas.
Tonkawa [TAHNG huh wuh]	Central and eastern Texas	Hunters and gatherers without permanent homes	The Tonkawa tribal office is located in Tonkawa, Oklahoma.
Cherokee [CHAIR o kee]	Beginning in the 1800s, north of present-day Nacogdoches	Farmers, hunters, lived in towns	Many still live in Texas, as well as in Oklahoma, where they have their western headquarters.

Native Americans in East Texas Today

Today there is one reservation in eastern Texas. It is the Alabama-Coushatta (koo SHAH tuh) Reservation, which is located near the city of **Livingston.** The Alabama-Coushatta were farmers and hunters who came to Texas from Alabama and Louisiana in the 1780s. They continue to practice many traditions from their culture.

In addition, many thousands of Native Americans live in East Texas. They are descendants of many different groups of Native Americans.

REVIEW Where in East Texas do Native Americans live today?
Summarize

Summarize the Lesson

- **The Caddo lived in farming villages in the Piney Woods.**
- **The Karankawa were nomads who lived near the Gulf Coast.**
- **Today some Native Americans live on reservations, while thousands of others live in cities and on farms.**

▶ **An Alabama-Coushatta girl**

LESSON 2  **REVIEW**

Check Facts and Main Ideas

1. ↻ **Compare and Contrast** On a separate sheet of paper, complete this diagram to show how the Karankawa and the Caddo ways of life were alike and different.

Alike	**Different**

2. What did the Caddo trade and why?
3. Name three different Native American groups of East Texas. Tell one thing about each.

4. How did the lives of the Caddo and the Karankawa change after the 1500s?
5. **Critical Thinking: *Draw Conclusions*** Why do you think the Caddo and Karankawa ruled themselves in different ways?

Link to ⚬━⚬ Geography

Learn About the Mound Builders Go to the library or search online to learn more about the Mound Builders. Gather information about Emerald Mound in Mississippi, Serpent Mound in Ohio, Cahokia in Illinois, and any other Mound Builder sites you can find. Mark these sites on a map to see how widespread the Mound Builders' culture was.

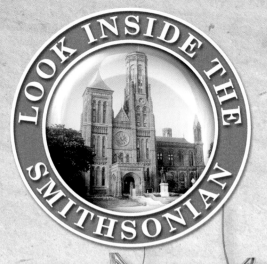

Native American Artifacts

By the time Europeans began exploring the Americas, North America had been home to many different groups of Native Americans for thousands of years. The artifacts on this page represent some of the workmanship of Native Americans from areas throughout North America.

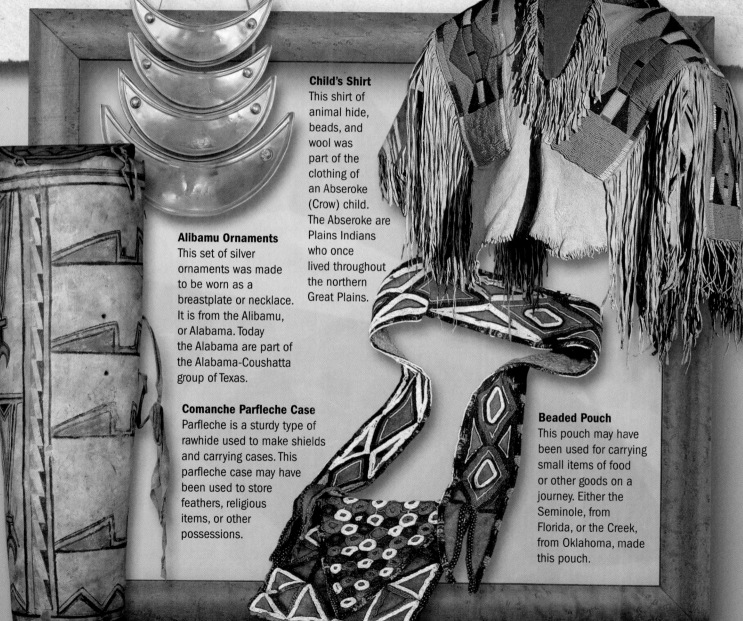

Child's Shirt
This shirt of animal hide, beads, and wool was part of the clothing of an Abseroke (Crow) child. The Abseroke are Plains Indians who once lived throughout the northern Great Plains.

Alibamu Ornaments
This set of silver ornaments was made to be worn as a breastplate or necklace. It is from the Alibamu, or Alabama. Today the Alabama are part of the Alabama-Coushatta group of Texas.

Comanche Parfleche Case
Parfleche is a sturdy type of rawhide used to make shields and carrying cases. This parfleche case may have been used to store feathers, religious items, or other possessions.

Beaded Pouch
This pouch may have been used for carrying small items of food or other goods on a journey. Either the Seminole, from Florida, or the Creek, from Oklahoma, made this pouch.

Artifacts are from the ✳ Smithsonian Institution.

Ysleta

Eagle
Pass

PREVIEW

Focus on the Main Idea
Many different groups of
Native Americans have lived
on the plains and in the
mountains and basins of
West Texas.

PLACES
Ysleta
Eagle Pass

VOCABULARY
pueblo
adobe
government
tepee
travois

People of the Mountains and Plains

You Are There The blazing sun beats down upon you as you hike in New Mexico's Bandelier National Monument. You look up at the sheer-walled canyons. Carved into the rock walls hundreds of feet above you are old cliff dwellings. From this distance, they look a bit like apartments. On the ground below these dwellings, you see some of the earliest examples of pueblo houses. These houses were made from wood and dried mud. Nearly 800 years ago, the Anasazi lived here. The Anasazi were farmers and hunters, but they also were artists who made beautiful and useful pottery. You wipe your brow and continue your hike, wondering what happened to the Anasazi.

▶ Anasazi canteen designed to look like an antelope

Compare and Contrast As you read, think about the ways of life of the Pueblo Jumano and the Comanche. How were they similar and how were they different?

▶ A beanfield in the Southwest

The Jumano

Some historians believe that the Pueblo people of today are the descendants of the Anasazi. **Pueblo** is a Spanish word that means "village." When the Spanish explored the Southwest region, they found villages made from adobe. **Adobe** is a type of brick made from straw and mud. Many different groups lived in villages such as these. The Spanish gave all these groups the name *Pueblo.*

About 1,100 years ago, the Jumano (hoo MAH noh) lived near the Rio Grande, in the Mountains and Basins region of Texas. Historians call them the Pueblo Jumano because they lived in villages. Each Jumano village had its own leader and its own government. **Government** is a system for ruling or running a town or country.

Like other Pueblo people, the Jumano were farmers. Because they lived in such a dry land, it was hard to farm. Just as many modern Texas farmers do, the Jumano irrigated their crops by bringing water from nearby streams.

A Spanish explorer wrote that the Jumano used a hollow gourd and hot stones to cook their food. They filled the gourd with water and placed hot stones in the water until it boiled.

"As soon as it boils they put into it what they want to cook, always taking out the stones as they cool off and throwing in hot ones to keep the water steadily boiling."

The Jumano traded with other groups for things they could not grow or make. They traded foods such as dried corn, squash, and beans for buffalo hides and meat. They also traded for cloth, shells, salt, and other goods.

There are no Jumano villages in Texas today. A small number of Jumano descendants still live in Texas.

REVIEW How were the Jumano able to farm in such a dry climate? **Main Idea and Details**

▶ *Comanche Feats of Horsemanship* by George Catlin, painted 1834–1835

The Comanche

The Comanche moved into Texas from the northern Great Plains in the 1700s. They were powerful hunters and fighters. Like other Plains Indians, the Comanche were nomads. They lived in **tepees,** or large tents made of long poles covered with buffalo hides. They followed buffalo herds and hunted them for food and supplies. From the buffalo, the Comanche got nearly everything they needed: clothing, blankets, food, and hides for tepees. The Comanche used a wooden frame called a **travois** (tra-VOY) to carry their possessions from place to place. At first, dogs pulled the travois.

By the 1600s the Spanish had brought horses to North America. The Comanche quickly became experts at horseback riding. A horse could pull a travois farther and faster than a dog. Breeding and training large herds of horses became a sign of wealth. The Comanche moved farther south in search of more buffalo and more horses. This is how they came to Texas.

Soon after the Comanche arrived in Texas, they gained control of the regions we know as the Great Plains and Central Plains. To keep control of this land, the Comanche fought with other Native Americans and with Europeans who traveled through the plains.

The Comanche traveled in bands. Each band had a leader. During raids or wars, bands would unite and choose a war chief to lead them. During times of peace, the Comanche traded buffalo goods and horses for food with the Caddo and Wichita.

By 1875 the Comanche no longer controlled the plains. Texas was part of the United States. Most Comanche were moved to a reservation in Indian Territory, which is now Oklahoma. Today about 10,000 Comanche live throughout the United States.

REVIEW How did horses affect the lives of the Comanche? **Summarize**

FACT FILE

The Jumano and Comanche were not the only Native Americans to live in what is now Western Texas. This table shows other Native American groups that lived in the plains and the mountains.

Other Native Americans of the Plains, Mountains, and Basins

Name of Native American Group	Where They Lived	How They Lived	How Their Lives Have Changed
Concho [KON cho]	In Mexico and in western Texas, where the Rio Concho and the Rio Grande meet	Farmers who also hunted, gathered, and fished	The Spanish enslaved them to work in mines. Many died from slavery and disease. Those left became part of the Jumano in the 1700s.
Kiowa [KEE o wa]	In and around the Texas Panhandle	Nomads and buffalo hunters, similar to the Comanche	The Kiowa have a reservation near Carnegie, Oklahoma.
Mescalero Apache	Along the Rio Grande	Nomads, hunters, and gatherers	The Mescalero Apache have a reservation in Mescalero, New Mexico.
Lipan Apache	On the south Texas plains between present-day Rio Grande City and San Antonio	Nomads, buffalo hunters, and gatherers	The Lipan Apache were removed to the Mescalero Apache reservation in the early 1900s.

Native Americans in West Texas Today

Today there are two reservations in West Texas. The Tigua, who are part of the Pueblo culture, live in Ysleta, near El Paso. The Tigua have lived in Texas for about 350 years. The home of the Kickapoo Traditional Tribe of Texas is near the Rio Grande, just south of Eagle Pass. Though Eagle Pass is in the far western part of the Coastal Plains region, its landscape is more like that of West Texas. The Kickapoo once lived in what is now Michigan. They came to Texas in the 1800s. There are many other Native Americans living in West Texas. They are the descendants of many different groups.

▶ A Tigua gathering

REVIEW Where in West Texas do Native Americans live today? Summarize

Summarize the Lesson

- The Pueblo Jumano lived in adobe villages in the Mountains and Basins region.
- The Comanche are Plains Indians who were known as expert horseback riders and buffalo hunters.
- Today some Native Americans live on reservations, while thousands of others live in cities and on farms.

LESSON 3 REVIEW

Check Facts and Main Ideas

1. **Compare and Contrast** On a separate sheet of paper, complete this diagram. List ways the Comanche's and the Pueblo Jumano's ways of life were alike and different.

Alike

Different

2. Why was trade important to the Jumano and the Comanche? What did they trade?
3. Name three different Native American groups of West Texas. Tell one thing about each.

4. How was the government of the Jumano different from that of the Comanche?
5. **Critical Thinking: *Make Inferences*** None of the Native American groups who lived in Texas when the Europeans arrived live in Texas today. Why do you think this is so?

Link to 〜 **Science**

Create a Resource Diagram Go to the library or online to learn more about how the Native Americans of West Texas used natural resources such as water, soil, plants, and animals. Create a simple diagram that shows what you learned.

PATRISIA GONZALES

1959–

Patrisia Gonzales lives in San Antonio. She is part Kickapoo, part Comanche, and part Mexican.

Patrisia grew up in Fort Worth, surrounded by a large family. She learned to respect older people and to work hard. She also heard many stories about her great-great grandmother. "Mama Mencha" was a Kickapoo. She was born in 1823 and lived to be 114 years old!

Patrisia Gonzales prizes this photo of her great-great grandmother, Mama Mencha.

In school, Patrisia earned good grades, but she didn't have many friends. "When I looked in the mirror," she says, "I thought I wasn't pretty because I didn't look like the . . . Americans on TV."

Today Gonzales leads a happy life. She teaches people about Native American ways. She is also an award-winning newspaper columnist. Gonzales says that she found success "because I followed my heart and because I believed in justice. I had a purpose on this earth."

Gonzales has this advice for fourth graders:

"Open your hearts to all the endless possibilities that life might want to give you. And never, never give up on living a happy and fulfilling life."

Learn from Biographies

What did Patrisia Gonzales learn from her family? What can you learn from older members of your family?

For more information, go online to *Meet the People* at **www.sfsocialstudies.com.**

LESSON 4

Tikal
Tenochtitlan
Cuzco

PREVIEW

Focus on the Main Idea
Great empires once thrived in Central and South America.

PLACES
Tikal
Tenochtitlan
Cuzco

VOCABULARY
empire
city-state
slave
tribute

1300	1400	1500

1325
The Aztecs build Tenochtitlan.

1450
The Mayan empire weakens.

1521
The Spanish defeat the Aztecs.

1527
The Incan empire ends.

Civilizations of the Western Hemisphere

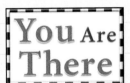

You Are There You, your guide, and other tourists are hiking on a hazy trail through the great jungles of northern Guatemala. You hear the shrieks of howler monkeys. What a strange sound! Suddenly you see great stone temples poking through the tops of trees. You are entering Tikal, a huge Mayan city. You come upon a temple that's shaped like a narrow pyramid. It is so tall that you have to climb five ladders to reach the top. From up here, you can see the ruins of plazas and temples. Your guide tells you that as many as 100,000 people once lived here. You peer over the ruins into the lush jungle and wonder what life was like here long ago.

Compare and Contrast As you read, compare the Maya with the Aztec and the Inca civilizations.

The Maya

At one time, Tikal was the capital of the Mayan empire. An **empire** is a group of governments under the control of one ruler. The Mayan empire lasted from about 300 to about 1450. As many as one hundred Mayan cities were located throughout the tropical forests of southern Mexico and Central America. These cities were called **city-states** because each city had its own government.

The Maya built beautiful cities, each with pyramids, temples, palaces, and many other buildings. Skilled artists made pottery, jewelry, and clothing. In the countryside, farmers lived in one-room houses. They grew corn, beans, squash, peppers, and other crops. The people who lived in the cities depended on these farmers for food.

The Maya developed an alphabet and a writing system. They were also among the first people to understand the use of zero. They studied the stars and planets and created a calendar.

The Mayan civilization began to weaken around 1450. City-states fought against each other. Farmers faced many seasons of dry weather. Crops failed and there was not enough food. Then, in the 1500s, Spanish explorers arrived and conquered what was left of the Mayan empire.

Today, descendants of the Maya live in Central America. They speak a language similar to the Mayan language and practice some of the old Mayan traditions.

REVIEW Why did the Mayan empire become weak? *Cause and Effect*

▶ **Temple at Tikal, Guatemala**

Empires of the Western Hemisphere

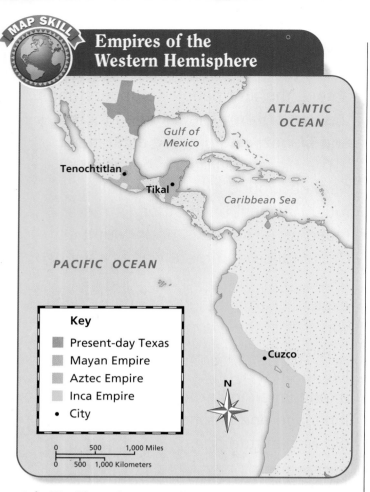

Key
- Present-day Texas
- Mayan Empire
- Aztec Empire
- Inca Empire
- City

ATLANTIC OCEAN

Gulf of Mexico

Tenochtitlan

Tikal

Caribbean Sea

PACIFIC OCEAN

Cuzco

N

0   500   1,000 Miles
0   500   1,000 Kilometers

▶ **The Maya, Aztecs, and Inca built empires in Central and South America.**

MAP SKILL Understand Continents *Which empires are in North America?*

The Aztecs

The Aztecs built a rich empire in the Valley of Mexico. They were also known as the Mexica (may SHEE ka). This is where the name "Mexico" comes from.

The Aztecs were once nomads and hunters. Around 1168, they began to migrate from the mountains in the north. By 1325, they had begun to build a city on an island in Lake Texcoco. This city, **Tenochtitlan** (te nawch tee TLAHN), became the center of the Aztec empire. The city was home to as many as 300,000 people.

In 1519, when Spanish explorers saw Tenochtitlan for the first time, they were amazed. Bernal Díaz, a Spaniard, later wrote,

"These great towns and pyramids and buildings rising from the water, all made of stone, seemed like an enchanted vision. . . ."

The Aztecs were warriors. By waging and winning wars, they built an empire of five million people. The Aztecs made some of these people their slaves. A **slave** is a person who is owned by another person. The Aztecs were governed by one strict ruler who controlled lands from the Gulf of Mexico to the Pacific Ocean. The Aztecs grew rich on tribute they demanded from the people they ruled. **Tribute** is a payment in goods or money made to a ruler. The Aztecs had many different classes of people, including priests, nobles, soldiers, merchants, workers, and slaves.

The Aztecs were very rich and powerful, but they were conquered by the Spanish. Today, descendants of the Aztecs live in Mexico. Some of them still speak the Aztec language. In fact, some words we use come from the Aztec language, including *chili, tomato,* and *chocolate.*

REVIEW How did the Aztecs build such a large, rich empire?
Cause and Effect

The Inca

The Inca lived in the Andes Mountains of South America, from Ecuador to northwestern Argentina. They used knotted strings to keep detailed records of their empire's population and lands. They dug irrigation systems to bring water to their crops. They built stone cities such as **Cuzco,** their capital. They also built at least 14,000 miles of roads high in the mountains. In 1527, a war weakened the Inca empire. Soon after, Spanish explorers arrived and conquered them. Today descendants of the Inca still live in the Andes Mountains.

REVIEW Name three accomplishments of the Inca. **Main Idea and Details**

Summarize the Lesson

- **The Mayan empire covered parts of Mexico and Central America.**
- **The Aztec empire spread from the Gulf of Mexico to the Pacific Ocean.**
- **The Inca built an empire in the Andes Mountains of South America.**

▶ **An Inca girl**

 LESSON 4 **REVIEW**

Check Facts and Main Ideas

1. ⟳ **Compare and Contrast** On a separate sheet of paper, fill in the chart below to show similarities and differences between the Maya and the Aztecs.

   Similarities   **Differences**

2. Why were farmers important to the Mayan empire?

3. Explain how the Aztecs built their empire.

4. What happened to the descendants of the Maya, Aztecs, and Inca?

5. **Critical Thinking:** *Draw Conclusions* Why do you think the Inca built so many roads?

Link to ∞ **Mathematics**

Calculate Distance The Inca built at least 14,000 miles of roads across their empire. The most direct route from Washington, D.C., to San Francisco, California, is about 2,800 miles. How many times would you have to travel this route to equal the distance of the roads the Inca built?

CHAPTER 3
REVIEW

Chapter Summary

Compare and Contrast

On a separate sheet of paper, fill in similarities and differences between the Comanche and the Caddo.

▶ **Comanche medicine bag**

Alike

Both groups were traders.

Different

The Caddo had a confederacy.

The Comanche were led by chiefs.

Vocabulary

Complete each sentence with the correct word from the box.

artifact (p. 92)   **adobe** (p. 103)

confederacy (p. 97)   **travois** (p. 104)

dugout canoe (p. 98)   **tribute** (p. 110)

1 The Jumano built homes of _____ bricks.

2 Caddo groups joined together to form a _____.

3 The Aztecs became rich from _____ paid to their rulers.

4 A Karankawa might have used a _____ to travel the waterways.

5 A Comanche family used a _____ to carry their possessions from camp to camp.

6 An ancient arrowhead is an example of an _____.

Places

List one important fact about each of the following places.

1 **Bering Strait** (p. 91)

2 **Caddoan Mounds** (p. 97)

3 **Livingston** (p. 100)

4 **Ysleta** (p. 106)

5 **Tikal** (p. 109)

6 **Tenochtitlan** (p. 110)

Facts and Main Ideas

1. What Native Americans gave us the name *Texas*? What does *Texas* mean in their language?

2. How would you describe the homes of the Jumano?

3. In what ways was the horse a major part of Comanche life?

4. **Main Idea** What is one theory that explains why people migrated to North America thousands of years ago?

5. **Main Idea** What Native American groups settled in villages in what is now Texas?

6. **Main Idea** What Native American groups traveled through Texas in search of food?

7. **Main Idea** How did the Aztecs build their empire?

8. **Critical Thinking:** *Make Inferences* Name three ways in which land features affected how people lived in Texas long ago.

Internet Activity

To get help with vocabulary, places, and terms, select the dictionary or encyclopedia from *Social Studies Library* at **www.sfsocialstudies.com.**

Write About History

1. **Write a story** about what life might have been like for the First Americans.

2. **Write a paragraph** comparing two of the Native American groups described in Chapter 3. Include information about their ways of life and the ways in which they governed themselves.

3. **Write a brochure** in which you describe the Aztec city of Tenochtitlan. You may have to do some research to learn more about the city.

Apply Skills

Use Reference Sources

Compare the reference sources below. Then answer the questions.

1. Which reference source can you use to find the correct pronunciation of *travois*?

2. Which reference source can you use to see where the Bering Strait is located?

3. List two sources where you can find information about Native Americans.

CHAPTER 4

Europeans Come to Texas

Lesson 1

Palo Duro Canyon 1540
Coronado searches for cities of gold.

1

Lesson 2

San Antonio 1718
A group of Spanish priests and settlers build missions and bring their culture to Texas.

2

Why We Remember

About 500 years ago, Spanish explorers sailed to the Western Hemisphere. At first, they explored islands in the Caribbean Sea. Then they made their way to the land we know as Mexico. Explorers from both Spain and France traveled to the land we know as Texas. Some of them journeyed north from Mexico. Some of them sailed from the Caribbean or Europe. Some explorers even landed on the coast of Texas by accident! No matter how they got to Texas, their arrival changed the land and its people forever.

Palo Duro Canyon
Galveston Island
Garcitas Creek

1500 **1550** **1600** **1650** 17

1492
Christopher Columbus lands in the Americas.

1528
Cabeza de Vaca reaches Texas.

1540
Coronado's search for gold begins.

1685
La Salle builds a fort in Texas.

PREVIEW

Focus on the Main Idea
Stories of gold, silver, and other riches led Spain to send explorers into Texas.

PLACES

Galveston Island
Palo Duro Canyon
Garcitas Creek

PEOPLE

Christopher Columbus
Moctezuma II
Alvar Núñez Cabeza de Vaca
Estéban
Francisco Vásquez de Coronado
René-Robert Cavelier, Sieur de La Salle

VOCABULARY

conquistador
colony

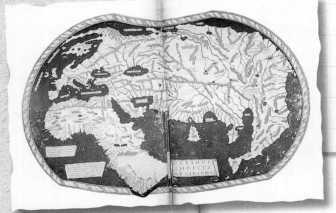

116 ▶ World map, c. 1489

Exploration Leads to Texas

You Are There

Friday, October 12, 1492

It's about two o'clock in the morning. You are on watch with your shipmate, Rodrigo. Your ship, the *Pinta,* has been sailing since August 3, along with two other ships, the *Niña* and the *Santa María*. Your commander, Christopher Columbus, has set his sails toward Asia. You've been looking for land for a long time now—for too long, you think.

Suddenly, Rodrigo shouts for joy. He points into the night. There in the moonlight you see it. Land! The *Pinta* fires its cannon to signal the other ships that this part of your journey is over. But a great journey of exploration is just beginning.

Compare and Contrast As you read, note the similarities and differences among the explorers' experiences.

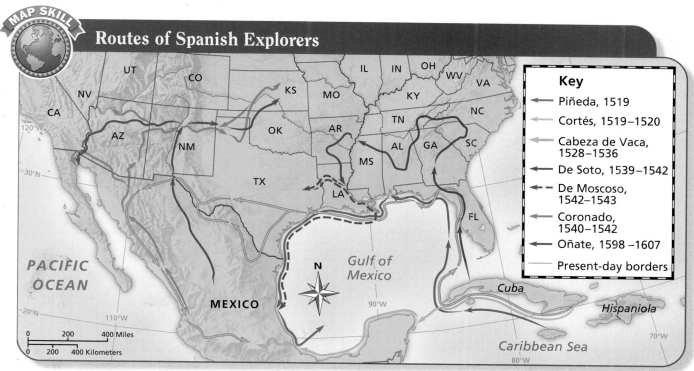

Routes of Spanish Explorers

Key
← Piñeda, 1519
← Cortés, 1519–1520
← Cabeza de Vaca, 1528–1536
← De Soto, 1539–1542
- - - De Moscoso, 1542–1543
← Coronado, 1540–1542
← Oñate, 1598–1607
— Present-day borders

▶ Many Spanish explorers followed Columbus to North America.

MAP SKILL Movement *Which explorers passed through Texas or along the Texas coastline?*

Spain Reaches the Western Hemisphere

In the 1500s, a new group of people began to travel through Texas— explorers from Europe. The story begins with Christopher Columbus.

Christopher Columbus was a sea captain and a trader. Europeans traded with countries in Asia for many goods, including spices such as pepper and cinnamon. But routes east from Europe to Asia were long and difficult. Columbus thought he could save time by sailing west across the Atlantic Ocean. He convinced the king and queen of Spain to let him test this plan.

In 1492, Columbus set out. For more than two months, his ships sailed westward. When Columbus landed, he thought he was close to

China or Japan. In fact, he was on an island near modern-day Florida. He had not reached the rich ports of Asia. He had reached the Americas. The Spanish explorers who followed Columbus quickly learned that the Americas had riches too—gold, silver, and plenty of land. The Spanish began to explore.

The rulers of Spain had three main goals for exploring the Americas. The first was to collect riches. The second was to teach Native Americans about the Roman Catholic religion. The third was to conquer the land and the people they came across and to claim the land as their own.

REVIEW What reason did Columbus have for exploration? **Main Idea and Details**

Cortés Comes to Mexico

In 1519, a Spaniard named Hernando Cortés arrived in what is now Mexico. Cortés was a **conquistador** (kohn KEES tah dohr), which means "conqueror." It did not take long for Cortés and his army of more than 500 soldiers to reach the grand Aztec city of Tenochtitlan. Cortés wanted to claim the city's treasure, but first he had to conquer the Aztecs and their leader, **Moctezuma II** (mok teh ZOO muh). It took two years, but Cortés and his army finally defeated the Aztecs and claimed their riches and their land. The Spanish came to call this land New Spain. Tenochtitlan later became Mexico City.

REVIEW How did the Spaniards gain control of the Aztec empire? **Cause and Effect**

▶ **Cabeza de Vaca and other crew members washed up on the shore.**

Cabeza de Vaca

In 1528, a group of about 600 Spaniards landed near Tampa Bay in what is now Florida. One of the members of the party, **Alvar Núñez Cabeza de Vaca** (ahl vahr NOO nyes kah BEHZ zuh day VAH kah), was about to have a great adventure.

The explorers left their ship to explore. They could not find their way back to the ship. They built rafts and tried to sail along the coast to Mexico, but a storm carried them far from shore. The men thought they might never reach land. Then early one morning Cabeza de Vaca heard the sound of breaking waves. The men on his raft awoke to a big surprise.

"Close to shore a wave took us and hurled [threw] the barge a horse's length out of water."

It was November 6, 1528. Cabeza de Vaca and his crew had landed in Texas, on **Galveston Island.**

Fifteen men had survived the voyage. Native Americans met the Spaniards on the beach, gave them food, and treated them well. But many of the sailors soon died or wandered off. Only four of them would make it to Mexico. That would take more than seven years.

For a time, Cabeza de Vaca traveled between Native American groups, trading shells for animal skins. After several years, Cabeza de Vaca went in search of other Spaniards. He was captured by another Native American group. There he met three men who had been shipwrecked with him—two Spaniards and an enslaved African named **Estéban** (es TAY bahn). They were also captives. Together, they escaped.

The four men walked throughout South Texas, looking for other Spaniards. They traveled west, perhaps as far as California. In 1536, they came to Mexico City. They told the Spanish leaders about their journey. The Spaniards were especially interested in a story the travelers had heard from some Native Americans about cities of gold. Soon the Spanish leaders were making plans to search for the Seven Cities of Cíbola (SEE boh lah).

REVIEW Why do you think it took Cabeza de Vaca so many years to get to Mexico City? **Draw Conclusions**

Literature and Social Studies

Cabeza de Vaca had many adventures on his journey. Here, in his own words, translated into English, he tells how he helped a Native American.

Here they brought to me a man who, they told, a long time ago had been shot . . . with an arrow, the head of which stuck close to his heart. He said it gave him much pain. . . . I touched the region of the body and felt the arrowhead. . . . So, with a knife, I . . . got it out; it was very long. Then, with a deer-bone . . . I made two stitches. After I had extracted [taken out] the arrow, they begged me for it, and I gave it to them. The whole village came back to look at it, and they sent it farther inland that the people there might see it also.

► **Cabeza de Vaca's journal**

▶ Pueblos such as North Taos, in New Mexico, shone golden in the sun.

Cities of Gold?

The Spanish decided to send a search party to see if the rumors of seven golden cities called Cíbola were true. A priest named Fray Marcos de Niza (MAHR cohs day NEE suh) led the group. Estéban was ordered to act as a guide and a scout. In 1539, they began their search. Estéban was killed on this journey, but Fray Marcos returned to Mexico. He said he had seen the golden cities, but he had not really seen cities of gold. He had seen adobe villages shining in the desert sunlight.

Spanish officials asked a nobleman to claim the cities for Spain. His name was **Francisco Vásquez de Coronado** (frahn SEEZ koh VAHS kez day kor oh NAH doh). In 1540, Coronado and many hundreds of soldiers began their journey.

When Coronado arrived at a pueblo he called Cíbola, he fought and won a battle with the Zuñi (ZOO nyee) people who lived there. After searching the pueblo, Coronado learned the truth. There was no gold at Cíbola.

REVIEW Which explorer thought he saw the golden cities? Which explorer discovered the truth about them?
Main Idea and Details

Coronado Explores Texas

Coronado would not give up. He sent search parties throughout the Southwest. One party even reached the Grand Canyon. Coronado and his soldiers searched pueblo after pueblo, but still they found no gold.

In one pueblo Coronado met a Pawnee Indian who told him about a land of riches called Quivira (key VEHR uh). Once again, Coronado set out in search of gold. The Pawnee acted as a guide. The Spanish called him *El Turco,* or "the Turk."

In April 1541, the explorers reached the Caprock Escarpment. When they climbed to the top, the Spaniards were amazed by the vast plain that stretched before them. Coronado called this plain *Llano Estacado* (YAHN noh es tah KAH doh), or "staked plains." We call it by the same name today.

Coronado's group traveled for days over the prairie until they came to Palo Duro Canyon. There they rested. Palo Duro Canyon was beautiful, but it held no gold. Coronado marched on.

Finally, Coronado reached Quivira. Many people think it was in present-day Oklahoma or Kansas. Quivira was a village of grass dwellings. There was no gold there either.

El Turco admitted that he had lied. The people of his pueblo had asked him to lead the Spaniards into the plains and to lose them. In anger, Coronado had El Turco killed. Coronado returned to Mexico empty-handed.

REVIEW What parts of Texas did Coronado and his party pass through? **Main Idea and Details**

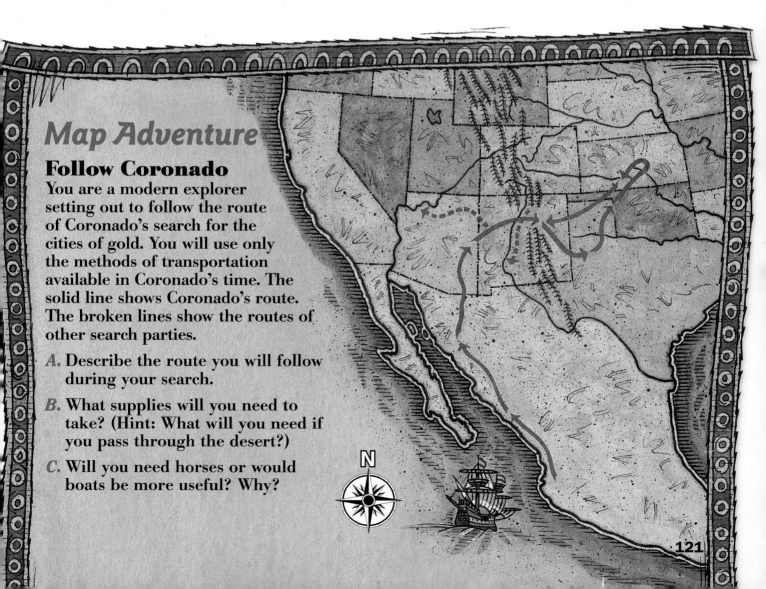

Map Adventure

Follow Coronado

You are a modern explorer setting out to follow the route of Coronado's search for the cities of gold. You will use only the methods of transportation available in Coronado's time. The solid line shows Coronado's route. The broken lines show the routes of other search parties.

A. Describe the route you will follow during your search.

B. What supplies will you need to take? (Hint: What will you need if you pass through the desert?)

C. Will you need horses or would boats be more useful? Why?

N

FACT FILE
More Explorers in Texas

Álonso Alvarez de Piñeda was the first Spanish explorer to reach Texas. In 1519, he sailed along the Gulf Coast looking for good places to settle. He drew the first maps of the Texas coastline.

Hernando de Soto explored what is now the southeastern United States. In 1541, he reached the Mississippi River but died soon after.

Luis de Moscoso then led de Soto's group through East Texas. They did not find gold, but Moscoso noticed oil shimmering on the water near the coast.

Juan de Oñate led a group of explorers through what is now West Texas to settle in New Mexico. Oñate called the place where they crossed the Rio Grande "El Paso del Norte"— the pass to the north. Today the site is known as El Paso.

La Salle Reaches Texas

In 1685, a French explorer, **René-Robert Cavelier, Sieur de La Salle** (ruh NAY roh BEHR kah veh LYAY, SYOOR duh lah SAHL), came to Texas. Several years before, he had traveled down the Mississippi River. He claimed the land around the river for France. He called it Louisiana in honor of the French king, Louis XIV.

When he returned to France, he convinced the king to give him ships to take people to Louisiana. The king agreed that La Salle could start a colony there. A **colony** is a settlement of people who have left one country to live in another.

La Salle missed Louisiana by at least 400 miles. Instead, he landed to the west, on the shore of Matagordo Bay on the Texas coast.

La Salle built a small fort on **Garcitas Creek,** inland from the bay. From there he hoped to find his way to Louisiana by land. It was not a good place to live though. The land was marshy and unhealthful. Some of the French settlers became sick and died. La Salle left to seek help, but on the journey his own soldiers turned on him and killed him. Meanwhile, the Karankawa attacked the French fort.

In 1689, Spanish soldiers arrived, ready to fight for land they claimed was theirs. They found La Salle's fort, but it was ruined and empty. Still, by building their fort, the French colonists had threatened Spain's claim to East Texas. The Spanish grew more determined to hold on to their land.

REVIEW Why did La Salle build a fort in Texas? *Cause and Effect*

Summarize the Lesson

1492 Christopher Columbus landed in the Americas.

1528 Cabeza de Vaca reached Texas.

1540 Coronado began searching for the golden cities of Cíbola.

1685 La Salle built a fort in Texas.

▶ **Archaeologists uncovered La Salle's ship, the *Belle*.**

★ LESSON 1
REVIEW

Check Facts and Main Ideas

1. ↻ **Compare and Contrast** On a separate sheet of paper, complete the diagram to show how the journeys of Cabeza de Vaca and Coronado were alike and different.

Alike

Different

2. Who was Columbus and why is he important to the history of Texas?

3. Who was La Salle and why is he important to the history of Texas?

4. Why did Spain send explorers into Mexico and the lands to the north?

5. **Critical Thinking:** *Draw Conclusions* Why do you think the Spanish were not quick to set up colonies in Texas?

Link to ⌗⌗ **Reading**

Read City Stories Go to the library or online to research the Seven Cities of Cíbola, the fabled cities of gold. Then write a report about what you read. Draw pictures to illustrate your report.

FRANCISCO VÁSQUEZ DE CORONADO

c. 1510–1554

Francisco Vásquez de Coronado was born in Salamanca, Spain. At the age of 25, Coronado came to Mexico. He was an assistant to the first Spanish viceroy, or regional ruler. About three years later, Coronado married the daughter of New Spain's colonial treasurer.

Coronado did very well in Mexico. He was able to stop an uprising of Spanish slaves. He became the governor of a Mexican province. He was wealthy.

When the Spanish rulers heard about golden cities to the north, Viceroy Antonio de Mendoza chose Coronado to lead the search for them. Although the expedition left Mexico with high hopes, Coronado did not find any gold or treasure. He returned to Mexico with only about 100 men. The viceroy declared the expedition a total failure.

BIOFACT

Coronado and Viceroy Mendoza spent their own Spanish money equal to four million dollars—to search for the "cities of gold."

Coronado's luck did not get much better after that. He was still governor of the Mexican province for a few years. Then he was accused of mistreating Native Americans under his control. He was cleared of these charges, but in 1544 he lost his position as governor. He went to live in Mexico City, where he died ten years later.

Learn from Biographies

How do you think Coronado's early life influenced him to search for the "cities of gold"?

For more information, go online to *Meet the People* at **www.sfsocialstudies.com**.

California Exploration

At the same time that Coronado's troops returned to Mexico City in 1542, Juan Rodríguez Cabrillo (kah BREE yoh) led another Spanish expedition to the west coast of North America. These explorers were looking for land and treasure too. Along the way, Cabrillo's group met Native Americans, the Chumash, who lived in what is now southern California. Today Cabrillo is remembered as the first European to explore the California coast.

PACIFIC OCEAN

ALTA CALIFORNIA

Arkansas R.

San Diego Bay

BAJA CALIFORNIA

Rio Grande

Key
← Coronado, 1540–1542
← Cabrillo, 1542–1543

▶ Cabrillo first sailed to the present-day San Diego Bay. His troops explored the coast there and then traveled northward to Monterey Bay.

▶ *Point Lobos, Monterey, California* by Thomas Moran

▶ Statue of Cabrillo, Cabrillo National Monument, San Diego

LESSON
2

1650   1700   1750   1800

1682
Mission Ysleta
is founded.

1720
Mission San
José is founded.

Ysleta

San Antonio

PREVIEW

Focus on the Main Idea
Spain built missions to strengthen its hold on Texas lands.

PLACES
Ysleta
San Antonio

VOCABULARY
mission
presidio
villa

Spaniards Settle in Texas

You Are There Since the end of winter, your family and friends have been helping to build the new mission in honor of Saint Joseph—San José. In fact, you spend most of your time there now. You and your father help lay tiles on the roof of the church and the houses. Your mother and your sisters cook meals and tend to the garden.

You miss your old village. But the mission does have some good points. You like the fresh food from the garden. You're learning to read and write. Best of all, you've made new friends.

The bells ring out. It's chapel time. After you say your prayers, you might speak to the priest. You can ask him if the Spanish plan to stay in this place. You wonder if they will live here for a long time.

Compare and Contrast As you read, think about how life in the missions differed from life in Native American villages.

Spanish Missions in Texas

In Lesson 1, you read about La Salle's French colony. That colony failed, but Spanish leaders still worried that France would try to claim more land in Texas.

With help from the Roman Catholic Church, the Spanish built **missions,** or religious settlements, in Texas. Missions often included a church, houses, and farm buildings. The Spanish believed that the missions gave them a strong claim to the land.

The Spanish usually built missions near places already settled by Native Americans. A priest, or padre (PAH dray), was in charge of each

▶ **Mission San José**

mission. *Padre* is the Spanish word for "father." The padres taught the Native Americans about the Roman Catholic religion and introduced them to other Spanish customs.

▶ **Mission Ysleta**

Corpus Christi de la Isleta (ee SLAY tah), the first Spanish mission in Texas, was built more than 300 years ago, in 1682. It still stands today near El Paso. You may know it as Mission Ysleta. The city of **Ysleta** grew up around the mission.

In the early 1700s the Spanish built more missions. Five of them, all still standing, were located around the source of the San Antonio River. The nearby water, trees, and stones were used as building materials. Mission San José y San Miguel de Aguayo—Mission San José, for short—was so important to the community of **San Antonio** that it became known as the "Queen of the Missions." People still attend church services there today.

REVIEW What are some similarities and differences between Mission Ysleta and Mission San José?

↻ **Compare and Contrast**

Missions, Presidios, and Villas in Texas

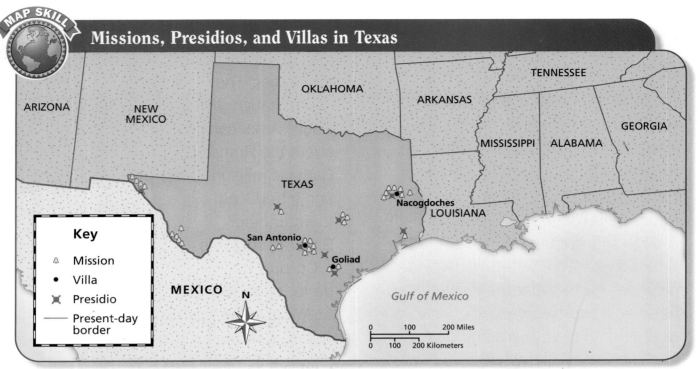

Key

- △ Mission
- • Villa
- ✳ Presidio
- — Present-day border

▶ This map shows the relationships among some Texas missions, presidios, and villas.

MAP SKILL Use a Map Key *What villa has the most missions near it?*

Missions, Presidios, and Villas

Mission buildings were usually surrounded by high stone walls. Spanish settlers and local Native Americans attended church and school there. At mission workshops, they made goods such as pottery, baskets, and tools.

Some Native Americans chose to move their families to the missions. The missions offered food and shelter in payment for work. But at some missions the Spanish forced Native Americans to live and work there.

Some groups of Native Americans were angry that the Spanish had settled on their land. They attacked the missons. To protect themselves, the Spanish built **presidios,** or forts, near the missions. Soldiers in the

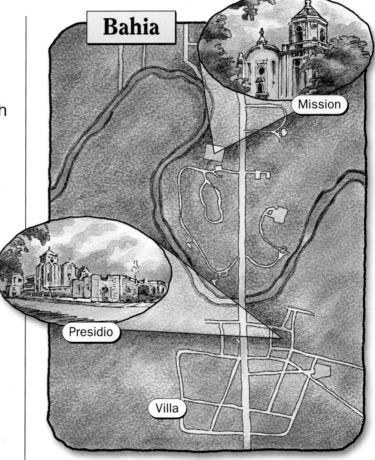

Bahia

Mission

Presidio

Villa

▶ Bahia, near Goliad, is an example of a presidio and villa that grew near a mission.

128

forts defended people in the missions during attacks. **Villas,** or towns, often grew up between and around the missions and presidios to provide goods and services to both. Most settlers in the villas were people from northern Mexico. They were seeking good farming and ranching land. People from Africa and from Spain's Canary Islands also lived in the villas. Both men and women planted and harvested crops. Everyone helped with the animals. Some people in the villa offered services, like trading or blacksmithing. For enjoyment, the people had dances, concerts, and *fiestas*, or celebrations.

REVIEW Why were presidios built near missions? **Cause and Effect**

A New Culture

Throughout history, people from many different backgrounds settled in the land we know as Texas. Each group—from hunters of the plains to woodland farmers—introduced its own culture.

Spaniards brought horses and European cattle with them to the Americas. It did not take long for Native Americans to see that riding horses and herding cattle could enrich their lives.

In the missions, Spaniards introduced foods such as onions, grapes, and wheat to the Native Americans. In turn, Native Americans

▶ **Native American flute and rattle**

showed the Spanish how to grow and prepare corn, tomatoes, beans, and potatoes.

Some Native Americans were interested in the church music of the mission. Many learned to play European instruments. Here is what a Spanish priest, Father Solis, wrote in 1767:

"Most of [the Native Americans] play some musical instrument, the guitar, the violin or the harp. All have good voices, and on Saturdays . . . a choir of four . . . with musical accompaniment, sings so beautifully that it is a delight to hear it."

Like the music, the new culture was no longer just Spanish or Native American. Instead, it was a blend of many cultures that had come together in the missions and other areas north of the Rio Grande.

REVIEW What parts of their culture did Native Americans share with Spaniards? **Main Idea and Details**

129

A Texas Mission

Workers' Quarters and Workshops

Workers' Quarters and Workshops

Well

Workers' Quarters and Workshops

Oven

Well

Church

Grape Arbor

Gate

Granary

Spanish Residence

Flour Mill

DIAGRAM SKILL *Use the diagram to explain how a mission could meet the needs of the people who lived there.*

Spanish Heritage in Texas

Today Texas is filled with signs of its Spanish heritage. Many Texans speak Spanish. Many places bear Spanish names such as Laredo, the Brazos River, Atascosa County, or Guadalupe Street. Tex-Mex foods are a blend of Native American and Spanish ways of cooking. Some homes, offices, and churches are built in the style of the Spanish missions.

If you look at and listen to the arts in Texas, you'll often notice a Spanish flair. Music, theater, the visual arts, dance—yes, the Spanish influence on Texas culture is everywhere. It reminds Texans of the people who helped create the Texas we know today.

REVIEW What are some reminders of the Spanish heritage in Texas?
Main Idea and Details

Summarize the Lesson

1682 Mission Ysleta was founded near present-day El Paso.

1720 Mission San José was founded on the San Antonio River.

Today Texans are surrounded by signs of their Spanish heritage.

▶ These dancers help keep Spanish and Mexican culture alive in Texas.

★ **LESSON 2** **REVIEW**

Check Facts and Main Ideas

1. **Compare and Contrast** On a separate sheet of paper, complete the diagram. Tell how the lives of Native Americans who lived in the missions and the lives of Native Americans you read about in Chapter 3 were alike and different.

Alike	Different
	Those living in missions learned Spanish customs.

2. When and where did the Spanish build their first mission in Texas?

3. Why did the Spanish build missions in Texas?

4. Name three ways in which Spanish traditions are a part of life in Texas today.

5. **Critical Thinking:** *Analyze Information* How did missions, presidios, and villas work together as part of Texas settlements?

Link to Art

Draw a Mission Job Think of a job you might have done at a mission. Draw a picture of yourself doing that job. Include details to show how your work helps others in the mission.

Map and Globe Skills

Find Latitude and Longitude

What? **Latitude** and **longitude** are sets of lines drawn on a map or a globe. These numbered lines give the exact "address" of any place on Earth.

Lines of latitude extend east to west. The latitude line that goes around the middle of Earth is known as the **equator**. Lines of latitude are measured in degrees. The equator is at 0° (zero degrees) latitude. Lines of latitude are called **parallels**. They run parallel, or side-by-side, around Earth and never meet.

Longitude lines, or **meridians**, run from north to south. The **prime meridian** is the starting line for measuring longitude. It is at 0° longitude. Lines of longitude are not parallel. These lines meet at the North Pole and at the South Pole.

Why? Latitude and longitude lines help you find places on Earth. You can give the location of a place by naming the latitude and longitude lines closest to it.

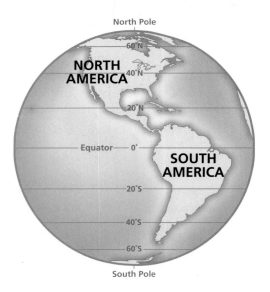

Lines of Latitude

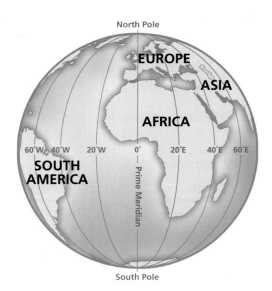

Lines of Longitude

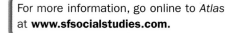
For more information, go online to *Atlas* at **www.sfsocialstudies.com**.

How? Compare the globes on page 132. Notice that the lines of latitude north of the equator are labeled *N*. Lines south of the equator are labeled *S*. Lines of longitude east of the prime meridian are labeled *E*. Those west of the prime meridian are labeled *W*.

Lines of latitude and longitude together form a grid—a crisscross pattern of lines. Study the grid on the map of Texas below.

Find the city of Midland. Look for the line of latitude closest to Midland. Write down this number. Then find the line of longitude closest to this city. Write down the number after the latitude number. When naming latitude and longitude, be sure to include the direction labels, *N* or *S* and *E* or *W*.

Think and Apply

❶ What lines of longitude and latitude meet near El Paso?

❷ Which line of latitude is closest to Austin? Which line of longitude is closest?

❸ Which two cities shown on the map are closest to 28° N latitude?

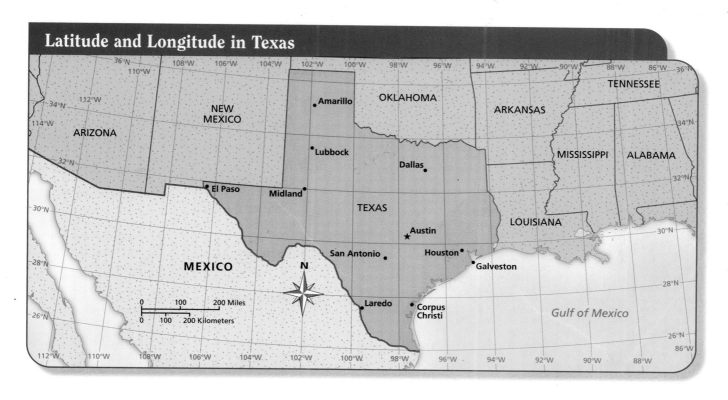

Latitude and Longitude in Texas

1450   1500   1550

1492
Columbus landed in the Americas.

1528
Cabeza de Vaca reached Texas.

1540
Coronado's search for gold began.

Chapter Summary

Target Skill

Compare and Contrast

On a separate sheet of paper, list the similarities and differences between Cabeza de Vaca's journey in Texas and La Salle's experience in Texas.

Similarities

Differences

Vocabulary

Use each vocabulary word in a sentence that explains its meaning.

1. **conquistador** (p. 118)

2. **colony** (p. 122)

3. **mission** (p. 127)

4. **presidio** (p. 128)

5. **villa** (p. 129)

▶ **Conquistador's helmet**

People

Match each person with the correct description.

1. **Christopher Columbus** (p. 117)

2. **Moctezuma II** (p. 118)

3. **Cabeza de Vaca** (p. 118)

4. **Estéban** (p. 119)

5. **Coronado** (p. 120)

6. **La Salle** (p. 122)

a. Aztec leader defeated by Cortés

b. Spanish explorer who lived with Native Americans

c. French explorer who built a fort in Texas

d. Spanish explorer led a search for gold

e. Explorer sent by the rulers of Spain to find a faster route to Asia

f. African who scouted cities of gold

1600	1650	1700	1750

1682
Mission Ysleta was founded.

1685
La Salle built a fort in Texas.

1720
Mission San José was founded.

Facts and Main Ideas

1 What did Coronado discover about the "cities of gold"?

2 What happened to La Salle's colony in Texas?

3 What two duties did Spanish padres have in the missions?

4 **Time Line** How many years went by between Cabeza de Vaca's landing in Texas and the founding of Mission Ysleta?

5 **Main Idea** Why did Spain send explorers north from Mexico?

6 **Main Idea** Why did the Spanish set up missions in Texas?

7 **Critical Thinking:** *Draw Conclusions* How do you think the arrival of the Spanish in Texas changed the lives of Native Americans? Name two ways.

Internet Activity

To get help with vocabulary and people, select the dictionary or encyclopedia from *Social Studies Library* at **www.sfsocialstudies.com.**

Write About History

1 **Write a paragraph** about the explorer with whom you would most like to have traveled. Give reasons for your choice.

2 **Write a letter** to a friend as a member of Coronado's expedition. Describe three amazing things you have seen on the journey.

3 **Write a comparison** that explains what life was like for Native Americans before and after the Spanish missions were built. What were the good points and bad points about each way of life?

Apply Skills

Find Latitude and Longitude

Use the map below or on page 133 to answer the questions.

1 What is the line of longitude closest to Amarillo and Lubbock?

2 What is the line of latitude closest to Houston?

3 What Texas city is about 28°N latitude and 98°W longitude?

CHAPTER 5

Texas Colonies and Conflicts

Lesson 1

**San Felipe de Austin
1824**
Stephen F. Austin
founds a city.

1

Lesson 2

**Mexico City, Mexico
1833**
Stephen F. Austin
asks for rights
for Texas.

2

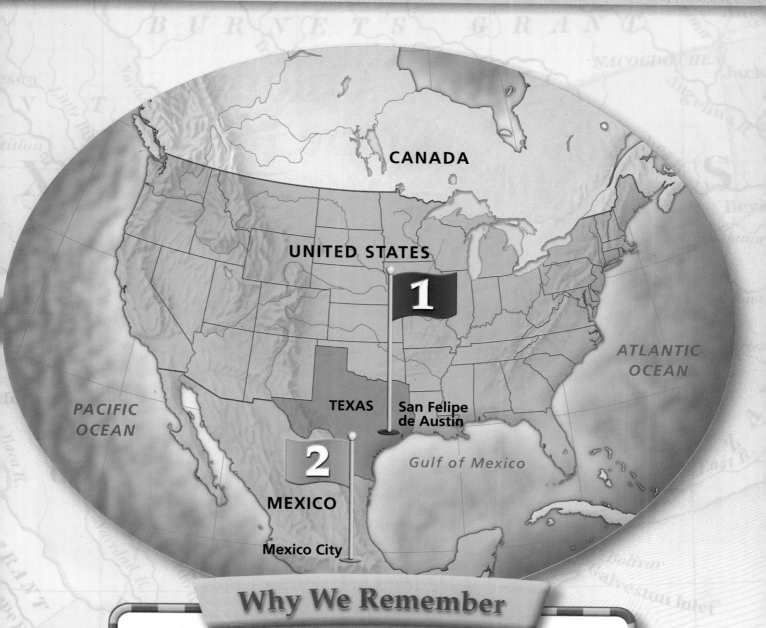

CANADA

UNITED STATES

1

ATLANTIC
OCEAN

PACIFIC
OCEAN

TEXAS   San Felipe
de Austin

2

Gulf of Mexico

MEXICO

Mexico City

Why We Remember

Today Texas and Mexico are close neighbors, separated by a national border. Fewer than two hundred years ago, they were one colony ruled by Spain. Then, in 1821, Mexico, including Texas, gained its independence. New settlers from the United States and Europe began to enter Texas. They met Mexican settlers who were already there and Native Americans who fought to protect their land.

San Felipe de Austin
Victoria
Dolores

PREVIEW

Focus on the Main Idea
Mexico gained independence from Spain as people from the United States began to move to Texas.

PLACES
Dolores, Mexico
San Felipe de Austin
Victoria

PEOPLE
Father Miguel Hidalgo
Moses Austin
Stephen F. Austin
Jane Long
Gail Borden
Erasmo Seguín
Martín de León
Patricia de la Garza de León
Lorenzo de Zavala

VOCABULARY
revolution
immigrant
empresario
militia
cash crop
vaquero

TERMS
Old Three Hundred

Colonists Come to Texas

You Are There

Who? Father Miguel Hidalgo, you, and other people of the town

Where? Dolores, a small town in Mexico

When? September 16, 1810

What? Early in the morning, you hear loud voices in the churchyard. Father Hidalgo is speaking to a large group of angry people. Father Hidalgo raises a banner and shouts, "Down with bad government!" Then he strides away. The people follow him.

Why? Native Americans and Mexicans in Dolores are upset. They want to have more power in their government.

What happens next changes the future of Mexico.

▶ Father Miguel Hidalgo

Summarize As you read, summarize the events that led to the formation of the colonies in Texas.

Mexico's Independence from Spain

What caused Father Miguel Hidalgo to speak out against the Spanish government? By about 1800, many Mexicans disliked the high taxes and other ways Spain tried to force them to give money to the Spanish king. Some Mexicans felt that their country should not be under Spanish rule. They believed they could handle their own affairs.

In 1803, Fr. Hidalgo traveled to the town of Dolores to help the poor people in that part of Mexico. He taught the farmers there to grow olives and grapes so they could earn a living.

However, Spanish leaders wanted Mexicans to buy olives and grapes from Spain. They had made laws against growing these crops in Mexico. The Spanish leaders chopped down the olive trees and grapevines that Fr. Hidalgo had helped the farmers plant.

Fr. Hidalgo took action. On September 16, 1810, he gave a speech that is remembered as "el grito de Dolores," or "the cry of Dolores." His speech called for a government that would be fair to all people. This demand started a **revolution,** or an organized fight against the government.

The Spanish government had Fr. Hidalgo killed, but the struggle continued. In 1821, after a long war, Mexicans won their independence. As you will see, these events had a big effect on the part of Mexico now known as Texas.

REVIEW How did Fr. Hidalgo's ideas about olive trees and grapevines differ from those of the Spanish government? ➲ **Compare and Contrast**

Then and Now

Mexican Independence Day

Each year, many Texans celebrate *Diez y Seis de Septiembre*, or September Sixteenth, Mexican Independence Day. Children break colorful piñatas and dance to Mexican folk songs. Bands perform on stages decorated with streamers of red, green, and white—the colors of the Mexican flag. Families enjoy delicious Mexican foods.

Celebrations may also include a performance of Father Hidalgo's famous speech.

▶ This mariachi band celebrates Mexican independence.

139

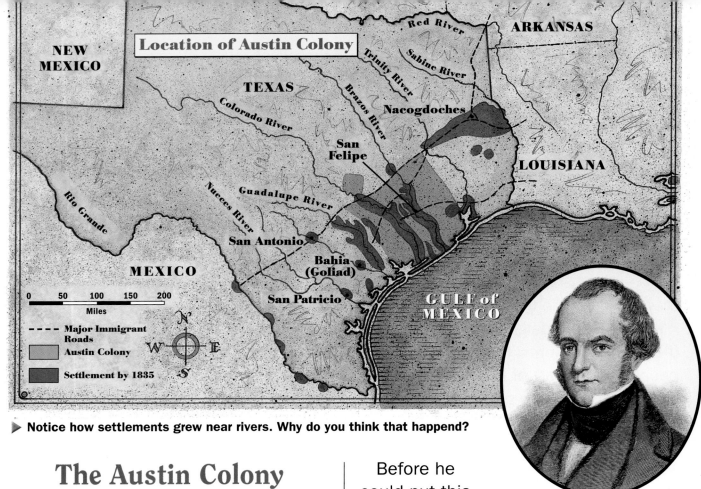

Location of Austin Colony

NEW MEXICO

TEXAS

Red River

Trinity River

Sabine River

ARKANSAS

Colorado River

Brazos River

Nacogdoches

San Felipe

LOUISIANA

Nueces River

Guadalupe River

Rio Grande

San Antonio

Bahia (Goliad)

MEXICO

San Patricio

GULF of MEXICO

0 50 100 150 200
Miles

- - - Major Immigrant Roads

Austin Colony

Settlement by 1835

N W E S

▶ Notice how settlements grew near rivers. Why do you think that happend?

▶ Stephen F. Austin

The Austin Colony

In addition to the revolution, the Spanish government had trouble settling Texas. Few Spaniards and Mexicans wanted to move there. Bands of outlaws were raiding in Texas. The Spanish government thought that a settlement of dependable Anglo American landowners might help protect Texas from its enemies.

American businessman **Moses Austin** heard that the Spanish government was offering grants, or gifts, of Texas land. In December 1820, he traveled from Missouri to San Antonio to ask the Spanish governor, Antonio María Martínez, for permission to start a colony. The governor agreed that Austin could bring 300 families to Texas.

Before he could put this plan into action, Moses Austin died. His son, **Stephen F. Austin,** carried out the plan. Austin visited Texas in 1821 to choose land for the colony. Between the Colorado and Brazos Rivers, he found land that was "as good in every respect as man could wish for. . . ."

Austin wrote letters and placed ads in newspapers telling about his plan. Austin looked carefully at each reponse he received. He wanted to find honest, hard-working people who would make the colony a success. Today Stephen F. Austin is known as the "Father of Texas."

The first of the Austin colonists arrived at the end of 1821. Then Austin heard that the revolution in Mexico had ended. The Spanish had lost. Austin traveled to Mexico City. He hoped that the new Mexican government would honor his father's agreement with Martínez. The Mexican leaders allowed Austin to set up the new colony. They appointed him as its judge and made him responsible for governing and defending the colony.

In 1821, Austin visited a site on the Brazos River, near the center of his colony. There was plenty of fresh water and trees for timber. He founded a city called San Felipe de Austin at the site in 1824. By 1828, the city had a blacksmith shop, a hotel, stores, and about 40 log cabins.

Jane Long joined the Austin colony in 1824. She had come to Texas earlier with her husband, James, a soldier. While James was away, Jane spent the harsh winter of 1821 at a fort near Galveston Island. Her two young children and a twelve-year-old servant girl, Kian, were the only other people there.

Sometimes Jane Long fired the fort's cannon to convince the Karankawa, who lived nearby, that the fort was full of soldiers. Long and Kian fished and gathered oysters. Later they learned that James Long had died. After the family moved to Austin's colony, Jane Long ran a hotel with Kian's help. Jane Long is known as the "Mother of Texas."

▶ Jane Long

The Mexican government allowed more American immigrants into Texas. An immigrant is a person who comes to live in a new region or country. By 1831 the Mexican government had signed agreements with 25 more empresarios. An empresario was a person who brought settlers into a colony, divided up the land, and enforced the law. Like Stephen F. Austin, these empresarios brought Anglo Americans to Texas.

Soon "Texas Fever" swept the United States. Thousands of people headed for Texas. Most hoped to make money by growing cotton. Many came because of the low cost of land. Some settlers wrote GTT—"Gone to Texas"—above their doors as they left their old homes.

REVIEW What impact did Mexico's independence from Spain have on events in Texas? Draw Conclusions

The First Colonists

How did these settlers get to Texas? Many bumped along rough, muddy trails in covered wagons. Others rode flatboats down the Mississippi River to New Orleans. From there they traveled by ship to Galveston. Some settlers rode horses with all their possessions strapped to their saddles.

▶ Gail Borden

The first 297 families who settled in Austin's colony were known as the **Old Three Hundred.** Most were ranchers or farmers from Louisiana, Alabama, Arkansas, Tennessee, and Missouri. Some enslaved African Americans were brought by their owners.

Life could be hard for the settlers. They lived in rough log cabins with dirt floors. At first, they tried to grow crops that were not well suited to the Texas climate. They also faced conflicts with nearby Native Americans such as the Karankawa. Austin's colony was built on the Karankawa's traditional land. The Karankawa were angry that the colonists claimed the land as their own. They raided the settlements. To defend themselves, the colonists organized militias. A **militia** is a group of volunteer soldiers.

Some colonists used their talents to make life in the colony better. **Gail Borden,** a publisher and inventor, came to live in San Felipe de Austin in 1830. He started a newspaper called the *Telegraph and Texas Register*. Years later, Borden saw a child die from drinking spoiled milk. He spent five years working on a new product—condensed milk. This kind of milk came in a can and would not spoil. It made Borden famous and wealthy. He and his wife gave some of their money to schools and other good causes.

▶ Gail Borden's machine for condensing milk

▶ An 1887 advertisement for Borden's Condensed Milk

REVIEW Why did Gail Borden develop condensed milk?
Cause and Effect

▶ A replica of Stephen F. Austin's dog-run cabin in San Felipe de Austin State Historical Park

Everyday Life in the Austin Colony

After the colonists chose their land, they built homes using the materials available to them: stones, mud, and timber. Neighbors often helped newcomers with the hard work.

Many settlers' homes were simple log houses called dog-run or dog-trot cabins. These houses had only two rooms, connected by an open breezeway. The breezeway was a good place for the family dogs to nap. The breezes cooled the rooms. Fireplaces in both rooms provided heat and light.

The colonists made their own furniture from the wood of nearby trees. They stuffed goose feathers or cornhusks into mattresses and swept the dirt floors with brooms made from grass.

Family members worked together. When they were not in school, younger children milked cows, gathered eggs, and fed the livestock. Men and boys hunted deer and wild game. The whole family plowed fields and planted crops such as cotton, corn, and sugarcane. Women and girls weeded the gardens, sewed clothes, made candles, and cooked.

As they settled into their new lives, some families began to grow enough crops to sell. These **cash crops,** or crops that are grown to be sold at a market, included cotton and sugarcane. Other settlers raised and sold cattle for beef and hides.

REVIEW Why do you think colonists made their own furniture?
Draw Conclusions

Tejanos and Tejanas

Long before the first U.S. colonists arrived, Spaniards and Mexicans had lived in Texas. They, as well as those who came later with empresarios, were called *Tejanos* (men) and *Tejanas* (women). Many Tejanos and Tejanas lived near the Rio Grande. Others settled in and around towns such as San Antonio and Goliad.

When Moses Austin first came to Texas, Tejano rancher and politician Erasmo Seguín welcomed him. Later, Seguín and his son, Juan, did business with Stephen F. Austin and became his friends.

In the 1820s, empresario Martín de León, a Texas rancher, brought more than 100 families from Mexico to Texas. De León and his wife, Patricia de la Garza de León, founded the town of Victoria on the Guadalupe River. In 1829, empresario Lorenzo de Zavala, received a land grant for 500 Mexicans to settle northeast of the Austin colony. Still, Texas drew more settlers from the United States than it did from other parts of Mexico. By 1831, Texas settlers from the United States outnumbered Tejano settlers by at least four to one.

REVIEW Who were the Tejanos and Tejanas, and where were their colonies located? **Summarize**

FACT FILE
Empresarios

Martín and Patricia de León founded the only colony in Texas that was almost entirely Mexican. Patricia de la Garza de León started a school and a church in Victoria. After her husband died, she ran the settlement.

Erasmo Seguín served as postmaster for San Antonio for many years. He also served the governments of both Mexico and the Republic of Texas. His son, Juan Seguín, was a hero of the Texas Revolution.

Lorenzo de Zavala held important posts in Mexico both before and after the Mexican Revolution. He helped write the constitution of the Republic of Texas, and served as its first vice president. He was also the author of a book about the history of Mexico.

Ranchos and Vaqueros

Many Tejanos were ranchers. Their *ranchos*, or ranches, were among the first in Texas. Ranching supplied people with meat, leather, and tallow, an animal fat used in making candles.

The Spaniards had started ranching in southeast Texas missions in the 1700s. Over time, their herds had grown. By the late 1700s some herds had thousands of animals.

Vaqueros (vah KAY rohz), or cowboys, drove cattle from southern Texas to Louisiana. They traded the cattle for needed supplies. Many vaqueros were Native Americans who lived in missions. Others were Spaniards and Mexican citizens who had settled on ranches.

Vaqueros spent most of their days on horseback, rounding up cattle and driving herds hundreds of miles to market. They used lariats, or ropes, made of braided leather or plant fibers.

▶ **Vaquero boots with iron spurs**

Vaqueros wore large hats called *sombreros* for shade. Later, other cowboys adopted the clothing, traditions, and equipment of the vaqueros.

REVIEW What group of people adopted the vaquero tradition?
Main Idea and Details

Summarize the Lesson

- **1820** Moses Austin arrived in San Antonio to ask permission to start a colony.
- **1821** Mexico won its independence from Spain, and the first U.S. colonists arrived in Texas.
- **1824** Stephen F. Austin founded San Felipe de Austin.

 LESSON 1 **REVIEW**

Check Facts and Main Ideas

1. Summarize Complete the diagram on a separate sheet of paper by listing at least one accomplishment of each Texas empresario named below. Then summarize their contributions to the settlement of Texas.

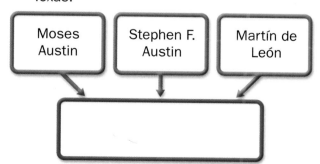

| Moses Austin | Stephen F. Austin | Martín de León |

2. What happened on September 16, 1810?

3. Who was Gail Borden, and why is he important to Texas history?

4. Describe life in the Austin colony.

5. Critical Thinking: *Make Generalizations* Who were the vaqueros, and how did they affect life in Texas?

Link to 🔗 **Geography**

Make a Ranching Chart Use an atlas to find other places in the world where cattle ranching is an important business. Find out about the climate and landforms in these places. Find ways in which they are similar to or different from the climate and landforms of Texas. Make a chart that shows your findings.

A Decision for Democracy

Lorenzo de Zavala had great respect for the ideals of democracy. Because of his beliefs, he had to make a very hard choice.

Lorenzo de Zavala was born in Mexico. Soon after he left school, Zavala began writing in support of democracy. But at that time, Mexico did not have a democratic government. It was still a part of Spain. Zavala's writing got him in trouble. When he was only 26, Zavala was put in prison for speaking out about his democratic beliefs. He spent three years in jail. But that didn't stop him from supporting democracy.

After he was set free, he put his ideas to work. He held many important jobs in the Mexican government. During this time, Mexico became independent of Spain. It set up its own democratic government.

Zavala also had strong ties to Texas. In 1829, he received a grant to found a colony of 500 families there. By 1835, he had to make a hard choice. The president of Mexico had become a dictator. That means he had taken power for himself. Mexico was no longer a democracy.

BUILDING CITIZENSHIP
Caring
★ Respect
Responsibility
Fairness
Honesty
Courage

Zavala decided to give up his role in the Mexican government and live in Texas. But, as he wrote to a friend, he was pulled in two directions:

"I, a Mexican by birth and always partial to [fond of] my native country, have been torn between opposing duties and sentiments [feelings]."

Zavala decided to support Texas's fight for independence. Leaders in Texas often turned to him for advice. He knew plenty about government, politics, and democracy. In 1836, he signed the Texas Declaration of Independence. He became vice president of the new Republic of Texas, and he helped write its constitution. Because of his respect for democratic ideals, Lorenzo de Zavala earned the respect of both Mexicans and Texans.

Respect in Action

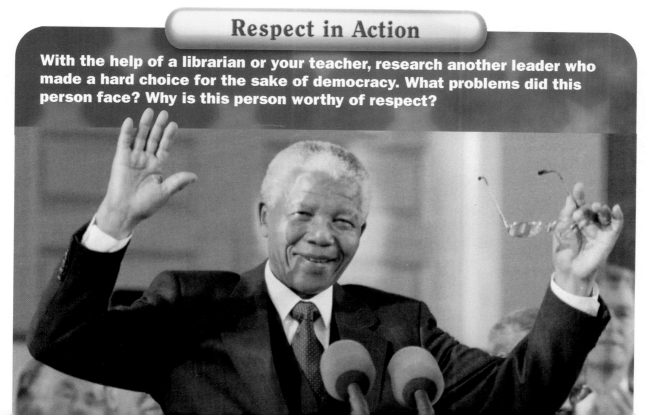

With the help of a librarian or your teacher, research another leader who made a hard choice for the sake of democracy. What problems did this person face? Why is this person worthy of respect?

San Felipe
de Austin

Saltillo

Mexico
City

1830   1835

1830
Law of April 6
is passed.

1832
Texans meet for
the first of two
conventions.

1833
Austin takes Texans'
concerns to Mexico.

Trouble Brews in Texas

PREVIEW

Focus on the Main Idea
Texas leaders tried to solve problems with the Mexican government.

PLACES
San Felipe de Austin
Mexico City, Mexico
Saltillo, Mexico

PEOPLE
Antonio López de Santa Anna

VOCABULARY
right
convention

TERMS
Law of April 6

You Are There

It is a winter day. You are standing in front of a government office in Saltillo, Mexico. Suddenly, you see Stephen F. Austin. He enters the building.

Minutes later, you learn that Austin has been arrested! Shocked, you ask what happened.

"Austin wrote to Texan officials, suggesting that they go ahead and set up a state government for Texas," a young man replies. "Now the Mexican government thinks that Austin wants to start a revolution."

Austin does not want to start a revolt. He simply wants to mend the problems between the Mexican government and the Texas colonists.

Compare and Contrast As you read, look for details that help you compare and contrast the Mexican colonists and the settlers from the United States.

Trouble in Texas Colonies

Under the Mexican Constitution of 1824, Texas became part of the Mexican state of Coahuila and Texas. United States citizens who moved to Texas during the 1820s and 1830s became Mexican citizens. Problems soon arose. These problems led to the arrest of Stephen F. Austin.

First, there was a language problem. Most people who lived in Mexico spoke Spanish. But most Anglo Americans spoke only English.

Second, there were religious differences. The Mexican government required its citizens to be Roman Catholic. But many Anglo Americans were Protestants, who held different Christian beliefs from Catholics. When settlers signed on to receive land in Texas, they agreed to become Roman Catholics. However, most of them did not do so.

A third problem was slavery. In Mexico, slavery was against the law. But some U.S. citizens had the **right,** or freedom, to own slaves, especially in the South. Many slave owners thought that they needed slave labor to make money on their crops. Mexican leaders wanted settlers to make money on their crops too. They allowed new settlers to bring slaves to Texas. But some settlers worried that the Mexican government might change its mind.

Mexican leaders began to worry that Texans might try to form their own government. In 1830 Mexican leaders passed the **Law of April 6.** This law said that very few United States citizens—and no slaves—could immigrate to Texas. The law also placed a tax on certain goods that passed through Texas ports. Texans feared this decree would separate them from their families in the United States and hurt their businesses.

REVIEW What caused the Mexican government to pass the Law of April 6?
Cause and Effect

▶ **Stephen F. Austin's Mexican citizenship papers**

149

Texans Meet to Take Action

In October 1832, and again in April 1833, the colonists gathered in San Felipe de Austin for conventions, or formal meetings. The colonists wanted Mexico to allow U.S. citizens to immigrate to Texas again. They also wanted Texas to become a separate state within Mexico so they could make some of their own decisions.

Stephen F. Austin was chosen to discuss this plan with the leader of Mexico, Antonio López de Santa Anna. Santa Anna was president of Mexico. By 1833, he had taken power for himself. He had become a dictator.

Austin arrived in Mexico City in July 1833. He waited many months before Santa Anna met with him. Then, before Austin could leave Mexico, he was arrested in Saltillo and jailed.

REVIEW What did the colonists decide at their conventions?
Main Idea and Details

Summarize the Lesson

— **April 6, 1830** The Mexican government passed the Law of April 6.

— **October 1832 and April 1833** Texans gathered in San Felipe de Austin.

— **July 1833** Stephen F. Austin arrived in Mexico.

 LESSON 2 **REVIEW**

Check Facts and Main Ideas

1. **Compare and Contrast** On a separate sheet of paper, complete the following chart to show the similarities and differences between the Anglo American immigrants in Texas and the Mexican government.

Similarities	Differences
Both wanted a say in the government.	Language was different.

2. How did Mexican laws cause problems for Anglo American settlers in Texas?

3. Why did the colonists hold conventions in San Felipe de Austin?

4. Why did Stephen F. Austin go to Mexico City?

5. **Critical Thinking:** *Point of View* Why did the Mexican leaders think that Stephen F. Austin might be planning a revolution?

Link to ⚭ **Writing**

Write a Letter Write a letter to Santa Anna from the point of view of a Texas settler, explaining why Texas should remain open to immigrants from the United States. Or, write a letter from Santa Anna's point of view, explaining to Texas settlers why Mexico should limit immigration from the United States.

STEPHEN F. AUSTIN
1793–1836

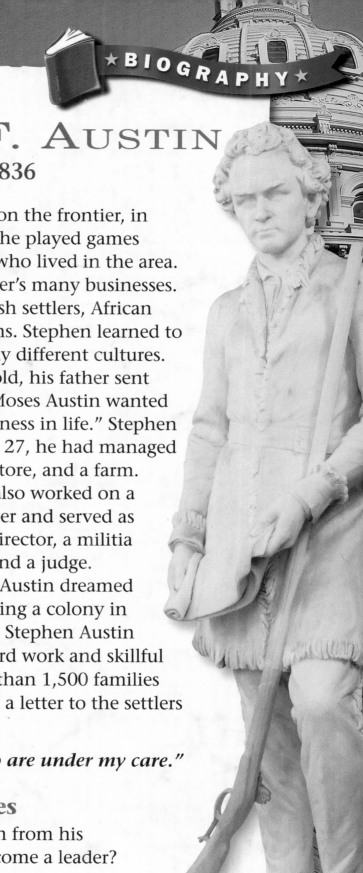

Stephen Fuller Austin grew up on the frontier, in the Missouri Territory. As a boy, he played games with Native American children who lived in the area. Stephen often played in his father's many businesses. There, he met French and Spanish settlers, African Americans, and Native Americans. Stephen learned to get along with people from many different cultures.

When Stephen was ten years old, his father sent him to school in Connecticut. Moses Austin wanted his son to be prepared for "greatness in life." Stephen returned home at age 16. By age 27, he had managed the family's lead mine, general store, and a farm. He had also worked on a newspaper and served as a bank director, a militia officer, and a judge.

Moses Austin dreamed of founding a colony in Texas. When Moses Austin died, Stephen Austin fulfilled this dream. Through hard work and skillful leadership, Austin helped more than 1,500 families settle in Texas. He once wrote in a letter to the settlers that he looked upon them

BIOFACT

Stephen F. Austin's settlement grew into an independent republic. Today, he is known as the Father of Texas.

". . . as one great family who are under my care."

Learn from Biographies

What did Stephen F. Austin learn from his experiences that helped him become a leader?

For more information, go online to *Meet the People* at **www.sfsocialstudies.com**.

Chart and Graph Skills

Compare Line and Bar Graphs

What? A graph is a special kind of picture. It shows and compares information. Two common kinds of graphs are line graphs and bar graphs.

A **line graph** shows how something has changed over time. A line on the graph goes up or down to show these changes. For example, the line on the line graph below shows how the population of Texas has changed from 1850 to 2000.

A **bar graph** can also show how something has changed over time. The bar graph below shows the same information as the line graph.

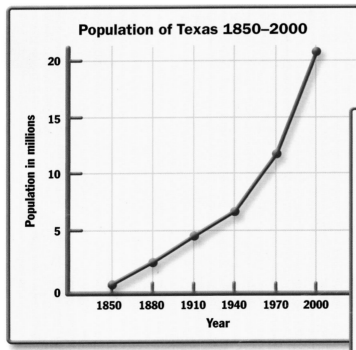

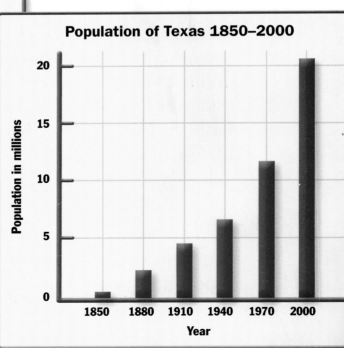

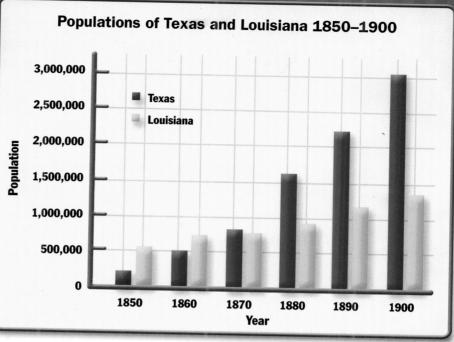

Populations of Texas and Louisiana 1850–1900

A bar graph can also be used to compare amounts. This bar graph compares how the populations of Texas and Louisiana changed between 1850 and 1900.

Why? Line graphs and bar graphs show facts in a clear, simple picture. They help you find information quickly and easily. They also help you compare information. Choose the correct type of graph for the information you want to show.

How? Always read the title of a graph and the labels on the graph. This information tells you what the graph is showing.

Look at the line graph on page 152. The dates at the bottom tell you when the population was measured. The numbers at the left show the number of people living in Texas. Each dot stands for the total number of people living in Texas in a given year. Did the population of Texas grow slowly or quickly from 1940 to 2000?

Look at the bar graph on page 152. It shows another way of presenting the same information that is in the line graph. How is this bar graph different from the line graph? Now look at the bar graph above. How is it different from the bar graph on page 152?

Think and Apply

1. Would you choose a bar graph or a line graph to show changes in your height each year since your birth? Why?

2. Suppose you wanted to compare the number of workers in two Texas industries. What kind of graph would best show that information?

3. Look at the graphs on page 152. In which 30-year period did the population of Texas grow the fastest? How did you find your answer?

CHAPTER 5
REVIEW

1820

1825

1820
Moses Austin arrived in Texas.

1821
Mexico gained its independence.

First U.S. colonists arrived in Texas.

1824
Stephen F. Austin founded San Felipe de Austin.

Chapter Summary

Compare and Contrast

On a separate sheet of paper, list similarities and differences between the problems that Mexican colonists had with Spain in 1810 and the problems American settlers to Texas had with the Mexican government in 1830.

Similarities

Both wanted to have more say in government.

Differences

Vocabulary

Match each word with its correct definition.

1 **immigrant** (p. 141)

2 **empresario** (p. 141)

3 **vaquero** (p. 145)

4 **right** (p. 149)

5 **convention** (p. 150)

a. freedom

b. cowboy

c. a formal meeting

d. a person hired to bring settlers to an area

e. a person who comes to live in a new country

People, Places, and Terms

Write a sentence describing each of the people, places, or terms listed below.

1 **Dolores, Mexico** (p. 139)

2 **Moses Austin** (p. 140)

3 **San Felipe de Austin** (p. 141)

4 **Jane Long** (p. 141)

5 **Gail Borden** (p. 142)

6 **Martín de León** (p. 144)

7 **Lorenzo de Zavala** (p. 144)

8 **Law of April 6** (p. 149)

1830

1835

1830
Law of April 6
was passed.

1832
Texans held the first
of two conventions.

1833
Austin took Texans'
concerns to Mexico.

Facts and Main Ideas

1 Who were the Old Three Hundred?

2 When did ranching begin in Texas? Who started the first ranches?

3 Why did Texans oppose the Law of April 6?

4 **Time Line** For how many years had United States immigrants to Texas lived in Texas before the Law of April 6 was passed?

5 **Main Idea** What is one reason that Stephen F. Austin is important to Texas history?

6 **Main Idea** Why did most colonists want Texas to be a separate Mexican state?

7 **Critical Thinking:** *Cause and Effect* Why did the Mexican government pass the Law of April 6? How did Texans react to the new law?

▶ **Stephen F. Austin**

Write About History

1 **Write a set of questions** that you might have asked Father Miguel Hidalgo if you had been a newspaper reporter in the early 1800s in Mexico.

2 **Write a poem** about everyday life as a colonist in Texas.

3 **Write a newspaper article** about the events leading to Stephen F. Austin's arrest.

Apply Skills

Use the line and bar graphs on page 152 to answer the questions.

1 Using either graph, estimate how much the population of Texas grew between 1850 and 1910.

2 Using either graph, estimate how much the population of Texas grew between 1970 and 2000.

3 Using the information on these graphs, what conclusion can you draw about how quickly the population grew in the 60 years before 1910 and in the 30 years after 1970?

Internet Activity

To get help with vocabulary, people, and terms, select the dictionary or encyclopedia from *Social Studies Library* at **www.sfsocialstudies.com**.

The Diary of Mary Austin Holley

Some good places to find out about the lives of Texas's women are in letters, journals, and diaries written by the women themselves. Mary Austin Holley kept a diary. In it she told of her travels. In 1831 and again in 1835, she visited the Texas colony of her cousin Stephen F. Austin. Her writings about Texas were published in a book in 1836. Many people in the United States read *Texas* and decided to move there. Here are some excerpts from her diary.

(January) 25
Foggy—warm enough with out fire—Birds are singing & hens cackling. When Mrs. Perry returned . . . her house was full of eggs. The hens had taken possession (of) beds, closets, bureaus, every place was a nest.

Jany (January) 26
Started on horse back with Mrs. Perry for Quintana. The road lying all through the prairie—It was very wet from late rains & the day was cloudy, still the ride was most charming. . . .

156

Friday (February) 9

Took a ride to mouth of the Bernard (River) in a light wagon—very pleasant over the prairie—12 miles—galloped over the beach—hard as a floor, with great delight. You can ride thus from Matagorda to Galveston, having to cross the mouths of the rivers and bayous. The latter are full of oysters— you can see them in piles above the surface wherever there is mud. . . .

Thursday (February) 15

Had a very cold night with ice. The high grass of the prairie is covered with sleet and looks like a vast field of snow. . . .

Friday (February) 16

Water froze solid in my room during the night. The prairie was like a sea of glass glittering in the sunshine. It continued shining and freezing all day. . . .

Main Ideas and Vocabulary

TEST PREP

Read the passage below and use it to answer the questions that follow.

Thousands of years ago, people first came to the land we call Texas. At first, they were hunters and gatherers. After many years, some of these early peoples learned to farm. They began living in villages. Over time, they developed a variety of new <u>cultures</u>.

Some peoples, such as the Jumano and the Caddo, lived in villages in what is now Texas. They farmed the land. Others, such as the Comanche and the Karankawa, continued to travel and hunt.

During the 1400s and 1500s, Europeans began exploring the Americas. Spanish rulers wanted the explorers to claim lands and bring back riches. They also wanted them to teach Native Americans about the Roman Catholic religion.

The Spanish built missions in Texas. They introduced Native Americans to the Spanish way of life. In turn, Native Americans shared their cultures with the Spaniards.

At first, Spain ruled Mexico, including the part known as Texas. In the early 1800s, Mexico won independence from Spain. During this time, Stephen F. Austin set up a new colony in Texas. Texas settlers became Mexican citizens.

Problems developed between Mexico and the settlers. The Mexican <u>government</u> passed laws to limit settlers' rights. Many colonists wanted Texas to become a Mexican state. In 1833, Stephen F. Austin went to Mexico to talk to the president. Before he could leave Mexico, Austin was jailed.

1 What caused some of the earliest Americans to settle in one place?
A hunting and gathering
B developing cultures
C meeting explorers
D learning to farm

2 In this passage, the word *cultures* means—
A people who travel
B people who live in the same village
C ways of life
D food that is planted

3 Which of these caused problems between the Mexican government and the Texas colonists?
A conflicts among Tejanos
B conflicts with Native Americans
C Spanish missions
D laws that limited rights

4 In this passage, the word *government* means—
A a system of running a town or country
B a colony
C to watch over someone
D a Mexican state

People and Places

Write a sentence using each of the people and places listed below. You may use two people or places in one sentence.

1. **Alibates Flint Quarries National Monument** (p. 92)

2. **Eagle Pass** (p. 106)

3. **Cuzco** (p. 111)

4. **Garcitas Creek** (p. 122)

5. **San Antonio** (p. 127)

6. **Father Miguel Hildago** (p. 139)

7. **Erasmo Seguín** (p. 144)

8. **Patricia de la Garza de León** (p. 144)

9. **Antonio López de Santa Anna** (p. 150)

10. **Saltillo** (p. 150)

Apply Skills

Graph Your Community With the help of a teacher or librarian, gather facts and numbers about your community. Facts could include how the population of your community has changed over time or the number of people who work at different jobs in your community. Use these facts and numbers to create a bar or a line graph. Compare your graph with classmates' graphs.

Write and Share

Present Texas History Give a presentation about the history of Texas, from the earliest Texans to the first U.S. colonists. Work in groups to research topics of Texas history covered in this unit. Each group should gather information and pictures about its topic. Groups should then present what they learn to the class.

Read on Your Own

Look for books like these in the library.

On the Spot

Life was often challenging for America's early settlers, as well as for Native American groups who had lived in Texas for hundreds of years. Make a documentary about their experiences.

1 Form a group and choose a Native American group or a group of early European settlers who settled in Texas.

2 Write sentences about their experiences and observations. Include a variety of topics.

3 Make a diorama or model to show the environment and settlements. Include where they lived, other buildings, and the physical setting.

4 Present your documentary. Show the diorama or model to the class.

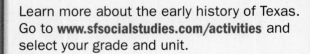

Learn more about the early history of Texas. Go to **www.sfsocialstudies.com/activities** and select your grade and unit.

Independence and Statehood

What do Texans believe is worth fighting for?

UNIT 3

Begin with a Primary Source

1835   1840

October 1835
Texans battle
Mexican troops
in Gonzales
and Goliad.

March 2, 1836
Texans declare
independence.

March 6, 1836
Texans lose the
Battle of the Alamo.

April 21, 1836
Texans win the
Battle of San Jacinto.

September 1836
Sam Houston is elected
President of the Republic.

162

"Texas must be defended and liberty maintained."

—Sam Houston, in a letter to Texas president David G. Burnet, April 20, 1836

William H. Huddle's painting, **Surrender of Santa Anna,** illustrates the surrender of the Mexican army to the Texan army.

1845

1850

December 29, 1845
Texas becomes a state.

April, 1846
U.S. and Mexican soldiers fight near the Rio Grande.

May 13, 1846
Mexican War begins.

1848
Mexican War ends.

UNIT 3

Meet the People

David Crockett

1786–1836

Birthplace: Tennessee

Frontiersman, political and military leader

- Served as elected official from Tennessee to U.S. Congress 1833–1834
- Moved to Texas in 1835, looking for wealth and adventure
- Volunteered to join the fight for Texas independence and died at the Battle of the Alamo

Sam Houston

1793–1863

Birthplace: Rockbridge County, Virginia

Political and military leader

- Left home in Tennessee at age 16 to live with the Cherokee
- Led Texas to independence at the Battle of San Jacinto
- Became the first elected president of the Republic of Texas in 1836

José Navarro

1795–1871

Birthplace: San Antonio, Texas

Political and military leader

- One of three Mexicans to sign the Texas Declaration of Independence in 1836
- Helped write the state constitution of Texas in 1845
- Served two terms in the Texas state senate

Anson Jones

1798–1858

Birthplace: Great Barrington, Massachusetts

Doctor, political leader

- Practiced medicine in the states of New York and Pennsylvania
- Served as a doctor in the Texas army during the fight for independence
- Served as the last president of the Republic of Texas from 1844 to 1846

1785	1795	1805	1815	1825	1835

1786 • David Crockett   1836

1793 • Sam Houston

1795 • José Navarro

1798 • Anson Jones

1798 • Mirabeau B. Lamar

1799 • Greenbury Logan

1806 • Juan Seguín

c. 1814 • Susanna Wilkerson Dickinson

For more information, go online to *Meet the People* at **www.sfsocialstudies.com**.

Mirabeau B. Lamar

1798–1859

Birthplace: Near Louisville, Georgia

Political and military leader

- Enjoyed riding horses, fencing, writing poetry, and painting as a child
- Served as the second president of the Republic of Texas from 1838 to 1841
- Nicknamed "Father of Texas Education" for proposing an education system

Greenbury Logan

1799–Unknown

Birthplace: Kentucky

Soldier in Texas Revolution

- Born into slavery, but later was freed
- Received a land grant in Austin's third colony in 1831
- Fought in the Battle of Velasco, the Battle of Concepcion, and the siege of Bexar during the Texas Revolution

✓ **Juan Seguín**

1806–1890

Birthplace: San Antonio, Texas

Rancher, military leader, and mayor

- Led Sam Houston's army during the Texas Revolution
- Served as mayor of San Antonio
- Served as the only Mexican Texan in the Senate of the Republic of Texas

Susanna Wilkerson Dickinson

c. 1814–1883

Birthplace: Williamson County, Tennessee

Survivor of the Battle of the Alamo

- Captured by Mexican troops at the Battle of the Alamo
- Is thought to have been sent by Santa Anna to carry a message of warning to Sam Houston

| 1845 | 1855 | 1865 | 1875 | 1885 | 1895 |

1863

1871

1858

1859

1890

1883

Independence and Statehood

Cause and Effect

Cause		Effect
Why did it happen?	→	What happened?

- A *cause* is why something happened. An *effect* is what happened.

- A cause can have more than one effect. An effect can have more than one cause.

- Sometimes writers use clue words such as *because*, *so*, *if*, *then*, or *since*. These words help you figure out what happened and why.

Read the following paragraph. Cause and effect have been highlighted.

In Unit 2, you read that Texans wanted more power. What caused them to seek more power? The Mexican government said that no more U.S. citizens could move to Texas. Mexico taxed goods from the United States. The effect was a revolution against Mexico, which led to Texas independence.

The Texas Declaration of Independence

By 1835, problems between Texans and the Mexican government had increased. Santa Anna, the Mexican leader, had taken more power than Mexico's constitution allowed. Because of these actions, Stephen F. Austin was angry with Santa Anna. Austin called for Texans to break free of Mexican rule.

Fighting between Texans and Mexicans began in the town of Gonzales. The Texans defeated the Mexican troops. Then they went on to defeat Mexican troops in Goliad and San Antonio.

These defeats angered Santa Anna. He wanted to defeat the Texan soldiers at San Antonio, so he led his troops toward the city.

Meanwhile, Texas leaders met to discuss independence. The leaders decided to form a new government. They wrote a Declaration of Independence from Mexico and signed it on March 2, 1836. They declared that Texas was now a free country.

Next, Texas leaders made a plan of government. Now, more than ever, Texans were ready to defend their independence. It is not hard to understand Santa Anna's anger about the news that Texans would no longer obey his rule.

Use the reading strategy of cause and effect to answer these questions.

1 What caused Stephen F. Austin to become angry with Santa Anna?

2 What effect did the Texans' defeat of Mexican troops in Gonzales, Goliad, and San Antonio have on Santa Anna?

3 What caused Texans to be more determined than ever to defend their country?

CHAPTER 6

The Republic of Texas

Lesson 1

Washington-on-the-Brazos March 2, 1836
Texans declare independence from Mexico.

1

Lesson 2

San Antonio March 6, 1836
Texans lose the Battle of the Alamo to Santa Anna's army.

2

Lesson 3

San Jacinto Battlefield, near Harrisburg April 21, 1836
Texans win the Battle of San Jacinto and gain their independence.

3

CANADA

UNITED STATES

2 1

3

PACIFIC OCEAN

ATLANTIC OCEAN

San Antonio
Washington-on-the-Brazos

Harrisburg
Gulf of Mexico

MEXICO

Why We Remember

One year can make a big difference in history. For example, the events that occurred in Texas from 1835 to 1836 changed the way you live today. During that time, settlers became unhappy with Mexican rule. They met to declare their independence. Many Texas soldiers died in battles defending this newly declared freedom. Today many schools and streets in Texas are named for these Texas heroes. Even more, today's Texans are proud of the independent Texas spirit that began in early Texas.

1835   1836

1835
Stephen F. Austin returns to Texas.

1835
In October, Texans battle Mexican troops in Gonzales and Goliad.

1835
In November, Texans meet at San Felipe for the Consultation.

1835
In December, Texas troops force the Mexican army from San Antonio.

1836
In March, Texas declares independence and sets up a new government.

Washington-on-the-Brazos

San Antonio • Gonzales • Goliad

PREVIEW

Focus on the Main Idea
Growing unhappiness with Mexican rule led Texas colonists to revolt and finally to declare independence.

PLACES
Gonzales
Goliad
San Antonio
Washington-on-the-Brazos

PEOPLE
Juan Seguín
James Bowie
James Fannin
Ben Milam
Sam Houston
Greenbury Logan
David G. Burnet

VOCABULARY
petition
Bill of Rights

EVENTS
March on San Antonio
Consultation
Convention of 1836

The Revolution Begins

You Are There
It is a hot and humid August evening in Gonzales. Usually, you and Papa would be taking a cool swim in the creek. But tonight all the adults you know are meeting at your house. You are playing outdoors with the other children. It is not a happy event, though. You have heard your parents talk about a dangerous time ahead. They believe the Mexican army is on its way to Texas. The sound of adult voices drifts through the open windows. It is a worried sound. You wonder whether life will ever return to normal.

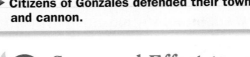

▶ Citizens of Gonzales defended their town and cannon.

 Cause and Effect As you read, look for causes and effects of events leading up to the Revolution.

170

Early Battles

In 1835, Stephen F. Austin returned to a troubled Texas. Earlier, you read that Austin had been held in a Mexican prison. This made Texans angry. They were also angry because Santa Anna, Mexico's dictator, was demanding that Texans pay taxes on goods from the United States. He wanted Texans to trade with Mexico instead.

Texans wanted Santa Anna to pay attention to the Mexican Constitution of 1824, the plan of government Mexico adopted after it won independence from Spain. Many rights in it were important to the Texans. But Santa Anna wanted more power than that constitution gave him.

Santa Anna sent troops into Texas, and on October 2, 1835, fighting began. A commander in the Mexican army had ordered his soldiers to take a cannon from the town of **Gonzales.** The people of Gonzales placed a white flag on the cannon. The flag had a picture of a cannon on it, and the words "Come and Take It." What a dare it was!

The battle for the cannon lasted only a few minutes. The men of Gonzales, along with a group of Texas soldiers, easily defeated the Mexicans.

A week later, on October 9, Texans attacked a Mexican fort at **Goliad.** They wanted to protect settlers from the Mexican soldiers there. Once again, victory was theirs.

These two battles gave Texans courage. They believed they were on the road to revolution. They also knew that they could defeat Santa Anna's army. And they had a purpose. As one colonist said:

> *"We have either to fight for our homes or fly and leave them."*

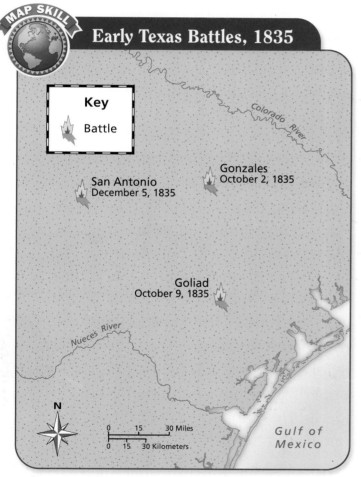

MAP SKILL
Early Texas Battles, 1835

Key

⚔ Battle

San Antonio
December 5, 1835

Gonzales
October 2, 1835

Colorado River

Goliad
October 9, 1835

Nueces River

N

0   15   30 Miles
0   15   30 Kilometers

Gulf of Mexico

▶ Texas soldiers won early battles at Gonzales and Goliad.

MAP SKILL Understand Cardinal Directions
In what direction did Mexican troops have to travel to reach Goliad from Gonzales?

REVIEW What caused Texans to take up arms against Santa Anna's forces?
↻ **Cause and Effect**

▶ Before the march on San Antonio, daily events on the city's Main Plaza included work and play.

March on San Antonio

About 300 Texan troops gathered at Gonzales to begin a **March on San Antonio.** Soldiers there had chosen Stephen F. Austin as their commander-in-chief. In **San Antonio** the Texan soldiers would face General Cós and about 1,100 soldiers—the last Mexican troops in Texas.

"On to San Antonio!" the Texans shouted. Volunteers joined the troops as they marched. Among these were 37 men led by **Juan Seguín.**

Austin sent 90 soldiers ahead with commanders **James Bowie** and **James Fannin.** They were to find a safe place for the troops to camp near San Antonio. However, this small group was attacked by about 275 Mexican soldiers. Even so, the Texans overpowered the Mexicans.

Soon the other Texas troops arrived. Eager to attack the Mexican army, Texas leader **Ben Milam** shouted, "Who will go with old Ben Milam into San Antonio?" Three hundred men answered his call.

On December 5, 1835, Milam and Frank Johnson led an attack on Mexican soldiers in San Antonio. The fighting went on for four days. Milam was killed. But in the end, the Texans won the battle. The Mexican army returned to Mexico.

Texans hoped the fighting had ended. But Santa Anna had other ideas. He planned to lead an army into Texas himself.

REVIEW What event may have caused Ben Milam's call to arms?
↻ **Cause and Effect**

A New Government

While Texas soldiers were at San Antonio, other Texans were meeting in San Felipe. This meeting was called the **Consultation.**

First, the Texans talked about their beliefs. One group at the meeting wanted to remain loyal to Mexico and the Constitution of 1824. Other people wanted to declare independence from Mexico.

Next, the people at the meeting created a temporary government for Texas. They elected Henry Smith as governor and **Sam Houston** as commander-in-chief of the army.

▶ **Santa Anna led Mexican troops against Texan soldiers.**

The new government had problems from the beginning. Governor Smith argued with those who wanted to remain part of Mexico. Sam Houston was in charge of the army, but he had no money to pay soldiers. Leaders, including Stephen F. Austin, were sent to the United States to raise the money needed to fight Santa Anna.

The Texas leaders agreed to meet again in March of 1836. At that time, they would continue with plans to fight against Santa Anna. Meanwhile, Santa Anna himself was on the move. By early February of 1836, he and his troops had crossed the Rio Grande. His army was on the march to San Antonio.

REVIEW What caused problems for the new Texas government?
↻ **Cause and Effect**

▶ **The Mexican flag of 1824 symbolized Mexico's independence from Spain.**

Texas Declares Independence

As planned, Texas leaders met again on March 1, 1836, at the town of **Washington-on-the-Brazos.** Meanwhile, Santa Anna had arrived in San Antonio. Texas soldiers were defending themselves at the Alamo. You will read more about this historic battle in the next lesson.

The meeting at Washington-on-the-Brazos was called the **Convention of 1836.** People gathered in an unfinished building owned by a blacksmith. This time there was no argument. Santa Anna's ongoing attacks had made one thing clear. The Texans must fight him in order to gain their independence from Mexico.

First, the leaders decided to declare independence from Mexico. Then they could form the government for a new country—the Republic of Texas.

▶ The meeting hall that stands today at Washington-on-the-Brazos is like the original hall of 1836.

George C. Childress was in charge of writing the declaration. He and his group based it on the United States Declaration of Independence. The purpose of the declaration was to explain why Texas wanted to be independent from Mexico. The declaration listed the problems Texans had with Mexico's rule. For example, Texans did not have freedom of religion. They did not have the right to a jury trial. Texans did not have the right to **petition,** or make requests of the government.

On March 2, every person at the convention voted in favor of the Declaration of Independence. Today, Texans celebrate March 2 as Texas Independence Day.

REVIEW What are some reasons why Texas declared independence from Mexico? ↺ **Cause and Effect**

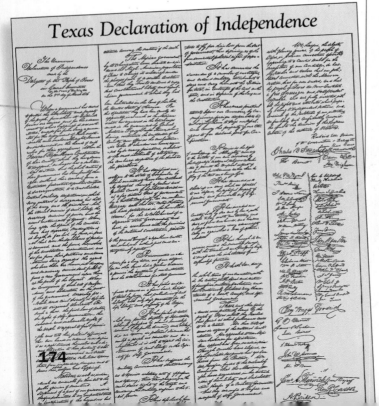

Texas Declaration of Independence

▶ The Texas Declaration of Independence was signed on March 2, 1836.

174

A New Constitution

Even though Texas was still a part of Mexico, Texans now considered themselves an independent nation. Texas's citizens needed their own constitution. The purpose of the Texas Constitution was to establish how the new government would work. The leaders at Washington-on-the-Brazos worked for two weeks on a plan. Then they wrote it down.

The Texas Constitution of 1836 was much like the U.S. Constitution. It called for three branches of government.

The Constitution also contained a **Bill of Rights.** This bill stated that certain rights belonged to all Texans. For example, Texans would now enjoy the freedoms of speech and religion. They would also have the right to a trial by jury. The bill also encouraged people to move to Texas.

However, the Constitution did not free slaves living in Texas. Even free African Americans would have to get permission from the new government to stay in Texas. This rule even applied to African Americans who were fighting against Mexico. African Americans such as Sam McCullough, Hendrick Arnold, and **Greenbury Logan** would now have to ask permission to stay in the very land they defended.

In fact, Greenbury Logan wrote a petition about the new Texas Constitution of 1836. Twenty-two other African Americans signed Logan's petition. Logan said that the constitution deprived him of "every privilege dear to a freeman . . . no vote or say in any way." Despite the petition, the constitution remained unchanged.

REVIEW Why did Texas need a constitution? ⟲ **Cause and Effect**

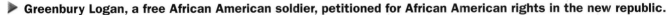

▶ Greenbury Logan, a free African American soldier, petitioned for African American rights in the new republic.

Temporary Government

Texas was at war with Mexico. There was no time to hold elections, but the new nation needed leaders to govern it. So the leaders at Washington-on-the-Brazos set up a temporary government. David G. Burnet, a Texas lawyer and landowner, was chosen to be president of Texas. Lorenzo de Zavala was named vice president.

When the officials were sworn in on March 17, 1836, they had a serious question on their minds. Would the Texas army be able to protect the new republic?

REVIEW Why did the Texas leaders set up a temporary government?
 Cause and Effect

Summarize the Lesson

- **1835** Stephen F. Austin returned to Texas from Mexico.
- **October 1835** Texans battled Mexican troops in Gonzales and Goliad.
- **November 1835** Texans met at San Felipe for the Consultation.
- **December 1835** Texan troops forced the Mexican army from San Antonio.
- **March 1836** Texas declared independence and set up a new government.

★ LESSON 1 REVIEW

Check Facts and Main Ideas

1. **Cause and Effect** On a separate sheet of paper, fill in two effects of Santa Anna's actions against Texas.

Cause

Santa Anna sent troops into Texas. He demanded that Texans pay taxes.

Effects

2. Describe what happened at Gonzales and at Goliad. Explain the Mexican and the Texan points of view.

3. What was the Consultation at San Felipe? What did each of the two groups at the Consultation want?

4. What three important things happened at the Convention of 1836 in Washington-on-the-Brazos?

5. **Critical Thinking: *Draw Conclusions*** Why do you think some people wanted Texas to remain a part of Mexico?

Link to ⚭ Writing

Express an Opinion Write a short persuasive speech you might have made at the Consultation at San Felipe. Choose one opinion represented at the Consultation. Provide details and examples to support your opinion.
- Texans should remain loyal to Mexico.
- Texans should declare independence from Mexico.

JUAN SEGUÍN
1806–1890

You have read that Juan Seguín was a leader in Texas during the Texas Revolution. As a Tejano, he fought Mexican soldiers to help Texas become independent. He later explained:

". . . I embraced the cause of Texas at the sound of the first cannon. . . ."

Juan's father, Erasmo Seguín, was a Tejano rancher who believed that Texas should be free of Mexican rule.

When Juan was fifteen, he went to Louisiana with his father. They met Stephen F. Austin and a group of people. These families were coming to settle in Texas. Juan's father would be their guide as they traveled to San Antonio.

Juan's father had always urged his son to read and write. As a young man, Juan Seguín used these skills to help Texas gain independence. He helped keep many Texans informed about events in Texas and Mexico. Later, he led a group of soldiers in the last battle of the Texas Revolution.

Juan Seguín was elected to the San Antonio town council when he was only 22 years old. In 1841, he became mayor of San Antonio.

Learn from Biographies

Why do you think Juan Seguín chose a career in politics?

For more information, go online to *Meet the People* at **www.sfsocialstudies.com.**

Identify Primary and Secondary Sources

What? A **primary source** is information that comes from an eyewitness, a person who was at the event. Letters, diaries, eyewitness accounts, interviews, some Web sites, and some newspaper articles can be primary sources. Photographs, drawings, tools, and artifacts can also be primary sources.

A **secondary source** is information that comes from someone who was not present at an event. Encyclopedias, biographies, some computer software programs, some Internet sources, and social studies books, such as your textbook, are secondary sources.

Thursday, March 10 1836

Fine weather, and we have got comfortably fixed in our new lodging. The eating at our house is becoming sorry — no butter, no milk, no sugar, little or no vegetables, and not much meat except pork.

The business of the Convention moves slowly. The Constitution is a good one, on the whole.

No news yet from the Alamo, and much anxiety is felt for the fate of the brave men there. It is obvious that they must be surrounded and all communication with them cut off.

▶ The source shown at left is from the diary of Colonel William F. Gray, a lawyer and an author. He was present at Washington-on-the-Brazos as Texas leaders met to declare independence from Mexico.

▶ The source shown below is from this book.

Texas Declares Independence

As planned, Texas leaders met again on March 1, 1836 at the town of **Washington-on-the-Brazos.** Meanwhile, Santa Anna had arrived in San Antonio. Texas soldiers were defending themselves at the Alamo. You will read more about this historic battle in the next lesson.

The meeting at Washington-on-the-Brazos was called the **Convention of 1836.** People gathered in an unfinished building owned by a blacksmith. This time there was no argument. Santa Anna's ongoing attacks had made one thing clear. The Texans must fight him in order to gain their independence from Mexico.

First, the leaders decided to declare independence from Mexico. Then they could form the government for a new country—the Republic of Texas.

▶ The meeting hall that stands today at Washington-on-the-Brazos is like the original hall of 1836.

George C. Childress was in charge of writing the declaration. He and his group based it on the United States Declaration of Independence. The purpose of the declaration was to explain why Texas wanted to be independent from Mexico. The declaration listed the problems Texans had with Mexico's rule. For example, Texans did not have freedom of religion. They did not have the right to a jury trial. Texans did not have the right to **petition,** or make requests

Texas Declaration of Independence

Why? Primary sources can help you learn firsthand how people lived. They can also help you understand how people felt about the events of their time. As you study a primary source, history can seem to come alive.

Secondary sources give you a wider view of events. They pull together information from many primary sources. In this way, they can show you how a single event fits into a larger piece of history. They can also help you find facts about an event.

How? Follow these steps to tell the difference between primary and secondary sources:

• Read the two excerpts shown on page 178. What information does each one give you?

• As you read, look for clues that signal a primary source. A primary source might contain present-tense verbs such as *is* and *are*. It might contain the opinions of the author. The author of a primary source might refer to himself or herself.

• Look for clues that signal a secondary source. A secondary source will not use firsthand details to describe an event. It may present more than one point of view. The author of a secondary source does not usually refer to himself or herself.

Think and Apply

❶ Which excerpt on page 178 is a primary source? Which is a secondary source? Tell how you know the difference.

❷ Go to your school library and find one primary and one secondary source about an event that took place in Texas or the United States. Explain how the sources are alike and different.

❸ Use the primary and secondary sources you find to write a paragraph describing the event. Is your paragraph a primary or a secondary source?

1836 **1837**

February 23 Santa Anna's troops arrive in San Antonio.	**February 24** Fighting begins at the Alamo.	**March 3** James Bonham enters the Alamo.	**March 6** Texans lose the Battle of the Alamo.

San Antonio
Laredo

The Battle of the Alamo

PREVIEW

Focus on the Main Idea
The Texans lost the Battle of the Alamo, but that tragedy inspired them to win the war.

PLACES
San Antonio
Laredo

PEOPLE
Santa Anna
William B. Travis
David (Davy) Crockett
James Bowie
James Bonham
James Fannin
Susanna Dickinson

VOCABULARY
siege

You Are There "Hurry, my children!" Your father looks worried. Santa Anna's Mexican army is marching toward San Antonio. As you approach the Alamo, a woman with a small child opens the huge wooden door and welcomes you. Tears fill your eyes. You will miss your home. But you are glad to be in a safe place. Suddenly, you hear a familiar voice. It's your good friend, Enrique Esparza! His father and your father are joining the fight for Texas independence. They have come with Juan Seguín to help defend the Alamo. Your eyes look up past the walls of the old, roofless chapel to the sky above. A distant cannon shot rumbles like thunder. Santa Anna's troops are near!

Cause and Effect As you read, look for causes that explain why the Alamo is the most legendary landmark in Texas today.

Soldiers Gather

The year was 1836. In January, Texan soldiers gathered in the Alamo. On February 23, General **Santa Anna** and about 5,000 of his Mexican soldiers marched into **San Antonio.** They wore uniforms of red and blue. Two weeks before, their horses had taken them across the Rio Grande at **Laredo.** Santa Anna's army was ready to attack the Alamo. In a **siege,** they would surround the walls of the mission and force the Texans to surrender.

Remember that only months before, Mexican soldiers had surrendered to the forceful Texans in San Antonio. At that time,

▶ **General Santa Anna**

Mexican General Cós had raised a white flag above the Alamo. A white flag is a signal of surrender. The surrender had made Santa Anna furious! After all, Texas was still a part of Mexico. Santa Anna was set to defeat the Texan army and stop the revolution. He ordered a red flag to be flown over another church in San Antonio. The flag sent a chilling message to the soldiers in the Alamo: surrender or die.

The Texans responded by firing a cannon. This meant they were ready to fight. However, they numbered only about 150 men.

REVIEW What event caused Santa Anna to become furious?
↻ **Cause and Effect**

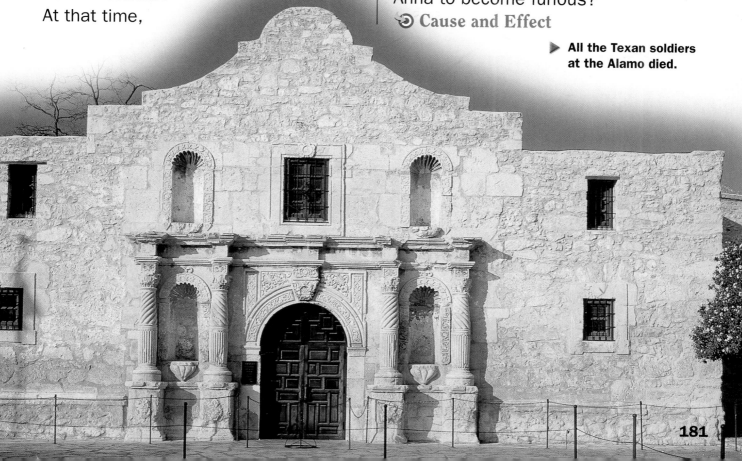

▶ **All the Texan soldiers at the Alamo died.**

The Fall of the Alamo

Among the leaders of the defenders of the Alamo were **William B. Travis, David (Davy) Crockett** and **James Bowie.**

This small group did not have uniforms. They did have good weapons. But what they needed most were more soldiers.

On February 24 the fighting began. Travis sent a letter "To the People of Texas & all Americans in the world." It was a plea for help.

"… I call on you in the name of Liberty, of patriotism & everything dear to the American character, to come to our aid. …"

The newly formed Texan force remained small, even though it grew to about 185 soldiers. On March 3, **James Bonham** dashed into the Alamo. He was the last Texan to enter its gates. He had gone to get help from **Colonel James Fannin** at Goliad. But one of Fannin's wagons had broken down along the way. Fannin and his troops returned to Goliad. This was bad news for the soldiers within the walls of the Alamo.

Legend has it that Colonel Travis then drew a line in the sand with his sword. He asked those who would stay with him to step over the line.

FACT FILE

Leaders Inside the Alamo, 1836

William Travis was a lawyer by profession. At age 26, he led the Texas force at the Alamo after James Bowie became too ill to command.

David (Davy) Crockett led a troop of 17 volunteers from Tennessee to fight for Texas's freedom at the Alamo. He called his rifle "Old Betsy." At times, he played his fiddle at the Alamo.

James Bowie was famous for the "bowie" knife he used. While he was getting Texas soldiers ready to fight, he became very ill. He was sick in bed during the battle.

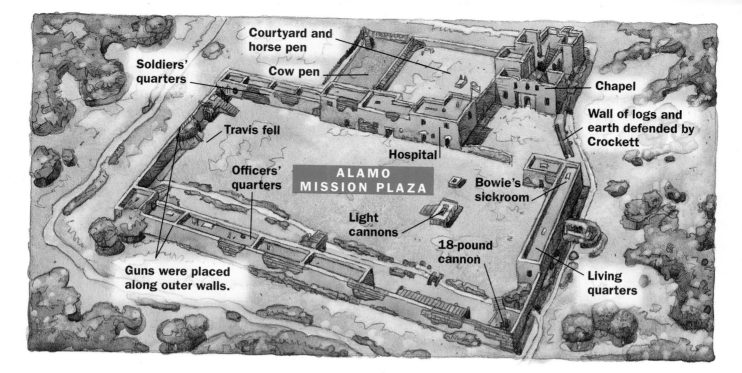

Courtyard and horse pen

Soldiers' quarters

Cow pen

Chapel

Wall of logs and earth defended by Crockett

Travis fell

Officers' quarters

Hospital

ALAMO MISSION PLAZA

Bowie's sickroom

Light cannons

18-pound cannon

Guns were placed along outer walls.

Living quarters

According to the story, only two men did not step over the line. One was Bowie, who had become too ill to walk. Someone carried him across the line on a cot. The other was Moses Rose, who escaped from the Alamo that night.

At dawn on March 6, Santa Anna was set to drive the Texans out of the Alamo. The Mexican government wanted to prove to the Texas army that Mexico still ruled Texas. This was the eleventh day of battle. The sleeping Texans awoke to the rumblings of enemy guns. Next, a bugle sounded. Then the Mexican band played the tune "El Degüello." The music meant that no mercy would be shown to the enemy.

Santa Anna's men rushed up the wooden ladders they had made to help them over the walls. The Texans sprang to their posts. They fought with all their might. It is said that these were Travis's last words:

"No rendirse, muchachos!"
(Don't surrender, boys!)

Within an hour, the fighting was over. Every Texan soldier died at the Alamo. For each one of them, about eight Mexicans died. Even though Mexico won the battle, both sides paid a tragic price.

Santa Anna spared the lives of some families inside the Alamo. Young Enrique Esparza was among the children who went free. The general also allowed some slaves to go.

Two of the survivors were **Susanna Dickinson** and her younger daughter, Angelina. Her husband, a Texas soldier, had been killed. It is said that Santa Anna sent her to Sam Houston to tell him of the Mexican victory.

REVIEW Why do you think Santa Anna wanted Sam Houston to know about the Mexican victory at the Alamo? **Draw Conclusions**

Remember the Alamo!

You can visit the Alamo in San Antonio today. It is a historic landmark. Why does it hold such special meaning in the hearts of modern-day Texans?

In the next lesson, you will discover how the bloody battle at the Alamo inspired Sam Houston's troops to win the war. Their battle cry soon became "Remember the Alamo!"

But many Texans honor the Alamo soldiers for yet another reason. These soldiers never knew they were fighting for a new nation. They had not heard that Texas had declared its independence on March 2. The brave Anglo American and Tejano soldiers of the Alamo knew only that it was worth a steep price—their lives.

▶ **The picture at the right is a plaque that honors the people who fought at the Battle of the Alamo.**

REVIEW Why does the battle cry "Remember the Alamo!" still hold meaning today? **Summarize**

Summarize the Lesson

- **February 23, 1836** Santa Anna's troops arrived in San Antonio.
- **February 24, 1836** Fighting began at the Alamo, and Travis sent out a letter.
- **March 3, 1836** James Bonham entered the Alamo.
- **March 6, 1836** Texans lost the Battle of the Alamo.

★ **LESSON 2** **REVIEW**

Check Facts and Main Ideas

1. 🔄 **Cause and Effect** On a separate sheet of paper, fill in the missing causes and effects of the major events from this lesson.

Cause	Effect
Santa Anna is furious.	→ Santa Anna leads siege at the Alamo.
	→
	→

2. Explain why Santa Anna was determined to take back the Alamo.

3. What did the Mexican army's music mean on March 6, 1836?

4. Why are the Texan soldiers who fought in the Alamo honored today?

5. **Critical Thinking:** *Point of View* Why did Santa Anna want to drive the Texans out of the Alamo?

Link to ⚭ Art

Draw a Picture Suppose your family is seeking safety inside the Alamo compound. Draw a detailed sketch showing what you see.

SUSANNA DICKINSON
(c. 1814–1883)

Susanna Wilkerson Dickinson is known as a hero of the Alamo. She lived through the bloody battle from inside the walls of the famous mission.

Susanna was born in Tennessee. In 1831, she traveled with her husband, Almaron Dickinson, to Texas. They helped settle the town of Gonzales, where the Texas Revolution would begin in 1834. Dickinson gave birth to a baby girl, Angelina, that year as well.

BIOFACT

In 2000, construction workers uncovered Susanna Dickinson's house in downtown Austin.

The Dickinsons moved to San Antonio during late 1835. Shortly before Mexican soldiers attacked the Alamo in March 1836, the family moved into it. Inside the mission walls, Angelina's father, Almaron, was killed.

It is said that after the battle, Santa Anna sent Susanna Dickinson to tell Sam Houston about the horrible battle. Santa Anna hoped the news would cause the Texans to surrender.

Learn from Biographies

What was Susanna Dickinson's special role in the Texas Revolution?

For more information, go online to *Meet the People* at **www.sfsocialstudies.com**

Read a Time Line

What? A **time line** is a diagram that shows important events and their dates. The events are given in the order in which they happened. Time lines are divided into equal time periods, as a ruler is divided into equal units. A time line might be divided into units that show a period of weeks, months, 1 year, 10 years, 25 years, 100 years, and so on.

The time line on this page is horizontal. It can be read from left to right. The earliest date appears at the left end of the time line. Time lines can also be vertical. Events in a vertical time line are read from top to bottom. The earliest date appears at the top of a vertical time line.

Why? How can you keep track of important events as you study history? One way is to use a time line. As you read across or down a time line, you begin to see connections. You understand how one event can lead to another.

The Alamo, 1836

January

February

January
Texas soldiers begin to gather at the Alamo.

Early February
The Mexican army crosses the Rio Grande into Laredo.

How? Follow these steps to help you read a time line:

- Look at the time line on pages 186 and 187. The time line shows important events in Texas history during a certain period. The events are shown in the order in which they took place. A description of each event appears above or below the date it happened.

- Notice the marks on the time line. They show units of time. They begin with January 1836 and end with April 1836. The space between each mark on this time line stands for one month.

- Find the event on the left side of the time line. This is the earliest event. It is when Texas soldiers began to gather at the Alamo.

- Look to the right of the first event. What is the next important event? When did this event happen?

Think and Apply

1 What amount of time does the time line cover?

2 What events took place on February 24?

3 About how much time passed between the first fights and the end of the battle?

4 How does a time line help you place events in order? Keep track of dates in the next lesson and make a time line of your own.

▶ **W. B. Travis**

February 24
Fighting begins at the Alamo, and W. B. Travis writes his famous letter—a plea for help.

James Bowie falls ill and is taken to a sickroom at the Alamo.

March 6
Mexican forces kill all Texan soldiers at the Alamo.

March

April

February 23
The Mexican army rides into San Antonio.

March 3
James Bonham returns to the Alamo with news that Col. J. Fannin cannot bring his troops.

▶ **Colonel James Fannin**

▶ **James Bonham**

Austin
Harrisburg
Houston
Gonzales
Goliad
Velasco
Columbia

March 11, 1836
The Runaway Scrape begins.

March 27, 1836
Fannin's troops are killed at Goliad.

April 21, 1836
Texans win the Battle of San Jacinto.

1839
Congress approves Austin as the new capital.

PREVIEW

Focus on the Main Idea
The Texans took Santa Anna by surprise and won the war.

PLACES

Gonzales
Goliad
Harrisburg
Velasco
Columbia
Houston
Austin

PEOPLE

General Urrea
Erastus "Deaf" Smith
Hendrick Arnold
Mirabeau B. Lamar

VOCABULARY

scout
monument
treaty
republic
congress
tax
debt

TERMS

San Jacinto Monument
Treaty of Velasco

EVENTS

Runaway Scrape
Battle of San Jacinto
188

Victory at San Jacinto

You Are There

March 14, 1836
Dear Cousin,
Life in Gonzales changed three days ago. A woman came with a message for Sam Houston from Santa Anna. I do not know whether Houston had heard about the horrible outcome at the Alamo. I do know that his face became very pale. What happened next may shock you, cousin. First, Houston told everyone in Gonzales to pack up and leave. Then his soldiers removed their supplies from the town. Finally, Houston's own soldiers burned our town to the ground! The Mexican army found only smoldering ashes. We would not let them take our town—at any cost!

Cause and Effect
As you read, look for causes that tell you how the Texans won the revolution.

More Fighting

"The Mexicans are coming!" Word about **Gonzales** spread quickly among Texas settlers. Santa Anna had ordered his troops to sweep across Texas, burning every settlement in their path. He wanted to stamp out the revolution for good.

During March 1836, people in Texas fled eastward toward the United States. They were fearful for their lives. This movement was called the **Runaway Scrape.**

Meanwhile, other battles were being fought in the revolution. Colonel James Fannin led one of them at **Goliad.**

A series of unfortunate decisions by James Fannin began on March 14. First, he did not lead his 350 men to Victoria for safety. Instead, he kept them inside a fort at Goliad. There he waited to hear from some of his troops fighting in nearby Refugio.

On March 18, Mexican **General Urrea** arrived in Goliad with about 450 soldiers. The two sides fought briefly.

Then Fannin decided to head toward Victoria after all. But it was too late. Urrea's army surrounded Fannin's troops near a creek.

Fannin decided that his troops must fight again. The Mexican army quickly stopped them, though. Fannin was forced to surrender.

On March 27, Urrea followed an order sent by Santa Anna. The Texas prisoners were marched onto the prairie near the fort. Then the Mexican soldiers shot most of them. The only survivors hid or ran from the firing squad.

The Goliad mass killing brought about another battle cry for the Texans: "Remember Goliad!"

REVIEW What two decisions led to Fannin's surrender? ↻ **Cause and Effect**

Literature and Social Studies

Noah Smithwick's Recollections

Noah Smithwick left Bastrop during the Runaway Scrape. He wrote about the abandoned houses there. This excerpt is from his book, *Evolution of a State.*

"Houses were standing open, the beds unmade, the breakfast things still on the tables, pans of milk moulding in the dairies. There were cribs full of corn, smoke houses full of bacon, yards full of chickens that ran after us for food, nests of eggs in every fence corner. . . . Forlorn dogs roamed. . . . Hungry cats ran mewing to meet us, rubbing their sides against our legs in token of welcome."

▶ **San Jacinto Monument**

Before the Last Battle

What would you have done if you were Sam Houston? The Texans could not lose many more men and win the revolution.

First, Houston decided to take some time to improve his main Texas force. For two weeks in April 1836, he taught the men how to work together to succeed in battle.

Next, Houston asked his **scouts** to help. A scout named **Erastus "Deaf" Smith** taught men how to ride ahead and gather clues about the enemy. **Hendrick Arnold,** a free African American scout, got into the Mexican army camps and pretended to be a runaway slave. He then brought information back to Houston.

Finally, Houston gathered more weapons. The citizens of Cincinnati, Ohio, sent two cannons. The Texans named them the "Twin Sisters."

On April 14, Houston's army marched toward **Harrisburg.** Five days later, his scouts told him that Santa Anna's army was camped on the San Jacinto River near Harrisburg. Houston's army was ready!

▶ Erastus "Deaf" Smi

REVIEW What steps did Houston take to improve his army?
Sequence

Map Adventure

Mapping Battle Sites

You are going to be a contestant on a quiz show about the Texas Revolution. How might you recall information about the main battles?

1. Think about the battles you have read about in Chapter 6.

2. On a sheet of paper, draw a time line showing the major battles.

3. With your finger on this map, follow the routes to battle sites. Refer to your time line to help you remember the most important dates.

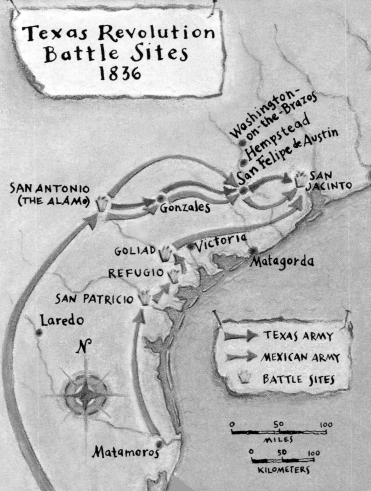

Texas Revolution Battle Sites 1836

Washington-on-the-Brazos
Hempstead
San Felipe de Austin
SAN JACINTO
SAN ANTONIO (THE ALAMO)
Gonzales
GOLIAD
Victoria
REFUGIO
Matagorda
SAN PATRICIO
Laredo
N

→ TEXAS ARMY
→ MEXICAN ARMY
BATTLE SITES

0   50   100
MILES

0   50   100
KILOMETERS

Matamoros

The Battle of San Jacinto

On April 20, Houston's army stopped where the San Jacinto River meets the Buffalo Bayou. The soldiers pitched camp in a grove of live oak trees. A wide prairie stretched in front of them.

That same day, a small group of Texan and Mexican soldiers started fighting. But when the Texans fired the Twin Sisters cannons, Santa Anna called off his men.

The next afternoon at 3:00, the training that Houston had given his troops paid off. The Mexican soldiers had waited all morning for the Texans to attack, then decided they were not coming. Houston decided to lead a surprise attack.

"Remember the Alamo! Remember Goliad!"

These were the battle cries that awoke the napping Mexican army on April 21, 1836. After only eighteen minutes, the Texans had won the battle. In the end, only nine Texans lost their lives in the **Battle of San Jacinto.** About 630 Mexicans lay dead.

What happened to the two generals? Houston suffered a shattered ankle. Santa Anna fled during battle.

A tall **monument,** or memorial, stands near the battleground today. The **San Jacinto Monument** is a reminder of the Texans' victory in the last battle of the Texas Revolution.

REVIEW Why did the Texan army win at San Jacinto? ⟳ **Cause and Effect**

► **Mexican army flag captured at San Jacinto**

MAP SKILL

The Battle of San Jacinto

Buffalo Bayou

San Jacinto River

Burnet's Bay

Lynch's Ferry

Houston's Headquarters

San Jacinto Bay

Santa Anna's Headquarters

Peggy's Lake

0   1/8   1/4 Mile
0   1/8   1/4 Kilometer

Key

■ Texas forces and their camp

■ Mexican forces and their camp

----- Ferry crossing

Hill: approximately 10 feet high

► **The Texans' victory at the Battle of San Jacinto won the war.**

MAP SKILL Use a Map Key and Symbols *How do the symbols and the key help you understand the battle?*

▶ Find Santa Anna in the painting. Why is he dressed in a common soldier's uniform?

The Treaty of Velasco

The next day the Texans found Santa Anna hiding in the woods. He was wearing the uniform of a common soldier. But when his men called out "El Presidente!" the Texans knew who he was.

Houston would not let his soldiers kill the Mexican general. Instead, he wanted Santa Anna to give Texas its freedom. So Santa Anna was made to stay with the Texas army.

At the same time, Houston had to take care of his own injured ankle. While Houston was in the hospital, the new president of the republic, David G. Burnet, met with Santa Anna at **Velasco.** There, the Mexican general signed a treaty that put an end to the war. A **treaty** is a formal agreement between two countries.

By signing the **Treaty of Velasco,** Santa Anna agreed to end the fighting against Texas. He also agreed to exchange prisoners of war and to remove all Mexican forces from Texas.

Santa Anna signed a second treaty too. It was a secret one. In it, he promised to urge the Mexican government to recognize the independence of Texas. Several months later, the defeated general returned to Mexico.

REVIEW Why do you think Santa Anna agreed to the terms of the Treaty of Velasco? **Draw Conclusions**

The New Republic

Texas was now an independent country. Its citizens had formed and defended a new republic. A **republic** is a type of government in which citizens choose leaders to represent them.

The Republic of Texas successfully set up its new government under the Constitution of 1836. Sam Houston was elected president. **Mirabeau B. Lamar** (MIR uh boh bee luh MAR) was elected vice-president. Texans elected a **congress,** or a group of elected representatives to make the nation's laws. A group of judges made decisions about the fairness of those laws. The new nation could collect taxes from its citizens. A **tax** is money paid to the government in exchange for services.

The new nation was successful in other ways too. Immigrants continued to arrive in Texas. The population grew by an average of 7,000 people per year. Several important private and religious schools, colleges, and universities were founded in the Republic of Texas.

REVIEW List ways in which the Republic of Texas was a successful new nation. **Main Idea and Details**

The Lone Star Flag

The flag that flies over Texas today was first adopted in 1839 as the national flag of the Republic of Texas. Its design reflected the new nation's nickname—the Lone Star Republic.

It is said that Joanna Troutman from Georgia made the first Lone Star flag. However, the Lone Star flag designed by Sarah Dodson from Harrisburg, Texas, most closely resembles the present Texas flag.

The Pledge to the Texas Flag
*Honor the Texas Flag.
I pledge allegiance to thee,
Texas, one and indivisible.*

▶ Joanna Troutman's flag, "Liberty or Death"

▶ Sarah Dodson's Lone Star flag

Challenges to the Republic

Have you ever gone through a change that was both exciting and difficult? Many Texans were thrilled with their new independence. But they also knew there were difficult challenges ahead.

One challenge was the new nation's **debt.** This money owed to others had been used to pay for weapons during the war. President Houston would plan ways to repay it.

Protection from attacks became another challenge. Some Texans feared more attacks from Mexico. Many settlers still wanted to claim the lands of Native Americans. This brought on more fighting with Native American groups.

A third challenge was the issue of statehood. Not all Texans believed that Texas should remain a separate country. Some thought it should become a U.S. state.

The Republic of Texas lasted from 1836 to 1845. During that time the people of Texas elected four presidents. The Fact File below tells about each one.

REVIEW What challenges did the new republic face? **Summarize**

FACT FILE

Presidents of the Republic of Texas

David G. Burnet served as a temporary president of the new republic from March 17 to October 22, 1836. During this time, Texas independence was won and the new government was formed.

Sam Houston served in the U.S. Congress. He later became governor of Tennessee. He was elected president of the Republic of Texas in 1836 and again in 1841.

Mirabeau B. Lamar is still known today as the "Father of Texas Education." He supported schools during his presidency, which lasted from 1838 to 1841.

Anson Jones served as the president of the Republic of Texas from 1844 to 1846. He was the last president of the Republic of Texas.

A New Capital

In 1836 the new leaders chose Columbia, a town on the Brazos River, as the new capital of Texas. Later that year, they moved the capital to Houston, a new town named for Sam Houston.

In 1839 the Texas Congress sent scouts to find a more central site for the state capital. The scouts selected a small frontier village named Waterloo on the banks of the Colorado River. They said Waterloo had a pleasant, healthful climate. It had fine water, plenty of stone, and good timber too.

The new capital's name was changed from Waterloo to Austin in 1839. The new name was in honor of Stephen F. Austin.

REVIEW What features caused the scouts to choose Waterloo?
Cause and Effect

Summarize

March 11, 1836 The Runaway Scrape began.

March 27, 1836 Fannin's troops were killed at Goliad.

April 21, 1836 Texans won the Battle of San Jacinto.

▶ The city of Austin, 1840

★ **LESSON 3** **REVIEW**

Check Facts and Main Ideas

1. **Cause and Effect** On a separate sheet of paper, fill in the missing causes of the major events from this lesson.

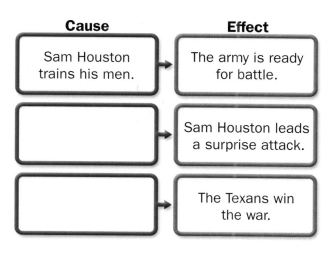

Cause	Effect
Sam Houston trains his men.	The army is ready for battle.
	Sam Houston leads a surprise attack.
	The Texans win the war.

2. How did Houston's strategy influence the outcome of the battle of San Jacinto?

3. Why did Santa Anna think he would win the Battle of San Jacinto?

4. Why was the Treaty of Velasco important to Texas?

5. **Critical Thinking:** *Cause and Effect* What event caused Santa Anna to lose the war, and how did that affect Texas and Mexico?

Link to **Writing**

Write a Dialogue Write a short conversation, or dialogue, about an event in the Texas Revolution. Check your work for correct spelling and punctuation. Did you write complete sentences? Ask two of your classmates to read the conversation aloud.

CITIZEN HEROES

Bringing Texans Together

Have you ever struggled with two sides of an argument when deciding what you should do? José Antonio Navarro tried to be fair to everyone when he worked with different groups in Texas.

José Antonio Navarro was born in San Antonio in 1795. He grew up to be a wealthy Tejano rancher, merchant, and lawyer. Navarro aimed for fairness. He tried to help both Anglo American and Mexican settlers in Texas understand each other better.

Navarro frowned upon actions that set people against one another. When a group of people tried to keep immigrants out of the country, Navarro felt that these people were being unfair. He said that they

> "... (do) not know just and generous ideas."

Navarro himself tried to be just and generous.

During the Texas Revolution, Navarro sent supplies from his store to the Texan army. Navarro said that Anglo Americans and Tejanos must work together for the good of all Texans.

Because he was so fair-minded, people often asked Navarro to help make decisions.

He represented San Antonio at the Washington-on-the-Brazos convention.

BUILDING
CITIZENSHIP
Caring
Respect
Responsibility
Fairness
Honesty
Courage

At this meeting, Texas decided to declare independence from Mexico. Navarro was one of three Tejanos to sign the Texas Declaration of Independence. He also convinced many Tejanos to support Texas in its struggle against Mexico.

Later, as a county judge, Navarro fought for the rights of Texans—especially Tejanos. He also believed that the government should help poor Texans and those who could not speak English.

Navarro was the only Texas-born leader at the Convention of 1845. When the leaders decided that Texas should join the United States, Navarro supported this decision. But he also insisted on basic rights for Tejanos. Navarro argued that Tejanos would be truly free only if they were given the right to vote.

Many of the choices Navarro made were difficult. But with each one, this leader tried to think fairly about all Texans. He wanted to bring justice to all those who needed it.

Fairness in Action

Link to Current Events Find out about a recent issue in the news that called for a fair leader to help solve it. What actions did the leader take that showed fairness?

Bolivia and Independence

During the 1800s many countries in the Western Hemisphere declared their independence. Bolivia, for example, fought for and won its independence from Spain in 1825. Today Bolivia is a republic, just as Texas became a republic after it won independence from Mexico. Bolivia shares other similarities with Texas as well.

▶ **Antonio José de Sucre led Bolivian forces in their battle for independence. He served as Bolivia's first president. The constitutional capital of Bolivia, Sucre, is named for him.**

▶ **Sam Houston led the Texan army to victory at the Battle of San Jacinto. He was the first elected president of the Republic of Texas. The city of Houston is named for him.**

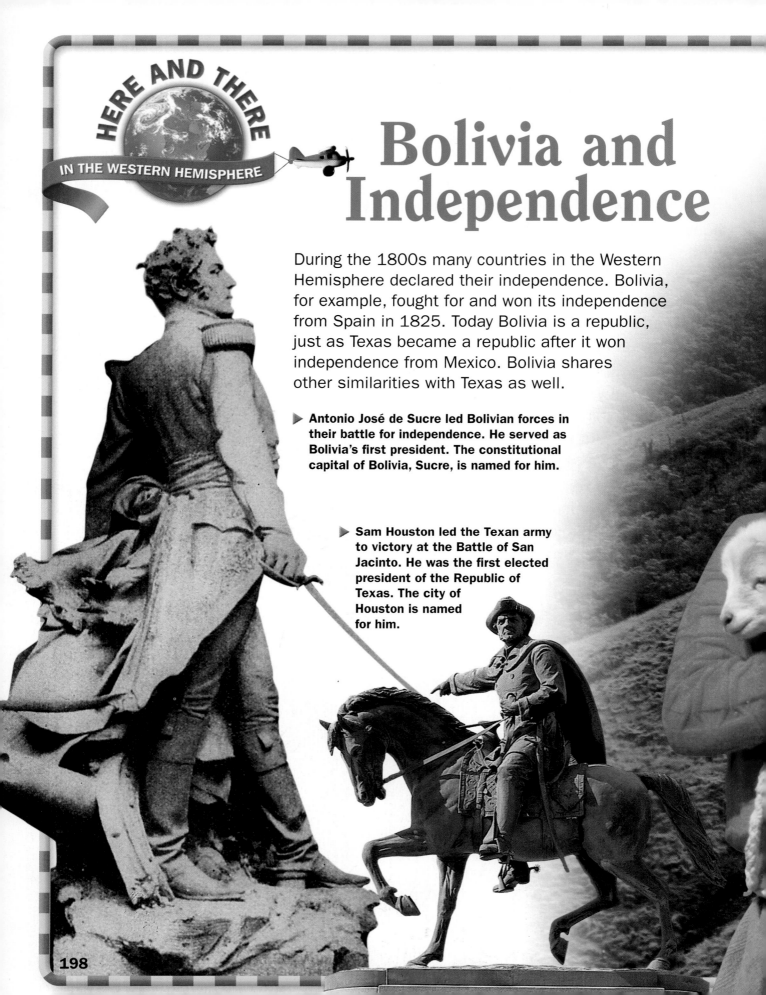

► Western Bolivia has high mountains, just as West Texas is a mountainous region. Bolivia's tallest mountains are more than 20,000 feet high.

► Bolivia is landlocked, which means it does not border an ocean, sea, or gulf. However, Lake Titicaca lies in Bolivia. At an elevation of 12,500 feet, Lake Titicaca is the highest lake in the world that can be navigated by commercial boats.

► Most people in Bolivia are descendants of Native Americans, Spanish settlers, or *mestizos*—a mixture of Spaniards and Native Americans.

► Bolivia also has lowland areas. Just as in Texas, some of these lowlands have a dry climate.

199

1835

1835	October 1835	November 1835	December 1835
Stephen F. Austin returned to Texas.	Texans battled Mexican troops in Gonzales and Goliad.	Texans met at San Felipe for the Consultation.	Texas troops forced the Mexican army from San Antonio.

Chapter Summary

 Cause and Effect

On a separate sheet of paper, fill in three effects that followed from Texans' desire to be free of Santa Anna's rule.

Santa Anna

Cause

Texans want to be free of Santa Anna's rule.

Effects

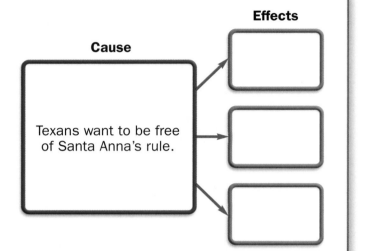

Vocabulary

Complete each sentence with the correct vocabulary word from the chapter.

1 Under Santa Anna's rule, Texans could not _____ the government for certain rights. (p. 174)

2 The Texas Constitution of 1836 included a _____, which stated that certain freedoms belonged to all Texans. (p. 175)

3 The Alamo was placed under a _____, by Santa Anna to force its surrender. (p. 181)

4 Houston asked Erastus "Deaf" Smith and other _____ to gather clues to help defeat Santa Anna. (p. 190)

5 Santa Anna signed a _____ that ended the war. (p. 192)

People and Events

Match the name of each person or event with the correct description.

1 **Consultation** (p. 173)

2 **David Crockett** (p. 182)

3 **William B. Travis** (p. 182)

4 **Susanna Dickinson** (p. 183)

5 **Hendrick Arnold** (p. 190)

a. Texas survivor of the fall of the Alamo

b. the commander of Texas forces at the Alamo after Bowie became ill

c. a scout who pretended to be a runaway slave

d. meeting to discuss Texas independence

e. a soldier who led men from Tennessee at the Alamo

February 24, 1836
Fighting began at the Alamo.

March 2, 1836
Texas declared independence and set up a new government.

March 6, 1836
Texans lost the Battle of the Alamo.

March 11, 1836
The Runaway Scrape began.

April 21, 1836
Texans won the Battle of San Jacinto.

Facts and Main Ideas

1 What happened at Gonzales on October 2, 1835?

2 As they fought at the Alamo, Texans were unaware of what fact?

3 **Main Idea** Toward the end of 1835, why did Texans believe they could defeat Santa Anna's troops?

4 **Main Idea** Why were the men of the Alamo willing to fight to their deaths?

5 **Main Idea** Why was the victory at San Jacinto important?

6 **Critical Thinking:** *Cause and Effect* How did the fall of the Alamo affect Texans?

Write About History

1 **Design a memorial plaque** that honors the men who gave their lives at the Alamo. Include a symbol that fits the spirit of the Alamo. Then write an explanation about your memorial design.

2 **Write a letter** from the point of view of a Mexican soldier who fought against the Texans during the revolution.

3 **Write a speech** from the point of view of a leader that celebrates the signing of the Texas Declaration of Independence.

Apply Skills

Identify Primary and Secondary Sources

Read the excerpt below. Then answer the questions.

Letter sent by William B. Travis to the citizens of Texas during the siege of the Alamo:

"*. . . The enemy is receiving reinforcements daily and will no doubt increase to three or four thousand in four or five days. If this call is neglected, I am determined to sustain myself as long as possible and die like a soldier who never forgets what is due his own honor and that of his country. VICTORY OR DEATH.*"

1 Is this a primary source or a secondary source? How do you know?

2 Would a book written last year about William B. Travis be a primary source or a secondary source? Explain your answer.

3 Why is this letter an especially useful source of information?

Internet Activity

To get help with vocabulary, people, and events, select the dictionary or encyclopedia from *Social Studies Library* at **www.sfsocialstudies.com.**

CHAPTER 7

The Lone Star State

Lesson 1

Austin
December 29, 1845
Texas becomes a state of the United States. Soon afterward, the U.S. flag replaces the Lone Star flag.

1

Lesson 2

Palo Alto
1846
The first major battle of the Mexican War is fought.

2

CANADA

UNITED STATES

1

2

TEXAS

Austin

MEXICO

Palo Alto

Gulf of Mexico

PACIFIC OCEAN

ATLANTIC OCEAN

Why We Remember

Texas was an independent nation for nine years. Citizens enjoyed new opportunities in the republic. Still, challenges arose. Many settlers thought Texas should become a state of the United States. In 1845, after much debate, a 28th star—for Texas—was added to the U.S. flag. Soon Mexico disagreed with where the Texas borders should be drawn. By 1846, the United States and Mexico were at war over land issues. In 1848, a treaty was signed. The United States won vast territory from Mexico.

1836	1841	184

1836 and 1841
Sam Houston is elected President of the Republic.

February 28, 1845
U.S. Congress passes a resolution allowing Texas to become a state.

July 4, 1845
Texas leaders meet to vote on the resolution.

December 29, 1845
Texas becomes the 28th state of the United States.

The Rise of the Lone Star State

PREVIEW

Focus on the Main Idea
Texas became one of the United States.

PLACES
Washington-on-the-Brazos
Austin
El Paso
New Braunfels
Panna Maria

PEOPLE
Anson Jones
José Antonio Navarro
James Pinckney Henderson
Prince Carl
Father Leopold Moczygemba

VOCABULARY
annexation
resolution
legislature

▶ **Statue of Sam Houston**

You Are There It is a warm summer morning in 1842. You stand with your father and a group of people outside the president's house. Suddenly, Sam Houston steps onto the back porch. He greets everyone warmly. Then he goes to the pump, takes out his razor, and begins trimming his sideburns. While he shaves, people chat with each other and with Houston. You marvel at how this tall Texan can entertain a crowd! One minute, he is sharing an amazing story. The next, he is telling a funny joke. Yet he also listens closely to people's ideas. You decide then and there that you would like to be a Texas leader when you grow up. But you wonder what Texas will be like then.

Cause and Effect To find causes as you read, ask yourself "Why?"

The Last Days of the Republic

If you had been able to talk with Sam Houston as he shaved, he might have told you his feelings about Texas. Houston loved Texas. But he did not feel that Texas should be a separate country. Instead, he supported annexation. That is, he wanted Texas to join with and become one of the United States. The U.S. Army protected its citizens. A U.S. postal system delivered mail to towns far and wide. Houston knew that such services cost money. At that time, Texas had very little money.

As president, Houston had tried to convince people of his views. Many Texans agreed with him, but others did not. They wanted Texas to become a powerful country like the United States.

People outside Texas also opposed Houston's ideas. Some U.S. leaders did not want to annex Texas. They knew that Texas laws allowed slavery. This meant that farmers could use the labor of enslaved workers—people who were not free. Certain southern states also had laws supporting slavery. Some leaders did not want to add another slave state to the United States. Many U.S. citizens did not want to take on the debt that Texas had.

REVIEW Why did some U.S. leaders oppose the annexation of Texas?
⟳ **Cause and Effect**

▶ **Paper money from the Republic of Texas**

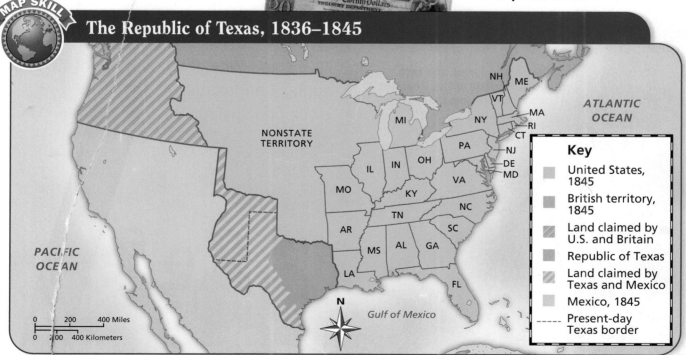

MAP SKILL

The Republic of Texas, 1836–1845

NONSTATE TERRITORY

NH
ME
VT
MI
NY
MA
RI
CT
PA
NJ
DE
MD
IL
IN
OH
VA
MO
KY
NC
TN
AR
SC
MS
AL
GA
LA
FL

ATLANTIC OCEAN

PACIFIC OCEAN

N

Gulf of Mexico

0   200   400 Miles
0   200   400 Kilometers

Key
- United States, 1845
- British territory, 1845
- Land claimed by U.S. and Britain
- Republic of Texas
- Land claimed by Texas and Mexico
- Mexico, 1845
- ----- Present-day Texas border

▶ **For nine years, Texas was an independent nation.**

MAP SKILL Use a Map Key *How was the shape of the Republic of Texas similar to and different from that of modern-day Texas?*

Texas Joins the United States

On February 28, 1845, the U.S. Congress passed a **resolution,** or decision. The resolution said that Texas could become a state. It went on to say that Texas would keep its public lands. But it must agree to give its forts to the U.S. government.

Many months would pass before Texas was officially a state. On July 4, 1845, Texas leaders met at **Washington-on-the-Brazos** to vote on the resolution. It passed with only one "no" vote.

In October, Texas voters also accepted the resolution. More than 4,000 people voted in favor of statehood. Only about 200 Texans voted against it.

Finally, on December 29, 1845, Texas became the 28th state of the United States. A few weeks later, Texans gathered in front of the state Capitol in **Austin. Anson Jones,** the last president of the Republic of Texas, was there. Lowering the flag of the republic, he announced, "The Republic of Texas is no more."

Feelings of sadness swept through the crowd. Writer Noah Smithwick later described the scene:

> *"Many a head was bowed, many a broad chest heaved, and many a manly cheek was wet with tears. . . ."*

But moments later, the mood changed. People began cheering as a new flag was raised. At last, the U.S. flag waved above the Texas Capitol!

REVIEW Why did a majority of Texans support annexation?
Draw Conclusions

▶ Anson Jones, the last president of the Republic of Texas, lowered the Texas flag.

▶ This Texas State Capitol building was completed in 1855. It was destroyed by fire in 1881.

The Constitution of 1845

Now that Texas was a state, it needed a state constitution. Think of it as if your school needed a new set of rules. You would probably feel honored if your principal chose you to write them. But you might also feel a little frightened.

This may be how the writers of the new constitution felt. They knew that the future of Texas would depend on their words. After all, the constitution would decide how all Texans would live.

Several men worked together to write the constitution. It took them two months. Only one of these men, José Antonio Navarro, had been born in Texas. The others came from the United States. The writers based their ideas on the constitutions written for the Republic of Texas and for the state of Louisiana.

The new constitution said that the Texas legislature would meet every two years. A legislature is a group of people who make new laws.

The constitution also said that Texans would elect a new governor every two years. The first governor of Texas, James Pinckney Henderson, took over as governor when Anson Jones stepped down from the presidency.

For many years, the only Texans allowed to vote were Anglo and Tejano men over the age of 21. Women, Native American men, and African American men did not have this right. They could not be elected to a public office either.

REVIEW Who was the first governor of Texas? **Main Idea and Details**

207

The Call of the Land

The story of Texas is a story of the land. It is also a story of change.

You may remember that Texas kept its public lands when it became a state. Leaders then gave away some of this land to attract people to the area.

This offer brought many immigrants to Texas after 1845. Most immigrants arrived from the southern United States. Others came from Mexico and Europe.

Many Mexicans settled in the southern part of Texas. They lived in towns such as San Antonio, Laredo, and Victoria. Some Mexican immigrants moved farther west, to places such as **El Paso** and Presidio.

European families left crowded cities and sailed to a new land. Some had to walk hundreds of miles from the Texas coast to reach their new homes. People often died on this difficult journey.

In the 1840s a group of Germans organized an association to bring Germans to Texas. One of their leaders, **Prince Carl** of Solms-Braunfels (solms BRAHN fels) in Germany, visited Texas and then wrote a book. He described "bays, rivers and creeks" swimming with "large and heavy fish," oysters, and crabs. "All are delicious," he concluded. What a rich world this was!

Prince Carl's words drew German families to Texas. Many settled in the central part of the state. There they built towns such as **New Braunfels** and Fredericksburg. They spoke German, read German newspapers, and ate German food. Today part of Central Texas is still called "the German Hill Country."

▶ Many immigrant families came to Texas to claim land.

208

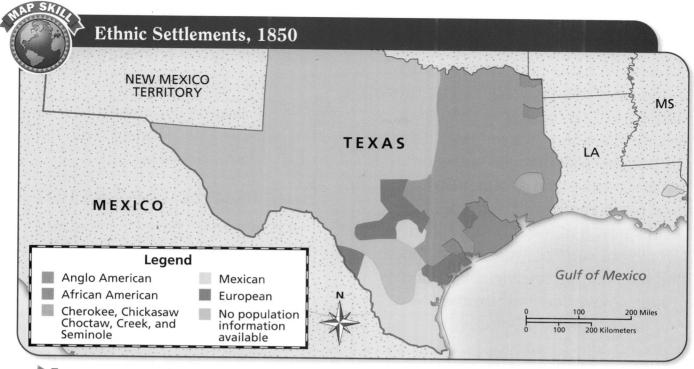

Ethnic Settlements, 1850

NEW MEXICO
TERRITORY

MS

TEXAS

LA

MEXICO

N

Gulf of Mexico

Legend

- Anglo American
- African American
- Cherokee, Chickasaw Choctaw, Creek, and Seminole
- Mexican
- European
- No population information available

0   100   200 Miles
0   100   200 Kilometers

▶ Texas was an attractive place for immigrants to settle.

MAP SKILL Movement *Why did a variety of ethnic groups settle in Texas?*

Some immigrants came to Texas from what are now the Czech and Slovak Republics. They settled in central and southeast Texas.

Father Leopold Moczygemba (LEE oh pold moh sheh GEM bah), a Polish priest, helped bring 100 families from Poland to Texas. Arriving on Christmas Eve in 1854, they founded the town of **Panna Maria.** This settlement is the oldest permanent Polish colony in the United States. The first Polish Catholic church and school are located there.

The immigrants brought new traditions and customs to the state. They spoke different languages. They ate different foods. Each group had its own ways of celebrating important events.

Take a look around Texas. What signs of the cultures of the various immigrants who settled here can you find? You may find clothing, such as a woven hat from Mexico. Or you may see a building of timber and stone like those the Germans built. Keep in mind that immigrants also brought new ideas to Texas—ideas about business, farming, and industry. These ideas have helped make Texas what it is today.

REVIEW Where was the first Polish settlement in Texas? **Main Idea and Details**

209

The New Texans

Some immigrants had been farmers in the countries they left behind. Others had worked as teachers, merchants, or tailors. But when they arrived in Texas, almost everyone had the same difficult tasks—buying land and growing food.

As more immigrants arrived, older towns grew and new towns formed. People opened hardware stores, hotels, and mills for processing cotton and grains. Texans worked together.

These settlers from other states, Mexico, and Europe answered the call of the land.

REVIEW Why do you think immigrants brought farming tools to Texas? **Draw Conclusions**

Summarize the Lesson

1836 and 1841 Sam Houston was elected president of the Republic of Texas.

February 28, 1845 U.S. Congress passed a resolution allowing Texas to become a state.

July 4, 1845 Texas leaders voted on and accepted the resolution.

December 29, 1845 Texas became the 28th state of the United States.

▶ **Immigrants from many lands made Texas their home.**

★ **LESSON 1** **REVIEW**

Check Facts and Main Ideas

1. **Cause and Effect** Draw the chart below on a sheet of paper. Fill in the effect.

Cause	Effect
The new state gives away some of its public land. →	

2. List two events that happened between February 28, 1845, and December 29, 1845.
3. Name three countries from which immigrants came to the new state.
4. Name two laws created by the Constitution of 1845.

5. **Critical Thinking: *Analyze*** You read that Texas had little money before it became a state. How do you think the new immigrants helped Texas get more money?

Link to ∞ **Writing**

Write an Advertisement You read that an association brought Germans to Texas. This group wrote ads to convince people that Texas was a good place to live. Suppose you are part of a group that wants to bring more people to your area today. Your group decides to advertise on the Internet. Write a paragraph for an advertisement convincing people to move to your area. List three locations that you would show in photos. Check your spelling and punctuation in your message.

SAM HOUSTON
1793–1863

When Sam Houston was sixteen, he worked in the village store near his home in Tennessee. But spirited Sam was more interested in adventure.

Sam ran away from home and stayed for most of the next three years with a group of Cherokee who lived across the river from the pioneer settlement.

The Cherokee chief, Oolooteka, took a liking to young Sam and adopted him as his son. Sam admired the Cherokee too. He learned their language, dressed like them, and practiced their customs. Houston later wrote:

Cherokee chief Oolooteka gave Sam Houston a Native American name, "The Raven."

"(M)y early life among the Indians was a necessary portion of that wonderful training that fitted me for my destiny."

As president of the Republic of Texas and later as a United States senator, Houston worked for the rights of Native Americans.

Learn from Biographies

How did his years with the Cherokee help Houston later in life?

For more information, go online to *Meet the People* at **www.sfsocialstudies.com**.

Should Texas Become a State?

Or should it remain its own republic?

After Texas became independent from Mexico in 1836, some Texans thought the new republic should stay independent. They did not want to give up the rights they had fought so hard to win. Others thought being part of the United States would improve their lives.

People in the United States disagreed on this issue too. Some did not want Texas to become a state. At that time, half of the states let people own slaves. It was legal to own slaves in Texas. People who were against slavery were worried that the United States would have more slave states than free states if Texas joined the Union.

There were other problems too. Mexico said Texas still belonged to it— even though Santa Anna had signed the Treaty of Velasco. Also, the United States did not want to take on the huge debt that Texans had brought about during the revolution. The United States was afraid of a war with Mexico.

Finally, in 1845, it was agreed that Texas should become a state. In 1846, a new star—the 28th—appeared on the American flag.

Sam Houston believed Texas should become a state. "Texas, with peace, could exist without the United States, but the United States can not . . . exist without Texas. . . . Texas would invite the commerce of all nations to her ports."

Sam Houston

"The annexation of Texas is a great offense against humanity."

Abiel Abbot
Texas minister, 1845

"None can fail to see the danger to our safety and future peace if Texas remains an independent state or becomes an ally . . . of some foreign nation more powerful than herself. Is there one among our citizens who would not prefer perpetual peace with Texas to occasional wars?"

James K. Polk
Presidential Inaugural Address, 1845

"Surely Mexico could be induced to surrender title to territory already lost."

Jane McManus Cazneau *1844(?),*
writer of newspaper articles

Issues and You

Suppose that you live in Texas in 1844. Everyone you know is arguing about whether Texas should become a state. What do you think? Find someone in your class who disagrees with you. Take turns trying to convince each other to adopt a new point of view.

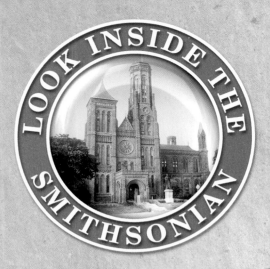

American Life in 1845

Americans enjoyed a growing spirit of adventure, expansion, invention, and creativity as the nation matured during the first half of the nineteenth century.

Bride's Quilt
Using 1,001 skeins of silk thread, Mary Jane Green made this beautiful quilt in 1845 in honor of her upcoming 1846 marriage to John J. Moran.

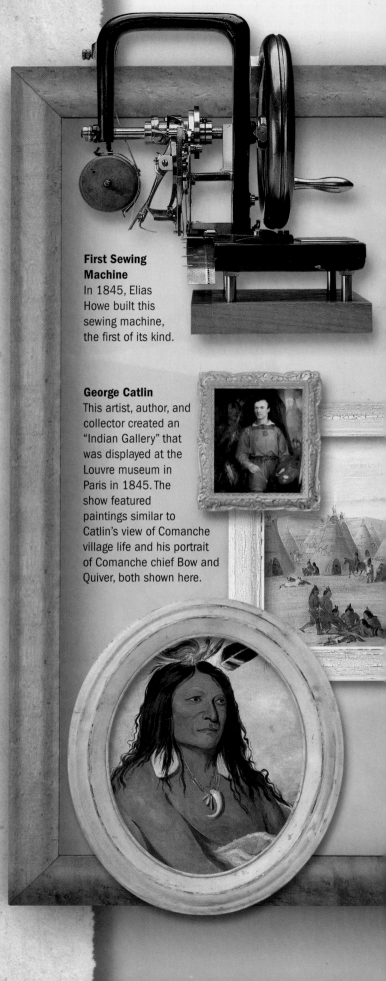

First Sewing Machine
In 1845, Elias Howe built this sewing machine, the first of its kind.

George Catlin
This artist, author, and collector created an "Indian Gallery" that was displayed at the Louvre museum in Paris in 1845. The show featured paintings similar to Catlin's view of Comanche village life and his portrait of Comanche chief Bow and Quiver, both shown here.

John Tyler

Although Texas became a state during President Polk's term of office, Texas won its long fight to join the Union in 1845 when President Tyler signed the bill approving its statehood.

Telegraph Machine

Samuel F. B. Morse sent the first successful electric telegraph message from Baltimore to Washington, D.C., in 1844, using the dot and dash code also invented by him. This telegraph set was designed in 1845.

1845 Bank Note

This paper money, dated 1845, was issued by the Bank of Corning in New York. It was typical for banks at that time to print their own money.

Conestoga Wagon

Conestoga wagons, very common in 1845, hauled wheat, flour, furs, and other goods across southern Pennsylvania and Maryland. Covered wagons similar to the Conestoga carried homesteaders into the farther frontiers of the West.

Artifacts are from the Smithsonian Institution.

LESSON 2

Palo Alto •

Guadalupe
Hidalgo •

1845   185

April 1846
U.S. and Mexican
soldiers fought near
the Rio Grande.

May 13, 1846
Mexican War
began.

February 1848
Mexican War
ended.

PREVIEW

Focus on the Main Idea
Disagreements between Mexico
and the United States led to
war between the two countries.

PLACES
Palo Alto
Guadalupe Hidalgo, Mexico

PEOPLE
James K. Polk
Zachary Taylor
Jane McManus Cazneau
Winfield Scott

VOCABULARY
expand
boundary
skirmish

EVENTS
Mexican War
Treaty of Guadalupe Hidalgo

The United States and Mexico at War

It is a hazy morning in the Gulf Coast town of Indianola. What's that wonderful smell? Cake? You hurry downstairs. Your mother and brother are busily working in the kitchen. "What's going on?" you ask in your native German. Your mother stops to brush flour off her hands. "Today's the first day of a new year—1846," she says. "Only ten years ago, Texas fought to become its own nation. Then, only a few days ago, Texas became the 28th state." Those are good reasons to bake a cake, you think. After all, how would your family know that another war was about to break out?

Cause and Effect As you read, look for the causes of war between the United States and Mexico and the effects of that war on the two nations.

216

Boundary Disputes

Many U.S. citizens felt that the country had a right to **expand**, or spread out. The Mexican government refused to give up northern Mexico—known as Texas. U.S. President **James K. Polk** wanted to buy Mexico's northern land. Mexican officials were not interested.

Mexico and the United States also disagreed over the boundary between the two countries. A **boundary** is a line that separates one place from another. Mexico claimed that the Nueces River was the boundary.

The United States said it was the Rio Grande.

Soon President Polk sent troops led by General **Zachary Taylor** marching toward the Rio Grande. In April 1846, Mexican soldiers defeated the U.S. soldiers in a **skirmish**, or minor battle. President Polk asked the U.S. Congress to declare war on Mexico. On May 8, 1846, a major battle began at **Palo Alto.** It would be the first battle of a new war.

REVIEW How did boundary disagreements lead to war?
↺ **Cause and Effect**

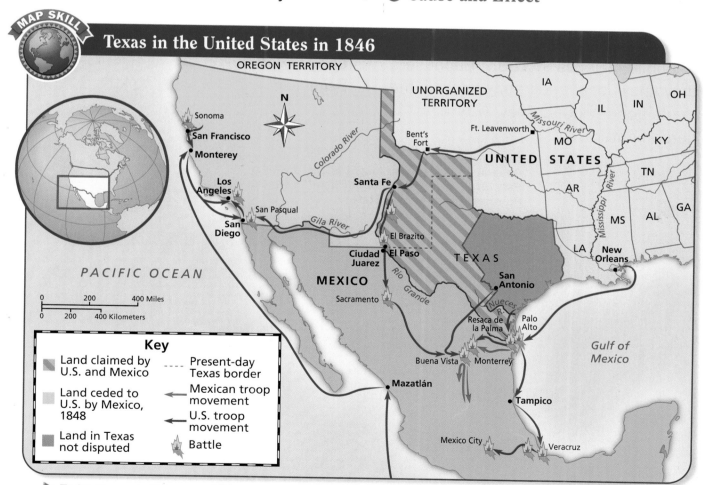

MAP SKILL

Texas in the United States in 1846

OREGON TERRITORY

UNORGANIZED TERRITORY

IA

IL   IN   OH

Ft. Leavenworth

Bent's Fort

Missouri River

MO

KY

N

Sonoma

San Francisco

Monterey

Los Angeles

San Pasqual

San Diego

Colorado River

Gila River

Santa Fe

UNITED STATES

TN

AR

MS   AL   GA

Mississippi River

PACIFIC OCEAN

El Brazito

Ciudad Juarez   **El Paso**

MEXICO

Sacramento

Rio Grande

TEXAS

LA

New Orleans

San Antonio

Nueces R.

Resaca de la Palma

Palo Alto

0   200   400 Miles
0   200   400 Kilometers

Mazatlán

Buena Vista   Monterrey

Gulf of Mexico

Key

■ Land claimed by U.S. and Mexico
□ Land ceded to U.S. by Mexico, 1848
■ Land in Texas not disputed

---- Present-day Texas border
← Mexican troop movement
← U.S. troop movement
⚜ Battle

Tampico

Mexico City   Veracruz

▶ Today Texas is the second-largest state in the United States. Texas was even larger when it first became a state in 1845.

MAP SKILL Location *How do present-day Texas boundaries compare to those of 1846?*

The Mexican War

On May 13, 1846, the U.S. Congress declared war on Mexico. This war became known in the United States as the **Mexican War.** Some Americans were against the war, but many Texans were ready to fight. They remembered other conflicts with Mexico. They wanted to put an end to Mexico's threats.

Other Texans were moved to fight by posters they saw. "To arms!" read one of the posters. It offered 160 acres of land to those who were willing to volunteer.

Even the Texas Rangers joined the war. They were a group of volunteers who officially formed to defend the Republic of Texas in 1835. Because they knew local geography so well, they made good scouts. They were also fierce fighters.

In spite of many U.S. battle victories, the war dragged on. In November 1846, the U.S. government sent a writer named **Jane McManus Cazneau** (jayn mac MAN us CAZ noh) to Mexico City. The government wanted her to help seek peace with Mexico. Cazneau failed to win a peace agreement. But she succeeded as the only female newspaper reporter in the Mexican War.

In the fall of 1847, General **Winfield Scott** led the U.S. Army and the Texas Rangers into Mexico City. His soldiers captured Mexico's capital city. At last, it was time to talk about peace.

REVIEW What important event happened just before the United States and Mexico began talking about peace? **Sequence**

General Zachary Taylor fought in The Battle of Palo Alto (below). He later became the twelfth President of the United States.

A Treaty Is Signed

Leaders from the United States and Mexico met in the village of **Guadalupe Hidalgo** (gwah dah LOO pay ee DAHL go), near Mexico City. On February 2, 1848, they signed a treaty that ended the war. The **Treaty of Guadalupe Hidalgo** was a written agreement stating that the Rio Grande was the border of Texas. It also gave the United States more than half a million square miles of land. This land included present-day California, Nevada, and Utah, as well as parts of Arizona, New Mexico, Colorado, and Wyoming. In return, the United States paid Mexico $15 million. Finally, peace with Mexico had come.

REVIEW What problem might the treaty have caused people who lived in the new U.S. territory?
Draw Conclusions

Summarize the Lesson

- **April 1846** A skirmish between U.S. and Mexican soldiers led President Polk to call for war.
- **May 13, 1846** War was declared between the United States and Mexico.
- **February 2, 1848** The Treaty of Guadalupe Hidalgo ended the Mexican War.

★ **LESSON 2** **REVIEW**

Check Facts and Main Ideas

1. **Cause and Effect** On a separate sheet of paper, fill in the missing causes of the major events from this lesson.

Cause → **Effect**

Cause	Effect
United States and Mexico disagree over boundaries.	United States and Mexican soldiers fight.
	United States and Mexico sign treaty.
	United States gains more territory.

2. Explain the boundary disagreement between the United States and Mexico.

3. How did Texans help win the Mexican War?

4. How did Texas change as a result of the Mexican War?

5. **Critical Thinking: *Draw Conclusions*** How did gaining new lands help the United States?

Link to 〜 Mathematics

Solve a Money Problem Suppose eight members of your family responded to the poster described on page 218. How many acres of land would your family get?

Map and Globe Skills

Use an Inset Map

What? An **inset map** is a small map that is set within a larger map. How do you recognize an inset map? It is usually enclosed in a box in a corner of the larger map. The large map below shows the location of Palo Alto National Battlefield. The smaller map, or inset map, shows where and how the Battle of Palo Alto was fought during the Mexican War. This battle was the first battle to be fought in Texas territory.

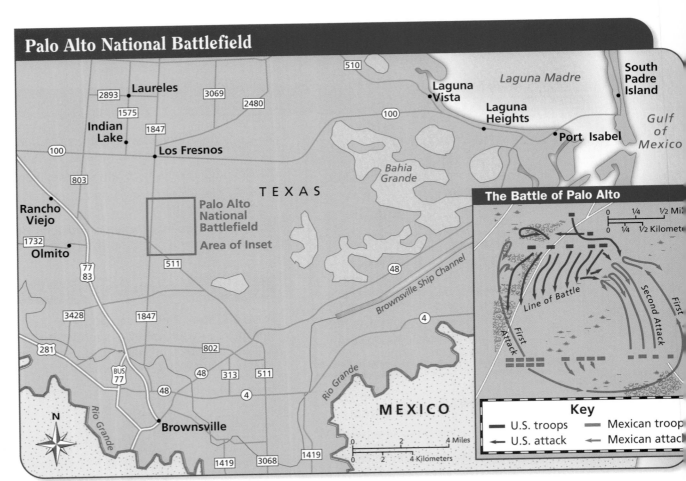

▶ The site of the Battle of Palo Alto is now a National Park Service site.

MAP SKILL Use a Map Scale *Which map has a larger scale? Why?*

Why? Inset maps give you more information about a place. Have you ever viewed something through a magnifying glass? An inset map is like this. It shows you one part of a map in greater detail. Inset maps can also show places that are outside the area covered on a main map. For example, Hawaii and Alaska are often shown on inset maps within a main map of the United States.

How? Follow these steps to use an inset map.

• Look at the large map on page 220. What information does the main map provide? How do you know?

• Now find the small box labeled "Area of Inset" on the main map. This helps you know what area the inset map covers. It may help to put your finger on this box as you study the inset map.

• Look more closely at the inset map. What does the inset map show? How do you know?

• Does the inset map have symbols? How can you find out what these symbols stand for?

Think and Apply

1 What do the symbols in the inset map stand for?

2 What city on the main map is nearest the area shown in the inset map?

3 How are inset maps helpful?

For more information, go online to the *Atlas* at **www.sfsocialstudies.com**.

CHAPTER 7
REVIEW

1835   1840

1836 and 1841
Sam Houston was elected President
of the Republic of Texas.

Chapter Summary

Cause and Effect

Target Skill

On a separate sheet of paper, fill in the missing effects.

Cause	Effect
Texans vote for annexation.	
After 1845, Texas leaders gave away public land.	
U.S. and Mexican leaders sign a treaty at Guadalupe Hidalgo.	

Vocabulary

Match each word with the correct definition
or description.

1 **annexation** (p. 205)

2 **resolution** (p. 206)

3 **legislature** (p. 207)

4 **boundary** (p. 217)

5 **skirmish** (p. 217)

a. a formal decision of a government body or group

b. a line that separates one place from another

c. a minor fight

d. the joining of one place with another place

e. a group of people who help make laws

People and Events

Write a sentence explaining why each person
or event was important in the early years of
Texas statehood.

1 **Anson Jones** (p. 206)

2 **José Antonio Navarro** (p. 207)

3 **Prince Carl** (p. 208)

4 **James K. Polk** (p. 217)

5 **The Mexican War** (p. 218)

February 28, 1845 United States passed Congressional resolution allowing Texas statehood.

July 4, 1845 Texas leaders voted on statehood resolution.

December 29, 1845 Texas became a state.

April 1846 U.S. and Mexican soldiers fought near the Rio Grande.

May 13, 1846 Mexican War began.

February 1848 Mexican War ended.

Facts and Main Ideas

1 Why did Sam Houston want Texas to join the United States?

2 Who was the first governor of Texas?

3 Why were many Texans ready to go to war with Mexico in 1846?

4 **Time Line** When was the treaty that ended the Mexican War signed?

5 **Main Idea** What important task did Texas leaders face soon after Texas became a state?

6 **Main Idea** Name two causes of the war between the United States and Mexico.

7 **Main Idea** Where was the treaty signed that named the border of Texas?

8 **Critical Thinking:** *Cause and Effect* What caused many people to move to Texas after 1845?

Apply Skills

Use an Inset Map

Look at the map on page 220. Then answer the questions.

1 What information does the inset map show that is not found on the larger map?

2 Which of the two maps has the smaller scale?

3 On a large map of your town, what information might be shown on an inset map?

Internet Activity

To get help with vocabulary, people, and events, select the dictionary or encyclopedia from *Social Studies Library* at **www.sfsocialstudies.com.**

Write About History

1 **Design a poster** that calls for volunteers in the Mexican War. Use some place names that you read about in Lesson 2.

2 **Write a poem** about the gathering at the state Capitol, when the flag of the Texas Republic was lowered and the U.S. flag was raised. Write from the point of view of a girl or boy about your age who attended the event.

3 **Write a newspaper article** from the point of view of a Mexican woman who was present at the signing of the Treaty of Guadalupe Hidalgo.

Angel of the Alamo

text by Lisa Waller Rogers • illustrated by Gwen Thigpen

Andrea Castañón Villanueva was born in the desert near Laredo and grew up in Texas with her family. She became a curandera, or folk healer. In the book, Andrea is known as the Angel of the Alamo. Her caring ways helped many people. In this excerpt, she helps take care of James Bowie in the Alamo.

Santa Anna is coming! People began leaving San Antonio in **caravans**.
But Andrea was not leaving. She had been given an official duty.
A letter had arrived at her home from General Sam Houston,
her old friend and the commander-in-chief of the Texas army. It said:

> *Candelarita* (his pet name for Andrea),
> *Go and take care of Bowie,*
> *my brother, in the Alamo.*
> *Houston*

Andrea had rushed to the Alamo. She had found Bowie lying on a cot,
gravely ill with **pneumonia**. He was as white as a sheet. . . . Now he had
only enough strength to say a few words. He had been forced to give
up his Alamo command. From then on, Andrea stayed by Bowie's side.
She left only to run brief errands in town.

caravan:
a company
of travelers
on a journey,
especially across
a desert

pneumonia:
a disease of the
lungs caused by
infection

Test Talk

Narrow the answer choices. Rule out answers you know are wrong.

Main Ideas and Vocabulary

TEST PREP

Read the passage below and use it to answer the questions that follow.

By early March 1836, the Texans had won several battles against Mexican troops. They had declared themselves a free country. Texas leaders had elected a president. They had also written a constitution and a <u>Bill of Rights</u>.

Santa Anna was determined to stop the Texas revolution. He marched his forces to San Antonio in February 1836. About three months earlier, Texans had defeated his army there. Now the Mexican leader ordered his troops to surround the Alamo. William Travis, James Bowie, and others inside the Alamo saw that they were outnumbered. Still, they fought bravely. Every Alamo defender died at the Alamo.

Fighting continued in other places. Mexican soldiers captured and killed James Fannin's troops in Goliad.

But at San Jacinto, Sam Houston's men surprised Mexican soldiers and defeated them. Santa Anna agreed to a treaty that ended the fighting. Texans were independent from Mexico. The Republic of Texas lasted from 1836 to 1845.

In December 1845 Texas joined the United States. Problems with Mexico developed, though. For one thing, the United States and Mexico disagreed over the Texas <u>boundary</u>. In 1846, a skirmish between U.S. and Mexican troops led the U.S. Congress to declare war on Mexico.

Aided by the Texas Rangers, U.S. soldiers defeated Mexico. A treaty was signed in 1848. At last, Texans could return to the business of building a strong state. There was no longer a threat of war with Mexico.

1 What was the result of the Battle of the Alamo?

A Texans declared independence from Mexico.
B Santa Anna gained an important victory.
C Fannin's troops were killed.
D A treaty with Mexico was signed.

2 In this passage, *Bill of Rights* means—

A a declaration of war
B an agreement to end fighting
C a statement of freedoms
D a plan of government

3 What group declared war on Mexico in 1846?

A The U.S. Army
B Texas leaders
C The U.S. Congress
D The Texas Rangers

4 In this passage, the word *boundary* means—

A a line that separates one place from another
B a republic that has become a state
C a statement of citizens' rights
D an agreement between two nations

Vocabulary and People

Match each word or the name of each person with the correct definition or description.

1 David Crockett (p. 182)

2 congress (p. 193)

3 republic (p. 193)

4 resolution (p. 206)

5 expand (p. 217)

6 Jane McManus Cazneau (p. 218)

a. lawmaking body in a government

b. writer who tried to seek peace with Mexico during the Mexican War

c. spread out

d. type of decision

e. government in which people choose leaders to represent them

f. volunteer who fought at the Alamo

Apply Skills

Make a Time Line Create a time line poster that shows important events in Texas history from 1835 to 1848. It can be vertical or horizontal. Work with a partner to choose six to eight events to show on the time line. If there is space on the poster, illustrate one or more of the events from the time line.

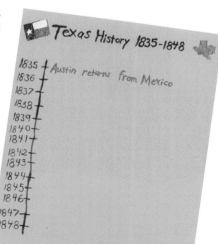

Write and Share

Present a Panel Discussion With your classmates, write a script for a discussion program. In the program, several people from Texas history will discuss their points of view about the Texas Revolution. Choose five or six men and women from the period of time you read about in Unit 3. Include Santa Anna and Sam Houston as panelists. If possible, perform your panel discussion for another class in your school.

Read on Your Own

Look for books like these in the library.

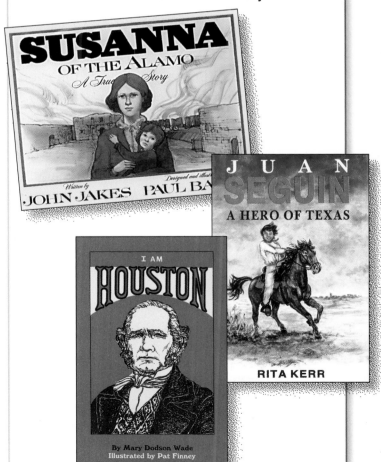

This Just In

Report breaking news in Texas's history.

1 Choose an important event in Texas's history.

2 Choose roles to play for a press conference about the event: government officials or experts, news reporters, eyewitnesses, and other participants.

3 Research the event, focusing on one or two important details of the event. Work together to write questions and answers about the event.

4 Create a poster that a TV news station might use to announce breaking news about the event.

5 Hold your press conference as a class activity.

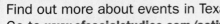

Internet Activity

Find out more about events in Texas's history. Go to **www.sfsocialstudies.com/activities** and select your grade and unit.

A Changing State

How did the Texas frontier change?

Begin with a Primary Source

1850			1860		

1850
More immigrants
come to Texas.

1861
The Civil War
begins.

1863
Lincoln issues
Emancipation
Proclamation.

1865
Slaves
are freed
in Texas.

1866
Texas cattle
drives begin.

"I rode the range, when it was new ... and many a pleasant memory is mine as I hark back to cow camps, long before barbed wire fence days."

—trail driver J. E. Pettus, recalling his trail life of the 1870s to 1882

The Old Chisholm Trail, painted by Clara McDonald Williamson in 1952, recalls the days of long cattle drives.

1870
Railroads boom in Texas.

1874
Joseph Glidden invents an improved barbed wire.

1875
Plains Indians are forced to leave Texas.

1886
The first Texas State Fair is held.

1890
The West Texas open range comes to an end.

UNIT 4

Meet the People

Jesse Chisholm

1805(?)–1868

Birthplace: Hiwassee region, Tennessee

Trader, guide, interpreter

- Spoke twelve Native American languages
- Interpreted for Sam Houston in Native American treaty councils
- Blazed a famous cattle trail between Texas and Kansas

Joseph Farwell Glidden

1813–1906

Birthplace: Charleston, New Hampshire

Inventor, businessman

- Patented an improved type of barbed wire in 1874
- Installed barbed wire fences on his Frying Pan Ranch in Texas
- Became one of the wealthiest men in the United States

Charles Goodnight

1836–1929

Birthplace: Macoupin County, Illinois

Rancher

- Moved to Texas when he was nine years old
- Started the first cattle ranch in the Texas Panhandle in 1876
- Led cattle to Wyoming in 1868 on a trail that soon took his name

Mary Ann Dyer Goodnight

1839–1926

Birthplace: Madison County, Tennessee

Rancher and volunteer

- Together with husband, Charles Goodnight, ran the JA Ranch in the Texas Panhandle
- Helped establish the Goodnight Buffalo Herd
- Helped establish many churches, schools, and service organizations

| 1805 | 1820 | 1835 | 1850 | 1865 | 1880 |

1805(?) • Jesse Chisholm — 1868

1813 • Joseph Farwell Glidden

1836 • Charles Goodnight

1839 • Mary Ann Dyer Goodnight

c. 1845 • Quanah Parker

1857 or 1858 • Johanna July

1870 • William

For more information, go online to *Meet the People* at **www.sfsocialstudies.com**.

Quanah Parker

c. 1845–1911
Birthplace: Unknown
Chief of the Comanche
- Son of Cynthia Ann Parker, a Texas settler, and Peta Nacona, a Comanche chief
- Became a Comanche chief
- Mediator between Native Americans and United States government after the Civil War

Johanna July

1857 or 1858– sometime after World War II
Birthplace: Mexico
Vaquera
- Fished and hunted to provide for her family as a child in Mexico
- Became responsible for taking care of her family's animals after her father's death
- Became a skilled horse trainer

William "Bill" Pickett

1870–1932
Birthplace: Jenks-Branch, Texas
Cowboy
- Became well known for "bulldogging," an exciting rodeo event
- Performed in the famous 101 Ranch Show
- Became the first African American to be inducted into the Rodeo Hall of Fame

1895	1910	1925	1940	1955	1970

1906

1929

1926

1911

"Bill" Pickett   1932

A Changing State

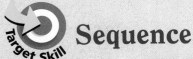

Sequence

First

↓

Next

↓

Finally

- *Sequence* means the order in which things happen.
- Clue words such as *first*, *next*, and *finally* show sequence.
- Dates and times of day also show sequence.
- Sometimes events are told out of order. Verb tenses or clue words can help you figure out sequence.

Read the following paragraph. The sentences that show sequence have been highlighted.

In Chapter 8, you will read about changes on the Texas frontier in the mid-1800s. First, you will read about people who moved to the new state. Next, you will read about the Civil War. Texas joined other Southern states to fight against the Northern states. Finally, you will read that Texas rejoined the United States after the Civil War.

Texas in the Mid-to-Late 1800s: A Changing State

By the mid-1800s, people from other parts of the world were moving into Texas. Native Americans who lived on the plains feared that these settlers would take away their land. The new settlers fought with the Native Americans over the land.

First, in 1867, leaders in the U.S. government met with a group of Native American chiefs. The U.S. leaders told the Native Americans to move to reservations. Next, some Native Americans refused to go. During 1874 and 1875, the Native Americans lost battles fought against U.S. soldiers. Finally, the soldiers forced the Native Americans to leave the Texas plains.

With more land now available, large cattle ranches sprang up in Texas. On horseback, cowhands drove their cattle over long trails to railroad towns in other states. The cattle were then shipped by train to eastern states.

By 1890, fences began to appear on the land. The fences helped farmers protect their crops, but they marked the end of cattle drives. Soon farmers began to settle along railroad lines in Texas. They shipped crops and received supplies by rail.

Use the reading strategy of sequence to answer these questions.

1 What are some clue words, dates, and phrases in the passage that show sequence?

2 What sequence of events led to the forcing out of Native Americans from the Texas plains by U.S. soldiers?

3 What sequence of events marked the rise and fall of cattle drives in Texas?

Lesson 1

**New Braunfels
1850s**
People from Europe and the United States move to Texas.

1

Lesson 2

**Galveston
1863**
The Confederacy wins a battle at Galveston.

2

Lesson 3

**Austin
1870**
Texas rejoins the United States.

3

CANADA

TERRITORIES

1

3

UNION STATES

2

CONFEDERATE STATES

PACIFIC OCEAN

ATLANTIC OCEAN

Galveston

New Braunfels

Austin

Gulf of Mexico

MEXICO

Why We Remember

During the 1850s more settlers came to Texas from many countries. Then, in 1861, the Civil War broke out in the United States. The Northern states and Southern states fought each other. One of the causes was the issue of slavery. Many Anglo American Texas settlers owned African American slaves. Thousands of Anglo American men and boys left their homes in Texas to fight for the South. The South lost, and slavery ended. This change created new challenges for all of Texas.

New Braunfels

1850	1865
1850 Texas sells land to the United States.	**1865** Texas population is more than 500,000.

PREVIEW

Focus on the Main Idea
People who moved to the new state of Texas settled on farms and ranches and started new businesses.

PLACES
New Braunfels

VOCABULARY
frontier
free enterprise
profit

Life on the Texas Frontier

You Are There

The year is 1855. You are traveling by stagecoach to your aunt's farm. Your back aches from the long, bumpy ride. Suddenly the stagecoach wheel slams into a rock. Crack! Then you hear the driver shout, "Whoa!" As he checks the wheel, a man next to you begins to jot down notes. This visitor, Frederick Law Olmsted, is writing an

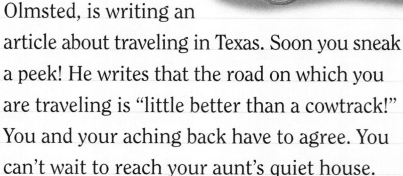

article about traveling in Texas. Soon you sneak a peek! He writes that the road on which you are traveling is "little better than a cowtrack!" You and your aching back have to agree. You can't wait to reach your aunt's quiet house.

 Sequence As you read, look for words that show the order of events, such as *then, later, during,* and *before.*

A Frontier State

By 1855 the state's borders were the same as we know them today. In 1850 the United States had paid Texas $10 million to give up parts of present-day New Mexico, Colorado, Wyoming, Oklahoma, and Kansas.

Texans agreed to sell this land because the state needed money. With this money, the state of Texas paid off debts from the time of the Republic.

In 1855, Texas still seemed like a frontier to some settlers. A **frontier** is the farthest part of a settled country, next to lands that are not yet settled.

Many of the new settlers were from other states, such as Arkansas, Tennessee, and Alabama. Some were merchants and tradespeople. Some were ranchers and farmers. Many shipped their goods from Texas to other places by stagecoach, wagon, or steamboat. People often brought their slaves with them. Other new settlers, such as those in **New Braunfels** whom you read about in Unit 3, were from European countries. By 1865 more than half a million people lived in Texas.

The new settlers caused problems for Native Americans who had lived in Texas for centuries. For example, as new settlers moved west, they killed or drove away buffalo and other animals that the Native Americans needed for food and trade. Most settlers used the land for agriculture. Many settlers built communities on land that the Native Americans called their own. This caused many Native Americans to attack the settlers. Such conflicts continued in Texas for another 20 years.

REVIEW What group of people was the first to live in Texas? ➔ Sequence

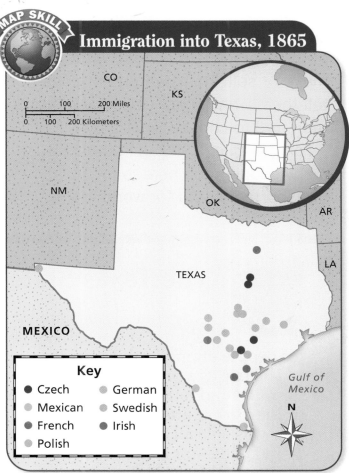

MAP SKILL

Immigration into Texas, 1865

CO
KS
NM
OK
AR
TEXAS
LA
MEXICO
Gulf of Mexico
N

Key
- Czech
- German
- Mexican
- Swedish
- French
- Irish
- Polish

▶ Many people moved to Texas from Europe and Mexico during the mid-1800s.

MAP SKILL Location *In what parts of Texas did most immigrants settle during the mid-1800s?*

▶ Settlers in New Braunfels

Growth of Free Enterprise

As more people moved to Texas, the need for goods and services grew. As in the rest of the United States, Texas businesses developed under the free enterprise system. **Free enterprise** is an economic system in which producers and consumers have the right to make choices. Producers are the people or businesses that make and sell goods or offer services. Consumers are the people or businesses that buy goods or use services. Under the free enterprise system, producers choose what they make or sell. The government does not tell them what to do. Consumers are then free to choose what they will buy.

For example, in Texas in the 1850s, many people rode horses for transportation and for work. Many people needed to buy and own saddles. A saddle maker had the freedom to decide how to design the saddles and how much to charge for them. A person who wanted to buy a saddle could choose to buy from one saddle maker or another, based on the price and the quality of the saddle.

Under the free enterprise system, producers usually make and sell goods in hopes of making a profit. A **profit** is the money a producer has left over after all the costs of making or selling the goods or services are paid. In the case of the saddle maker, the price of the saddle would include the price of materials and labor, and the cost of selling the saddle. The saddle maker

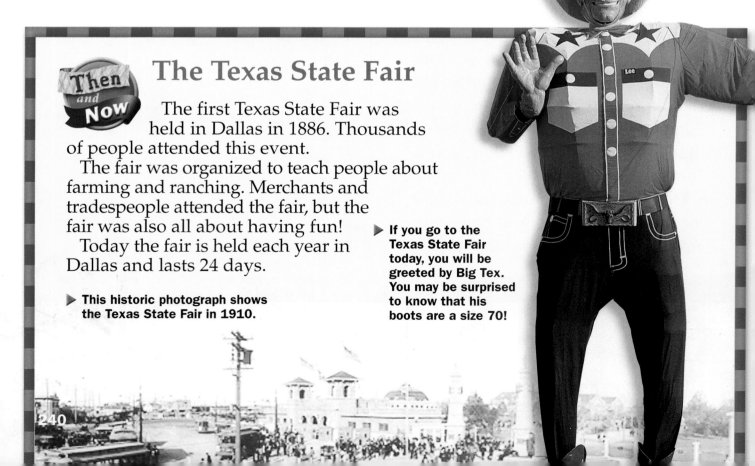

The Texas State Fair

Then and Now

The first Texas State Fair was held in Dallas in 1886. Thousands of people attended this event.

The fair was organized to teach people about farming and ranching. Merchants and tradespeople attended the fair, but the fair was also all about having fun!

Today the fair is held each year in Dallas and lasts 24 days.

▶ This historic photograph shows the Texas State Fair in 1910.

▶ If you go to the Texas State Fair today, you will be greeted by Big Tex. You may be surprised to know that his boots are a size 70!

would set a price for the saddle that was higher than the sum of these expenses. That extra money would be the saddle maker's profit.

Free enterprise works on a system of supply and demand. The number of items that a producer is willing to offer at a particular price is called the supply. The number of items that consumers are willing to buy at a particular price is the demand.

For example, if many people wanted to buy saddles, demand would be high. The saddle maker might choose to set a higher price for saddles. If the saddle maker had a large supply of saddles, and people weren't buying them at the price set, the saddle maker might choose to lower the price of the saddles so that more people would buy them.

The free enterprise system is the basis of our economy. This system encourages inventions and new technologies. As you read this book, look for more examples of the free enterprise system.

REVIEW

Put the following steps in order:
a. Need for goods and services increases.
b. Population grows.
c. New businesses develop.
⟳ Sequence

Summarize the Lesson

— **1850** Texas sold land to the United States.

— **1865** Texas's population was more than 500,000 people.

★ LESSON 1 — **REVIEW**

Check Facts and Main Ideas

1. ⟳ **Sequence** Draw the chart below on a sheet of paper. Fill in the missing sentence to show what the saddle maker must do before he or she can sell a saddle.

> **First,** a saddle maker makes a saddle.
>
> ↓
>
> **Next,** _____
>
> ↓
>
> **Last,** a customer buys the saddle.

2. How did the growth of the population in Texas help the growth of free enterprise?

3. Name three ways settlers earned a living in Texas during the 1850s.

4. How were businesses in Texas in the 1850s like businesses in Texas today?

5. **Critical Thinking:** *Make Inferences* Why do you think a producer wants to make a profit?

Link to ⚭ Writing

Write About the Fair Learn more about the Texas State Fair by going online or by looking in books. Draw a picture of Big Tex. Include two facts from your research in a speech bubble.

1860   1870

1860
Abraham
Lincoln is
elected
President of
the United States.

1861
Texas
secedes
from the
Union.

1861
The Civil War
begins.

1865
The last battle of the
Civil War is fought,
and slaves in Texas
learn of their
freedom.

Texans and the Civil War

PREVIEW

Focus on the Main Idea
Texas joined other Southern states to fight a war against the Northern states.

PLACES
Gulf of Mexico
Galveston Harbor
Sabine Pass
Brownsville

PEOPLE
Abraham Lincoln
Jefferson Davis
Robert E. Lee
Ulysses S. Grant
John B. Magruder
Santos Benavides

VOCABULARY
plantation
nullify
secede
cavalry
blockade

EVENTS
Civil War

You Are There The year is 1864. You live on a farm near Newton. A group of enslaved men gather around a warm fire in the barn where you are playing. One of the men whispers to the group, "This war can't last much longer! Freedom's coming, and when it does I'm going to take my family and leave this farm." Another man says, "I hope I can stay right here in Texas and live as a free man." The other men join in the hushed discussion. They talk of hopes and plans for the future. Listening to them, you feel both excitement and fear. How will your life change if freedom comes?

▶ **A Texas Confederate soldier**

Sequence As you read, pay attention to the order in which events occurred in Texas after 1860.

Plantations and Slavery

Many enslaved African Americans in Texas lived on small farms and large plantations. A **plantation** was a large farm that produced crops to sell. Some enslaved Texans lived in cities and towns.

People who were enslaved had no rights. Landowners bought and sold them and forced them to work. Enslaved African Americans could not even leave the property where they lived without permission.

On plantations, some enslaved adults worked as carpenters, blacksmiths, or housekeepers. But most labored in the fields from sunup to sundown. They hoed, planted seeds, and picked cotton. Sometimes slaves sang songs as they worked. Many of these songs held secret codes, or messages, that told of ways to escape slavery. One song was "Follow the Drinking Gourd." The drinking gourd was a code for the Big Dipper. It helped slaves find the North Star to follow during an escape:

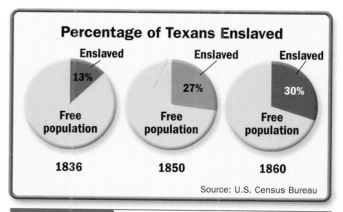

North Star (Polaris)

▶ The North Star is at the end of the handle of the Little Dipper (above). Two stars in the Big Dipper point to this star.

The river ends between two hills,
Follow the Drinking Gourd.
There's another river on the other side,
Follow the Drinking Gourd.

A few free African Americans also lived in the new state. Many had settled in Texas before the Texas Revolution. These Texans were free, but they did not enjoy the same rights as other Texans.

REVIEW Why should escaped slaves follow the North Star?
Draw Conclusions

▶ Most slaves had to work long hours in the fields for no pay.

Percentage of Texans Enslaved

Enslaved 13%	Enslaved 27%	Enslaved 30%
Free population	Free population	Free population
1836	1850	1860

Source: U.S. Census Bureau

GRAPH SKILL As enslaved Texans increased in number, what happened to the percentage of the free population?

243

A Nation Divided

During the 1850s cotton was exported to faraway countries in Europe. This was good news for plantation owners, who grew wealthy from the sale of cotton.

But the demand for cotton also created a need for more workers. As a result, the plantation owners forced more and more enslaved African Americans to come to Texas. By 1860, more than one in every four Texans was an enslaved African American.

The question of slavery had divided the nation for years. Many Southern Anglo Americans claimed they could not grow crops and make money without slave labor. By the mid-1800s, a growing number of people in the Northern states were against slavery. They believed that humans should be free. Some Texans agreed that slavery was wrong.

The issue of states' rights also divided the nation. Many Northerners felt that states should follow all national laws. Most Southerners disagreed. They believed that states could **nullify,** or reject, national laws that they did not like. Many Southern Anglo Americans thought that a new national law soon would be passed to end slavery. This would hurt their cotton production and trade.

In November 1860, a new President of the United States was elected. His name was **Abraham Lincoln.** President Lincoln was against the spread of slavery. "As I would not be a slave, so I would not be a master," he once said. Some Southerners worried that, with Lincoln's election, the national government would end slavery. They began to talk about separating from the United States.

REVIEW What did Northerners and Southerners most disagree about?
Main Idea and Details

▶ A South Carolina newspaper announces secession.

▶ Abraham Lincoln was President of the United States during the Civil War.

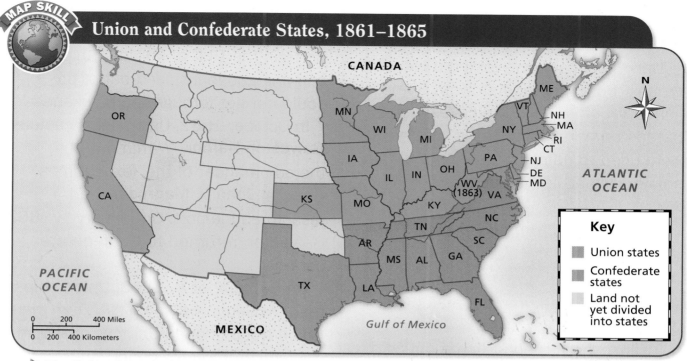

CANADA

ATLANTIC OCEAN

PACIFIC OCEAN

MEXICO

Gulf of Mexico

N

0   200   400 Miles
0   200   400 Kilometers

Key
- Union states
- Confederate states
- Land not yet divided into states

▶ The Union states had a much larger population than did the Confederate states.

MAP SKILL Use Cardinal Directions *In what part of the United States were the Confederate states located?*

Texts Secedes

The first state to **secede,** or separate, from the nation was South Carolina. Other states quickly followed, including Texas on March 2, 1861. At that time, seven cotton-producing Southern states formed a new country called the Confederate States of America, or the Confederacy. In all, eleven Southern states joined the Confederacy. **Jefferson Davis,** of Mississippi, was named president of the Confederacy. The states that remained in the United States were called the Union.

On April 12, 1861, Confederate cannons fired on Fort Sumter, a Union fort in South Carolina. This marked the beginning of a terrible war that would last for four years. By the war's end, **Robert E. Lee** was the leading Confederate general, and **Ulysses S. Grant** led the Union troops.

This **Civil War,** or "War Between the States," saw brothers killing brothers and friends wounding friends. Families were torn apart as family members took different sides. Texan David Carey Nance, a Confederate soldier at the age of 18, later explained, "My father was bitterly opposed to my enlistment, but my mother favored it."

More than 60,000 Texans fought in the war. Most fought on the side of the Confederacy.

REVIEW What was the first state to secede from the Union?
↻ Sequence

▶ Jefferson Davis was President of the Confederacy.

Texans and the Civil War

Many Texas soldiers joined units, or groups, from their hometowns. Some joined **cavalry** units. The cavalry fought battles on horseback. Texas cavalrymen were used to riding horses. As a British soldier visiting Texas observed,

> *". . . no Texan walks a yard if he can help it. . . ."*

Texas units fought in most major Civil War battles.

Texans who stayed at home during the Civil War kept farms and businesses running. Some women made uniforms, tents, blankets, and bandages for the soldiers. Other women worked in hospitals caring for wounded soldiers.

Most Civil War battles in Texas took place near ports. As the map shows,

Union ships would **blockade,** or block, ports in the **Gulf of Mexico.** Ships carrying goods into and out of ports could not get through the blockades.

In October 1862, Union ships captured **Galveston Harbor.** Within months, the commander of the Texas forces, General **John B. Magruder,** had recaptured the port. On January 1, 1863, Galveston returned to Confederate control.

On September 8, 1863, Union ships tried to capture **Sabine Pass.** From there, Union troops hoped to move inland. Confederate troops at a fort fired cannons at the ships. They damaged two ships. The rest turned back.

Other battles were fought in Texas. Colonel **Santos Benavides,** the highest ranking Mexican American to serve in the Confederacy, defeated Union troops at the Battle of Laredo.

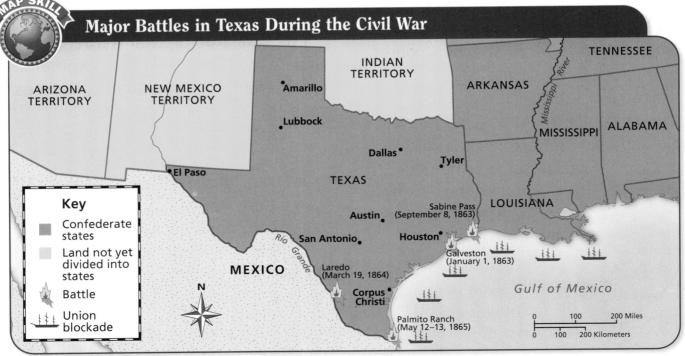

MAP SKILL

Major Battles in Texas During the Civil War

► Civil War battles in Texas took place on land and in the Gulf of Mexico.

MAP SKILL Understand Map Symbols *How many Civil War battles were fought on the Texas Gulf Coast?*

▶ These nurses cared for wounded soldiers in hospitals.

Benavides and his Texas Cavalry Regiment were among the Texans who fought in the last battle of the Civil War. Even though Lee had surrendered to Grant more than a month earlier, Union and Confederate forces clashed at the Battle of Palmito Ranch near **Brownsville** on May 13, 1865. Although they had just gotten word of the surrender, some Texan troops stayed on to defeat the Union troops in this final battle.

REVIEW Why did most Texas Civil War battles take place near ports? **Cause and Effect**

Summarize the Lesson

- **March 2, 1861** Texas seceded from the Union.
- **April 12, 1861** Confederate cannons fired on Fort Sumter, and the Civil War began.
- **May 13, 1865** The last battle of the Civil War was fought.

★ LESSON 2
REVIEW

Check Facts and Main Ideas

1. ↻ **Sequence** Draw the chart below on a sheet of paper. Fill in the missing events.

```
In 1860 _____ is elected President
of the United States.
        ↓
South Carolina secedes from the Union.
        ↓
Texas secedes from the Union in _____.
        ↓
Texans fight in the Civil War as Confederates.
```

2. Why were enslaved African Americans brought to Texas?

3. How did the growing of cotton in the South contribute to Texas's part in the war?

4. How did the Civil War affect the lives of Texans who stayed at home?

5. **Critical Thinking:** *Analyze* Why did many Anglo Americans in Texas support slavery?

Link to ⊂⊃ Mathematics

Find a Fraction In 1860, almost 200,000 enslaved African Americans lived in Texas. The total population of Texas was more than 600,000. What fraction of the population was made up of slaves?

Thinking Skills

Recognize Point of View

What? **Point of view** is the way someone thinks or feels about a subject or an issue. Have you ever disagreed with a friend about something? For example, you may think that your town needs a new movie theater. Your friend may think that your town has enough theaters already. You and your friend have different points of view.

The passage below is from a book about the Civil War. In the book are many points of view about the war. One excerpt is by John T. Poe of Longview. After four years of fighting, Poe agreed with Sam Houston, who had advised Texans not to enter the war.

I heard Sam Houston make a speech during the days just before secession, in which he said: "Bring on the war, gentlemen, as you now propose to do, and whether you whip in the fight or not, you'll meet a taxgatherer at every street corner!" How true! General Houston urged us to remain in the Union and fight for our rights under the Stars and Stripes. I think he was right.

Why? Thinking about point of view is important. It helps you understand how someone thinks or feels about a subject. It can also help you form your own point of view. The passage on page 248 will help you understand one point of view about the Civil War.

How? To recognize a writer's point of view, follow these steps.

- First, figure out the subject or topic. Read the passage. Then finish the following statement: *This passage is about _____.*

- Next, look for things that can be proven true. Remember that an opinion is a judgment or a belief. It cannot be proven true or false.

- Then look for words or phrases that tell how the writer feels about the subject.

- Finally, put together the information from the first three steps. Ask yourself, *What does the author know about the subject? What does the author believe? How does he or she feel about the subject?* The answers will help you understand and talk about the writer's point of view.

Think and Apply

❶ What is the topic of the passage on page 248?

❷ What is one fact from the passage?

❸ What is a word, phrase, or sentence from the passage that shows point of view?

❹ What is the point of view of the writer of this passage?

1860 ── 1870

1863 The Emancipation Proclamation is issued.

1865 The Civil War ends.

1865 Enslaved Texans are freed.

1870 Texas rejoins the United States.

Austin ★

PREVIEW

Focus on the Main Idea
The end of the Civil War brought years of difficult changes to Texas.

PLACES
Austin

PEOPLE
Gordon Granger
Matthew Gaines
Edmund Davis

VOCABULARY
sharecropper

TERMS
Emancipation Proclamation
Freedmen's Bureau

EVENTS
Reconstruction

War and Slavery Come to an End

You Are There

The date is April 9, 1865. General Robert E. Lee, General Ulysses S. Grant, several soldiers, and you meet at Appomattox Court House, a town in Virginia.

General Lee sits at a table in the center of a room. Around him, several soldiers stand in silence. General Grant sits nearby. No one smiles. You are General Lee's helper. You watch him from the back of the room. He slowly takes off his gloves and hat and places them on the table. A soldier hands him a pen. He signs a paper and stands up. Robert E. Lee has surrendered. The Union Army has won the Civil War.

Sequence As you read, look for words, phrases, and dates that show the order of events.

Freedom for Slaves

On April 9, 1865, the Union won the Civil War. Confederate general Robert E. Lee surrendered to Union general Ulysses S. Grant in Virginia. The Civil War had ended at last.

Two years earlier, Abraham Lincoln had issued the **Emancipation Proclamation.** A proclamation is an order. Lincoln's order had freed all enslaved people in Confederate states. But many people did not learn about this order until after the war.

Union soldiers landed in Galveston about two months after Lee surrendered. On June 19, 1865, Union general **Gordon Granger** announced that all enslaved Texans were free under United States law. For the next six weeks, he rode through Texas telling everyone the news.

One by one, Texas planters had to call together the enslaved African Americans who lived on their land. The planters explained that the workers could now come and go as they pleased. Some African Americans shouted for joy when they heard this news. But they faced new challenges. After all, they did not know what would happen to them after freedom. Where would they live? Where would they find jobs? Sarah Ford, who was about fourteen at the time, said,

"When freedom [came] I didn't know what [that] was."

REVIEW What happened in Virginia about two months before General Granger came to Texas to announce that all Texas slaves were free?
↺ Sequence

Then and Now

Juneteenth

On June 19, 1866, African Americans in Texas celebrated their first year of freedom. They gave thanks, listened to speeches, sang, and enjoyed picnics. This tradition continues today. Each year, on the nineteenth of June, families still celebrate what many call "Juneteenth." They listen to speeches about the state of affairs for African Americans.

▶ On Juneteenth, people from many cultures gather together to watch parades, dance, and share picnics. This joyful day often ends with a baseball game or a rodeo.

251

After the Civil War

It was time for the North and South to reunite. This period of rebuilding was known as **Reconstruction.** It lasted more than ten years.

Life was difficult for almost everyone during this time. African Americans had to find jobs and housing. Many farmers had to learn to grow crops without using the labor of enslaved people.

Some Anglo Americans were angry because African Americans had new rights. This anger often led to acts of hatred. Some African Americans were beaten up and even killed.

In 1865, the U.S. government set up the **Freedmen's Bureau.** For a short time, it helped African Americans find jobs and homes. It also opened about 150 schools in Texas for African American children and adults.

Many African American leaders worked to help set up the new government. One such leader, **Matthew Gaines,** was elected to the Texas Senate in 1869.

Some African Americans decided to stay on the land where they had always lived. They became sharecroppers. A **sharecropper** is a farmer who pays part of the crops he or she grows to a landowner. The landowner provides housing and the right to work the land.

If the weather failed, crops did not grow. Then the sharecroppers could not get out of debt to the landowners, so they could not move to a new place.

REVIEW What was Reconstruction?
Main Idea and Details

▶ The time of Reconstruction brought challenges to most people in the South.

Early Spanish explorers posted this flag during the 1500s.

La Salle claimed Texas for France in 1685.

The Mexican flag flew over Texas during the early 1800s.

The first official flag of the Republic of Texas was adopted in 1839.

In 1861 the flag of the Confederate States of America flew over Texas.

The United States flag first flew over Texas in 1846 and again after 1870.

Texas Rejoins the Union

On March 30, 1870, Texas rejoined the United States of America. Once again, the United States flag flew over the Capitol building in **Austin.** But problems soon arose. Many Anglo Americans in Texas did not support the new governor, **Edmund Davis.** They thought that he spent too much state money and was too eager to help African Americans. In 1876, Texas leaders adopted a new state constitution. It gave less power to the governor and other state officers.

REVIEW Why was Edmund Davis unpopular among many Anglo American Texans? **Cause and Effect**

Summarize the Lesson

- **January 1, 1863** Abraham Lincoln issued the Emancipation Proclamation.
- **April 9, 1865** The Civil War ended.
- **June 19, 1865** General Granger announced that enslaved Texans were free.
- **March 30, 1870** Texas rejoined the United States.

LESSON 3 REVIEW

Check Facts and Main Ideas

1. **Sequence** On a sheet of paper, draw the chart below. Fill in the missing details.

________ ________ issues the Emancipation Proclamation.
↓
The Civil War ends in ________.
↓
General Granger announces that enslaved Texans are free.

2. What purpose did the Emancipation Proclamation serve?
3. How did life change for African Americans after General Granger rode through Texas?
4. What challenges did African Americans face during Reconstruction?
5. **Critical Thinking: *Evaluate*** *The Freedmen's Bureau helped all Texans, not just African Americans.* Do you agree or disagree? Explain your answer.

Link to Writing

Write to a Friend Sarah Ford did not know what to expect when she learned that she was free. Suppose you could tell her what you have read. Write a few sentences telling Sarah how her life may change.

1850   1855

1850
Texas sells land to
the United States.

Chapter Summary

 Sequence

On a separate sheet of paper, complete a chart such as the one shown. List the events in the order in which they happened.

- Texas rejoins the United States.
- The Civil War begins.
- Texas slaves know they are freed.
- Abraham Lincoln becomes President of the United States.
- The Civil War ends.

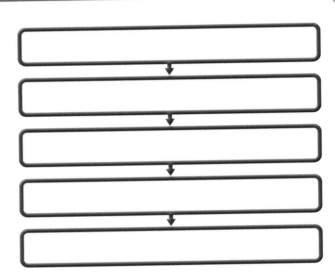

Vocabulary

Match each word or term with the correct definition or description.

1. **frontier** (p. 239)
2. **free enterprise** (p. 240)
3. **plantation** (p. 243)
4. **secede** (p. 245)
5. **sharecropper** (p. 252)

a. an economic system in which producers and consumers have the right to make choices

b. to separate

c. the farthest part of a settled country

d. a farmer who pays some of the crop he or she grows to the landowner

e. a large farm that produces cash crops

People and Events

Write a sentence describing what you learned about each person, term, or event in the lesson.

1. **Abraham Lincoln** (p. 244)
2. **Jefferson Davis** (p. 245)
3. **Robert E. Lee** (p. 245)
4. **Ulysses S. Grant** (p. 245)
5. **Civil War** (p. 245)
6. **Gordon Granger** (p. 251)
7. **Reconstruction** (p. 252)

1860   1865   1870

1861
Texas seceded from the Union.

1863
Lincoln issued the Emancipation Proclamation.

1865
Slaves were freed in Texas.

1870
Texas rejoined the United States.

Facts and Main Ideas

1 How did most Texans earn a living in the 1850s?

2 What was the main crop in Texas during the 1850s?

3 Why was life difficult for African Americans during Reconstruction?

4 **Time Line** How many years after Texas seceded from the Union did it rejoin?

5 **Main Idea** During the 1850s, how were goods shipped from Texas to other areas?

6 **Main Idea** What is one reason that Texans voted to secede from the United States?

7 **Main Idea** What was the Emancipation Proclamation?

8 **Critical Thinking:** *Compare and Contrast* What rewards and challenges do you think emancipation brought slaves?

Write About History

1 **Write a journal entry** as a young African American whose family has just been granted freedom.

2 **Write about a picture** shown in one of the lessons of this chapter. Explain its meaning.

3 **Write a paragraph** from the point of view of either a Northerner or a Southerner. Explain why the Civil War took place.

Apply Skills

Point of View

Read the quote by Sam Houston about Texas's secession from the Union. Then answer the questions.

"To secede from the Union and set up another government would cause war. If you go to war with the United States, you will never conquer her, as she has the money and the men."

1 What is Sam Houston's point of view on secession?

2 How do you know?

Internet Activity

To get help with vocabulary, people, and terms, select the dictionary or encyclopedia from *Social Studies Library* at **www.sfsocialstudies.com.**

CHAPTER 9

The Close of a Century

Lesson 1

Indian Territory
1870s
Plains Indians lose their land to the U.S. government.

Lesson 2

South Texas
1800s
The lariat is used by Mexican vaqueros, early Texas ranchers.

Lesson 3

San Angelo
1870s
Texas cattle trails lead to northern railroads.

Lesson 4

Clarendon
1880s
Texas towns grow along railroad lines.

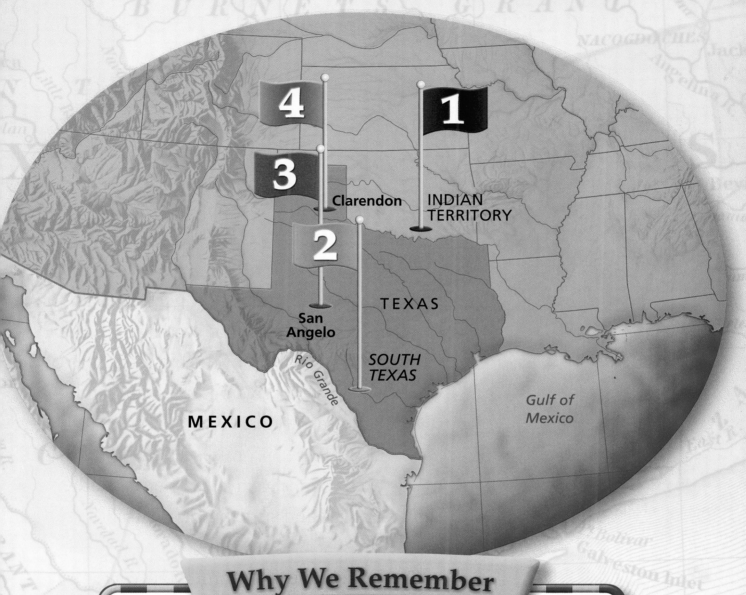

Why We Remember

The Civil War had ended, but fighting in Texas continued. Soldiers now battled Plains Indians, who fought to protect their land. The U.S. government soon forced Plains Indian groups to move away from Texas. On the open plains, large ranches were built. Cowhands drove herds up dusty trails to northern railroad cities. The coming of railroads and fences to Texas would close the open range. This, in turn, would change the people who lived there.

INDIAN TERRITORY

TEXAS

1865   1870   1875

1867
Some Plains Indian chiefs agree to move to reservations.

1873
Anglo American buffalo hunters enter Texas.

1874
Plains Indians are defeated in the Battle of Adobe Walls.

1874–75
Plains Indians are defeated in the Red River War.

PREVIEW

Focus on the Main Idea
To defend their territory, Plains Indians fought with new settlers in Texas. The U.S. Army responded by sending soldiers and by building forts to protect the settlements.

PLACES
Indian Territory

PEOPLE
Satanta
Quanah Parker
Colonel Ranald S. Mackenzie

VOCABULARY
Buffalo Soldiers

EVENTS
Battle of Adobe Walls
Red River War
Battle of Palo Duro Canyon

The Indian Wars

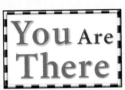
You Are There
You watch as the eleven-year-old Comanche stands up straight and tries to look brave. He is telling his father good-bye. The Comanche are riding off to battle again. His father has told him about the big army that wants his people to give up their land and go to live on reservations. "I will not let that happen," his father promises again. "We will live as we have always lived." Then his father rides off, swift and sure, on his beautiful horse.

The boy sits near his family tepee and pulls a warm blanket around himself. He is frightened. He hopes with all his might that his father will be safe. Now his main worry is that his life is about to change.

Sequence As you read, pay attention to the order of the events described.

Conflict on the Frontier

While the Civil War was raging, another conflict, or struggle, was going on in Texas. Anglo American settlers were claiming land in Texas as their own. They often fought with the Plains Indians, Native Americans who lived or hunted on this land, such as the Comanche and Kiowa.

This struggle between the settlers and the Plains Indians had begun before the Civil War. During the war, however, the conflict grew. Both sides became more violent. Each group wanted to drive the other off the Texas plains.

Among the Plains Indians, the Comanche were well known as hunters and traders. The Comanche honored men and women who defended their people in battle. Comanche warriors joined with warriors from other groups to raid Texas frontier settlements. The warriors destroyed many farms and homes.

After the Civil War, settlers wrote to the national government in Washington,

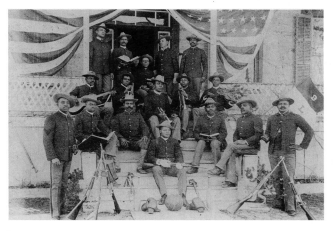

▶ The Buffalo Soldiers fought against the Plains Indians on the Texas frontier.

D.C. They asked the government to send soldiers to protect them from the Plains Indian raids. As a result, the U.S. Army moved troops into Texas. The troops built forts to house soldiers. The soldiers fought the Plains Indians and tried to force them onto distant reservations.

African American troops were among those sent to Texas and the Southwest to fight against the Plains Indians. These soldiers were famous for their strength, courage, and skill. The Plains Indians called them **Buffalo Soldiers.**

REVIEW List in order three or four events that led to the conflict on the frontier. ↺ Sequence

▶ A Plains Indian family on horseback

End of the Buffalo Days

In 1867 the U.S. government met with some Plains Indian chiefs, or leaders, in Kansas. The government asked them to sign a peace treaty. Some chiefs agreed to move their people to reservations in **Indian Territory**. This was an area set aside in the 1830s as a homeland for Native Americans. Today it is the state of Oklahoma.

Other leaders disagreed. **Satanta**, a famous Kiowa chief, said,

> *"I love to roam over the prairies. There I feel free and happy, but when we settle down we grow pale and die."*

Because Native Americans lacked a central government, this disagreement meant that many groups stayed on the Texas plains. Their warriors continued to fight with the Texas settlers.

▶ Satanta

▶ After the Civil War, railroads brought buffalo hunters to the Great Plains, bringing an end to a way of life for the Plains Indians.

▶ **Buffalo hide**

Another problem arose for the Plains Indians. They depended on the buffalo for many of their needs. They had a great respect for these mighty animals. Since Anglo American settlement began, Plains Indians had traded buffalo hides to merchants in settlements for tools and other supplies. In the 1870s, there was a great increase in demand for buffalo hides for use in clothing and in factories.

Eager to make money, buffalo hunters came to the plains. They used powerful guns to kill thousands of buffalo. They skinned the buffalo and then left the big bodies to rot. Such waste made the Plains Indians angry and sad. Chief Satanta explained it this way: ". . . they kill my buffalo; and when I see that, my heart feels like bursting; I feel sorry."

The U.S. Army also killed buffalo. They thought that peace with the Plains Indians would happen only when all the buffalo were gone. By 1887 the

huge buffalo herds had been reduced to only a few hundred animals.

REVIEW Why did hunters and soldiers kill the buffalo? **Cause and Effect**

The Battle of Adobe Walls

Just before dawn on June 27, 1874, a large group of Plains Indians galloped on horseback toward Adobe Walls. Adobe Walls was a group of a few stores near an old trading post. That day, a group of buffalo hunters was gathered in the stores with the storekeepers. The Plains Indians, led by Comanche chief Quanah, later called **Quanah Parker,** were angry over the slaughter of the buffalo herds. The Plains Indians planned to attack everyone in the stores.

Here is what one of the hunters saw when he looked out that morning:

> *". . . fighting men . . . mounted upon their finest horses, armed with guns and lances, and carrying heavy shields of thick buffalo hide, were coming like the wind."*

The startled people inside the stores fired bullets through holes they had knocked in the walls. The battle lasted most of the day. The buffalo hunters, with their big buffalo guns, were able to hit the Plains Indians at long range. In all, four men in the stores died in the attack. Many more Plains Indians were killed.

The Plains Indians leaned down from horseback and picked up their dead and wounded friends. Then they carried them away. One of the wounded was Quanah.

The Plains Indians finally gave up their fight and left. However, this **Battle of Adobe Walls** would lead to the Red River War of 1874–75.

REVIEW In your own words, retell the important events of the Battle of Adobe Walls. **Summary**

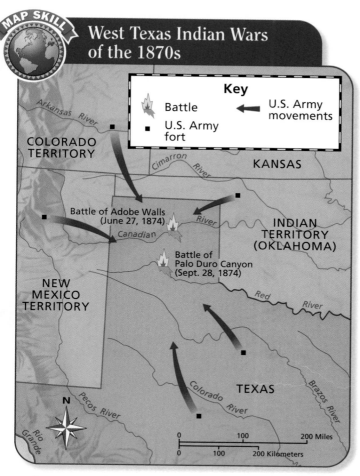

MAP SKILL
West Texas Indian Wars of the 1870s

Key
- ★ Battle
- ■ U.S. Army fort
- ← U.S. Army movements

Arkansas River

COLORADO TERRITORY

Cimarron River

KANSAS

Battle of Adobe Walls (June 27, 1874)

Canadian River

INDIAN TERRITORY (OKLAHOMA)

Battle of Palo Duro Canyon (Sept. 28, 1874)

NEW MEXICO TERRITORY

Red River

Pecos River

Colorado River

TEXAS

Brazos River

Rio Grande

N

0   100   200 Miles
0   100   200 Kilometers

▶ Plains Indians fought to defend their land.

MAP SKILL *Movement According to this map, in which directions did U.S. Army soldiers travel to fight Plains Indians?*

The Red River War Begins

After the Battle of Adobe Walls, the defeated Plains Indians rode back to their camps. Their defeat made them more determined to rid their land of settlers and buffalo hunters. At the same time, soldiers were moving in to protect the hunters and settlers. The resulting conflict was called the **Red River War.**

All through the summer of 1874, the Plains Indians attacked settlers on the plains. To help defend the settlers, the U.S. government sent about 3,000 soldiers to the Texas Panhandle. The soldiers moved to the Red River and its branches, where they thought the Plains Indians were camping. They circled the area and blocked all the escape routes.

The soldiers' goal was to chase the Plains Indians into Indian Territory. They kept the Plains Indians on the move. The Plains Indians had little time to rest, to graze their animals, or to hunt for food.

The fall of 1874 brought cold, wet weather. Shivering and weary, both sides suffered. The Plains Indians began calling the Red River War "The Wrinkled Hand Chase." The weather was so damp that the warriors' hands often looked as if they had been soaked in water!

REVIEW What did the soldiers think might force the Plains Indians into Indian Territory? **Cause and Effect**

The Battle of Palo Duro Canyon

Colonel Ranald S. Mackenzie led the U.S. Army in the last major battle of the Red River War. The **Battle of Palo Duro Canyon** is considered the turning point of the war.

Before dawn on September 28, 1874, Mackenzie's soldiers surprised the Plains Indians. Camps of Kiowa, Comanche, and Cheyenne were scattered through the Palo Duro Canyon. Mackenzie and his soldiers led their horses down the steep sides of the canyon. The sleeping Plains Indian families awoke to the military attack. The camps could not come together quickly enough to form a defense. Most of the Plains Indians fled on foot. They left their horses and other belongings behind.

▶ The Palo Duro Canyon in the Texas Panhandle was the site of the last battle of the Red River War.

Tepees, blankets, buffalo robes, food, and weapons lay scattered across the canyon floor. The Plains Indians' horses and mules had been unable to escape up the steep canyon walls. Mackenzie ordered his men to gather the Plains Indians' belongings into heaps and set them on fire.

Then he asked them to round up the animals. Slowly the men led more than 1,400 animals up the canyon walls, back to the army's supply camp. There Mackenzie ordered the soldiers to shoot most of the mules and horses. The best of the animals—340 of them— were saved for the military.

The Plains Indians were now stranded without horses to help them fight. Their shelter, weapons, and other belongings—including the entire winter food supply—had been burned.

Mackenzie and his troops had achieved their goal. The Plains Indians were forced to turn to the Oklahoma reservations for food and shelter. They did not want to leave behind the open plains that had been central to their way of life.

REVIEW Tell what events happened first, next, and last in the Battle of Palo Duro Canyon. ↻ **Sequence**

Plains Indians Leave Texas

In June 1875, only Quanah's group of Comanche lingered on the plains. Colonel Mackenzie persuaded Quanah to surrender. The great chief recalled that his mother, an Anglo American woman, had long ago lost her home too. Quanah led his people toward a strange new life on a reservation, saying,

"If my mother, Naduah, could learn the ways of Comanche, I can learn the ways of the white man."

Indeed, Anglo Americans had killed the buffalo herds and forced Quanah's people from the Texas plains. The region was now open to cattle ranchers and other settlers.

REVIEW Why did the remaining Plains Indians move to reservations?
Main Ideas and Details

Summarize the Lesson

- **1867** Some Plains Indian chiefs agreed to move to reservations.
- **1874** Plains Indians were defeated in the Battle of Adobe Walls.
- **1874–1875** Plains Indians were defeated in the Red River War.

★ **LESSON 1** **REVIEW**

Check Facts and Main Ideas

1. ↻ **Sequence** On a separate sheet of paper, fill in the missing information.

> Some Plains Indians signed a treaty saying they would _____.

↓

> Some Plains Indians stayed in Texas and fought in the Red River War.

↓

> _____ was the last Comanche chief to surrender to U.S. soldiers.

2. How did the lives of the Plains Indians change as settlers and buffalo hunters moved onto the plains?

3. What was the role of the buffalo in the lives of the Plains Indians?

4. Why did buffalo hunters kill so many buffalo?

5. **Critical Thinking: *Draw Conclusions*** Why do you think Chief Quanah finally surrendered to Colonel Mackenzie?

Link to ⛓ **Geography**

Research the Setting The Battle of Palo Duro Canyon was fought in an unusual setting, or place. Read more about the Palo Duro Canyon to decide how the steep canyon walls helped Mackenzie's army.

Quanah Parker
c.1845–1911

Quanah Parker was born about 1845. His mother, Cynthia Ann Parker, was Anglo American. She had been captured by the Comanche at a young age. They called her "Naduah." When she grew up, she became the wife of a Comanche chief. Quanah was their first child.

Quanah rose to leadership in the Kwahadi group of the Comanche. Like other Plains Indians, he was known by only one name. In 1875, he moved to a reservation. There he learned that his mother had died. In honor of her, he took her last name, Parker.

BIOFACT

Quanah Parker wore a feathered warbonnet as he rode a horse in a parade with President Theodore Roosevelt in 1905.

In the years that followed, Quanah Parker spoke out for his people in Washington, D.C. He earned money for reservation families by renting tribal land to cattle ranchers. Quanah also encouraged Plains Indians to set up their own schools.

In 1910, a few months before his death, Quanah Parker told a crowd at the Texas State Fair,

". . . I am a citizen of the United States. I pay taxes the same as you people do. We are the same people. . . ."

Learn from Biographies

Name three things that Quanah Parker did to help his people after he moved to a reservation.

For more information, go online to *Meet the People* at **www.sfsocialstudies.com**.

South Texas

King Ranch

1800
Large *ranchos* operate in South Texas.

1865
Five million longhorn cattle roam wild in Texas.

1880
Several large ranches expand in Texas.

PREVIEW

Focus on the Main Idea
After the Civil War, the Texas ranching industry grew.

PLACES

South Texas
King Ranch

PEOPLE

Charles Goodnight
Richard King
Henrietta King

VOCABULARY

open range
brand
line rider
roundup

The Texas Cattle Kingdom

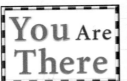

May 5, 1881
Dear Diary,

    This has been the most exciting day! A new family moved into the ranch house near ours. There are three children near my age. I hope we become friends. It has been a while since I have had a playmate here at the ranch.

    The children's papa is a fine vaquero—one of the best I have ever seen. I am amazed to see him use the lasso! He will be of great help at the cattle roundup.

    All the excitement has made me sleepy. But tomorrow is sure to be another exciting day.

    Goodnight, Diary.

Sequence As you read, think about the steps ranchers took to run their ranches.

The Open Range

The story of cattle in Texas begins in the 1500s. Spanish explorers brought a lean type of cattle with them when they came to Mexico. Later, after 1820, Anglo American settlers brought cattle into Texas from other parts of the United States. These cattle weighed more than the Spanish cattle. After a while, some of the heavier cattle drifted into **South Texas.** Vaqueros rounded them up and added the heavier cattle to the leaner herds owned by Tejano ranchers. The two types of cattle mixed to form the Texas longhorn.

Longhorn cattle are strong animals with long legs and curved horns. The tips of the horns are usually about six feet apart. Some measure eight feet across! Longhorn cattle can travel many miles without water. Recalling this hearty Texas animal, writer J. Frank Dobie wrote:

> *"They could horn off the fiercest wolf, smell out the most cunning panther . . . (they) did not hesitate to engage with grizzly bears."*

Before the 1880s, Texas ranchers did not build fences. Their cattle roamed the grassy plains, or the **open range.** Some of the range belonged to ranchers. Other parts belonged to the state. By the time the Civil War ended, there were about 5 million longhorn cattle in Texas.

REVIEW In the proper order, list three events that led to the presence of longhorns on the open range.
🔄 **Sequence**

▶ The longhorn is a Texas symbol. It is the official Texas large mammal. Today longhorns live in some Texas state parks. Ranchers also raise longhorns.

Ranching and Roundups

After the Civil War, many cattle owners brought their herds into Texas. Other ranchers caught enough wild longhorns to form a herd. They began to mix other types of cattle with the Texas longhorn.

The large ranches shown in the Map Adventure below opened in the late 1800s. Some were owned or managed by well-known ranchers such as **Charles Goodnight**, **Richard King**, and **Henrietta King.** The **King Ranch** still operates today.

In the 1880s, a rancher could buy land from the state or from a private owner. Ranchers could also run cattle on state lands. The grass and water there were free for the taking. Ranching on the open range had its challenges too. For example, it was sometimes hard to tell which cattle belonged to which rancher. That is why ranchers branded their cattle.

A **brand** is a design burned into the hide of a cow. All cattle with the same brand belonged to one rancher.

► After her husband, Richard, died, Henrietta King ran the large South Texas King Ranch for forty years.

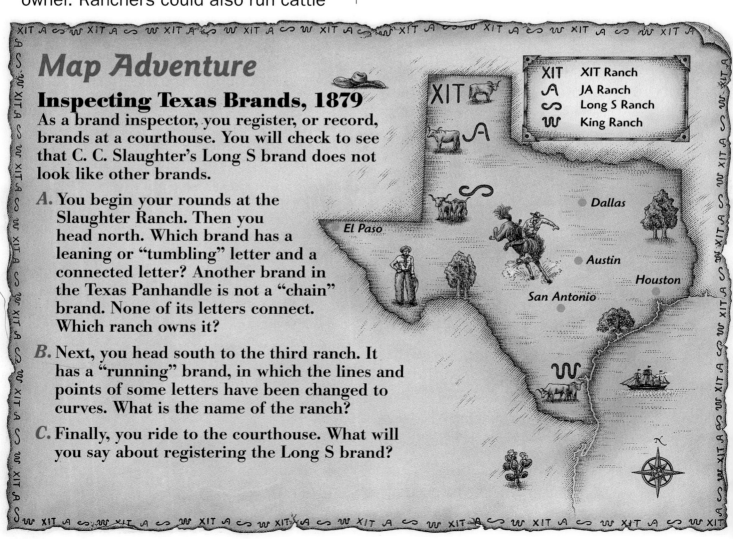

Map Adventure

Inspecting Texas Brands, 1879

As a brand inspector, you register, or record, brands at a courthouse. You will check to see that C. C. Slaughter's Long S brand does not look like other brands.

A. You begin your rounds at the Slaughter Ranch. Then you head north. Which brand has a leaning or "tumbling" letter and a connected letter? Another brand in the Texas Panhandle is not a "chain" brand. None of its letters connect. Which ranch owns it?

B. Next, you head south to the third ranch. It has a "running" brand, in which the lines and points of some letters have been changed to curves. What is the name of the ranch?

C. Finally, you ride to the courthouse. What will you say about registering the Long S brand?

XIT	XIT Ranch
JA	JA Ranch
S	Long S Ranch
W	King Ranch

Dallas

El Paso

Austin

Houston

San Antonio

Ranchers hired cowhands to brand and tend their cattle. Many cowhands were African American, Hispanic, or Native American. Cowhands kept the cattle from straying. **Line riders** rode up and down the borders of the ranch to watch the cattle. Often they camped out at night, alone.

But some cattle still got lost. So every spring and fall, the ranchers held a **roundup.** Cowhands from different ranches drove all the cattle they found into one area. Then everyone helped separate the cattle by brands. Cowhands branded new calves that had been born on the range. They were easy to find because they stayed close to their branded mothers.

REVIEW Why did ranchers brand their cattle? **Cause and Effect**

▶ **Cattle brands such as these help ranchers identify their cattle.**

Summarize the Lesson

- **1800** Large Tejano ranches operated in South Texas.
- **1865** Five million longhorn cattle roamed wild in Texas.
- **1880** Several very large ranches opened in Texas.

★ LESSON 2 **REVIEW**

Check Facts and Main Ideas

1. ↻ **Sequence** On a separate sheet of paper, fill in the missing steps of a roundup.

> First, cowhands gathered together all the cattle they found on the range.

↓

> Next, _____.

↓

> Finally, _____.

2. What makes the longhorn a valuable breed of cattle?

3. Who owned the first ranches in Texas? What were the cowhands called?

4. What was the open range and how did ranchers use it?

5. **Critical Thinking:** *Draw Conclusions* What kind of person might have chosen to become a cowhand?

Link to ⚭ **Art**

Design Your Brand You are the owner of a large Texas ranch. Give your ranch a name. Then design a brand for the ranch.

Charles Goodnight
1836–1929

Charles Goodnight was born in Illinois on March 5, 1836, three days after Texas declared its independence from Mexico. Goodnight would later say that he and Texas were born together like twins.

Charlie played and did chores with the other children in his family. He also liked to daydream. He spent many days in the woods observing wild animals and plant life.

When Charlie was nine, his family moved to Texas in two covered wagons. Charlie rode the entire 1,000-mile trip on his young horse, Blaze. Once again, Charlie's life crossed paths with Texas history. He arrived on Texas soil in 1845, just as Texas was becoming the 28th state in the nation.

BIOFACT

Charles Goodnight's longhorn steer Old Blue led the other cattle on the trail drive.

Later, as a young horseman, Goodnight guided military troops through unsettled areas of Texas. He also blazed cattle trails for taking his herds long distances. About his days on the cattle trail, Goodnight said,

"When all went well, there was no other life so pleasant."

Learn from Biographies

How did Charles Goodnight's days in the woods help him later on?

For more information, go online to *Meet the People* at **www.sfsocialstudies.com.**

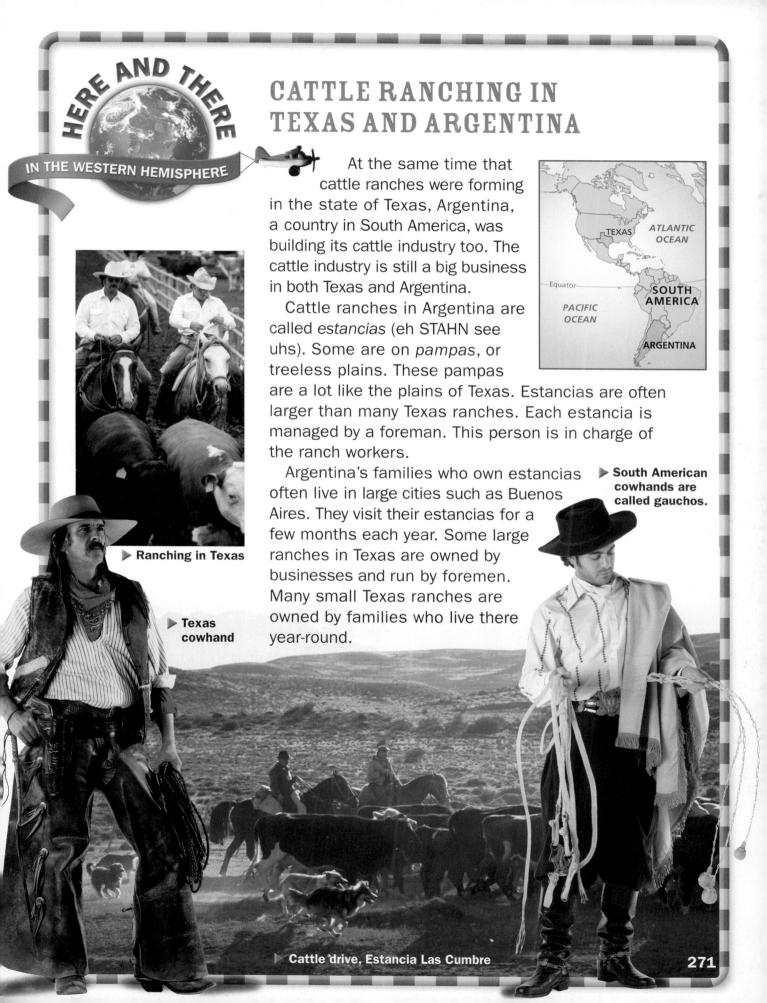

CATTLE RANCHING IN TEXAS AND ARGENTINA

At the same time that cattle ranches were forming in the state of Texas, Argentina, a country in South America, was building its cattle industry too. The cattle industry is still a big business in both Texas and Argentina.

Cattle ranches in Argentina are called *estancias* (eh STAHN see uhs). Some are on *pampas*, or treeless plains. These pampas are a lot like the plains of Texas. Estancias are often larger than many Texas ranches. Each estancia is managed by a foreman. This person is in charge of the ranch workers.

Argentina's families who own estancias often live in large cities such as Buenos Aires. They visit their estancias for a few months each year. Some large ranches in Texas are owned by businesses and run by foremen. Many small Texas ranches are owned by families who live there year-round.

▶ Ranching in Texas

▶ Texas cowhand

▶ South American cowhands are called gauchos.

▶ Cattle drive, Estancia Las Cumbre

271

Going Beyond the Call of Duty

Has anyone ever depended on you? When did you promise to help someone and then follow through? Many people depended on Mary Ann "Aunt Molly" Dyer Goodnight. She was a responsible citizen who did more than her share about 100 years ago.

Mary Ann Dyer was faced with harsh responsibility early in life. When she was a teenager, her parents died. Mary Ann was left to care for five younger brothers. She accepted a job teaching school in Weatherford, Texas. With her earnings, she supported herself and her brothers.

Later, Dyer married a Texas cowman named Charles Goodnight. In the late 1870s, the Goodnight couple, with the Dyer brothers, settled on the JA Ranch in the Texas Panhandle. Together they opened Goodnight College for youth of the Texas plains. They let some students live in their home.

Aunt Molly, as she was called, became known as "Mother of the Panhandle." She led an effort to build churches and an elementary school in the area. People often gathered at the Goodnight home to talk, learn, and pray. Aunt Molly cared for sick cowhands. She sewed missing buttons onto their shirts. She even gave them

▶ **Molly Goodnight helped save buffalo calves whose mothers were shot by the buffalo hunters.**

BUILDING
CITIZENSHIP
Caring
Respect
★ Responsibility
Fairness
Honesty
Courage

parties. People could borrow books from Aunt Molly's library and often admired the flowers she planted in her window boxes and garden. Charles Goodnight later wrote about his beloved wife:

> *"She took life's varied gifts, and made her home a house of joy."*

As a rancher, Aunt Molly saw that buffalo might disappear from the plains. They could not escape the buffalo hunters' guns. Aunt Molly knew this was wrong. She felt a responsibility to help save the great herds that thundered across the plains of her state and her country.

Aunt Molly took action. She asked her brothers to rope a few buffalo calves. She especially hoped to rescue the calves lost from their mothers. The cowhands brought her the calves to raise, and she took special care of them. They grew up and had more calves. The Goodnight Buffalo Herd became famous.

Responsibility in Action

Link to Current Events Read a newspaper to find out more about a citizen hero showing responsibility today. How does that person show responsibility?

LESSON 3

Dodge City • Sedalia
Fort Worth •
• San Angelo

| 1860 | 1870 | 1880 | 1890 | 1900 |

1866
Texas cowhands begin driving cattle up long trails to sell them in other states.

1874
Joseph Glidden develops an improved barbed wire.

1890
Fences and windmills close off most of the West Texas open range.

1900
Farming is an important industry in Texas.

PREVIEW

Focus on the Main Idea
Cattle trails helped build the Texas cattle business until the closing of the open range.

PLACES

Fort Worth
San Angelo
Sedalia, Missouri
Dodge City, Kansas

PEOPLE

Charles Goodnight
Jesse Chisholm
Elizabeth "Lizzie" Johnson Williams
Johanna July
Joseph Farwell Glidden

VOCABULARY

stampede
barbed wire

Cattle Drives on Texas Trails

You Are There

It's dusty as the cattle and horses move along the trail. You're thirsty. But you don't want to bother your father. Being the trail boss, he has a lot on his mind. After all, he's leading this whole outfit toward Kansas.

"I'll ride up front to the chuck wagon," you think. You know the cook will have a bucket of water and a dipper. The dust shouldn't be so bad there either.

You wonder what stories you'll hear around the campfire meal tonight. Last night, Hank told about Abilene, Kansas. He says it's some town. Just two more days and you'll see it for yourself.

▶ Cowhands on trail drives paused for meals from the chuck wagon.

Sequence As you read, notice the order of the events that changed the cattle industry in Texas.

274

Cattle As Big Business

In the 1860s, cattle drives solved a problem for Texas ranchers. Raising cattle was inexpensive on the state's open range. Ranchers needed to find a way to sell the cattle at a good price. In 1865, cattle were worth only three or four dollars apiece in Texas. But in the eastern United States, they sold for ten times as much!

How could Texas ranchers get their cattle to eastern cities? At that time, Texas had few railroads. Anglo American ranchers began doing what Spanish and Mexican ranchers had done for years. They hired cowhands to help drive their cattle over long trails to cattle markets in other states.

Cowhands worked and slept outside in blistering heat and freezing cold. They fought off attacks by cattle thieves. They worried about stampedes. A **stampede** occurs when a herd of cattle becomes frightened and runs wild.

Cattle drives began in Texas towns such as **Fort Worth** and **San Angelo.** They ended in railroad towns such as **Sedalia, Missouri,** and **Dodge City, Kansas.** There the ranchers sold their cattle. Then buyers shipped the cattle by train to the East. Ranchers used the money they earned to buy supplies.

Some cattle trails were named in honor of the people who first blazed, or traveled, them—cowmen such as **Charles Goodnight** and **Jesse Chisholm. Elizabeth "Lizzie" Johnson Williams** was a trailherder from Texas too. She raised cattle, branded them, and drove them over the long trail to market.

Ranches and cattle drives needed strong workhorses. Some cowhands were expert horse trainers. One such trainer was **Johanna July.** Cowhands, such as Bill Pickett, became known for their skillful ways of handling the cows.

REVIEW List in order three steps in moving cattle from Texas to the eastern United States.
⟲ Sequence

▶ **The cook worked mostly from the rear of the chuck wagon, which folded out.**

Texas Trailherders

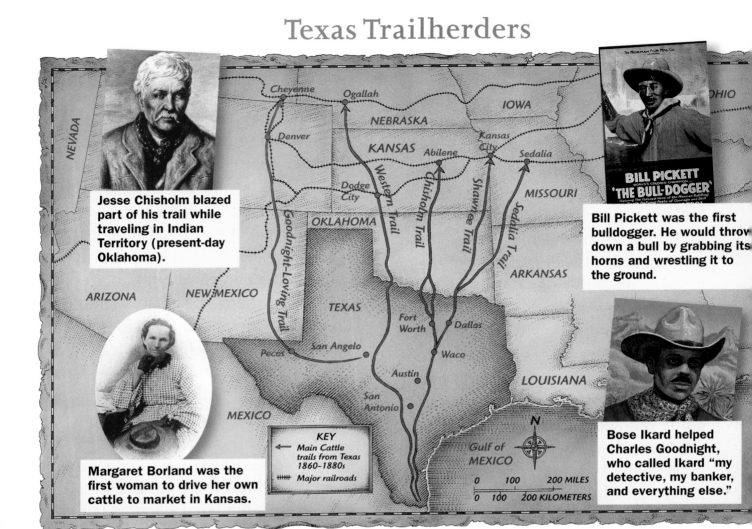

Jesse Chisholm blazed part of his trail while traveling in Indian Territory (present-day Oklahoma).

Margaret Borland was the first woman to drive her own cattle to market in Kansas.

Bill Pickett was the first bulldogger. He would throw down a bull by grabbing its horns and wrestling it to the ground.

Bose Ikard helped Charles Goodnight, who called Ikard "my detective, my banker, and everything else."

KEY
← Main Cattle trails from Texas 1860–1880s
++++ Major railroads

0   100   200 MILES
0   100   200 KILOMETERS

Spanish Words on Texas Trails

Spanish explorers brought cattle to Texas. Vaqueros herded wild cattle in South Texas. Later, Texans learned about trail driving and ranching from Mexican ranchers. It is no surprise, then, that many words used in the cattle business came from the Spanish language.

Some Spanish words, such as *rodeo* and *corral*, stayed the same after Texas ranchers began using them. Others changed. For example, the Spanish word *rancho* became *ranch. La reata* (lah ray AH tah)—a rope used to catch cattle—became *lariat* (LEHR ee ut). Vaqueros wore leather pants called *chaparreras* (shop ah RAY rahs). Texas cowhands called them *chaps* (shaps, or chaps).

REVIEW Name two ranching words that came from the Spanish language. Then give the English words that mean the same thing. **Main Idea and Details**

276

Fencing the Open Range

In 1874, **Joseph Farwell Glidden** invented the first commercially successful **barbed wire.** It is a twisted wire with very sharp points, or barbs. It is strung between posts as a fence for cattle.

Many Texans did not want to put fences around ranch land. Some did. For example, farmers in West Texas were angry because roaming cattle ate their crops. Ranchers with prize cattle wanted to keep them safe.

As fences sprang up, so did new challenges. Fences blocked cattle from creeks and lakes. To get water to their herds, some ranchers now had to build windmills.

Windmills were used to pump underground water up to ground level. Cattle then drank this water from a tank.

Fencing also blocked the trails that the cattle followed northward. By 1890 barbed-wire fencing and windmills had closed off most of the open range. Ranchers still raised cattle. But with railroads closer to home and fences across the range, the long trail drives were gone forever.

REVIEW What two problems did barbed-wire fences cause for some ranchers? **Cause and Effect**

Literature and Social Studies

I'm Going to Leave Old Texas Now

With the closing off of most of the open range, some cowhands moved on. This song shows how one cowhand felt about the change.

I'm going to leave old Texas now;
They have no use for the Longhorn cow.

They plowed and fenced my cattle range,
And the people here all seem so strange.

I'll take my horse and I'll take my rope,
And I'll hit the trail upon a lope.

I'll bid adiós to the Alamo,
And set my face toward Mexico.

Farmers Look Forward

Barbed-wire fences helped protect farmers' crops from cattle. Windmills pumped water to use in farmhouses. But in the late 1800s, windmills were not yet used for irrigation. Instead, farmers planted the crops that grew best in their part of Texas. These crops were watered only by the rain.

In the next lesson, you will read about railroads coming to Texas. This new way to ship crops and receive supplies would help farmers. By 1900, farming had become a more important industry than ranching in Texas.

REVIEW How did the windmill help farmers? Cause and Effect

Summarize the Lesson

- **1866** Texas cowhands began driving cattle up long trails to sell them in other states.
- **1874** Joseph Glidden thought of a new idea for barbed wire.
- **1890** Fences and windmills closed off most of the West Texas open range.
- **1900** Farming had become an important industry in Texas.

REVIEW

Check Facts and Main Ideas

1. **Sequence** How did barbed wire change the open range? On a separate sheet of paper, fill in the missing details.

> Joseph Glidden developed an improved barbed wire. Texans used it to build _____.

⬇

> Fences helped keep cattle from _____.

⬇

> Windmills pumped _____ for people and livestock.

2. Describe some contributions of Mexican and Spanish people to the cattle industry in Texas.

3. What caused the days of the cattle trails to end?

4. How did cattle trails help make ranching an important industry in Texas?

5. **Critical Thinking: Predict** In what other ways might the coming of the railroad have changed Texas in the 1800s?

Link to ⚭ **Art**

Make a Drawing Draw a scene from a cattle drive. Include details to show what is happening.

Johanna July
1857 or 1858–unknown

As a child, Johanna July hated being indoors. She was happiest when she was outside with the animals. For example, she loved to fish and wander through the hills. She herded goats and cattle. Her father, Elijah, taught her to rope and ride horses.

Johanna was born in Mexico. In 1871, when she was 13 or 14, her family moved to Texas to live with other African American and Seminole families. Her father died, and she took over responsibility for tending to the animals.

BIOFACT

Johanna July trained horses to accept a saddle and bridle, such as this one.

Johanna rode bareback. One of her jobs was to "gentle" wild horses, to train them to accept a saddle and bridle. This vaquera, or cowgirl, had her own special way:

> *"I would lead them right into the Rio Grande and keep them in there until they got pretty well worried. . . . I would swim up and get him by the mane and ease up on him."*

July eventually married and had children and grandchildren. She continued to be a vaquera, breaking horses and mules.

July died sometime after 1945. She is buried in the Seminole Cemetery in Brackettville, Texas.

Learn from Biographies

In what way was Johanna July's life unusual for her time?

For more information, go online to *Meet the People* at **www.sfsocialstudies.com**.

Cowboys and Cowgirls

You have read about how cowboys began riding the ranges of Texas. Driving cattle to the railroads required courage and energy, and most cowboys took pride in their work. This work attracted people who were independent and who relied on themselves. During the days of the cattle trails, very few women could be called "cowgirls." Still, some women, such as Lizzie Johnson Williams and Margaret Borland, raised and sold cattle. Borland even led a cattle drive. Today you can see cowgirls and cowboys as they compete in rodeos. They use roping and riding skills that were useful years ago on the cattle trails.

Flying the Flag
The birthplace of American ranching, Texas was an important part of the "Wild West."

Skillful Lady
Although very few women rode the range, in recent years women have proven that they can ride as skillfully as men. This rodeo cowgirl is competing in a demonstration of range skills.

The powerful mustang—an ideal cow pony

A light touch of the rein to the horse's neck guides the horse around the barrel.

Silver concha

North American cowboy wearing batwing chaps

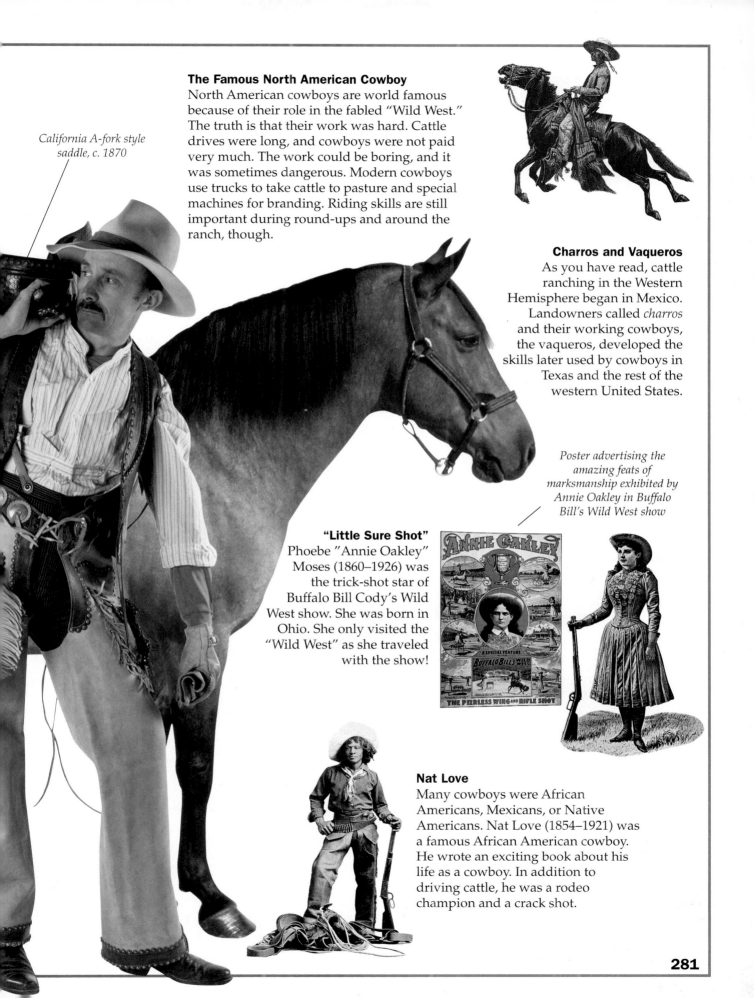

The Famous North American Cowboy

North American cowboys are world famous because of their role in the fabled "Wild West." The truth is that their work was hard. Cattle drives were long, and cowboys were not paid very much. The work could be boring, and it was sometimes dangerous. Modern cowboys use trucks to take cattle to pasture and special machines for branding. Riding skills are still important during round-ups and around the ranch, though.

California A-fork style saddle, c. 1870

Charros and Vaqueros

As you have read, cattle ranching in the Western Hemisphere began in Mexico. Landowners called *charros* and their working cowboys, the vaqueros, developed the skills later used by cowboys in Texas and the rest of the western United States.

Poster advertising the amazing feats of marksmanship exhibited by Annie Oakley in Buffalo Bill's Wild West show

"Little Sure Shot"

Phoebe "Annie Oakley" Moses (1860–1926) was the trick-shot star of Buffalo Bill Cody's Wild West show. She was born in Ohio. She only visited the "Wild West" as she traveled with the show!

Nat Love

Many cowboys were African Americans, Mexicans, or Native Americans. Nat Love (1854–1921) was a famous African American cowboy. He wrote an exciting book about his life as a cowboy. In addition to driving cattle, he was a rodeo champion and a crack shot.

281

1860   1870   1880   1890   1900

1861
Texas has 400 miles of railroad track.

1870s
Texas railroad boom begins.

1900
Texas is on its way to having more miles of railroad track than any other state.

Clarendon
Childress
Fort Worth
Marshall

Railroads Reach Texas

PREVIEW

Focus on the Main Idea
Railroads in Texas changed the way people lived and worked.

PLACES

Fort Worth
Marshall
Childress
Clarendon

VOCABULARY

boom
locomotive
junction
depot

You Are There
It is a thrill to be waiting at the Fort Worth depot. The train from Denver will arrive any minute. Soon you will hear a loud *screeeeeeech* as the wheels grind to a halt on the tracks.

It has been six years since you saw Grandma. Back then, there were no train tracks through the Panhandle. You made the long trip in a stagecoach with Mama and Papa.

"I'm glad the new tracks are finished," Papa says. "So many people along the rail line will be able to travel now." Suddenly, you hear a loud whistle. You're sure you can smell the coal burning. "Look!" you gasp. Then you see Grandma smiling through the window.

Sequence As you read, think about the order of events that shaped the railroad industry in Texas.

Trains in Texas

In the 1850s, the coming of railroads to Texas changed the way people lived. Businesses and new towns grew. Goods could be transported more easily. Riding on trains also made it easier for people to get together and visit. Indeed, the Texas frontier had come to an end.

In 1860, Texas had only about 400 miles of railroad track. During the 1870s and 1880s, the railroad boom hit Texas. A **boom** is a time of rapid growth. The Texas boom began at the Gulf coast ports. Then it stretched

▶ **Railroads in Texas were built by Chinese and other workers.**

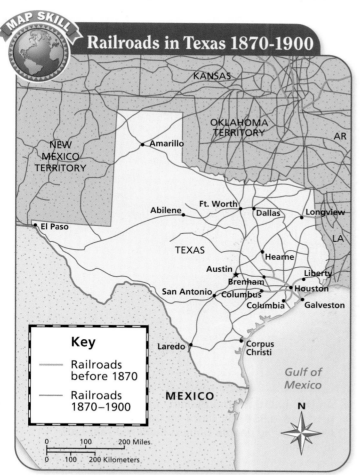

Railroads in Texas 1870-1900

MAP SKILL

KANSAS

OKLAHOMA TERRITORY

NEW MEXICO TERRITORY

AR

Amarillo

Abilene Ft. Worth
Dallas Longview

El Paso

LA

TEXAS

Hearne

Austin
Brenham Liberty
San Antonio Columbus Houston
Columbia Galveston

Laredo Corpus Christi

Gulf of Mexico

MEXICO

N

Key

— Railroads before 1870

— Railroads 1870–1900

0   100   200 Miles
0 100 200 Kilometers

▶ **Railroads helped businesses grow and changed the ways that Texans lived.**

MAP SKILL Understand Map Symbols *What parts of the state had the most railroad lines?*

northward. In about 30 years, under tough conditions, workers laid more than 8,000 miles of railroad track.

Before the 1870s, Texans traveled mainly by horse, wagon, or stagecoach. By the 1880s, they could travel by rail through many parts of their state. They could even travel to other countries. Some Texas railroads were linked to Mexican lines.

Railroads brought newcomers to Texas too. They came from other states and from other countries. Among these newcomers were Chinese rail workers— probably the first Chinese people in Texas. These workers earned $20 plus food each month for 26 days of work. Most of the workers planned to return to China. But some liked Texas. They stayed and found success in other kinds of work.

REVIEW Where did the railroad boom begin in Texas? Where did it go from there? ↻ **Sequence**

The Boom Changes Texas

More railroads in Texas meant more people in Texas. During the boom, the population of Texas grew from about 800,000 to more than 2 million people. The arrival of new people meant the arrival of new cultures in Texas. New kinds of music and art, new religions, new ideas—all of these had an impact on Texas. The **locomotive**, or train engine, had become a symbol of change.

Railroad companies advertised in other states. They wanted to persuade people to move to Texas. The companies ran special trains called "homeseeker" trains. New settlers could ride these trains into Texas at lower rates.

Railroad companies also taught farmers better ways to farm. If the farmers raised more crops, the railroads took in more money. The railroads earned money by shipping out farmers' products and bringing back more supplies.

As railroads pushed into the frontier, new towns sprang up along the lines. Steam engines needed water to make steam. The engines could go only about 30 miles without adding more water. So every 30 miles along the track, railroad crews drilled a water well. Trains then stopped at each well to take on water. The railroad company sold land on which to build homes near the wells. People knew that wherever trains stopped, businesses could grow. Even today, many Texas towns are about 30 miles apart.

REVIEW Why did railroad companies teach farmers new ways of farming? **Cause and Effect**

▶ As this painting, *The Building of the Railroad* (c. 1949–1950) by Clara McDonald Williamson, shows, many people helped build the railroads in Texas.

Growing Businesses

Beginning in the 1870s, railroad companies helped many Texas businesses grow. In East Texas, for example, companies built railroads through huge pine forests. This helped the lumber industry. Businesses cut trees from the forests. Then trains shipped lumber to buyers in distant places.

Railroad companies also helped form new factories. One railroad company helped start a fruit and vegetable cannery in the Rio Grande Valley. Railroads helped build the sugar and meatpacking industries in Texas. Railroads profited by transporting goods made in these factories.

Businesses grew along the Gulf coast as well. Railroads connected to the port of Galveston. Goods from far away were shipped to Texas by boat and then by train to towns far from the coast. Texas products could be shipped out as well.

Railroads changed the Texas cattle business too. Railroad companies built tracks close to ranches. Cowhands could now load cattle onto rail cars nearby. By 1890 the cattle drives had disappeared. Many towns grew up around cattle-shipping points. Meanwhile, ranchers began to sell some of their cattle land to farmers. Ways of earning a living in Texas were changing.

REVIEW Why do you think the railroad companies wanted to build railroads in Texas? **Draw Conclusions**

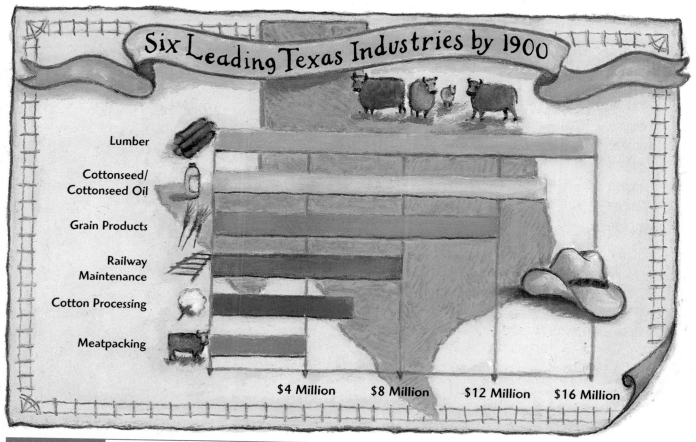

Six Leading Texas Industries by 1900

Lumber

Cottonseed/ Cottonseed Oil

Grain Products

Railway Maintenance

Cotton Processing

Meatpacking

$4 Million $8 Million $12 Million $16 Million

GRAPH SKILL *Which industry led all others in Texas in 1900?*

Growing Cities

By 1900, Texas was on its way to having more miles of railroad tracks than any other state. Each major city in Texas had a population of more than 10,000 people. Most of these cities also had two or more railroads. These cities were junctions. A **junction** is a place where two or more rail lines meet.

Cities along the railroads attracted businesses and trade. More and more workers came to help with the businesses. **Fort Worth,** for instance, was home to stockyards and meatpacking plants. "Cowtown," as the city is still called, used railroads to ship beef to markets around the country.

At junctions, rail companies often built repair shops. In the city of **Marshall,** workers repaired locomotives and other train cars. The Panhandle city of **Childress** had repair shops too. Walter Chrysler worked as a manager at these shops. Later he became an automobile maker and formed the Chrysler Corporation.

Sometimes train companies laid tracks several miles away from a town. When that happened, towns often grew toward the railroad line. If the town was large enough, the train company would build a **depot,** or train station, there. In 1887, the people of **Clarendon** moved their houses and other buildings about five miles nearer to a busy railroad route. They realized the importance of a railroad to the growth and life of a town.

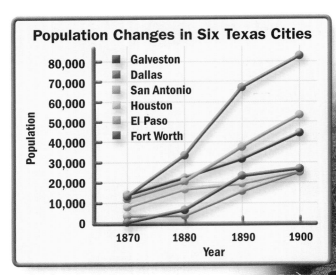

Population Changes in Six Texas Cities

- Galveston
- Dallas
- San Antonio
- Houston
- El Paso
- Fort Worth

Population / Year: 1870, 1880, 1890, 1900

GRAPH SKILL *Which Texas city grew the most from 1870–1900?*

▶ Cotton planters wait for cotton buyers in Palestine, Texas, in 1890. Cotton was shipped from Texas by rail.

By 1910, Texas had more miles of railroad track than any other state in the country! This is still true today. Five major rail lines, as well as many smaller ones, run through Texas.

REVIEW How might Texas's large size relate to the number of railroad miles in the state? **Draw Conclusions**

Summarize the Lesson

- **1861** Texas had 400 miles of railroad track.
- **1870s** The Texas railroad boom began.
- **1900** Texas was on its way to having more miles of rail than any other state.

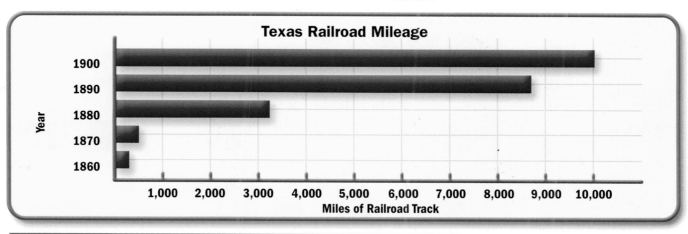

GRAPH SKILL *When were the most miles of railroad laid?*

LESSON 4 REVIEW

Check Facts and Main Ideas

1. **Sequence** An early railroad line is being built across an unsettled area of Texas. On a separate sheet of paper, fill in the missing information.

> A steam engine needs water every 30 miles.

↓

> The railroad company drills a _____ at a 30-mile mark.

↓

> The train _____.

↓

> Many towns grow _____.

2. Why did more people move to Texas cities during the railroad boom?
3. How did railroads help businesses in Texas? Give two examples.
4. How did the railroads change Texas cities and industries?
5. **Critical Thinking:** *Generalize* Explain how railroads changed the Texas landscape.

Link to ⛓ Writing

Write a Speech Write the speech you might give to persuade the people in Clarendon to move their town about five miles to be closer to the railroad. Draw a diagram to show to your audience. Give your speech to classmates.

287

Map and Globe Skills

Use Map Scale

What? A **map scale** helps you compare distances on a map with actual distances. Maps are much smaller than the areas they show. For example, two cities that are actually 100 miles apart may be only one inch apart on a map.

Map A, below, shows major railroads in Texas. Find the map scale in the lower left corner of the map. The scale shows that, on this map, one inch stands for 250 miles.

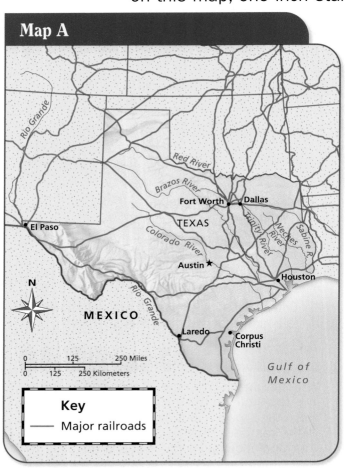

Map A

Key
— Major railroads

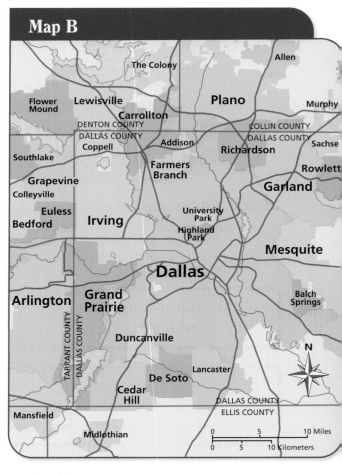

Map B

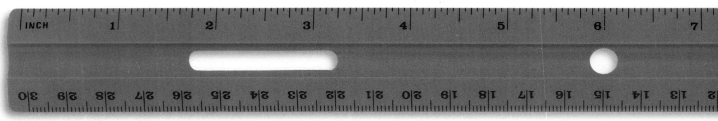

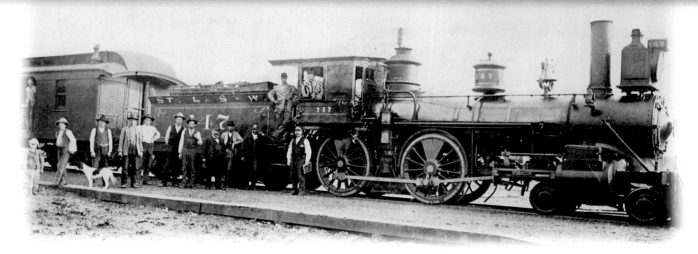

Why? Travelers, drivers, and businesses often need to know the distance between one place and another. The distance shown on a map scale depends on the size of the map and the area the map covers. Map B shows railroads around Dallas. The map scale for Map B is one inch for every 10 miles. You can see more detail on Map B than on Map A.

How? Use the scale on Map A to find the distance between Fort Worth and Houston. First, find these cities on the map. Next, place a ruler in a straight line between them. Measure the distance. How many inches apart are these cities? Write this number down. Then multiply this number by the number of miles that equal one inch on the map scale. The product is the distance in miles between the cities. Fort Worth and Houston are about one inch apart on the map. The map scale is 250 miles per inch. That means that Fort Worth and Houston are about 250 miles apart.

Think and Apply

❶ What information does a map scale give?

❷ On Map A, about how many miles apart are El Paso and Laredo?

❸ On Map B, about how many miles apart are Plano and Garland?

❹ On Map A, find a city you know about or live in. Find another city you want to visit. Find the distance between these cities in miles.

For more information, go online to the *Atlas* at **www.sfsocialstudies.com**.

1800	1865	1870

1800
Large *ranchos* operated in South Texas.

1866
Texas cowhands drove cattle on cattle trails.

1867
Some Plains Indians moved to reservations.

1874
Joseph Glidden developed an improved barbed wire.

Chapter Summary

Sequence

On a separate sheet of paper, complete a chart such as the one shown. List the events in the order in which they happened.

- Texas had more miles of railroad track than any other state.

- Several very large ranches opened in Texas.

- The Spanish brought cattle to the Southwest.

- Plains Indians were defeated in the Red River War.

- Most of the West Texas open range was fenced off.

- Some Plains Indian chiefs agreed to move to reservations.

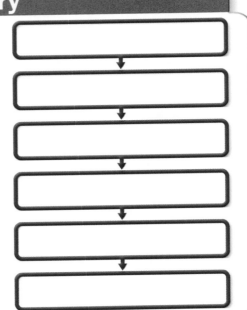

Vocabulary

Complete each sentence with the correct word from the box.

Buffalo Soldiers (p. 259)

barbed wire (p. 277)

open range (p. 267)

locomotive (p. 284)

brand (p. 268)

junction (p. 286)

1. Before fences, cattle roamed the _____.

2. Cattle from the same herd are marked with the same _____.

3. One type of fence is made of _____.

4. The train engine, or _____, was a symbol of change.

5. Two rail lines meet at a _____.

6. African American troops who fought Plains Indians were called _____.

People and Events

Write a sentence describing what you learned about each person or event in the lesson.

1. **Satanta** (p. 260)

2. **Quanah Parker** (p. 261)

3. **Colonel Ranald S. Mackenzie** (p. 262)

4. **Red River War** (p. 262)

5. **Battle of Palo Duro Canyon** (p. 262)

6. **Charles Goodnight** (p. 268)

7. **Richard King** (p. 268)

8. **Jesse Chisholm** (p. 275)

9. **Elizabeth "Lizzie" Johnson Williams** (p. 275)

10. **Joseph Glidden** (p. 277)

1875	1880	1885	1890	1895	1900

1874
Plains Indians were defeated in the Battle of Adobe Walls.

1875
Plains Indians were defeated in the Red River War.

1880
Several very large ranches expanded in Texas.

1890
Fences and windmills closed off most of the West Texas open range.

1900
Farming had become an important industry in Texas.

Facts and Main Ideas

1. Why did Texas settlers and the Plains Indians fight?

2. Why did ranchers brand their cattle?

3. How did Texas cattle reach states in the eastern U.S.?

4. **Time Line** How did the invention of an improved barbed wire in 1874 help cause the disappearance of the open range in 1890?

5. **Main Idea** Why did the Plains Indians leave Texas?

6. **Main Idea** Why were longhorn cattle important to Texas ranchers?

7. **Main Idea** How did the invention of an improved barbed wire fence call for the increased use of windmills in Texas?

8. **Critical Thinking:** *Summarize* How did the Indian Wars, the Cattle Kingdom, and the railroads change Texas at the end of the 1800s? Write a brief summary. Use three or four sentences.

Write About History

1. **Write a letter** from the point of view of a Texas cowhand who has just finished a long cattle drive. He has driven the cattle to a railroad town. Now he is ready to return to Texas.

2. **Write a list of questions** you might ask Quanah Parker. Include questions about his new life on a reservation.

3. **Write a newspaper article** dated 1900. Tell how life in a small Texas town has changed because of the railroad.

Apply Skills

Use a Map Scale

Look at Map A on page 288. Then use a ruler to answer the questions.

1. On this map scale, how many miles equal one inch?

2. About how many miles are between Laredo and Corpus Christi?

3. About how how many miles are between El Paso and Laredo?

Internet Activity

To get help with vocabulary, people, and events, select the dictionary or encyclopedia from *Social Studies Library* at **www.sfsocialstudies.com.**

291

Cowboy Poetry

Buck Ramsey worked as a cowboy on a ranch in the Texas Panhandle. One day his horse threw him, injuring his legs for life. After that, he read many books by famous writers and poets. He took English and poetry courses. He wrote poems that described his memories of being a cowboy.

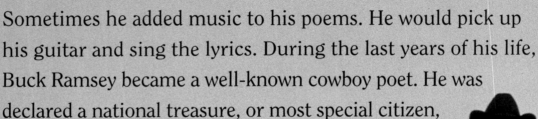

Sometimes he added music to his poems. He would pick up his guitar and sing the lyrics. During the last years of his life, Buck Ramsey became a well-known cowboy poet. He was declared a national treasure, or most special citizen, by the Smithsonian Institution in Washington, D.C.

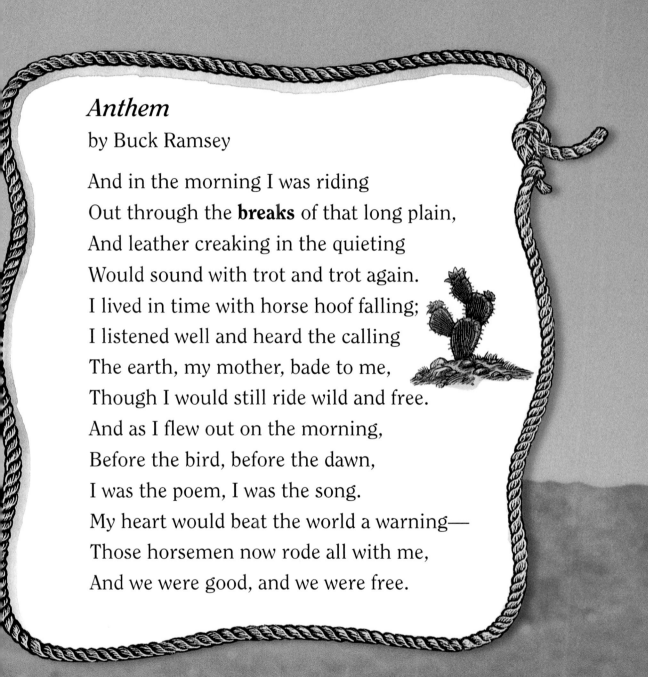

Anthem

by Buck Ramsey

And in the morning I was riding
Out through the **breaks** of that long plain,
And leather creaking in the quieting
Would sound with trot and trot again.
I lived in time with horse hoof falling;
I listened well and heard the calling
The earth, my mother, bade to me,
Though I would still ride wild and free.
And as I flew out on the morning,
Before the bird, before the dawn,
I was the poem, I was the song.
My heart would beat the world a warning—
Those horsemen now rode all with me,
And we were good, and we were free.

breaks: places on
plains where small
canyons form.

Unit Review

Main Ideas and Vocabulary

Read the passage below and use it to answer the questions that follow.

More people had come to Texas by the 1850s. Many of them farmed or ranched. Many were slaves. They worked on farms or plantations. Most of them tended cotton fields.

Many people in the North were against slavery. Many Anglo Americans in the South depended on the work of slaves. This difference caused problems. Texas voted to <u>secede</u> from the nation in 1861. That same year, the Civil War began.

In 1865 the Civil War ended. Slaves in Texas learned of their freedom about two months later.

Many Anglo Americans moved to Texas. They settled an area they called the <u>frontier</u>.

The building of railroads helped farmers and ranchers. Farmers and ranchers shipped crops and cattle by rail. Railroads brought supplies to them. By 1900, farming was a major Texas industry.

Railroads changed the way many Texans lived and worked. More people came to the state. Steamship lines connected to railroads at Texas ports. The frontier of Texas was disappearing fast.

1 What issue caused problems between Northern and Southern states?

A the hunting of buffalo
B the use of slavery
C problems with Native Americans
D the coming of railroads

2 In this passage the word *secede* means to—

A vote
B fight
C join
D separate

3 In this passage the word *frontier* means—

A the farthest part of a settled country, next to lands that are not yet settled
B settled areas such as towns and cities
C areas with mountains and valleys
D areas settled by Native Americans

4 Which of these brought many new people to Texas?

A railroads
B the end of the Civil War
C barbed-wire fences
D windmills

Vocabulary

Match each word with its definition.

1. **free enterprise** (p. 240)

2. **plantation** (p. 243)

3. **open range** (p. 267)

4. **roundup** (p. 269)

5. **barbed wire** (p. 277)

6. **boom** (p. 283)

a. a twisted wire with very sharp points

b. a large farm that produced crops to sell

c. a time of rapid growth

d. freedom to make choices in selling and buying

e. an event where cowhands herd together cattle from different areas for branding

f. grassy plains without fences

Apply Skills

Create a Map That Shows Scale Draw a map of a cattle ranch in the 1800s. Show different parts of the ranch, such as a main house, a bunkhouse for cowboys, a barn, and a corral. Label each item. Then draw a one-inch scale. Decide how many feet or yards an inch will stand for on your map. Write this information near the scale. Then choose two places on the map. Write a sentence telling how many yards apart they are.

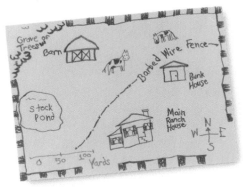

Write and Share

Make a Class Magazine Work in small groups to write articles. The articles will be about important events in Texas from 1850 to 1900. Draw a picture for each article. As a class, choose a title for the magazine. Then make a cover. Bind the articles and pictures together. Place the magazine in the class library.

Read on Your Own

Look for books like these in the library.

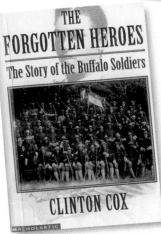

UNIT 4 Project

Point of View

People often have different ideas about an issue. Take sides and discuss different points of view.

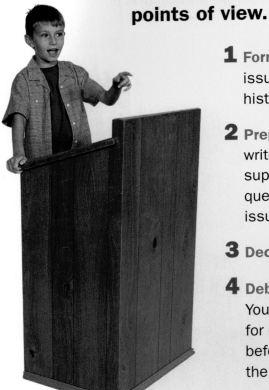

1 Form a group and choose an issue that was important to the history of Texas.

2 Prepare to debate the issue and write sentences with facts that support each side. Write several questions and answers about the issue as well.

3 Decide who will argue each side.

4 Debate your issue for the class. You may want to set a time limit for each side's presentation before taking questions from the class.

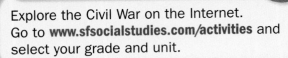
Internet Activity

Explore the Civil War on the Internet.
Go to **www.sfsocialstudies.com/activities** and select your grade and unit.

Texas Enters the Twentieth Century

Do you think change is good
for a state or for a country?

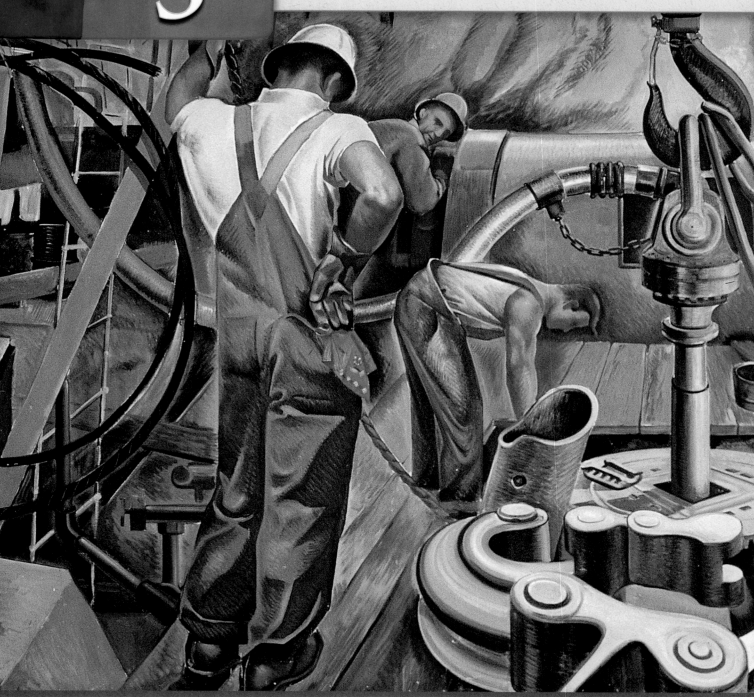

1900

1910

1920

1901
Oil is discovered
at Spindletop.

1917
The United
States enters
World War I.

1918
World
War I
ends.

1920s
The Roaring
Twenties bring
good times.

> ## "I came to the conclusion that this . . . was the greatest place on earth for oil and gas."
> —Pattillo Higgins, in an interview in the *Beaumont Enterprise*, 1941

Drilling for Oil, a mural painted by Xavier Gonzales in 1941, covers the wall of a post office in Kilgore.

1929
The Great Depression begins.

1930s
West Texans endure the Dust Bowl.

1933
The New Deal brings new jobs to Texas.

1930

1940

1941
The United States enters World War II.

1945
World War II ends.

1950

Elisabet Ney

1833–1907

Birthplace: Münster, Westphalia (Germany)

Sculptor

- Moved to Texas from Germany in the 1870s with her family
- Created sculptures of Stephen F. Austin and Sam Houston now on display in Texas Capitol
- Supporters founded the Texas Fine Arts Association in 1911 in her honor

Pattillo Higgins

1863–1955

Birthplace: Sabine Pass, Texas

Business owner and scientist

- Formed a business to produce oil and gas in Beaumont
- Started a project to drill for oil at Spindletop Hill
- Was a self-taught geologist, as well as a draftsman, cartographer, and engineer

Scott Joplin

1868–1917

Birthplace: near Linden, Texas

Composer and pianist

- Known as the "King of Ragtime"
- Played banjo and piano from the age of seven
- Composed many famous ragtime songs for piano, including "Maple Leaf Rag" and "The Entertainer"

Samuel (Sam) Taliaferro Rayburn

1882–1961

Birthplace: Roane County, Tennessee

Speaker of the U.S. House of Representatives

- Served in the Texas legislature for three years
- Served more than 48 years in the U.S. House of Representatives
- Served as Speaker of the House for 17 years

1830	1845	1860	1875	1890	1905

1833 • Elisabet Ney   1907

1863 • Pattillo Higgins

1868 • Scott Joplin

1882 • Samuel (Sam) Taliaferro

1885 • Jovita Idar

1891 • Katherine

Jovita Idar
1885–1946
Birthplace: Laredo, Texas
Teacher, political activist, journalist
- Taught elementary school in Ojuelos, Texas, under poor conditions
- Served as first president of the League of Mexican Women in 1911
- Wrote for Texas newspapers *El Progreso* and *La Crónica*

Katherine Stinson
1891–1977
Birthplace: Fort Payne, Alabama
Pilot
- Became the fourth American woman to earn a pilot's license
- Established the Stinson School of Flying with her family in San Antonio
- Was the first woman in the United States to master the loop-the-loop flying stunt

Doris (Dorie) Miller
1919–1943
Birthplace: Willow Grove, Texas
Member of U.S. Navy during World War II
- Stationed on the USS *West Virginia* at Pearl Harbor
- Awarded the Navy Cross in 1942 for heroism
- Lost his life during World War II
- Honored after his death when a Navy vessel, the USS *Miller*, was named for him

Cleto L. Rodríguez
1923–1990
Birthplace: San Marcos, Texas
Member of the U.S. Army and Air Force
- Served in the U.S. Army during World War II
- Awarded the Medal of Honor for his courage during battle in the Philippines
- Given the key to the city of San Antonio in 1946 for his bravery during World War II

Timeline: 1920 · 1935 · 1950 · 1965 · 1980 · 1995

1955
1917
Rayburn 1961
1946
Stinson 1977
1919 • Doris (Dorie) Miller 1943
1923 • Cleto L. Rodríguez 1990

Texas Enters the Twentieth Century

 Summarize

Important detail or event	Important detail or event	Important detail or event

Summary

A summary is a short statement that tells the main ideas of an article or story.

- Summarizing will help you recall and organize information.
- Choose important details or events in an article or story.
- Leave out unimportant details or events.
- Use no more than a few sentences in a summary.

Read the following paragraph. The most important ideas have been highlighted.

In the early 1900s new inventions made life easier in Texas. The automobile rolled onto Texas roads. People used the telephone to talk to friends far away. Electric lamps lit up homes and businesses.

Summary: The early 1900s brought new inventions such as the automobile, the telephone, and the electric lamp to Texas.

A Summary of Inventive Texans

In this unit, you will read about inventions that made Texans' lives easier. Did you know that some very important inventions were created by Texans?

As early as 1839, the Republic of Texas opened a patent office—an office that keeps records of inventions. Before Texas became a state, this office had listed 14 inventions. They ranged from new types of plows to a brickmaking machine.

There were many Texas inventors in the twentieth century. Ned Eastman Barnes opened an office in Houston in 1915. There he invented a brace to keep train tracks even, a projector that showed the times when trains arrived and departed, and other railroad devices.

James Field Smathers was born in Valley Spring. For a while, he worked as a typist. He thought that typing was hard work. In 1912, he thought of a way to make typing easier. He invented the electric typewriter.

In the 1950s in Dallas, Bette Graham invented another product that helped typists: correction fluid. With correction fluid, typists could just paint over a mistake and keep typing. They did not have to erase it or start all over.

Use the reading strategy of summarizing to answer these questions.

1 Which of these ideas is a main idea from the selection?
(a) There were many Texas inventors in the twentieth century.
(b) James Field Smathers was born in Valley Spring.

2 What is the most important idea in paragraph 5 of the selection?

3 How would you summarize the selection?

Lesson 1

**Dallas
Early 1900s**
Texans try out new inventions.

1

Lesson 2

**Beaumont
1901**
The discovery of oil at Spindletop brings jobs and wealth.

2

CANADA

UNITED STATES

1

2

ATLANTIC OCEAN

Dallas

PACIFIC OCEAN

TEXAS

Beaumont

Gulf of Mexico

MEXICO

Why We Remember

The first 15 years of the 1900s presented some surprises in Texas. For one, Texans struck oil! This meant more money and many new jobs. Inventions from other states made their way to Texas. For example, automobiles bumped across dirt roads made for buggies. People talked near and far on a new gadget called the telephone. Electric lights lit up homes and businesses. All of this excitement attracted people from around the world to the United States. Many came to live in the growing cities of Texas.

Fort
Worth • • Dallas
Lufkin •

1900   1910   1920

1901
Meatpacking companies come to Fort Worth.

1910
Some Texans own automobiles.

1913
Henry Ford opens a car factory in Dallas.

Changes and Growth

PREVIEW

Focus on the Main Idea
Texas cities and industries grew during the early 1900s.

PLACES
Dallas
Fort Worth
Lufkin

PEOPLE
Elisabet Ney
Henry Ford

VOCABULARY
rural
urban
invention
industry
manufacture
assembly line

You Are There

November 13, 1910
Dear Diary,
I'll never forget my first visit to Dallas. What a city! I had so much fun with Cousin Gloria, but how different our lives are! She rides in an automobile on paved streets, and I ride in a buggy on dirt roads. Her family cooks on a gas stove. My family uses a wood-burning stove. Our farmhouse has a fireplace for heat, but Gloria's house has a coal furnace. Someday I may live in a big city too. But for now, I like my home just the way it is. I'm too sleepy to write more about Dallas tonight. But tomorrow I'll tell you all about my trolley ride!

Sarah

Summarize As you read, remember to stop at the end of each section to summarize the main ideas.

Inventions Bring Change

In the early 1900s many Texans lived a rural life, a life in the countryside. Life was much as it had been years before. Mules pulled plows for planting. People rode in horse-drawn buggies and used wood-burning stoves for cooking and heat. Few homes had electricity.

People who lived an urban life, in a city such as Dallas, saw life change. They used newly created products called inventions. Instead of writing letters, Texans in cities could use a telephone. Light from electric lamps allowed people to work longer hours.

Electric streetcars, called trolleys, moved people quickly around the city.

By 1910, automobiles began to appear more often on Texas roads. With a car, a doctor could drive to see patients rather than walk or ride a horse. Cars use oil and gasoline, which is made from oil. Oil would soon become very important to Texas.

The line graph on this page shows that between 1900 and 1920, many Texans moved to cities. It also shows that Texas's population increased by more than 1.5 million people.

REVIEW How did Texas change during the early 1900s? ⟳ Summarize

FACT FILE

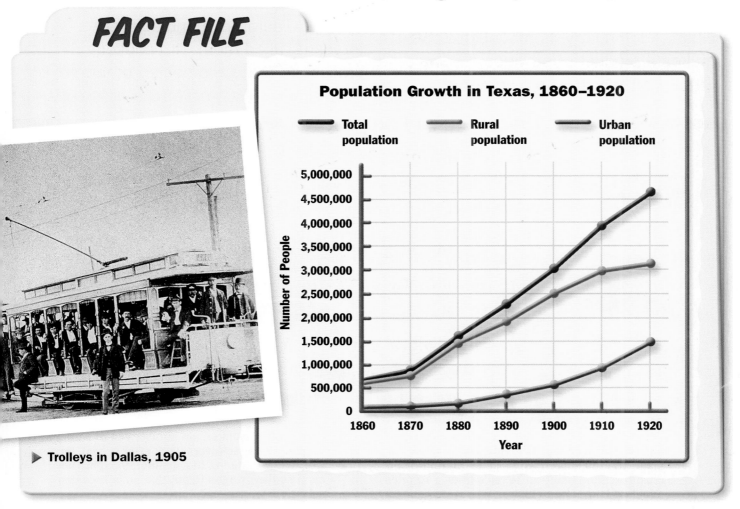

▶ Trolleys in Dallas, 1905

Population Growth in Texas, 1860–1920

— Total population   — Rural population   — Urban population

(Number of People vs. Year, 1860–1920)

New Industries

The new Texans immigrated to Texas from around the world. Many came from other states. Some came from nearby countries, such as Mexico. Others came from countries far away in Asia, Africa, and other continents. Artist **Elisabet Ney** came to Texas from Germany, a country in Europe.

During the early 1900s, people moved to cities for many reasons. Some wanted to be near urban schools and hospitals. Others enjoyed theaters and concerts. But most people moved to cities for one reason—well-paying jobs.

More jobs in industries meant larger cities. An **industry** is a business that makes a product or provides a service. Since **Fort Worth** was a center of the cattle trade, large meatpacking plants opened there. Many Texans worked in manufacturing industries. To **manufacture** means to make goods by hand or with machinery. Some industries made their own communities. Sawmill towns sprang up across East Texas to house workers who cut the big pine forests there. **Lufkin** became an important trading center for many sawmill towns.

Many industries were based on inventions. For example, some inventions kept trucks cold to help food stay fresh during shipping. Cans, like the ones you see today in the grocery store, also kept food from spoiling. Factories manufactured the cans, filled them with cooked or processed food, and sealed them.

Children at Work

Factories in the United States were busy in the 1900s. They needed lots of workers. Many of these workers were children!

▶ These children are working in a vegetable cannery. Many people thought it was wrong to make young children work. In 1903, reforms, or changes, were made to Texas's laws. Factories could no longer hire children who were younger than 12. Later, that age limit was raised to 15.

▶ Today young children are not allowed to work for wages. Many teenagers work after school, on weekends, or during the summer, though. They can use their wages to buy goods, or they can save their wages for future needs.

Now people in other parts of the world could eat foods grown in Texas.

Texas factories ran a lot like the first automobile factory. In 1903, **Henry Ford** built a factory to make cars in Detroit, Michigan. At first his workers made only a few cars each day. Then Ford put in an **assembly line.** The work was divided up. Riding on a moving platform, car after car passed by the workers. Each worker put together just one part of each car, over and over.

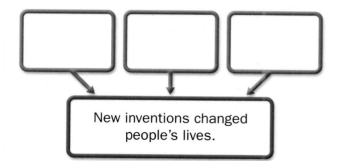

With each worker specializing in one task, Ford's company could make one car in about 90 minutes. In 1913, Henry Ford brought his assembly line to Texas. He opened an automobile factory in the Deep Ellum neighborhood of Dallas.

REVIEW Explain why people were moving to Texas cities during the early 1900s. ⟳ Summarize

Summarize the Lesson

1901 Meatpacking plants were established in Fort Worth.

1910 The automobile began to appear more often in Texas.

1913 Henry Ford opened an automobile factory in Dallas.

▶ **Workers on a 1913 Model T assembly line**

★ **LESSON 1** **REVIEW**

Check Facts and Main Ideas

1. ⟳ Summarize On a separate sheet of paper, complete the diagram. Fill in important details to show how new inventions changed the lives of Texans in the early 1900s.

[ ] → [ ] → [ ]

New inventions changed people's lives.

2. Where did immigrants to Texas come from in the early 1900s?

3. Name two reasons why people moved to cities during the early 1900s.

4. Name two new industries that came to Texas during the early 1900s.

5. **Critical Thinking:** *Apply Information* What do you think it would be like to work on an assembly line?

Link to ⚭ Writing

Write a Letter Reread the diary entry on page 306. Write a letter to Sarah or her cousin Gloria in which you describe either rural or urban life today. Describe some of the inventions that were new in the early 1900s and tell how they are used today.

Inventions in the Home

Scientists discovered how to produce electricity in 1831, but many years passed before electricity was used around the home. As people began to realize that electrical appliances could cut down on work in the home, mechanical items, such as the vacuum cleaner shown below, were replaced by electrical versions. Some of these items were very similar to those used today.

Electric Refrigerator

On the Boil
The Swan electric kettle of 1921 was the first with a totally immersed heating element. This means that when the kettle was in use, the part that heated the water was completely covered with water.

Easy Mixing
The 1918 food mixer had two blades driven by an electric motor.

Heating element

Bellows

Electric Cooker

Cleaning Up
This mechanical vacuum cleaner from the early 1900s needed two people to work the bellows to suck up dirt. William Hoover began to make electric vacuum cleaners in 1908.

ELISABET NEY
1833–1907

Artist Elisabet Ney spent the last 35 years of her life in Texas, but she was born and raised in what is today Germany. Young Elisabet always dreamed of becoming a sculptor. A sculptor is a person who carves images out of stone and other materials. However, in the 1800s, very few women became sculptors. Ney did not let that stop her.

When she was 19, Ney became the first woman to study sculpture at an art school in Munich, Germany. Ney showed great talent. After graduation, she was hired to create sculptures of

BIOFACT

Elisabet Ney used tools such as this brush, scribe, and chisel to shape her sculptures.

many important people living in Europe. She even created sculptures of kings. When asked why she became a sculptor, Ney replied,

> *"I wished to meet the great persons of the world."*

Ney moved to Texas in the 1870s. She created life-sized sculptures of Stephen F. Austin and Sam Houston. These sculptures can be seen in the state Capitol.

Learn from Biographies

What did Elisabet Ney do to achieve her dream?

For more information, go online to *Meet the People* at **www.sfsocialstudies.com.**

Thinking Skills

Identify Fact and Opinion

What? A **fact** is a statement that can be checked. It can be proved to be true. An **opinion** tells about personal feelings. It cannot be proved to be true or false.

Why? Every day you read and hear facts and opinions. Both help you understand the world. Why should you know the difference between them? This skill helps you know what is true about a subject. It also helps you know how other people feel about a subject.

   Writers often combine fact and opinion. They may use facts to support their opinions. They may also use opinions to make a story lively, or to try to persuade others to feel as they do.

   Callie Ross grew up in West Texas in the early 1900s. Cities such as Pecos were growing and changing, but Callie preferred life on her family's ranch in the country. Here are some of Callie's childhood memories:

   I had a sister and three brothers that were older than I and we all would head for the ranch as soon as the Pecos school year was over. As soon as school was out, we would take off and go to the ranch and spend the summer. Oh, I wish everybody could grow up in the country! It is a good, wholesome life.

   The roads were such that you didn't come back and forth a lot. In a wagon, a hack, or a buggy the fifty-four-mile trip took all day. But by the time I came along, we had gotten a car and we could make the trip in three or four hours (barring no flat tires or car trouble!).

How? To tell the difference between a fact and an opinion, follow these steps.

- First, read all the way through the information. Then go back and read one sentence at a time. Read and reread the information about Callie Ross's life on page 312.

- Ask yourself, "What statements can be proved to be true?" These statements are facts. You can use reference sources such as encyclopedias, almanacs, and maps to check facts. The first sentence of Callie's story is a fact. Family records would show that Callie had a sister and three brothers.

- Ask yourself, "What statements cannot be proved to be true or false?" These statements are opinions. Sometimes statements of opinion begin with clues such as *I believe* or *In my opinion*. Opinions are also signaled by describing words such as *wonderful*, *horrible*, *best*, and *worst*.

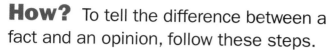

Think and Apply

1. What is an example of a fact from the passage on page 312? What is one way to prove that this fact is true?

2. What is an example of an opinion from the passage? What words signal the opinion?

3. How can reading for facts and opinions help you understand a passage?

LESSON 2

1900	1910	1920	1930

1901
Oil is discovered at Spindletop.

1928
Texas produces more oil than any other state.

Beaumont

PREVIEW

Focus on the Main Idea
The discovery of oil fields in Texas was the beginning of an important industry.

PLACES
Spindletop
Beaumont

PEOPLE
Pattillo Higgins
Anthony F. Lucas

VOCABULARY
oil refinery
petroleum

EVENTS
Lucas Gusher

Texas Gold!

You Are There

Who? Three drillers and you

Where? Spindletop, a field near Beaumont

When? January 10, 1901

What? You watch as three men work on a giant structure called a derrick. Suddenly, a rumbling noise comes from deep underground. Then BOOM! You run for cover. Flying rocks, mud, and even some pipes sail through the air.

Whoosh! A black liquid shoots toward the sky, soaring far above the derrick. Then it falls like heavy, black rain to the ground. You are covered in it, but the drillers don't care. They are shouting with joy.

Why? They have made a remarkable discovery—a discovery that will change the future of Texas.

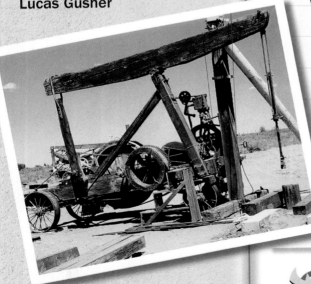

▶ Early oil-drilling machinery

Summarize As you read, remember to think about how the main ideas fit together.

314

Spindletop

Texas would never be quite the same after oil was discovered beneath a hill called **Spindletop**, near **Beaumont**. The story begins with **Pattillo Higgins.** He was a businessman. Higgins sometimes took his Sunday school class on picnics to Spindletop. On these visits, a strange smell caught his attention. It smelled like gas.

Higgins thought that the gas smell might mean that oil was under the ground. He convinced a miner to help him drill a well at Spindletop. The miner's name was **Anthony F. Lucas.**

On January 10, 1901, Lucas's drill struck oil 1,139 feet underground. What happened next amazed everyone. One historian described it in this way: "Without warning, . . . heavy mud shot out of the well with the sound of a cannon shot, followed by . . . gas, then oil. . . . "

This gusher, or blast of oil, rose more than twice the height of the derrick. It took workers nine days to gain control of it.

Spindletop was only a beginning. Texans would discover many more oil fields in the coming years. Texas would prosper, but Beaumont was set to boom.

REVIEW Write a sentence describing the events at Spindletop on January 10, 1901. ⟳ **Summarize**

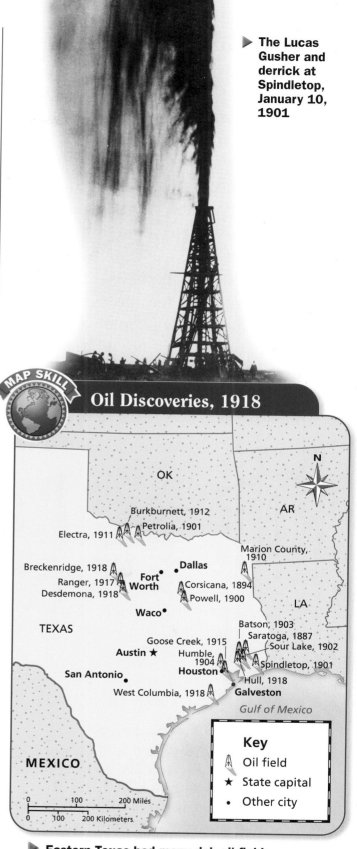

▶ The Lucas Gusher and derrick at Spindletop, January 10, 1901

Oil Discoveries, 1918

MAP SKILL

Burkburnett, 1912
Petrolia, 1901
Electra, 1911

OK

AR

N

Marion County, 1910

Breckenridge, 1918
Ranger, 1917
Desdemona, 1918

Dallas

Fort Worth

Corsicana, 1894
Powell, 1900

LA

Waco

TEXAS

Batson, 1903
Saratoga, 1887
Sour Lake, 1902

Goose Creek, 1915

Austin ★

Humble, 1904

Spindletop, 1901

Houston

Hull, 1918

San Antonio

West Columbia, 1918

Galveston

Gulf of Mexico

MEXICO

0   100   200 Miles
0   100   200 Kilometers

Key
🛢 Oil field
★ State capital
• Other city

▶ Eastern Texas had many rich oil fields.

MAP SKILL Understand Map Symbols
What is the symbol for an oil field? How many are shown on the map?

Oil Boom in Texas

News of the Lucas Gusher quickly spread around the world. Factories and machines needed oil and gas products. The demand for oil, or "black gold," was high. Thousands of people moved to the Spindletop area. They had hopes of getting rich. Within months, nearby Beaumont grew from a town of 9,000 to a city of 50,000. Beaumont suddenly had more than five times the people it had only a few months before!

Many of these new people were business people. They hoped to buy or sell oil wells, land, or drills. Workers also came to the growing city. They drilled for oil and laid pipelines to carry the oil. They also worked in oil refineries. An oil refinery is a factory where crude oil straight from the ground is cleaned, processed, and turned into useful oil products.

The first oil boom had begun. Soon oil wells were flowing in Electra, Burkburnett, and many other places in Texas. By 1928, Texas produced more oil than any other state in the nation. More oil meant more jobs and more money for Texans. Many refineries were built along the Gulf Coast. Texas oil was shipped to countries all over the world.

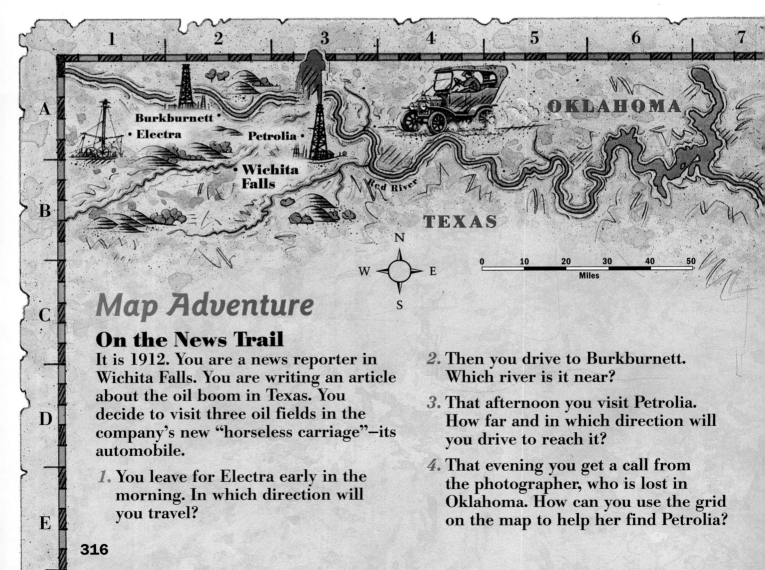

Map Adventure

On the News Trail

It is 1912. You are a news reporter in Wichita Falls. You are writing an article about the oil boom in Texas. You decide to visit three oil fields in the company's new "horseless carriage"—its automobile.

1. You leave for Electra early in the morning. In which direction will you travel?

2. Then you drive to Burkburnett. Which river is it near?

3. That afternoon you visit Petrolia. How far and in which direction will you drive to reach it?

4. That evening you get a call from the photographer, who is lost in Oklahoma. How can you use the grid on the map to help her find Petrolia?

During the boom, people quickly found new uses for oil. Railroad companies began to use it as fuel for trains. Factory owners burned oil instead of coal to power their machines.

Today oil, or **petroleum,** is used to make many products. Most lip balms for chapped lips contain petroleum products. So do many other household goods such as lotion, plastic wrap, and paint. Texas drivers use a common petroleum product every day. This is the gasoline that fuels most cars and trucks. Motor oil helps engines run smoothly. Petroleum is also used to make the pavement of many of the roads they drive on!

▶ **Pumps such as this one bring oil from deep underground.**

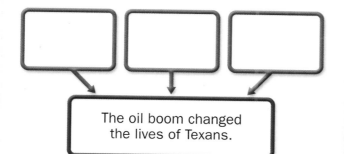

REVIEW Why do you think people wanted to find new uses for oil?
Draw Conclusions

Summarize the Lesson

1901 Oil was discovered at Spindletop.

1928 Texas became the leading oil-producing state in the nation.

Today Oil is used in a variety of petroleum products.

 LESSON 2 **REVIEW**

Check Facts and Main Ideas

1. 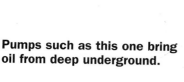 **Summarize** On a separate sheet of paper, complete the diagram. Fill in important details describing how the oil boom changed the lives of Texans in the early 1900s.

[ ] → [ ] → [ ]
↓   ↓   ↓

The oil boom changed the lives of Texans.

2. Who was Pattillo Higgins? What was his contribution to Texas history?

3. How did the Texas oil industry grow after the discovery at Spindletop?

4. Name three products that are made from petroleum.

5. **Critical Thinking:** *Cause and Effect* Why did the invention of the automobile help the oil industry?

Link to ⦵⦵ **Geography**

Where in the World? Use a world atlas and resource maps to find other states and countries that produce oil. Go to the library or do an Internet search to find out more about life in one of these states or countries.

Read a Cross Section Diagram

What? A **cross section diagram** shows the inside of something. The diagram on page 319 shows a cross section of an oil pumping unit. The diagram lets you see the machinery that pumps oil from the ground.

Why? A cross section diagram shows you what is not always easy to see. What does the inside of the human body look like? What does the inside of a car look like? A cross section diagram helps you know.

A cross section diagram can also show you how the parts of the item pictured work together. For example, a cross section diagram of a building might show how all the floors are connected by an elevator.

This diagram of a beam pumping unit shows that some of the important parts of the machine are located beneath the ground.

How? To read and understand a cross section diagram, follow these steps.

- First, read the labels on the diagram.
- Next, look at what the labels point to. Notice how the different parts of the diagram are related.
- Use what you have learned to understand the big picture.

Think and Apply

1. Why did the artist draw a cross section of parts of the pumping unit that are under the ground?

2. What part of the beam pumping unit is under the ground?

3. What else does the artist show in the cross section part of the diagram?

Beam Pumping Unit

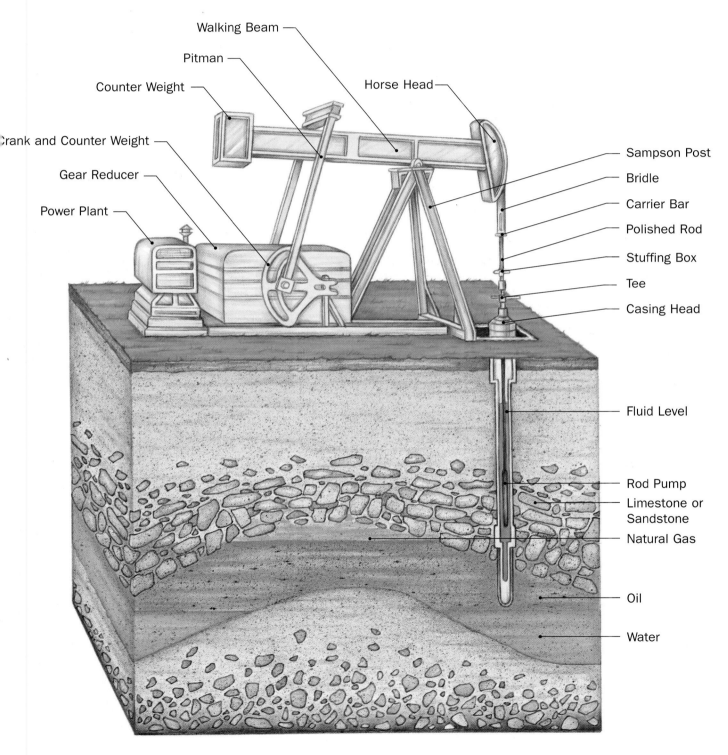

Walking Beam

Pitman

Counter Weight

Horse Head

Crank and Counter Weight

Gear Reducer

Power Plant

Sampson Post

Bridle

Carrier Bar

Polished Rod

Stuffing Box

Tee

Casing Head

Fluid Level

Rod Pump

Limestone or Sandstone

Natural Gas

Oil

Water

1900   1910

1901
Oil was
discovered at
Spindletop.

1901
Meatpacking plants
were established in
Fort Worth.

1910
Some automobiles
began traveling on
Texas roads.

Chapter Summary

Summarize

On a separate sheet of paper, complete
a chart such as the one shown. Fill
in details that show how Texas
changed in the early 1900s.
Then write a sentence
that summarizes
these changes.

People began
to move to
cities.

Summary

Vocabulary

Match each word or phrase with the correct
definition or description.

1 urban
(p. 307)

2 rural
(p. 307)

3 invention
(p. 307)

4 manufacture
(p. 308)

5 oil refinery
(p. 316)

6 petroleum
(p. 317)

a. in the countryside

b. to make by hand
or machine

c. a factory that
turns oil into other
products

d. a newly created
product

e. oil

f. in a city

People and Places

Write a sentence describing what you learned
about each person or place.

1 Elisabet Ney (p. 308)

2 Spindletop (p. 315)

3 Pattillo Higgins (p. 315)

4 Anthony F. Lucas (p. 315)

5 Beaumont (p. 315)

▶ Anthony F. Lucas

1920   1930

1913
Henry Ford
opened a car
factory in Dallas.

1928
Texas produced
more oil than
any other state.

Facts and Main Ideas

1 Tell about an invention that helped Texans in the early 1900s.

2 Why did Pattillo Higgins suppose there might be oil at Spindletop?

3 What was the Lucas Gusher?

4 Name two products made from oil.

5 **Time Line** What two events happened in Texas in 1901?

6 **Main Idea** How was urban life in Texas different from rural life in the early 1900s?

7 **Main Idea** How did the oil boom help Texans make money?

8 **Critical Thinking:** *Draw Conclusions* Name one petroleum product you often use or depend on. How would your life be different without that product?

Internet Activity

To get help with vocabulary, people, and terms, select the dictionary or encyclopedia from *Social Studies Library* at **www.sfsocialstudies.com.**

Write About History

1 **Write a poem** about the Lucas Gusher as if you had seen it. Use adjectives to bring the event to life.

2 **Write a journal entry** as a visitor to a Texas city in 1901. Describe what you saw and how you felt.

3 **Write an advertisement** for one of the new inventions in this chapter. Tell what it does, how it is used, and where people can find it.

Apply Skills

Fact and Opinion

Read the advertisement below. Then answer the questions.

1 What is being offered in this ad?

2 Name one fact from the ad. How do you know it is true?

3 Name one opinion from the ad. How do you know it is not a fact?

Felix Flyer—only $1250!
The best value in the U.S.A.
4 cylinders!
30 horse power!
108" wheel base!
Magneto and headlights!

CHAPTER 11

Texans at Home and Abroad

Lesson 1

**San Antonio
1917**
U.S. pilots train for duty in World War I.

1

Lesson 2

**Dallas
1920s**
The Jazz Age comes to Texas and the nation.

2

Lesson 3

**Texas Panhandle
1930s**
Texans live through the Great Depression and the Dust Bowl.

3

Otis Dozler "The Annual Move, 1936" Oil on masonite; 24 x 36″, Dallas Museum of Art, gift of Eleanor and C. Thomas May, Jr.

Locating Time and Place

CANADA

UNITED STATES

3

2

1

Texas
Panhandle

ATLANTIC
OCEAN

PACIFIC
OCEAN

TEXAS

Dallas

San Antonio

Gulf of Mexico

MEXICO

Why We Remember

The first half of the twentieth century indeed began with a bang. But after the discovery of oil at Spindletop, Texans lived through a roller coaster of events. War raged across the world. Then the Roaring Twenties brought jazz and good times. Suddenly, the stock market hit rock bottom, and many people went broke. A new president tried to bring the nation back to normal. Then BAM! Another war. Most Texans survived the roller-coaster ride. Some folks today can tell you about how they did it.

LESSON 1

San Antonio

Laredo

1910	1915	1920

1910
The Mexican Revolution begins.

1914
War breaks out in Europe.

1917
The United States enters World War I.

Preview

Focus on the Main Idea
Between 1900 and 1920, Texans dealt with conflicts along the Mexico border and in Europe.

PLACES
Laredo
San Antonio

PEOPLE
Jovita Idar
Woodrow Wilson
Katherine Stinson
Annie Webb Blanton

VOCABULARY
discrimination
bond
suffrage

EVENTS
Mexican Revolution
World War I

Troubles in Texas and Overseas

You Are There
The sun is setting on a long day in 1915. You and your family finally sit down to supper. Everyone is tired from working hard. The grown-ups look worried.

Your aunt Mercedes says the blessing. Her voice shakes. "Be with the Flores family as they are forced to leave their land."

Now you are worried too. How can this be? Mr. and Mrs. Flores were born on that ranch. So were their children. Will you ever see your best friends, Juan and Rosa, again? What will happen to *your* family's ranch?

Your father unfolds his napkin and picks up his fork. "We Tejanos must stick together," he says calmly. "We will never sell our land!"

Summarize As you read, stop from time to time to recall the important parts of the lesson.

Border Troubles

Why would Tejano families have to move from their land? The answer is not simple. In Chapter 7, you read about the Mexican War. During this war many Tejanos sided with Texas. But many Anglo Americans feared that because the Tejanos had ties to Mexico, they would take Mexico's side. Bad feelings grew. Some Anglo Americans discriminated against Tejanos. **Discrimination** is when one group denies rights to another.

In 1910, fighting broke out in Mexico. Mexican President Porfirio Díaz (pahrr FEER yoh DEE ahs) was removed from office. Two other men wanted to replace him. Battles broke out between supporters of these two men.

▶ **Jovita Idar**

This was called the **Mexican Revolution.** The fighting came very close to the Texas border. Discrimination got worse.

Some Anglo Americans forced Tejanos to sell their land to them. Many Tejano families lost their ranches.

Many Tejanos spoke out for their rights. **Jovita Idar** (hoh VEE tah ee DAHR) of **Laredo** was one of them. She worked for Tejano rights, first as a teacher and then as a writer. She wrote newspaper articles saying that Tejanos should have the same rights as Anglo Americans. She inspired many Tejanos to stand up for their rights too.

REVIEW How did the Mexican Revolution affect Tejanos?
↪ **Summarize**

▶ **Texas ranch house, early 1900s**

World War I

Trouble was also brewing across the Atlantic Ocean. In 1914, war broke out in Europe. This war would come to be known as **World War I.** Britain, France, Italy, and Russia were called the Allied Powers. They joined together to fight against Germany, Austria-Hungary, and the Ottoman Empire, or Turkey. This group was known as the Central Powers. People in Texas and the other states had family roots in all these countries. President **Woodrow Wilson** urged citizens not to take sides in the war.

In 1915 the German navy sank a British passenger ship, the *Lusitania.* Along with many other passengers, 128 Americans were killed. Many angry U.S. citizens wanted the United States to declare war on Germany. Still, the United States stayed out of the war until 1917, when German submarines stepped up attacks on merchant ships as well as warships. In April, the

▶ **Even children helped in the war effort.**

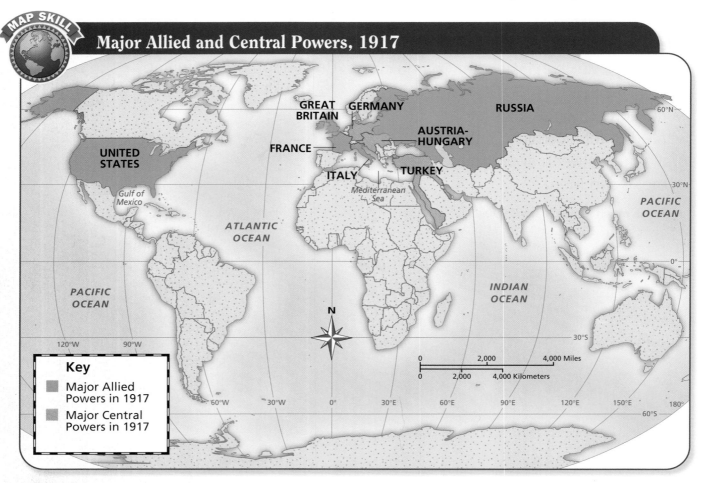

▶ Because so many nations were involved, World War I was called the "Great War."

MAP SKILL Understand Continents *On what continents were the major Allied and Central Powers located?*

United States entered the war on the side of the Allied Powers.

About 200,000 Texans served during World War I. About 450 of them were women who worked as nurses. At training camps in Texas, soldiers from around the United States trained for the war. The soldiers learned to work and to fight as a team.

▶ Planes of the American Expeditionary Force, 1918

▶ Red Cross workers in Bartlett, Texas

COMPLIMENTS OF CANTEEN COMMITTEE, BARTLETT, TEXAS.

Airplanes were a new and important part of the fighting in World War I. Some pilots trained at Kelly Field in San Antonio. Other pilots polished their skills at the Stinson School of Flying in the same city. This school was run by two women, Marjorie and Katherine Stinson and their two brothers.

Texans at home also supported the war effort. Some people worked for volunteer groups such as the Red Cross. Many women took factory jobs that had been left open by men who went to war. Other people helped the government raise money. They did this by buying government bonds. A **bond** is a certificate given in exchange for money. A person could cash in a bond at a later date and receive more money than he or she had paid for it. This extra money is called interest.

Because many farmers were away at war, and because so much food was needed to feed the soldiers, there were food shortages during the war. Many Americans grew their own vegetables so that more canned goods could be sent to soldiers. People also cut back on the foods they ate. On Tuesdays most Americans did not eat meat. On Mondays and Wednesdays, they did not eat wheat products.

In 1918 the Allied Powers won the war. Texans celebrated. They looked forward to welcoming the soldiers home.

Sadly, though, more than 5,000 Texans had died while serving in the war. Texans and all Americans hoped that this war would be "the war to end all wars."

REVIEW What events led the United States to enter World War I? **Cause and Effect**

Women Fight for Rights

Another battle was being fought in the early 1900s. It was the battle for women's suffrage. **Suffrage** means the right to vote—a right women did not have in the United States.

Many women in Texas fought this battle. Mary Eleanor Brackenridge wrote in support of women's rights. She organized women's suffrage groups.

Jessie Daniel Ames was the first president of the Texas League of Women Voters. She helped black and white women work together to win suffrage.

 Women's suffrage poster

Texas women won the right to vote in some state elections in 1918. That same year, teacher **Annie Webb Blanton** was elected State Superintendent of Public Instruction. She was the first woman elected to statewide office in Texas. In 1920, the Nineteenth Amendment granted women all over the United States the right to vote in national elections.

REVIEW Why did women fight for suffrage? **Draw Conclusions**

Summarize the Lesson

- **1910** The Mexican Revolution began.
- **1914** War broke out in Europe.
- **1917** The United States entered the war.
- **1918** World War I ended. Texas women won the right to vote in some state elections.

★ **LESSON 1** **REVIEW**

Check Facts and Main Ideas

1. ◉ **Summarize** On a separate sheet of paper, complete the diagram. Write a summary describing what Texans did during World War I.

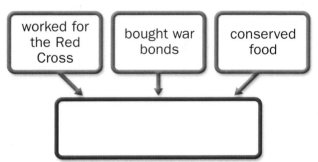

2. Who was Jovita Idar, and why is she important to Texas history?

3. What caused the United States to declare war on Germany?

4. Name two women who fought for women's voting rights in Texas and tell how they helped women take part in the democratic process.

5. **Critical Thinking: *Point of View*** How did the different points of view of Anglo Americans and Tejanos lead to conflict during the Mexican Revolution?

Link to **Science**

Wheatless Wednesdays! During World War I, many Texans gave up wheat products on Mondays and Wednesdays. Work with your teacher or librarian to make a healthful menu for a Wheatless Wednesday. Make sure it has servings from each food group.

KATHERINE STINSON
1891–1977

Young Katherine Stinson wanted to study music in Europe, but her family could not afford it. How could she earn the money herself? Stinson decided to become a stunt pilot. She found a teacher and quickly learned that she had a knack for flying planes. Soon flying was more important than her music.

At age 21, Stinson became the fourth American woman to earn a pilot's license. Known as the "Flying Schoolgirl," Stinson traveled around the country. At each stop she performed thrilling airplane stunts, such as doing the loop-the-loop and skywriting at night.

BIOFACT

Stinson wore these gloves as a part of her flight gear.

Katherine Stinson was the first woman to fly mail from city to city. In 1917, Stinson set a record by flying 610 miles from San Diego to San Francisco without stopping. Some of the flight was over rugged mountains. Still, Katherine Stinson said,

"I never had any fear."

Stinson got her whole family involved in flying. Her sister and two brothers became pilots. Together they opened the Stinson School of Flying in San Antonio.

Learn from Biographies

Name two qualities that you think helped Stinson become a successful pilot.

For more information, go online to *Meet the People* at **www.sfsocialstudies.com.**

Dallas

1920
Business booms in Texas.

1924
Texas elects its first female governor.

1928
There are more than 250,000 autos and trucks in Texas.

PREVIEW

Focus on the Main Idea
Between 1920 and 1929, a business boom changed the lives of many Texans.

PLACES
Dallas

PEOPLE
Miriam "Ma" Ferguson
Scott Joplin

VOCABULARY
jazz

TERMS
Roaring Twenties
Jazz Age

The Roaring Twenties

You Are There

Bang! Pop! What is that racket? You peek out the window to see your Grandpa climbing down from the seat of a brand new Model T Ford! This shiny, black car is so much fancier than the horse-drawn buggy sitting in the barn!

One by one, your neighbors get to ride in Grandpa's new car. Finally, it is your turn. But the ride is cut short when it begins to rain. The dirt road turns to mud. Grandpa fears the car will get stuck. Also, the car does not have windshield wipers. It is hard to see with rain splattering on the front window. Grandpa turns the car around and heads for home. You can't wait to take another ride!

Summarize As you read, think about the important ideas in each section.

Booms and Changes

Just as Grandpa did, many Texans had bought automobiles by 1920. World War I was over. Factories no longer made products for war. Now they made things people wanted to buy. Factories hired new workers to fill the orders that came pouring in.

Texas and the United States were in the midst of a business boom. This boom time between 1920 and 1929 is called the **Roaring Twenties.** More people than ever before had jobs. This meant they had more money to spend.

By 1928, Texans owned more than 250,000 cars and trucks. They needed gasoline to make them run. As you have read, Texas had plenty of oil. Gasoline companies built more oil refineries to manufacture gasoline. This boosted the oil industry. Cars also needed better roads on which to travel.

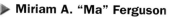

▶ **Miriam A. "Ma" Ferguson**

Sure enough, cars and trucks soon buzzed along new paved highways from city to city. As needs came about, new businesses formed to fill them.

Many people were able to buy their own homes, both in rural and urban areas. They bought new inventions, such as refrigerators, vacuum cleaners, and radios, to put in these homes.

There were big changes in the state government too. You have read that American women won the right to vote in 1920. It didn't take long for a woman to come to power in Texas. In 1924, **Miriam "Ma" Ferguson** was elected as Texas's first female governor after her husband had been removed from office. He had been accused of breaking the law.

REVIEW Why do you think the 1920s were called the Roaring Twenties? **Draw Conclusions**

▶ **Before roads were paved, it was common for cars to get stuck in the mud.**

The Jazz Age

Some people call the 1920s the Jazz Age. Jazz is a type of music that began in the southern United States. It was created by African Americans. Jazz became very popular during the 1920s. It had new sounds and strong, complex rhythms. It was exciting, just like the Roaring Twenties.

During the Jazz Age, people looked for new ways to have fun. Some women dressed in daring new styles, such as short "flapper" dresses. People learned new, lively dances. On weekends, people cheered at football games and went driving in their cars. Some Texans went to clubs such as those in Deep Ellum, a Dallas neighborhood, to dance and hear live musicians.

▶ Silent movie poster, 1923

In Texas, as in other states, families gathered around big radios in the evening. They might hear a jazzy "ragtime" tune written by Texas-born Scott Joplin. They might listen to news reports. Many families tuned in every week to listen to radio plays and comedy shows.

Movies were different then too. In the 1920s every "picture show" was black and white. There was neither color nor sound! In most theaters, piano players provided background music. "Talkies," or movies with sound, were not made until the late 1920s. The first major "talking picture" was called *The Jazz Singer*.

REVIEW Why were the 1920s called the Jazz Age? ⟳ **Summarize**

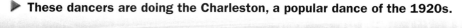

▶ These dancers are doing the Charleston, a popular dance of the 1920s.

Problems in the Twenties

There were serious problems in the 1920s too. Groups of white people that called themselves the Ku Klux Klan, or the KKK, hid their faces beneath hooded costumes. They harmed and killed African Americans, including women and children. They also hurt others whose race or religion they hated.

The KKK believed that only certain white people should have rights. They fought to keep all of the power in their own hands. The KKK tried to elect their supporters to office. For a while, they were successful.

African Americans and some whites protested the KKK's actions and goals.

Miriam Ferguson and others spoke out against the Ku Klux Klan. After "Ma" Ferguson was elected governor, the KKK began to lose power in Texas.

REVIEW Why did African Americans and whites such as "Ma" Ferguson oppose the Ku Klux Klan?
Draw Conclusions

Summarize the Lesson

1920 A business boom began in Texas.

1924 Texas elected its first female governor.

1928 The number of automobiles and trucks in Texas topped 250,000.

★ **LESSON 2** **REVIEW**

Check Facts and Main Ideas

1. **Summarize** On a separate sheet of paper, complete the diagram. Fill in details and summarize the business boom of the 1920s.

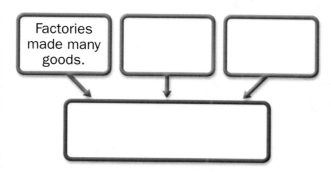

Factories made many goods.

2. In the 1920s many people bought automobiles. How did this affect the Texas oil industry?

3. Who was Miriam Ferguson and why is she important to Texans?

4. What was the Jazz Age like?

5. **Critical Thinking: *Draw Conclusions*** How did the increase in jobs affect the Texas economy?

Link to ⚬—⚬ **Reading**

Reading About the 1920s Find one or two books in the library that tell about life in the 1920s. As you read about the Roaring Twenties, notice how life was different then. Also notice how life then was similar to our lives today.

Deep Ellum and Harlem

During the 1920s the Deep Ellum district of Dallas became a center for blues music. The "blues" grew out of the songs, stories, and experiences of African Americans in the southern United States. At the same time, 1,600 miles away in New York City, African American painters, writers, and musicians began to gain fame in a neighborhood called Harlem.

▶ Blind Lemon Jefferson was a talented Texas blues singer, musician, and songwriter. He played in the clubs of Deep Ellum and made more than 80 recordings of his songs.

▶ Duke Ellington, shown below at the piano, was an important jazz composer, pianist, and bandleader. He and his orchestra became famous playing at Harlem's Cotton Club. He led his big band for more than 50 years.

Smithsonian Art Museum, Washington, D.C./Art Resource, Romare Beardon Foundation/Licensed by VAGA, New York, N.Y.

▶ Romare Bearden's collage called *Empress of the Blues* (1974) recalls the bright color and excitement of a Harlem jazz club. Jazz singer Bessie Smith was known as the "Empress of the Blues."

▶ Deep Ellum was settled by "freedmen," or former slaves, after the Civil War. By the 1920s, it had become an important center of business and entertainment for African Americans in Dallas.

▶ Victoria Spivey was one of the most famous of the Texas blues singers and songwriters. This "Queen of the Blues" began her music career in Houston. She performed in Deep Ellum and around the country.

335

Research and Writing Skills

Research on the Internet

What? You can find out more about a topic by doing **research.** One place to find lots of research information is on the **Internet.** The Internet is a huge network of computers. It contains many Web (World Wide Web) sites. One of the quickest ways to find information on the Internet is to use a **search engine.** A search engine is a special Web site that locates other Web sites that can provide information on the topic you are researching.

Why? A search engine can provide links to Web sites from all over the world. The search engine usually gives you the title of the Web site and a little information about it. From the search engine, you can choose a link to find out more about the topic you are researching.

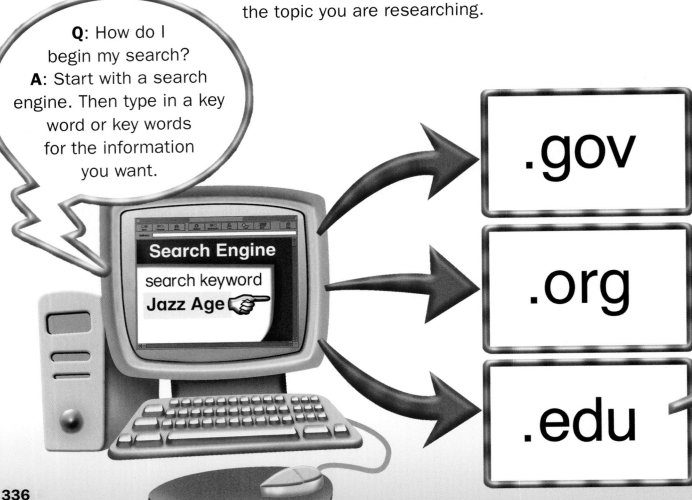

Q: How do I begin my search?
A: Start with a search engine. Then type in a key word or key words for the information you want.

Search Engine

search keyword
Jazz Age

.gov

.org

.edu

How? To use a search engine, follow these steps.

- First, select a search engine. A teacher or librarian can help you choose a search engine that will best help you conduct your search.

- Next, type in a key word or two. A key word is a word or phrase related to your topic, such as "Jazz Age." Then click on "Search." You may have to experiment with different words and phrases. If you need help, click on "Help" or "Search Tips."

- The search engine will show a list of Internet sites related to your key word. Decide which sites look as if they have the material you want. Click on one of the sites. The information will appear on your computer screen.

- If your search brings no results, try another key word or ask for help from someone with Internet experience.

- Check the information you find on the Internet with another source such as an encyclopedia.

Think and Apply

1. What is one way in which the Internet can be a useful research tool?

2. What words or phrases would you type in to begin a search for jazz performers in Texas?

3. How would you choose which sites to visit from the list created by a search engine?

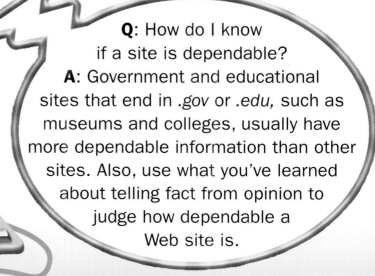

Q: How do I know if a site is dependable?
A: Government and educational sites that end in *.gov* or *.edu,* such as museums and colleges, usually have more dependable information than other sites. Also, use what you've learned about telling fact from opinion to judge how dependable a Web site is.

1925	1930	1935	1940	1945

1929
The stock market crashes.

1929
The Great Depression begins.

1933
President Roosevelt creates the New Deal.

1941
The United States enters World War II.

1945
World War ends.

Texas Panhandle

HAWAII

PREVIEW

Focus on the Main Idea
Between 1930 and 1945, the Great Depression, a terrible drought, and World War II caused hard times for Texans.

PLACES
Texas Panhandle
Pearl Harbor, Hawaii
Canyon

PEOPLE
Franklin D. Roosevelt
Sam Rayburn
Lyndon B. Johnson
Doris Miller
Cleto Rodríguez
Audie Murphy

VOCABULARY
stock
depression

TERMS
New Deal

EVENTS
Great Depression
Dust Bowl
World War II

Hard Times in Texas

You Are There
You look up from your game of marbles. Next door, Mr. Frank is hammering a "For Sale" sign into his front lawn. It is the third house to go up for sale on your street this month. Earlier, you heard Mr. Frank telling your mom that he had lost his job. He no longer has the money to make the payments on his house.

Your parents are trying hard to save money. It has been months since you have gotten a new pair of shoes or any new clothes. Your dad says his job at the grocery store is safe. Still, you worry about what might happen if the store closes. As you reach for your favorite marble, you wonder how long these hard times will last.

Summarize As you read, think about how you might retell the information in this lesson to a friend.

▶ *The Annual Move,* painted by Otis Dozier in 1936, shows the hard times of the Great Depression.

Otis Dozier "The Annual Move, 1936" Oil on masonite; 24 x 36", Dallas Museum of Art, gift of Eleanor and C. Thomas May, Jr.

The Great Depression

The 1920s began with a business boom, but they ended with a crash. Here is what happened.

When business was booming, many people had faith in American companies. They bought **stocks,** or shares of ownership, in companies, hoping to make a profit. When a company makes money, the price of its stock increases. But near the end of the 1920s, companies began to fail. In October 1929, stock prices fell across the country. People rushed to sell their stocks. Prices tumbled even lower.

Many people had borrowed money to buy stocks. Now their stocks were worth less than they paid for them. They could not pay back their loans. Some of the banks that had loaned the money could not do business unless the loans were repaid. These banks were forced to close their doors. Some people lost all their savings.

Since people had very little money to spend, companies had a hard time selling their products. Like some businesses do today, companies laid off workers. Many companies went out of business.

The period known as the **Great Depression** had begun. A **depression** is a period during which business slows down and prices fall. The Great Depression affected people in countries all around the world.

In Texas, as in other states, people had a hard time buying what they needed to live. Many lost their homes and were forced to beg for food. Others traveled from place to place looking for work.

REVIEW What happened during the Great Depression? ⟳ **Summarize**

339

The Dust Bowl

The Great Depression brought hard times to Texas farmers. People did not have money to spend on the farmers' crops. When farmers could sell their crops, prices were so low that they often could not make a profit.

Then Americans faced another big problem. Farmers need plenty of rain and sunshine to grow their crops. During the 1930s a large part of Texas and other Midwestern states suffered a drought. Also, some farmers had not conserved or enriched their soil. Much of the soil was thin and dry. Then the winds came.

On the Great Plains, dust storms raced across the dry farmland. Winds picked up the topsoil and blew it away.

Parts of the region became known as the **Dust Bowl.**

Dust storms harmed the land and ruined crops. They also made life miserable for people. Here is what Pauline Robertson, then thirteen years old, had to say about her first dust storm on the **Texas Panhandle:**

> *"We choked and gasped and ran as the air thickened with brown dust . . . everything went completely black. . . . I remember gasping, 'I can't breathe!'"*

Because of these hard times, many farmers left their farms to find jobs. Some left Texas to work on farms in California.

REVIEW What was the Dust Bowl?
Main Idea and Details

Literature and Social Studies

"Dust Bowl Refugee"©

Woody Guthrie wrote folk songs. He lived in Texas as a teenager and young adult. In this song, he tells about a farmer who has fled from the Dust Bowl to pick peaches in California.

....

I'm a dust bowl refugee,
Just a dust bowl refugee,
From that dust bowl to the Peach Bowl
Now the Peaches is killing me.
'Cross the mountain to the sea,
Come the wife and kids and me,
It's a hard old dusty highway
For a Dust Bowl refugee.

▶ **Migrant family on a California highway, 1937**

The New Deal

In 1932, Franklin D. Roosevelt was elected President of the United States. In 1933, he created a program to help the United States recover from the Great Depression. This program was called the New Deal.

The New Deal created new jobs. The government hired workers to build dams, repair roads, and plant trees. Workers even painted murals on post office walls! The parks, bridges, and government buildings in your area may have been built by workers as part of the New Deal.

Through these jobs, communities improved. New jobs boosted people's spirits. With the money they earned, people could buy groceries and pay for services. Companies hired new workers. Once again, money was changing hands in the country.

Some Texans did not agree with the New Deal. They thought it gave the U.S. government too much control and did not let the free enterprise system work as it should. Other Texans played important roles in the government during the New Deal. John Nance Garner from Uvalde served as President Roosevelt's vice president. Jesse Jones of Houston led an agency that gave New Deal loans to businesses. Sam Rayburn from Bonham was a member of Congress. He helped pass many New Deal laws.

▶ President Franklin D. Roosevelt meets Texas governor James Allred and Texan Lyndon B. Johnson in 1937.

In Texas a young man named Lyndon B. Johnson was in charge of a government program called the National Youth Administration. This program helped young people find jobs. This young man would one day become President of the United States.

REVIEW How did the New Deal seek to fight the effects of the Great Depression? **Main Idea and Details**

World War II

You have read that people hoped World War I would be "the war to end all wars." After the war ended in 1918, there was peace for 21 years, but peace time ended in 1939. In Europe, Germany attacked Poland. Soon many countries were involved in the fight. The Allies—Britain, France, and the Soviet Union—went to war against the Axis Powers—Germany, Italy, and Japan. This war is known as World War II.

The United States tried to stay out of the war. But on December 7, 1941, Japanese planes dropped bombs on Pearl Harbor in Hawaii. There were many U.S. ships in this harbor. A Texas sailor named Doris Miller was aboard the battleship USS *West Virginia* during the attack. He defended his ship by shooting at the attacking planes.

The next day, the United States declared war on Japan. The United States became one of the Allies. Once again, many Texans—about 750,000 of them—rushed to the aid of their nation. Among them was Cleto Rodríguez. His bravery helped win battles and save lives in the Philippines. Another Texan, Audie Murphy, was only eighteen when he joined the Army. By the time he was twenty, Murphy had earned more awards than any other U.S. soldier in the war! Both of these soldiers won the Medal of Honor—the nation's highest military award.

REVIEW What drew the United States into World War II? ➲ Summarize

FACT FILE

Some Texas Heroes of World War II

▶ **Oveta Culp Hobby** of Houston helped organize and run the Women's Army Corps, through which women could work for the war effort.

▶ **Admiral Chester Nimitz** from Fredericksburg commanded the United States Pacific Naval fleet.

▶ **General Dwight D. Eisenhower** from Denison was in charge of the Allied forces in Europe. He later became President of the United States.

▶ **Audie Murphy** of Farmersville was one of the war's most honored heroes. After the war, he became a movie actor.

▶ **Cleto Rodríguez** of San Antonio was one of 11 Mexican Americans to win the Medal of Honor during World War II. In 1975, a Texas school was named in his honor.

▶ The Congressional Medal of Honor

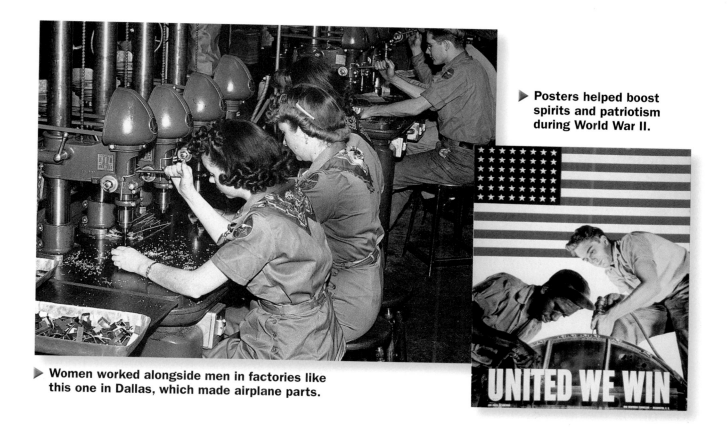

▶ Posters helped boost spirits and patriotism during World War II.

UNITED WE WIN

▶ Women worked alongside men in factories like this one in Dallas, which made airplane parts.

Industry and War

Suddenly, Texas industries were busy. The oil industry sprang back to life. Battleships, planes, and tanks all needed gasoline to run. The U.S. government looked to Texas oil companies to fill this need. Overall, about half of the oil used as fuel in the war came from Texas. Texas factories also produced rubber from petroleum for many wartime uses.

New factories hurried to produce war supplies. Steel mills in Houston and Daingerfield manufactured tons of steel. Factories in Fort Worth, Garland, and Grand Prairie shaped the steel into airplanes. Workers in shipyards along the coast also used steel to build warships.

All of this new business created thousands of new jobs. As they had in World War I, women took the jobs of men who had gone to war. People from all over the country moved into Texas cities to take wartime jobs. People even came across the border from Mexico to work in Texas's factories.

World War II ended in 1945 when the Axis Powers surrendered to the Allies. About 23,000 Texans died in the war. Those who made it home found that their state was much better off than it had been when they went to war. The Great Depression had come to an end, and Texas was a powerhouse of industry.

REVIEW What effect did World War II have on Texas industries?
Cause and Effect

Treasuring Texas History

In spite of wars and the Great Depression, Texans kept on treasuring their history and art in the 1900s. As you have read, this was a time of rapid change. New objects and inventions quickly replaced the old. Some Texans saw a need to save objects from the past. They built museums to house them. Inside the museums today, you can see artifacts from bygone days. These special objects give clues about the history of Texas.

The Panhandle-Plains Historical Museum is the largest and oldest state-owned museum in Texas. It was built in **Canyon** and opened in 1933. Inside you will find objects as large as a real windmill or a chuck wagon. Or you may see tiny things, like a perfect arrowhead.

In 1936, Texas celebrated 100 years of independence. As a result of this celebration, many museums were opened in the state. Among these was the San Jacinto Monument and Museum. The monument honors the heroes of the Battle of San Jacinto. The museum has displays on the history of Texas, Mexico, and the Southwest dating back to the days before Columbus arrived in the Americas.

Do you live near a Texas history museum? One way to find out is to search the Internet for names of Texas history museums. You may be surprised to find at least one near your home.

REVIEW What kinds of items are displayed in Texas history museums? **Main Idea and Details**

▶ **This chuck wagon is on display at the Panhandle-Plains Historical Museum in Canyon.**

FACT FILE

During the early 1900s many Texas artists left their mark on history. Their artwork often showed what was happening in the world then. Here are but a few of the artists who left us information through their works.

Texans with Tales

► Katherine Anne Porter (1890–1980) was born in Indian Creek. She is one of the best-known Texas authors of the early 1900s.

► J. Mason Brewer (1896–1975) wrote tales about African American life in Texas.

Texans with Tunes

► Bob Wills (1905–1975) created western swing music during the 1930s.

► Lydia Mendoza (Born 1916) was a well-known *conjunto* singer in the 1930s. *Conjunto* combines styles such as traditional Mexican music and German polkas.

Texans in the Visual Arts

► Alexandre Hogue (1898–1944) painted famous images of the Dust Bowl, such as *Drought-Stricken Area,* 1934.

► Kathleen Blackshear (1897–1988) often recalled her childhood in rural Texas in her paintings. *Marion with Book* was painted in 1940.

Alexandre Hogue, Drought Stricken Area, 1934, oil on canvas, '2002 Estate of Alexandre Hogue, courtesy of Cline Fine Art, New Mexico/Dallas Art Association Purchase, Dallas Museum of Art

Texas Culture and Art

A rich part of Texas history is alive and well today through the arts. You have read about artists such as Elisabet Ney and Isamu Taniguchi, who created statues and gardens that Texans enjoy. Texans come from many different cultures—Mexican American, African American, Native American, Asian American, and Anglo American.

Many Texas artists get ideas and inspiration from our rich mix of culture and scenery.

▶ The Mustangs of Las Colinas, by Robert Glen, are located in Irving, Texas.

REVIEW Where do some Texas artists get their ideas?
Main Idea and Details

Summarize the Lesson

1929 The stock market crashed. The Great Depression brought hard times to Texas.

1932 Franklin D. Roosevelt was elected President of the United States.

1941 The United States entered World War II.

1945 World War II ended.

★ **LESSON 3** **REVIEW**

Check Facts and Main Ideas

1. ⟳ **Summarize** On a separate sheet of paper, complete the diagram by describing life in Texas during the Great Depression. Then complete the summary statement.

> Many people lost their jobs.

> ↓

> Life in Texas during the Great Depression was _____.

2. Explain the causes and effects of the Dust Bowl storms.

3. Who were Audie Murphy and Cleto Rodríguez, and why do we remember them today?

4. Name and tell about three Texas artists from the early 1900s.

5. **Critical Thinking:** *Evaluate* Explain the New Deal and tell whether or not you think it was a good plan.

Link to ⫘⫘ **Art**

Dusty Drawings Using crayons or pastels and paper, draw a scene from the Texas Dust Bowl. Use what you read about the Dust Bowl to help you think of details to include.

SAMUEL TALIAFERRO RAYBURN
1882–1961

For 17 years Sam Rayburn served in the U.S. Congress as the Speaker of the House of Representatives, a very important and powerful job. His friends called him "Mr. Sam."

As a boy, Sam lived on a cotton farm in north Texas. Even then he knew that he wanted to work in politics. When he was twelve, he heard U.S. Representative Joe Bailey give a speech in Bonham, Texas. Sam rode his mule for miles through a heavy rain to reach the town. The roads were very muddy.

Once there, Sam looked at the crowd that had gathered in a tent. Many townspeople had come dressed in fancy clothes. Sam was soaking wet. He decided to stand outside in the rain and listen through a gap in the tent. Still, Sam was moved by Bailey's speech. He later remembered,

" . . . I scarcely drew a breath the whole time."

Afterwards, Sam was quite sure that he wanted to serve in the U.S. Congress like Joe Bailey.

Learn from Biographies

Even though it was difficult, Sam Rayburn managed to hear Joe Bailey speak. What do Rayburn's actions on that day tell you about his character?

BIOFACT

When he was young, Sam could often be heard giving political speeches to the animals in the family's barnyard.

For more information, go online to *Meet the People* at **www.sfsocialstudies.com**.

Courage Under Fire

Would you risk your life to save the lives of others? Doris Miller, an African American sailor, bravely helped his shipmates when his ship was attacked.

Doris "Dorie" Miller was born near Waco, Texas, in 1919. He was the son of a sharecropper. During the Great Depression, Miller helped support his family by working as a cook in a small restaurant. Miller joined the Navy shortly before he turned twenty. He was given a job in the dining hall of the battleship USS *West Virginia*. Because African Americans did not have equal rights then, kitchen jobs were some of the few positions open to them.

Miller's ship was docked at Pearl Harbor in Hawaii on December 7, 1941. About 90 other American ships were docked there too. Early that morning, Japanese airplanes attacked these ships. When the surprise attack began, Miller ran to his ship's main deck. Bombs were exploding. Gunfire rained down. Miller saw his captain lying on the deck, badly wounded. Miller ran to his captain and helped move him to safety. He also helped other wounded sailors nearby. Miller then jumped behind a deck gun and began shooting at the planes. At that time, African Americans were not trained to use these heavy guns. The brave young sailor later described his experience:

> "It wasn't hard. . . . I had watched the others with these guns . . . I guess I fired her for about fifteen minutes . . . [the planes] were diving pretty close to us."

In May 1942, Miller was awarded the Navy Cross by Pacific Fleet Admiral Chester Nimitz. This high honor is given to sailors who show outstanding bravery in battle. Miller was the first African American to receive the Navy Cross. Admiral Nimitz praised Miller for acting with courage and for risking his own life to save others. The next year Miller lost his life when his ship was torpedoed during the war.

BUILDING CITIZENSHIP

Caring
Respect
Responsibility
Fairness
Honesty
⭐ Courage

Courage in Action

Go to the library or use the Internet to research another Texan who won the Congressional Medal of Honor or another high award for courage. How did this person's courageous actions help others?

Read a Road Map

What? A **road map** shows routes, or roadways, from one city to another.

Why? A road map can help you plan a trip from one place to another. It can also guide you during your journey. Suppose you wanted to visit the cities of San Antonio, Houston, Dallas, and Fort Worth. A road map can help you plan the route you want to take. And it can help you find your way if you get lost.

How? To read and understand a road map, follow these steps.

• First, look at the map on page 351. Notice that each road is labeled with a number. The numbers are the "names" of the roads. By comparing the numbers on road signs with the numbers on the map, you can find your route.

• Next, look at the map key. What do the symbols show you? A double blue line stands for an Interstate highway—a wide, fast highway that links states together. A double orange line stands for a U.S. highway. A single orange line stands for a Texas state highway.

• Suppose that you plan to travel from San Antonio to Houston. Use your finger to follow different routes between these cities. What road appears to be the most direct route from San Antonio to Houston?

Think and Apply

1. What does a road map mainly show?

2. What U.S. highway goes from Laredo to Houston?

3. What Interstate highway links Houston and Dallas?

4. Using the map on page 351 as a guide, draw a simple road map that shows two ways to get from Abilene to San Angelo. Label each highway.

Road Map, Eastern Texas

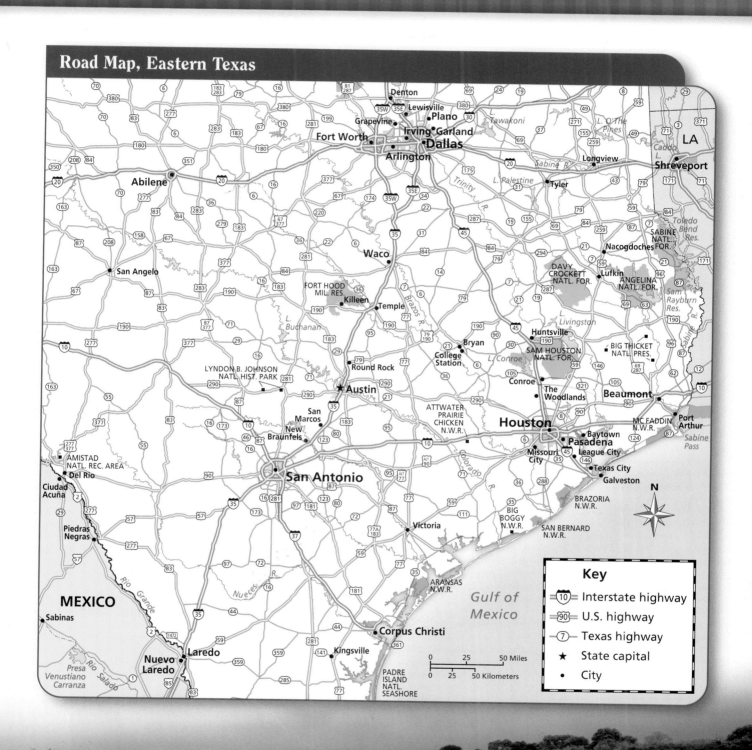

Key
- 🛣 **10** Interstate highway
- 🛣 **90** U.S. highway
- ⬭ **7** Texas highway
- ★ State capital
- • City

0   25   50 Miles
0   25   50 Kilometers

For more information, go online to the *Atlas* at **www.sfsocialstudies.com**.

1910

1920

1910
Mexican
Revolution
began.

1914
World War I
began.

1917
United States
entered World
War I.

1918
World
War I
ended.

1920
Business
boomed in Texas
and the U.S.

1924
Texas elected
its first woman
governor.

Chapter Summary

Summarize

On a separate sheet of paper, complete the diagram. Use the details to write a summary statement about why the United States entered World Wars I and II.

| United States does not want to go to war. | German navy attacks the *Lusitania*. | Japanese planes attack Pearl Harbor. |

▶ The AT-6 Texan, a World War II training fighter plane

Vocabulary

Match each word with the correct definition or description.

1 discrimination (p. 325)

2 bond (p. 327)

3 suffrage (p. 328)

4 jazz (p. 332)

5 stock (p. 339)

a. share of ownership in a company

b. denying rights

c. a certificate given in exchange for money

d. the right to vote

e. a type of music

People and Events

Write a sentence that tells why each person or event below is important in Texas history.

1 Jovita Idar (p. 325)

2 World War I (p. 326)

3 Miriam "Ma" Ferguson (p. 331)

4 Great Depression (p. 339)

5 Franklin D. Roosevelt (p. 341)

6 Sam Rayburn (p. 341)

7 World War II (p. 342)

8 Cleto Rodríguez (p. 342)

▶ Franklin D. Roosevelt

1930　　　　　　　　　1940　　　　　　　　　1950

1929
Great Depression began.

1932
Franklin D. Roosevelt was elected President of U.S.

1939
World War II began.

1941
The United States entered World War II.

1945
World War II ended.

Facts and Main Ideas

1. About how many Texans served in World War I? About how many of these were women?

2. Why did the oil business get a boost between 1920 and 1929?

3. What two problems did farmers face during the 1930s?

4. **Time Line** How long did the United States fight in World War II?

5. **Main Idea** How did Texans' lives change between 1900 and 1920?

6. **Main Idea** How did Texans' lives change between 1920 and 1929?

7. **Main Idea** How did Texans' lives change between 1930 and 1945?

8. **Critical Thinking: *Summarize*** How did the New Deal seek to help Texans?

Internet Activity

To get help with vocabulary and people, select the dictionary or encyclopedia from *Social Studies Library* at www.sfsocialstudies.com.

Apply Skills

Research Facts on the Internet

Choose a topic covered in this chapter. Search the Internet for more facts. Write a summary of what you learn. Include pictures. Tell the name of the Web site you used and why you like it.

Summary

Texans with Tunes
Josephine Lucchese was a famous opera singer. She was born in San Antonio in 1901. She learned to sing in Texas. She sang all over the United States and Europe. Then she taught others to sing opera at the University of Texas. She died in 1974.

Write About History

1. Write a **journal entry** from the point of view of a Texan who is living in the Roaring Twenties.

2. Write a **poem** from the point of view of a Texas farmer who is living during the Great Depression.

3. Write a **script for a radio newscast** about the effects of World War I on Texans at home. Add specific details from your reading about the war.

End with an Oral History

An oral history is a story about a person's life, told aloud by that person and recorded on tape or written down. This is an oral history told by W. Silas Vance. About 1920, Silas attended Lucky Ridge School in Wise County. His school had no sports equipment for playing outdoor games. Here he tells how he and his friends solved this problem.

Most of us at Lucky Ridge never saw a basketball or football or volleyball or tennis ball or golf ball or a store-bought baseball. Our constant game, in and out of school, was townball.

. . . Historians have suggested that baseball replaced [townball] before the end of the nineteenth century, but we were playing townball at Lucky Ridge down to at least 1920. For us it had . . . **advantages**. First, any number could play. . . . Second, it didn't require any equipment except a ball and

advantages: benefits

bat, and we didn't have any, not even a catcher's mitt. Third, the poorest player could take part with some success and enjoyment, since the pitcher had to deliver the ball with an underhanded pitch and usually served it as gently as possible to smaller boys and girls. Fourth, since a team [remained] "in bats" and "in town" . . . until every member was put out, the **inept** player was not the serious handicap he would be to a team in baseball.

inept: clumsy

If Silas and his friends didn't have any store-bought equipment, how did they get bats and balls to play "townball" with? This excerpt from a letter written by Josephine Ballard explains where the balls and bats came from.

. . . Since we had no store-bought balls or bats, we made our own. For balls we unraveled large socks and wound the ravels around a small stone until it got about as large as a baseball. It was then securely sewed to keep it from unwinding. (My mother made many of these.) For bats we used a strong stick or a board which we had shaped like a paddle so we could hold it. . . . ▪

Unit Review

Main Ideas and Vocabulary

Read the passage below and use it to answer the questions that follow.

The first half of the new century brought many changes to Texas. City people began using telephones and electric lamps in the early 1900s.

People came to Texas from all over the world. Most of them sought jobs. New <u>industries</u> sprang up. The state entered the modern age.

Oil was discovered at Spindletop in 1901. The demand for oil increased. Texas oil was shipped to countries all over the world.

In 1914 World War I broke out in Europe. The United States joined the war in 1917.

In 1918 the United States and its allies won the war. Business boomed. People had jobs and money to spend during the Roaring Twenties. The Jazz Age had begun.

The Great Depression brought an end to the Roaring Twenties. Banks closed their doors. People lost money, and workers lost jobs. Farmers could not sell their crops. Drought and dust storms added to farmers' problems.

In 1933, President Franklin D. Roosevelt created the New Deal. This program sought to provide jobs to fight the <u>depression</u>.

Then the world went to war again. The United States entered World War II in 1941. Texas manufactured many supplies for the war. Many Texans had jobs during wartime. This marked the end of the Great Depression. In 1945 the war ended.

1 In this passage, the word *industries* means—
   A inventors
   B jobs
   C cities
   D businesses

2 Oil was discovered at Spindletop in—
   A 1917
   B 1901
   C 1918
   D 1933

3 President Roosevelt created the New Deal to—
   A increase the demand for oil
   B help people during wartime
   C provide jobs
   D enter World War II

4 In this passage, the word *depression* means—
   A a business slow down
   B a dust storm
   C a valley
   D sadness

Use the map to help you find the answers.

People and Places

Match each person or place to its definition.

1. **Lufkin** (p. 308)
2. **Annie Webb Blanton** (p. 328)
3. **Scott Joplin** (p. 332)
4. **Pearl Harbor** (p. 342)
5. **Audie Murphy** (p. 342)

a. Texas-born ragtime composer

b. won many awards in World War II

c. site of Japanese attack in 1941

d. trading center for sawmill towns

e. first woman elected to statewide office in Texas

Apply Skills

Read a Road Map

1. Name one road near Corpus Christi International Airport.

2. What is the name of the road that passes by the Texas State Aquarium?

3. What route would you take to get from the airport to the aquarium?

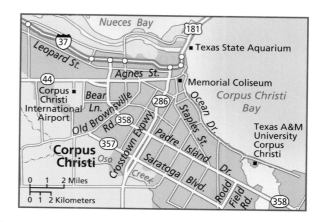

Read on Your Own

Look for books like these in the library.

Write and Share

Collect an Oral History
Talk to a parent, grandparent, or another adult about a favorite childhood memory. If possible, record their words on audio tape. Write down their story to share with your class. Then collect the oral histories into a class book.

Ad Sales

Healthy businesses are good for Texas's economy. Make your own infomercial about a product or a business.

1 **Form** a group. Choose a product or a business.

2 **Research** the product or business and write a list of facts about it.

3 **Write** a script for an infomercial about the product or business. Include the value and cost, as well as the history of the product or business. Give examples of its successes. Tell how it contributes to Texas's economy.

4 **Make** an advertisement on a poster or banner to use in your infomercial.

5 **Present** your infomercial to the class.

Internet Activity

Find out more about the twentieth century on the Internet. Go to **www.sfsocialstudies.com/activities** and select your grade and unit.

Texas, Our TEXAS

UNIT
6

What is important in the lives of Texas citizens?

1970s Demand for oil creates boom in Texas

1950   1960   1970   1980

1950s Segregation continues in Texas and other states.

1960s Many people join the Civil Rights Movement.

1969 Neil Armstrong walks on the moon.

1972 First Texas Folklife Festival begins in San Antonio.

"The more each of us knows and understands, the better our chances are for . . . building a . . . democracy . . . "

— Bill Moyers, 1997

The Capitol in Austin is the seat of state government.

1980s High-tech industry grows in Texas.   **1990s** High-tech industry brings new businesses to Texas.

1990   **2000**   **2010**

1992 First African American woman travels in space.

1993 Selena wins a Grammy award.

1996 First Texas Book Festival opens.

2001 Lance Armstrong wins his third Tour de France.

Meet the People

Lyndon Baines Johnson

1908–1973

Birthplace: Stonewall, Texas

Political leader

- Directed the National Youth Administration from 1935 to 1937
- Served in the U.S. House of Representatives and the U.S. Senate
- Became President in 1963 after the assassination of President John F. Kennedy

Henry B. González

1916–2000

Birthplace: San Antonio, Texas

Political leader

- Grew up in poverty
- Elected to the U.S. House of Representatives in 1961, the first Mexican American to represent Texas in Congress
- Awarded the John F. Kennedy Profile in Courage Award in 1994

Barbara Jordan

1936–1996

Birthplace: Houston, Texas

Political leader, teacher

- Served as a Texas State Senator and in the U.S. House of Representatives
- Delivered the keynote speech at the Democratic National Convention in 1976
- Inducted into the National Women's Hall of Fame in 1990

George W. Bush

1946–

Birthplace: New Haven, Connecticut

Political leader

- Served as managing partner of the Texas Rangers baseball team from 1989 to 1994
- Served as the 46th Governor of Texas from 1994 to 2001
- Elected as the 43rd President of the United States in 2000

| 1900 | 1910 | 1920 | 1930 | 1940 | 1950 |

1908 • Lyndon Baines Johnson

1916 • Henry B. González

1936 • Barbara Jordan

1946 •

1947 •

For more information, go online to *Meet the People* at **www.sfsocialstudies.com**.

Henry Cisneros

1947–

Birthplace: San Antonio, Texas

Political leader

- Served as a city council member in San Antonio
- Elected mayor of San Antonio in 1981, the first Hispanic mayor of a major U.S. city
- Served as Secretary of Housing and Urban Development under President Bill Clinton

Lance Armstrong

1971–

Birthplace: Plano, Texas

Professional cyclist

- Won the Iron Kids Triathlon at age thirteen
- Formed the Lance Armstrong Foundation in 1997 to support cancer research
- Became the 1999, 2000, and 2001 champion of the Tour de France, the toughest cycling race in the world

Selena Quintanilla Perez

1971–1995

Birthplace: Lake Jackson, Texas

Singer

- Began performing with a musical group at age ten
- Became a popular Tejano performer, recording songs in both Spanish and English
- Won a Grammy Award in 1994 for her album *Selena Live*

| 1960 | 1970 | 1980 | 1990 | 2000 | 2010 |

1973

2000

1996

George W. Bush

Henry Cisneros

1971 • Lance Armstrong

1971 • Selena Quintanilla Perez 1995

Texas, Our Texas

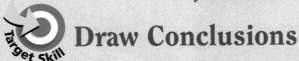

Draw Conclusions

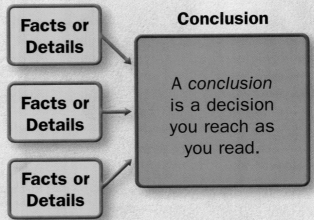

- Writers do not always explain everything. Often they let readers *draw conclusions*, or figure out some things, for themselves.

- You can use facts or details to draw conclusions about what you read. You can also use what you already know.

Read the following paragraph. **Facts** and the **conclusion** you can draw from them have been highlighted.

In Unit 5, I read that during the Great Depression, life was hard for many Texans. People did not have enough money to buy farmers' crops. Dust storms and drought added to farmers' problems. The writer does not say this directly, but I can conclude that some Texas farmers had a hard time paying bills during this time.

On the Fast Track

Could anyone have imagined how Texas would change in the last half of the 1900s? World War II ended in 1945. Texas soldiers returned home. The Great Depression had long passed. More and more Texans were leaving farms and ranches. They were finding jobs in towns and cities. Areas surrounding cities grew too.

African Americans and Hispanics gained more rights in the United States during the 1960s. The world's attention turned to Texas in 1969. That is when scientists near Houston helped put the first people on the moon.

By the 1970s the oil industry was booming. It was the leading industry in the state. During the 1970s and 1980s, people in Texas had more money to spend than ever before. They bought homes, cars, and televisions. People from other states and countries were drawn to Texas. They saw many opportunities.

By the late 1990s the computer industry was booming in Texas. This drew other related industries. Texas was moving forward in the second part of the twentieth century. It was moving fast!

Use the reading strategy of drawing conclusions to answer these questions.

1 What are two facts that you could use to draw a conclusion about changes that came to Texas in the second half of the 1900s?

2 What real-life experience can you add to the two facts to help you draw a conclusion?

3 What conclusion can you draw from the facts and your own experience in items 1 and 2?

CHAPTER 12

Modern Times in Texas

Lesson 1

**Houston
1969**
Workers at the Manned Spacecraft Center, now called the Johnson Space Center, near Houston help land the first man on the moon.

1

Lesson 2

**San Antonio
1972**
Texans celebrate the first annual Texas Folklife Festival.

2

Locating Time and Place

CANADA

UNITED STATES

2 **1**

ATLANTIC OCEAN

PACIFIC OCEAN

TEXAS

San Antonio   Houston

Gulf of Mexico

MEXICO

Why We Remember

Today we think of Texas as being a modern state. It is a state with large cities and growing industries. Modern Texas means inventions, technology, the arts, sports, and festivals. But that is not all. Texans have a strong sense of place—a feeling of belonging to a state with a rich history. Modern Texas is about the many kinds of people who call Texas their home. You are a part of Texas history. You are a part of the place we call Texas!

Dallas
Austin ★
Houston

1950	1960	1970	1980	1990

1950s
Segregation continues in Texas and other states.

1960s
Many people join the Civil Rights Movement.

1969
Neil Armstrong walks on the moon.

1970s
The demand for oil creates a boom.

1990s
The high-tech industry brings new businesses to Texas.

PREVIEW

Focus on the Main Idea
After World War II, Texans focused on equal rights and growing industries.

PLACES
Houston
Dallas
Austin

PEOPLE
Lyndon B. Johnson
Neil A. Armstrong
Mae C. Jemison

VOCABULARY
segregation
astronaut
aerospace
high-tech
technology

TERMS
Civil Rights Act
Internet

Moving Forward

You Are There

November 5, 1967
Dear Pen Pal,
Today our class took a field trip to our magnificent state Capitol building in Austin. We saw Barbara Jordan! Our teacher said it has been an entire century since an African American has served in the state senate. From the balcony we could see Jordan's big wooden desk, along with all the others. She leaned back in the leather chair. When she spoke, her voice sounded powerful. Come to Texas. Who knows—you might get to see Barbara Jordan!

Your friend,
Guess Who

 Draw Conclusions
As you read, use the facts and details, along with what you know, to draw conclusions.

Equal Rights

Barbara Jordan's election to office, along with many other victories during the 1960s, meant progress for all ethnic minorities in Texas. Why? Until then, many African Americans and Hispanics did not have the same rights as Anglo Americans. They could not go into some restaurants or movie theaters. They could not ride in the front seats of buses. Until a U.S. Supreme Court ruling took place in 1954, they even had to attend separate schools from Anglo Americans. These and other unfair types of racial separation, known as **segregation,** are now illegal in our country.

In 1964 the U.S. Congress, under President **Lyndon B. Johnson,** passed the **Civil Rights Act.** This law means

This sign is an example of segregation, which is now illegal in the United States.

that people must be treated alike, no matter what their race, religion, or gender is. Since then, many changes have taken place. But more work remains in the fight for equal rights.

REVIEW Why do you think the U.S. Congress and President Johnson passed the Civil Rights Act?
◎ Draw Conclusions

Working for Civil Rights

Then and Now

During the 1960s many people in the United States worked to gain civil rights, or basic rights, for all Americans. Dr. Martin Luther King, Jr., led a national movement to give all U.S. citizens equal rights.

In Texas, Christia Adair worked to end segregation in Houston's libraries and airports. Texans of all ethnic backgrounds joined in the Civil Rights Movement.

Today, discrimination based on race, religion, or gender is against the law. Many Americans continue to work together to make sure we all have equal rights.

Georgia minister Dr. Martin Luther King, Jr., led civil rights marches.

The Changing Oil Industry

More than a century has passed since the Texas oil industry began booming at Spindletop. Today Texas is a leader in the production of oil and natural gas. Until recently the oil and gas industry was the major industry in Texas.

By the 1970s the increased demand for oil caused oil prices to go up. Many Texans made money, or profited, in the oil business.

While some Texans grew wealthy drilling for oil, some others profited by drilling natural gas wells. Your home or school may use natural gas for heating or cooling.

The money from oil and natural gas drew immigrants to Texas, adding to the state's prosperity.

This boom to the Texas economy during the 1970s brought more jobs.

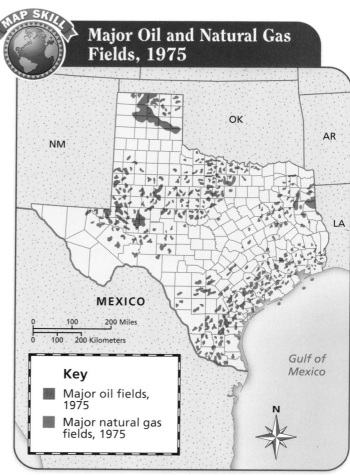

Major Oil and Natural Gas Fields, 1975

Key

Major oil fields, 1975

Major natural gas fields, 1975

▶ Oil and natural gas are important Texas resources.

MAP SKILL Use a Map Key *Which resource was more plentiful in the Panhandle of Texas in 1975, natural gas or oil?*

With the money they earned, Texans bought things. Cars, televisions, and many products came to Texas from other parts of the world.

The oil boom and warm climate of Texas attracted workers from northeastern states. Some industries in the Northeast, such as plants that manufactured steel and cars, were closing.

Other families came from faraway places such as North Korea, South Korea, Pakistan, India, the Philippines, and Vietnam. The face of Texas was changing!

Perhaps you have heard the saying "What goes up must come down." During the 1980s, less than a decade after the oil boom, the oil industry "went bust." The growth of many Texas industries slowed to a snail's pace. Leaders in Texas put their heads together. They decided to attract new industries to the state. No longer would Texas depend mostly on the oil industry.

REVIEW How might the oil and gas boom in the 1970s have affected the owner of a gift shop?

⊙ **Draw Conclusions**

FACT FILE

Other Changing Industries in Texas

AGRICULTURE

Currently three-fourths of Texas land is used for agriculture. Texas farmers normally raise more cotton, cattle, and sheep than do farmers in any other state.

INTERNATIONAL BUSINESS

Businesses around the world have offices in Texas cities such as Dallas, Houston, and San Antonio.

MANUFACTURING

Some Texas factories make airplanes, automobiles, and oil-field equipment. Others process foods and mill lumber.

SERVICE INDUSTRIES

Hospitals, schools, and repair shops are examples of service industries. More Texans work in these industries than in any other type.

TECHNOLOGY

Texas is a leader in high-tech industries. These industries make computers and other electronic equipment.

TRANSPORTATION

The Dallas-Fort Worth International Airport is one of the world's busiest airports.

▶ **Cotton is a major Texas crop.**

Space and Technology

On July 20, 1969, Neil A. Armstrong guided a tiny spacecraft called *Eagle* toward the surface of the moon. His heart raced as he searched for a perfect landing site. Minutes later, the spacecraft touched down. Armstrong began by saying

"Houston, Tranquility Base here. The Eagle has landed."

On the ground, cheers arose from excited workers in the Mission Control Center near Houston. After all, they had helped put the first people on the moon!

Today you can visit "Mission Control" at the Johnson Space Center. It is still the center of operations for our country's piloted space flights. Located in Clear Lake near Houston, the center was renamed in honor of President Lyndon B. Johnson in 1973.

Another part of the Johnson Space Center is the National Aeronautics and Space Administration, or NASA. This group runs the United States space program. NASA trains astronauts. Many young people dream of being an

Map Adventure

Space Center Houston

Look at the map of the visitor's center at the Johnson Space Center, called Space Center Houston. Then answer the questions.

1. You plan to see the displays in order. The Kids Space Place is first on your list. The Mission Status Theater is third. What will your second stop be?

2. What display will you visit next, if you are seeing the displays in order?

3. You would like to buy some freeze-dried pizza like the astronauts eat. Where is the gift shop located?

- IMAX Theatre
- Tram Tour
- The Feel of Space
- Kids Space Place
- Gift Shop
- Starship Gallery
- Mission Status Theatre

Space Center Plaza

Front Door

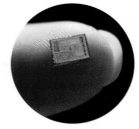

1950 **1955** **1960** **1965** **1970**

UNIVAC, an early computer first used by the U.S. Census Bureau in **1951**, weighed about 16,000 pounds.

This SAC-A satellite was placed in Earth orbit in 1998. The first human-made satellite was launched in **1957**.

The first integrated circuits, or microchips, were made in **1959**. This tiny microchip is from 1982.

An early version of the Internet was established by the U.S. military in **1969**. The Internet as we know it dates from 1983.

The first personal computers began to appear in the **mid-1970s**. This PC is from 1984.

astronaut, a scientist who explores and studies space.

The Johnson Space Center is part of the **aerospace** industry. This industry, which builds and operates spacecraft, brings many jobs to Texas. Specialists, such as scientists and engineers, work there. Other specialists, such as doctors, provide services at the center.

The first African American woman to travel in space, **Dr. Mae C. Jemison,** flew aboard the space shuttle *Endeavour* in 1992. Dr. Jemison has said that, as a child, she would "stare up at the stars and imagine myself among them."

Can you guess what special invention made Jemison's dream possible? It is the microchip. A microchip is much smaller than your little finger. Yet it is the "brain" that makes computers work. Computers can control space flights from the ground.

The microchip opened the door for the high-technology, or **high-tech,** industry. **Technology** is the use of scientific knowledge, skills, and tools

to help people meet their needs. The high-tech industry grew rapidly during the 1980s and 1990s. Texas soon became a center for this industry.

Computers and software made by Texas companies help people communicate and do business. Some of the largest computer companies in the United States are located in Texas.

The **Internet** allows people to share information almost instantly. Press a button on a keyboard in Texas. Zip! The connection could be to another computer across the world. People in many Texas schools, libraries, and businesses communicate daily over the Internet. Perhaps you use the Internet to help you research topics of interest.

These high-tech tools save business owners money and time. They help artists such as musicians and photographers create new and exciting sounds and images.

REVIEW List two details that support the conclusion that the high-tech industry has changed people's lives.
⟲ **Draw Conclusions**

Today and Tomorrow

Many high-tech companies have their main offices in **Dallas** and **Austin.** These companies provide jobs for experts in science and math. The success of the companies has caused these cities to grow larger.

As Texas grows, its citizens must be especially thoughtful about protecting the environment. Think back to information you read in Unit 1 that could help you lead others to make good decisions about the future of your state. How can industrial growth and caring for the Texas environment come about at the same time?

REVIEW How could city planners best deal with traffic jams caused by the many cars of high-tech workers and others coming into Texas cities?
◉ Draw Conclusions

Summarize the Lesson

1969 Neil A. Armstrong walked on the moon.

1970s The demand for oil created a boom.

1990s The high-tech industry brought new businesses to Texas.

★ LESSON 1 **REVIEW**

Check Facts and Main Ideas

1. **Draw Conclusions** On a separate sheet of paper, fill in the "Conclusion" box to answer this question: How might future developments in technology affect life in Texas?

2. What were some types of segregation during the 1950s and 1960s?

3. How did the population of Texas change during the 1970s?

4. What invention opened the door for the high-tech industry?

5. **Critical Thinking: *Conflict Resolution*** What are some challenges and solutions that might go along with working for equal rights?

Facts/Details

Technology has made space travel possible.

Computer technology has created new businesses.

Technology has allowed artists to create new works.

Conclusion

Link to ⚭ **Writing**

Write a Journal Entry Write a short journal entry of a worker at the Johnson Space Center. Describe the day when people reached the moon.

Lyndon Baines Johnson
1908–1973

Lyndon Johnson was born on a farm near Stonewall, Texas. He was the oldest of five children. The Johnson family became poor trying to farm their land.

Lyndon decided that he wanted to lead a different kind of life. When he was twelve years old, he told his classmates that someday he would become President of the United States.

BIOFACT

At the Lyndon Baines Johnson Library and Museum in Austin, a lifelike model of LBJ tells jokes and stories.

In high school, Lyndon's senior class elected him class president. Then he went to college and studied to become a teacher. He taught for one year.

Later, as a politician, Johnson, often called LBJ, fought to improve education for all children. He said,

"Once we considered education a public expense; we know now that it is a public investment."

LBJ became the 36th U.S. President in 1963. The Johnson Space Center near Houston was later named in his honor.

Learn from Biographies

How did Johnson's early career affect his later work as a politician?

For more information, go online to *Meet the People* at **www.sfsocialstudies.com**.

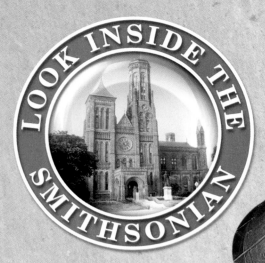

LOOK INSIDE THE SMITHSONIAN

Americans in Space

Engineers and scientists at the Lyndon B. Johnson Space Center in Houston, Texas, help guide the Americans who fly into space. Here are some images and objects from the Apollo moon missions and from more recent space shuttle flights.

Apollo 11 Command Module
Apollo 11's command module was called *Columbia*. Astronaut Michael Collins stayed in *Columbia* while Neil Armstrong and Edwin "Buzz" Aldrin landed the lunar module, named *Eagle*, on the moon.

FIRST MAN ON THE MOON

Moon Mail!
This postage stamp honors Neil Armstrong's first steps on the moon.

Lunar Rover
The Apollo astronauts trained with this lunar rover before their flights to the moon. It is almost identical to the rovers that American astronauts used during the Apollo 15, 16, and 17 moon missions.

Manned Maneuvering Unit
In 1984, Bruce McCandless was the first astronaut to test the manned maneuvering unit, or MMU, on a space shuttle flight. The MMU allows astronauts to do "spacewalks" without needing a lifeline attached to the shuttle.

Spacesuit
Commander David Scott wore this spacesuit on the Apollo 15 moon mission in 1971. Lunar spacesuits were custom-fitted to each astronaut.

Apollo 11 Lunar Module
This model of the lunar module was used in ground training. The original *Eagle* is still on the moon.

Moon Maps
The crew of Apollo 11 carried these lunar maps on the first mission to the moon.

Artifacts are from the Smithsonian Institution.

Map and Globe Skills

Read a Time Zone Map

What? A **time zone** is a region in which people use the same time. The world is divided into twenty-four time zones. The time is different in each time zone. Time zone maps show the difference in time from one region to the next. The map on this page shows the time zones in the United States. Most of Texas is in the Central Time Zone. When it is 12 noon in Lubbock, Texas, it is 1:00 P.M. in Philadelphia, Pennsylvania.

Honolulu

Anchorage

Portland

El Paso

Laredo

Atlanta

Time Zones of North America

Why? Suppose you work for a high-tech company in Austin. You need to make business calls to people around the country. The time in Austin is 10:00 A.M. What time is it in El Paso? in Seattle? in New York City? You can use a time zone map such as the one on page 378 to find out.

You can also use a time zone map when you travel. Will your trip take you to a city in a different time zone? What time will it be when you arrive?

How? To read and understand a time zone map, follow these steps.

• Look at the map. Notice that each time zone is shown in a different color. This makes it easier to tell time zones apart. You can see that parts of some states are in two different time zones. Find Austin and El Paso on the map. In what time zone is each city?

• Next, look at the clock face for each time zone. What times do the clock faces show? When it is 10:00 A.M. in Austin, what time is it in El Paso?

• Compare the times on all the clock faces shown above the map. Begin with the Eastern Time Zone. What do you notice as you move from east to west across the map? What is the time difference between Boston, Massachusetts, and Portland, Oregon?

Think and Apply

1. How many time zones does the United States have?

2. In which time zone is Austin? El Paso?

3. When it is 6:00 P.M. in Salt Lake City, what time is it in Detroit?

4. How can a time zone map help you plan a trip?

For more information, go online to the *Atlas* at **www.sfsocialstudies.com**.

▶ **While children in Texas enjoy lunch, children in Hawaii may be eating breakfast.**

1970   1980   1990   2000

1972
First Texas Folklife Festival opens in San Antonio.

1993
Selena wins a Grammy Award.

1996
First Texas Book Festival opens in Austin.

2001
Lance Armstrong wins his third Tour de France.

Cultural Expressions

PREVIEW

Focus on the Main Idea
Cultural events, cultural leaders, and the arts reflect ideas and ways of life in Texas.

PLACES
San Antonio
Art
The Women's Museum
The Bob Bullock Texas State History Museum
Austin

PEOPLE
Laura Bush
Lance Armstrong
Willie Nelson
Santiago Jimenez, Jr.
Flaco Jimenez
Selena Quintanilla Perez

VOCABULARY
heritage
quinceañera
bat mitzvah
bar mitzvah

EVENTS
Texas Folklife Festival
Kwanzaa
Lunar New Year
Ramadan
Texas Book Festival
Texas Independence Day
Fiesta San Antonio

You Are There

The thermometer reads 102 degrees Fahrenheit in San Antonio. No one at the Texas Folklife Festival seems to mind. Everyone, including you, is busy looking, listening, tasting, touching, and smelling. You are learning about the many cultures in Texas. You sample foods brought to Texas from countries around the world. Each dish tastes so different! You stop to watch Japanese folk dancers. You visit the artists' booths too. You remind yourself to save some time to pet the sheep, listen to bagpipes, and dance "The Cotton-Eyed Joe." Where else could you find such a celebration? Here, at your fingertips, is "The world of Texas"!

Draw Conclusions As you read, use the facts and what you know to draw conclusions about how different cultures make Texas a better state.

A State of Many Cultures

The Texas Folklife Festival in San Antonio has been an annual event since 1972. More than two million visitors have passed through its gates. You can learn about 40 or 50 countries there!

In Unit 2 you read that a culture is a way of life. It is shared by a group of people. You are a member of a culture. You may know culture as language, music, foods, and holidays. Cultures often center around religious beliefs and other beliefs too.

Each cultural group has its own heritage, or shared history. Heritage may be based on an ethnic group. This group of people may share things in common. Language, religious beliefs, and ways of life are examples.

Look at the graph. It shows the different ethnic groups of children who lived in Texas when the 2000 census was taken. About 57 of every 100 Texans younger than 18 belonged to ethnic groups other than white, or

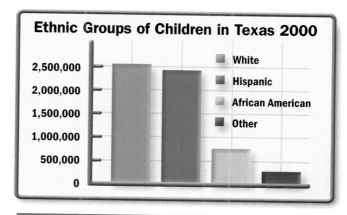

Ethnic Groups of Children in Texas 2000

Legend: White, Hispanic, African American, Other

y-axis values: 0, 500,000, 1,000,000, 1,500,000, 2,000,000, 2,500,000

GRAPH SKILL *The U.S. Census is taken every ten years. What is an example of something this graph tells you?*

Anglo.

Some ethnic groups have different ways of doing things. They each have customs. A custom is the way a group of people does something.

Your cultural group has customs. The types of food you eat and the way you eat are examples of customs.

REVIEW Why do you think the Texas Folklife Festival in San Antonio has attracted more than two million visitors? **◉ Draw Conclusions**

▶ Many artists demonstrate their skills at the Texas Folklife Festival.

Texas Traditions

People from many different cultures live in Texas. They often celebrate special events and keep their own customs. These celebrations and customs are called traditions. Parents and grandparents pass along traditions to their children and grandchildren.

Many Texas families enjoy a Mexican birthday tradition. Children swing a stick and try to break a candy-filled *piñata*. When the piñata breaks, children pick up all the treats. A Mexican girl might celebrate her **quinceañera,** a Hispanic tradition, on her fifteenth birthday with a religious service and a party.

Jewish people welcome their children to the responsibilities of adulthood with a special custom. Girls become a **bat mitzvah** and boys become a **bar mitzvah** when they reach age thirteen. Friends and family come together for a religious ceremony and a party.

Some traditional festivals are held to mark the seasons. Each November, families across Texas celebrate Thanksgiving, a harvest festival, with turkey and pumpkin pie.

Winter traditions in Texas bring cultural and religious celebrations. Christians celebrate the birth of Jesus on Christmas. On this day, it is a tradition for family and friends to exchange gifts.

▶ All across Texas, cultural groups celebrate their heritage through traditions.

Some African Americans celebrate **Kwanzaa,** a tradition based on African harvest festivals. It lasts seven days. It is an opportunity for people to learn about their connections to African culture.

If you are in Houston during January, you might see a grand parade with dragon floats. This is how Asian families in Texas observe the **Lunar New Year,** which is marked by a new moon.

Ramadan is the ninth month of the Islamic calendar. Muslims celebrate the whole month by thinking about their faith and thinking less about everyday things. They don't eat or drink between sunrise and sunset.

Different cultures share many Texas traditions. A new tradition, the annual **Texas Book Festival,** began in Austin in 1996. The festival's founder, First Lady **Laura Bush,** explained,

"By showcasing Texas writers and providing grants to expand library collections, we are investing in our children's future."

In Unit 3, you read that Texas declared its independence from Mexico on March 2, 1836. Many people celebrate **Texas Independence Day** with parades and parties. Citizens of San Antonio have a colorful festival called **Fiesta San Antonio.** It marks the Texans' final victory at San Jacinto on April 21, 1836.

REVIEW How are traditions in Texas alike? How are they different?
Compare and Contrast

▶ Texas First Lady Laura Bush (right) founded the annual Texas Book Festival.

Sports in Texas

You may play sports in school, as well as after school. Some Texans build a career in sports. Athletes in Texas, past and present, have received many awards in sports competitions. Sports are a part of the cultural fabric of Texas. Which of the famous Texas athletes in the Fact File below have you seen on television or in a newspaper?

Cyclist **Lance Armstrong**, from Austin, won the Tour de France in 1999, 2000, and 2001! He is a Texas hero for more reasons than one. You will read more about him on page 387.

REVIEW What is the role of sports in Texas? *Main Idea and Details*

FACT FILE
Sports Stars

Tara Lipinski (1982–)

The youngest world figure skating champion at age fourteen, she earned an Olympic gold medal for figure skating in 1998.

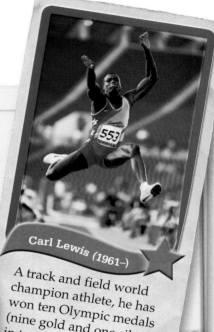
Carl Lewis (1961–)

A track and field world champion athlete, he has won ten Olympic medals (nine gold and one silver) in track and field events.

Mildred (Babe) Didrikson Zaharias (1914–1956)

She won 82 golf tournaments. In the 1932 Olympic Games, she won two gold medals and one silver medal in track and field events.

Lee Trevino (1939–)

He grew up in Dallas and later won the U.S. Open golf tournament twice and the Professional Golf Association (PGA) title two times.

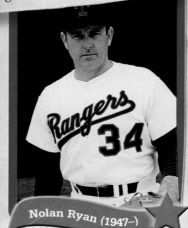
Nolan Ryan (1947–)

He is a member of the Baseball Hall of Fame and holds the career record for most strikeouts thrown.

Sheryl Swoopes (1971–)

A basketball player and Olympic gold medal winner, Swoopes led Texas Tech University to the 1993 national women's basketball title.

State of the Arts

How many states have a town named **Art**? Texas does! The tiny town is near the center of Texas on State Highway 29. But you do not have to live in Art to be a Texas artist.

In 2001 the Texas Cultural Trust Council announced the winners of a new set of awards. They are called the Texas Medal of Arts Awards. The first music award went to singer and songwriter **Willie Nelson.** Musicians and singers **Santiago Jimenez, Jr.,** and his brother **Flaco Jimenez** received the first folk arts award.

Artists in Texas often receive awards from outside Texas too. For example, in 2000, Texas playwright Horton Foote received a National Medal of Arts award.

Earlier, in 1993, singer **Selena Quintanilla Perez** won a Grammy Award for her album *Selena Live*. The Grammy Awards ceremony is telecast each year to an international audience of more than 1.5 billion people in 170 countries! Although Selena died at age twenty-three, her memory lives on through her recordings.

REVIEW What is an example of an award given in Texas to Texas artists? **Main Idea and Details**

▶ **Have you ever seen an electronic quilt? The Women's Museum has one that is 30 feet high!**

Two Museums

In the new millennium, some Texas communities have built museums. In Dallas and Austin, the museums have different purposes.

"Educate a woman and you educate a family." This quote by Jovita Idar is written along the main staircase of **The Women's Museum** in Dallas. This museum honors women from many places, both in and out of Texas. They are leaders in sports, the arts, medicine, politics, and other areas.

Just a few blocks from the Capitol in Austin, **The Bob Bullock Texas State History Museum** sits tall and wide. It tells "The Story of Texas." Each floor has a theme, such as "Encounters on the Land," "Building the Lone Star Identity," and "Creating Opportunity." Exhibitions, such as "It Ain't Braggin If It's True," show real artifacts from Texas cultures.

REVIEW Contrast the museums described above. **Compare and Contrast**

Filmmaking

What city has been called the "Hollywood of Texas"? It is your state capital, **Austin.** Why? During the mid-1990s, filmmakers in California and New York saw Austin and some other areas in Texas as good places to make movies. Austin offered them talented workers, a mild climate, and beautiful scenery.

In 1999 the Texas state government passed a new law to help the filmmaking industry. This law allows filmmakers to borrow money from Texas banks. Filmmakers must use the money to make movies in Texas.

REVIEW Why do you think Austin has been called the "Hollywood of Texas"? **Main Idea and Details**

Summarize the Lesson

1972 First annual Texas Folklife Festival in San Antonio was held.

1993 Selena Quintanilla Perez won a Grammy Award for an album.

1996 The first Texas Book Festival began in Austin.

2001 Cyclist Lance Armstrong won his third championship in the Tour de France.

2001 The first Texas Medal of Arts Awards were announced.

★ LESSON 2 **REVIEW**

Check Facts and Main Ideas

1. ⊙ **Draw Conclusions** On a separate sheet of paper, fill in the "Conclusion" box to answer this question: How do people in Texas feel about culture and the arts?

Facts/Observations

Texans hold festivals to celebrate different cultures.

Texans observe traditions to remind them of their heritage.

Texans honor artists with awards for their work.

Conclusion

2. What are some customs and traditions celebrated by cultural groups in Texas?

3. Name two Jewish celebrations that usually occur when a child turns thirteen and tell how those are different from a quinceañera.

4. Name some contributions of some ethnic and religious groups in Texas.

5. **Critical Thinking:** *Fact and Opinion* List facts about a Texas sports figure or artist. Then tell what you think about her or his accomplishments.

Link to 🔗 **Art**

Make a Storyboard Draw two pictures showing scenes from a movie you're making about a family who has just moved to Texas from another country.

Lance Armstrong
1971–

Lance Armstrong began winning triathlons as a boy living in Plano, Texas. A triathlon is a race that includes swimming, riding a bicycle, and running. He has written,

"When I was in fifth grade, my elementary school held a distance-running race. I told my mother the night before the race, 'I'm going to be a champ.'"

BIOFACT

In 1999, 2000, and 2001, Lance Armstrong completed about 2,200 miles in about 21 days to win the Tour de France.

Lance won the race. He went on to become a champ in many other ways too.

Armstrong became a world cycling champion in 1993. At age twenty-five, he learned that he had cancer. Armstrong fought hard to get well. Finally, his cancer was gone. Armstrong started riding his bicycle again.

Learn from Biographies

How do you think Armstrong's determination to succeed helped him when he was sick?

For more information, go online to *Meet the People* at **www.sfsocialstudies.com**.

TRADE ACROSS

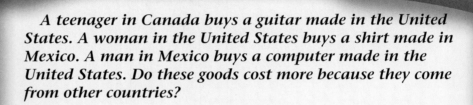

A teenager in Canada buys a guitar made in the United States. A woman in the United States buys a shirt made in Mexico. A man in Mexico buys a computer made in the United States. Do these goods cost more because they come from other countries?

The answer is no, because of NAFTA—the North American Free Trade Agreement. NAFTA is an agreement among the United States, Mexico, and Canada. These countries sell their goods to one another without paying tariffs.

A tariff is like a tax. Governments can charge money to import goods. The United States, Mexico, and Canada no longer charge one another tariffs. They hope that this will encourage the growth of industry and create more jobs.

Some people feel that NAFTA is harmful. They fear that workers in the United States will lose many jobs to Mexico. Mexican workers often are paid lower wages than workers in the United States. Also, some U.S. businesses have set up companies in Mexico to cut down on labor expenses. Some Texans worry about the effects of more trucks on Texas highways.

Some people argue that NAFTA is good for business. More businesses can sell their goods, they say. They point out that trade among all three countries is growing. They think NAFTA is making people's lives better. Here are some viewpoints on NAFTA.

BORDER$

"There never was much opportunity in Silao before. Now there are a lot of jobs."

Alfredo Gomez *automobile plant worker, Silao, Mexico*

"[My company has] had to fight for every new deal, because it seems free trade was meant for the big companies."

Irma Morales *manufacturing company export manager, Mexico*

"NAFTA has been a positive force in trade and investment growth for both the Mexican and U.S. economies."

Lucinda Vargas *economist*

Issues and You

The next time you go to a store, look for products made or grown in Mexico or Canada. Make a list of everything you find. Do the same thing with products that your family buys and uses. Bring your list back to class and discuss it with your friends. Discuss how your lives would be different without these products.

HECHO EN MÉXICO   MADE IN USA   FAIT AU CANADA

Research and Writing Skills

Read a Newspaper

What? A new museum is about to open in your town! How can you find out more about this exciting event? Check your local newspaper. A newspaper is usually printed daily or weekly. It contains news, articles of opinion, and features. It often carries advertising. Some newspapers tell about events in your country and around the world. Others tell about events in your town, county, or state. Some larger newspapers cover all these events.

Making history

Thousands learn about state's varied past on museum's first day for public

By Dick Stanley
AMERICAN-STATESMAN STAFF

[Sue Long] adjusted the souvenir spurs on 5-year-old son [Sam's] running shoes and spoke for many of the more than 3,000 people who toured the new Bob Bullock Texas State History Museum on Saturday at its unheralded public opening.

"It's one of those things you should do a little at a time," [Long] said, standing beneath the 10-ton Lone Star in the entrance plaza of the downtown museum at 1800 N. Congress Ave.

The Bastrop woman was leaving after almost three hours of [Sam's]

"having a ball" among the 34,000 square feet of exhibits on three floors: more than 400 years of Texas history, from Karankawa Indian family mannequins in a dugout canoe on the first floor, two flights up to a scale model of the 1969 *Eagle* moon lander, whose crew's first transmitted word from the moon was "Houston. . . ."

Much of the history is enjoyable. A whimsical Cadillac is studded with rhinestones. Glass cases display the gaudy Hollywood duds of "singing cowboy" Gene Autry and "Ezekiel's Wheel," an improbable aircraft with which an obscure East Texas inventor claimed to have beaten the Wright brothers into the air.

But there also is plenty of unpleasantness to think about and much printed material about it to linger over.

"Texas is rich in unredeemed dreams," a remark from Texas novelist Larry McMurtry, is carved in stone near the entrance.

—from the *Austin American-Statesman,* Sunday, April 22, 2001

Newspapers contain news stories and feature stories. They also contain editorials. Most news stories appear in the front section of a newspaper. These stories give facts about recent events.

Feature stories are detailed reports. They can be about a person, a subject, or an event. Editorials give opinions usually supported by facts. People who manage the newspaper often write the editorials. The newspaper story on page 390 tells about the new Bob Bullock Texas State History Museum.

Why? You cannot be everywhere at once, but you can find out about things that are happening around you. Reading newspapers is a good way to keep up on news at home and around the world.

How? Knowing about the different parts of a newspaper article can help you find information.

• Look at the article on page 390. It appeared in the *Austin American-Statesman*. Notice that the article begins with a headline. A headline tells the main idea of the article in just a few words.

• A byline appears below the headline. The byline gives the name of the person who wrote the story. Many news stories also have a dateline. The dateline tells where a story was written.

• Read the article. A well-written story should answer some or all these questions: *Who* is the story about? *What* is it about? *When* did it take place? *Where* did it take place? *Why* did this event happen? And *how* did the event take place?

Think and Apply

1. Is the article on page 390 a news story or an editorial? How can you tell?

2. How does the story on page 390 answer some or all of the questions *Who? What? When? Where? Why?* and *How?*

3. How can reading newspapers help you in school?

1950	1960	1970

1950s
Segregation continued in Texas and other states.

1960s
Many people joined the Civil Rights Movement.

1969
First people walked on the moon.

1970
Oil boom began.

Chapter Summary

Draw Conclusions

On a separate sheet of paper, fill in a conclusion that you can draw from the information in the three boxes.

By the 1970s many Texans could afford to buy new products.

Businesses in Texas were growing in the 1970s.

Some workers moved to Texas from northeastern states.

Conclusion

Vocabulary

Use each vocabulary word in a sentence that explains its meaning.

1. **segregation** (p. 369)
2. **astronaut** (p. 373)
3. **aerospace** (p. 373)
4. **technology** (p. 373)
5. **high-tech** (p. 373)
6. **heritage** (p. 381)
7. **quinceañera** (p. 382)
8. **bar mitzvah** (p. 382)

People and Events

Match the name of each person or event with the correct description.

1. **Neil A. Armstrong** (p. 372)
2. **Laura Bush** (p. 383)
3. **Lance Armstrong** (p. 384)
4. **Texas Folklife Festival** (p. 381)
5. **Texas Independence Day** (p. 383)
6. **Flaco Jimenez** (p. 385)

a. a celebration of cultures in Texas
b. founder of the Texas Book Festival
c. annual celebration on March 2
d. award-winning musician
e. famous Texas bicyclist
f. first person to set foot on the moon

1980	1990	2000

1972
First Texas
Folklife Festival
began.

1980
High-tech
industries
grew in Texas.

1992
First African
American woman
traveled in space.

1996
First Texas
Book Festival
was held.

2001
Lance Armstrong
won his third
Tour de France.

Facts and Main Ideas

1 In what ways did the Civil Rights Movement change Texas and other states?

2 What caused the oil industry to grow in the 1970s?

3 What is an example of a traditional celebration by a cultural group in Texas?

4 **Time Line** When was the first Texas Folklife Festival held?

5 **Main Idea** Name three ways that Texans' lives changed between 1950 and 2000.

6 **Main Idea** What are two ways in which Texans celebrate the arts in their state?

7 **Critical Thinking:** *Make Generalizations* How has Texas benefitted from having citizens from many different cultures?

Write About History

1 **Design a poster** that celebrates the mixture of cultures in Texas. Include a slogan, or saying, on the poster.

2 **Write a newspaper advertisement** that invites high-tech companies in other states to move their offices and factories to Texas.

3 **Write a brief speech** as the mayor of a growing Texas city in the 1950s. In the speech, explain to the citizens of your town why segregation is wrong.

Apply Skills

Read a Time Zone Map

Look at the time zone map and the clocks on page 378. Then answer the questions.

1 What information does a time zone map give you?

2 When it is 4:00 P.M. in Dallas, what is the time in San Francisco?

3 In what time zone is Denver, Colorado?

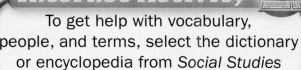

Internet Activity

To get help with vocabulary, people, and terms, select the dictionary or encyclopedia from *Social Studies Library* at **www.sfsocialstudies.com.**

CHAPTER 13

Government in Texas

Lesson 1

Austin
The Capitol of Texas is made of granite.

1

Lesson 2

Texas
Texans celebrate our nation's independence each year on July 4.

2

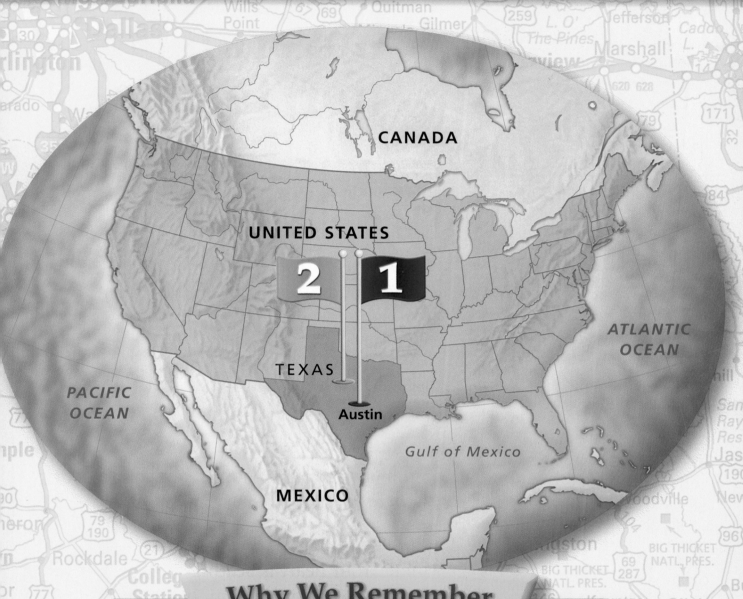

CANADA

UNITED STATES

2 1

TEXAS

ATLANTIC OCEAN

PACIFIC OCEAN

Austin

Gulf of Mexico

MEXICO

Why We Remember

Today's state government is a part of Texas's past and present. Texas government began before 1836, when Texas became an independent nation. Some of the ideas in our state government can be traced to Spanish and Mexican law. Other ideas are a lot like those in the U.S. government. Today's state laws are additions to those in the Texas Constitution of 1876. Of course, new leaders are elected to serve the state. These leaders affect your life in many ways every day.

PREVIEW

Focus on the Main Idea
Local, state, and federal governments provide important services for all Texans.

PLACES
Austin
Washington, D.C.

PEOPLE
Dwight David Eisenhower
Lyndon B. Johnson
George Herbert Walker Bush
George W. Bush

VOCABULARY
citizen
political party
municipal
county
county seat
special district
executive branch
veto
legislative branch
judicial branch
appeal

Government for Texans

You Are There

The election is finally over. The students in Mrs. Wong's class have voted for class president. You hope to win the election. You will be proud to speak for all the students in your class.

Whoever is elected class president gets to meet the mayor of your city. She is coming next week to visit your school. You have seen her on the local television news station.

You want to learn more about your mayor and the job she does. But right now, Mrs. Wong is about to announce the winner. Your heart is beating faster. You shake hands with the other candidate. Then you wait to hear who has won. Will it be you?

 Draw Conclusions After you read the lesson, stop to think about the jobs that Texas leaders do. What can you conclude about their responsibility to the people they represent?

What Is a Government Leader?

The students in Mrs. Wong's class have a type of government. As you know, governments are made up of people who lead and represent others.

Many leaders are elected, or chosen by vote. Would you like to be elected as a government leader such as a governor or senator? First, you would have to persuade people to vote for you. Then an election would take place. If you gain the most votes, you win!

Other people who work in government are appointed, or chosen without a vote, by leaders. For example, the Texas secretary of state is appointed by the governor.

Appointed leaders serve your needs as a citizen. A **citizen** is a member of a nation, state, county, or town.

Because Texas is part of the United States, national leaders serve Texans, along with all other U.S. citizens. Four Texans have served as President of the United States! These leaders have represented both the Democratic and Republican political parties. A **political party** is an organized group of people who share similar ideas about how to run the government.

Dwight David Eisenhower was born in Denison, Texas, in 1890. He was commander of the Allied forces during World War II. He became President of the United States in 1953.

On page 375, you read about **Lyndon B. Johnson.** He was elected Vice-President of the United States in 1961. He became President after President John F. Kennedy was killed in 1963. Johnson was elected President in 1964.

George Herbert Walker Bush and his son **George W. Bush** have both served as President. George H. W. Bush was born in Massachusetts. George W. Bush was born in Connecticut but grew up in Midland, Texas. Both men lived and worked in Texas for many years.

REVIEW Name four Texans who have been U.S. Presidents. Main Idea and Details

▶ Dwight D. Eisenhower (Republican) was U.S. President from 1953 to 1961.

▶ Lyndon B. Johnson (Democrat) was U.S. President from 1963 to 1969.

▶ George Herbert Walker Bush (Republican) was U.S. President from 1989 to 1993.

▶ George W. Bush (Republican) began his term as U.S. President in 2001.

Local Government

Texans have three types of local government: city government, county government, and special districts. Each type serves citizens in different ways. If you live in a Texas city or town, you may be governed by all three types of local government. Rural areas often have county government and special districts.

Municipal means "of a city." A city's self-government is often called a municipal government. It serves citizens in towns and cities. This type of government provides important services such as police and fire protection. It also takes care of city parks and libraries.

Suppose you see a broken swing at the park. You know that this can be dangerous. What should you do? In many towns, you could call the parks department. People in this department make sure that parks are safe and clean. They will want to know about any problems at city parks.

The chart on this page shows the two forms of municipal government. An elected mayor heads one form. An elected manager heads the other. In both, council members, who are elected by citizens, make laws and help run the government. Other departments, such as the police, fire, and parks department, report to the mayor or the manager.

Gordon Quan is a city council member in Houston, Texas. Here is what he has to say about municipal government:

"Voices from every community should be included in the decision-making process."

▶ What type of municipal government is in place in your city or a city near you?

▶ **Many courthouses in Texas, such as this one in Corsicana, are known for their attractive design.**

Another type of local government is **county** government. A county is one of the sections into which a state is divided. Most counties are larger than cities. Texas is made up of 254 counties. Each one has a county seat. A **county seat** is a city or town chosen to be the center of government for that county.

Four county commissioners, or people with special duties, and one county judge are elected to lead a county government. Counties also hold elections for sheriff. The sheriff makes sure that people obey county and state laws. The sheriff's department provides protection for people who do not live within a city or town.

County governments serve people in many ways. They keep records of births, deaths, and marriages. They register people to vote. Counties also operate jails and take care of certain roads.

The third type of local government is the **special district.** It is run by an elected group of people. Each special district has a certain purpose. Some special districts manage water resources in an area. Others provide fire protection in rural areas.

One special district you may know about is a school district. This district oversees all the schools in its area. What is the name of your school district?

Citizens in a school district vote for school board members, or trustees. This board decides how schools in the district will be run. How do trustees make decisions? You can see for yourself! All people who live in the district are welcome at most school board meetings.

REVIEW Why do citizens need three different types of local government?
⊙ Draw Conclusions

State Government

Austin is the center of state government in Texas. It is home to the governor's mansion and many state government office buildings. It is also home to the Capitol.

Texas state government is divided into three parts, or branches. They are the executive branch, the legislative branch, and the judicial branch. The Texas Constitution gives each branch certain powers.

Our state constitution also calls for the three branches to work separately. This balances power among the branches.

The executive branch makes sure that laws are enforced. The governor heads the executive branch. He or she provides leadership and appoints many state officials. Governors are elected by the people of Texas.

Suppose you are the governor of Texas. What would your duties and responsibilities be? You could suggest new laws for the legislature to pass. You would sign new laws. You would have veto power. This means that if you did not agree with a new law, you could veto, or refuse to sign, it. The law would then go back to the legislature. A vetoed law can still be passed if two-thirds of the legislators vote for it.

▶ The Texas government, like the United States government, has three branches.

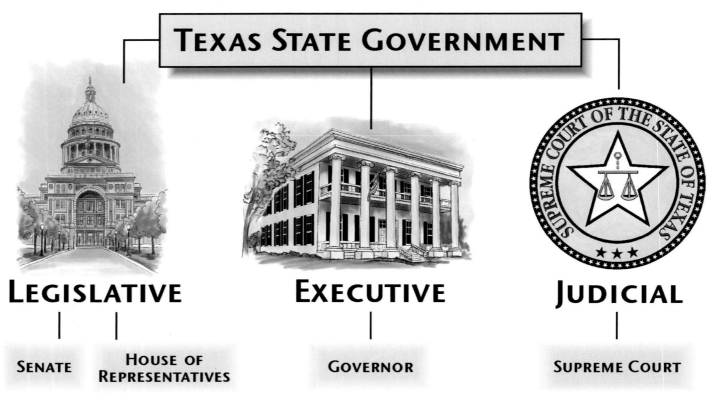

TEXAS STATE GOVERNMENT

LEGISLATIVE	EXECUTIVE	JUDICIAL
SENATE HOUSE OF REPRESENTATIVES	GOVERNOR	SUPREME COURT

▶ In Austin, Texas, laws are made inside the Capitol, where legislators meet to vote on them.

The executive branch has more than 200 agencies. Agencies are groups that make sure certain laws are followed. One of these agencies is the Texas Education Agency. It oversees all the schools in Texas.

The **legislative branch** makes the laws for our state. This branch has two groups. One is the Senate, with 31 members. The other is the House of Representatives, with 150 members. The state is divided into political districts. Voters from these districts elect senators and representatives.

The lieutenant governor heads the Senate. This person is elected by the people of Texas. The speaker of the house heads the House of Representatives. He or she is chosen by members of the House of Representatives.

The **judicial branch** is made up of courts and judges. Its job is to make sure that state laws are applied fairly.

Texas has more than 2,000 courts and nearly 3,000 judges. Many of these serve local areas. District courts are where some jury trials take place. The Texas Supreme Court and the Court of Criminal Appeals are the state's highest courts.

The Texas Supreme Court listens to and judges questions about the Texas Constitution. The Supreme Court's nine members are elected by the people of Texas. The Court of Criminal Appeals hears criminal cases. People who have been found guilty of a crime have the right to **appeal**, or ask for another trial. The Court of Criminal Appeals also has nine elected members.

REVIEW How do leadership roles differ between the executive branch and the legislative branch?
Compare and Contrast

401

How a Bill Becomes a Law

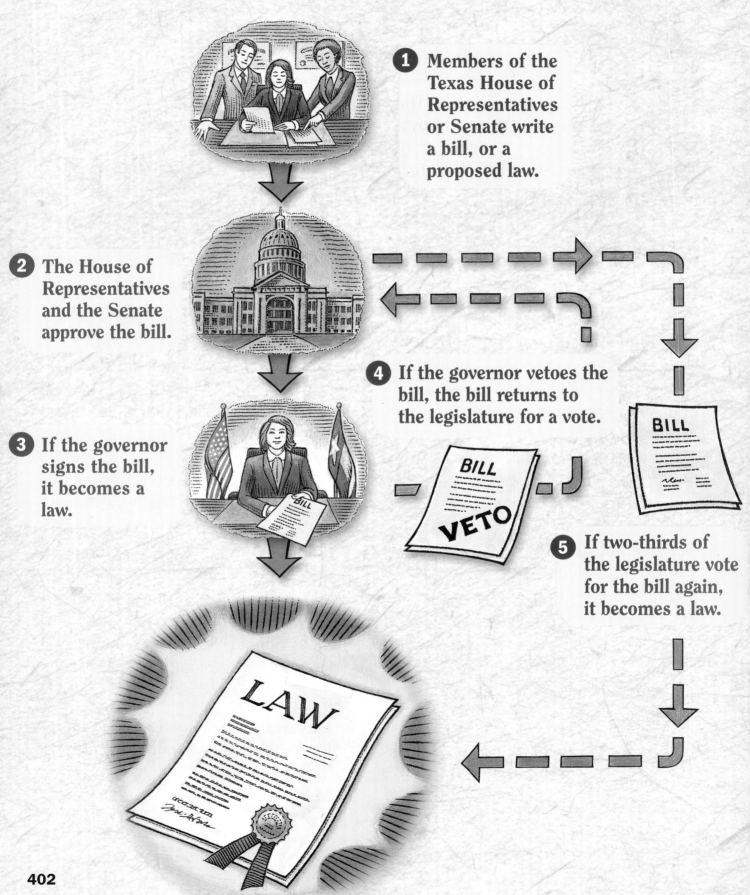

1. Members of the Texas House of Representatives or Senate write a bill, or a proposed law.

2. The House of Representatives and the Senate approve the bill.

3. If the governor signs the bill, it becomes a law.

4. If the governor vetoes the bill, the bill returns to the legislature for a vote.

5. If two-thirds of the legislature vote for the bill again, it becomes a law.

BILL

BILL VETO

LAW

The U.S. Government

Washington, D.C., is the capital of the United States. It is the center of the nation's government. Like the Texas government, it has three branches—legislative, executive, and judicial. The branches work together to govern the country and to protect the rights of all U.S. citizens. Many Texans have jobs in the U.S. government. They work to serve all the citizens of our country. You will read more about national government in Grade 5.

REVIEW Both the U.S. and Texas governments have three branches. What conclusion can you draw from this fact? ⦿ **Draw Conclusions**

Summarize the Lesson

- **Local government serves people in towns, cities, and counties.**
- **State government, based in Austin, serves all Texans and is made up of the executive branch, the legislative branch, and the judicial branch.**
- **Washington, D.C., is the capital of the United States.**

▶ **The U.S. Capitol in Washington, D.C.**

★ LESSON 1

REVIEW

Check Facts and Main Ideas

1. ⦿ **Draw Conclusions** On a separate sheet of paper, fill in the spaces to answer the following question: What qualities make a person a good leader?

    Facts

    | Leaders must know how the government works. |

    Conclusion

    What I Know from Experience

    | My representative cares about people in her district. She fought to get money for new roads here. |

2. Name three of the four Texans who have served as U.S. President.
3. What are three types of local government?
4. What are the three branches of the Texas government? What is the function of each branch?
5. **Critical Thinking:** *Cause and Effect* What is one result of separating powers among branches of a government?

Link to ⚬⚬ **Drama**

Stage a Local Government Meeting In a small group, discuss a local issue, such as whether or not to change the speed limit in a school zone. Take turns role-playing local government officials and other participating citizens.

IN THE WESTERN HEMISPHERE

Austin and Saltillo— Sister Cities

It may surprise you to know that a city in Mexico was once the capital of Texas. Remember that long before it became a republic, Texas was part of Mexico. In 1824, Mexico combined the land known today as Texas with the Mexican state of Coahuila.

Texas became a republic in 1836 and a state in 1845. Austin is now the capital of Texas, and Saltillo is the capital of the Mexican state of Coahuila.

▶ Aurelio and Rosa Marie Torres moved to Austin from Saltillo in 1988. Today they own and operate a restaurant in Austin. Aurelio Torres's family still visits Saltillo "to renew our batteries," he says.

▶ Saltillo Plaza is an outdoor public meeting place in Austin.

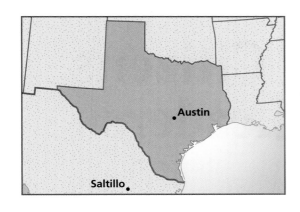

Saltillo is located in the mountains of northern Mexico. It is more than 400 years old. One of its most beautiful buildings is the Santiago Cathedral. This church took more than 200 years to build. There are many other public buildings to visit in Saltillo. One of these is the Palace of Government. It has a huge painting in the central patio. In 1968, leaders in Austin and Saltillo declared the two capitals "sister cities." Citizens in both cities celebrated the new bond.

In 1999, Austin named its new outdoor public square Saltillo Plaza. It was built like the open-air marketplaces in Mexico. People gather on the plaza for celebrations, food, and musical events.

► People in Saltillo, Mexico, gather for public events and to visit on this large, open plaza in front of Santiago Cathedral.

405

Houston

Texas Citizens and Leaders

PREVIEW

Focus on the Main Idea
There are different ways to become a citizen, but all citizens have certain rights and responsibilities.

PLACES
Houston

PEOPLE
Barbara Jordan
Kay Bailey Hutchison
Sheila Jackson Lee
Henry B. González
Henry G. Cisneros
John Tower

VOCABULARY
responsibility
volunteer
orator

> **You Are There**

Fireworks pop. Laughter fills your house in Rockport, Texas. Today your parents have become citizens of the United States. Your family and friends have come to celebrate!

Your mother places a tray of *bahn chung* on the table. Usually, this rich pastry is served only on special holidays such as *Tet*, the Vietnamese New Year.

You think back to when your family moved to Texas from Vietnam. You didn't speak English then. You are proud of everything your family has learned.

Your parents worked long and studied hard to become citizens. Now you and your parents enjoy the same rights as all other United States citizens. That's something to celebrate!

Draw Conclusions As you read, think about ways in which you might become more involved in your local and state government.

▶ **This doll wears a traditional dress from the Vietnamese city of Hue and plays an instrument called a Dan Ty Ba.**

The Role of the Individual

A citizen is a person who is protected by and obeys the laws of a particular country. Citizens are born in that country or, as the You Are There describes, have earned the right to become a citizen of the country.

In the United States, citizens have certain freedoms and rights. Freedom of speech, freedom of religion, and voting rights are some basic rights of citizens. Some of these rights, such as the right to vote, are limited. For example, you have to be at least eighteen years old to vote in an election.

Voting is both a right and a **responsibility,** or something that adult citizens should do. Another responsibility citizens have is to help solve problems where they live. Good citizens find ways to **volunteer,** or give their time, in their communities and state. For example, many volunteers help at senior citizen centers, hospitals, child care centers, and schools. Some people volunteer to help keep roadways, beaches, and waterways clean.

REVIEW What are some rights and responsibilities of citizens? **Summarize**

▶ **Texas citizens celebrate Independence Day.**

State and Local Leaders

Citizens vote in elections to choose leaders for local, state, and national offices. You have read about many Texans who hold those offices. When you are eighteen, you will be old enough to vote. But even today, you may contact your elected and appointed leaders to ask questions, offer your opinions, and state some facts. The Fact File below shows some ways in which citizens can contact their local and state leaders.

REVIEW Why might someone choose to contact a local or state leader?
⊙ Draw Conclusions

FACT FILE

How to Contact Your Local and State Leaders

Your elected and appointed leaders work for you. What matters most to you? saving native plants? keeping roadways clean? changing voting rules? You can call or write your local and state leaders to let them know what you think. Here are some ways to get in touch with state leaders.

Governor
P.O. Box 12428
Austin, Texas 78711-2428
1 (512) 463-2000

Speaker of the House
P.O. Box 2910
Austin, Texas 78768-2910
1 (512) 463-1000

Lieutenant Governor
P.O. Box 12068
Austin, Texas 78711-2068
1 (512) 463-0001

Supreme Court Justice
P.O. Box 12248
Austin, Texas 78711
1 (512) 463-1312

To learn more about your state government, you can go to these World Wide Web sites:
- http://www.senate.state.tx.us/kids/
- http://www.governor.state.tx.us/kids/index.html
- http://www.house.state.tx.us/
- http://www.courts.state.tx.us/publicinfo/overview.htm

Representing Texas in Washington, D.C.

What leadership qualities do leaders in your school share? Most people want leaders who are honest, caring, brave, and knowledgeable. You have read about Texas leaders like Lyndon Johnson. On page 411 you will read a biography of **Barbara Jordan** from **Houston.** In 1972 she became the first African American woman from the South to be elected to the U.S. Congress. Jordan, a Democrat, was well known as an **orator,** a skillful and powerful public speaker. Other Texas leaders, too, have represented Texas at the national level.

Senator Kay Bailey Hutchison was named "Texan of the Year" in 1997.

Kay Bailey Hutchison, a Republican, was the first woman to represent Texas in the U.S. Senate. She held jobs in business and in state government before being elected senator.

Sheila Jackson Lee, a Democrat, represents a part of Houston in the U.S. House of Representatives. She served on the Houston city council and as an associate municipal court judge for the city of Houston.

Sheila Jackson Lee was elected to the U.S. House of Representatives.

Henry B. González, a Democrat, served as a council member for the city of San Antonio and as a state senator. In 1961, he was elected to a seat in the U.S. Congress. He was the first Hispanic from Texas to hold that office. He served for 37 years.

▶ Henry B. González was the first Hispanic Texan elected to the Texas Senate in more than 100 years.

Henry G. Cisneros, a Democrat, was the mayor of San Antonio from 1981 to 1989. He was selected as one of the "Ten Outstanding Young Men in America" in 1981. In 1993, he became U.S. Secretary of Housing and Urban Development.

▶ Henry G. Cisneros was named "Outstanding Mayor" and "Hispanic Man of the Year."

Before his death in 1991, **John Tower,** a Republican, had a long career of service to Texas and the United States. In 1961, at age 35, he became the youngest person in the U.S. Senate.

▶ John Tower was the first Republican senator from Texas since 1870.

REVIEW What leadership quality is most important to you? Tell why.

Summarize

Into the Future

The year is 2030. As in the past, leaders have come together at the state Capitol to serve Texas citizens. Are you one of tomorrow's leaders?

You have already taken the first step toward leadership. That step is learning about the rights and duties of citizens. Other steps might include volunteering, reading about leaders, and finding other ways to serve your community. No step is too small. After all, you are helping shape the future of Texas.

REVIEW What kinds of people often grow up to become leaders?
Draw Conclusions

Summarize the Lesson

- All citizens have certain rights.
- All citizens have certain duties and responsibilities.
- Even though leaders can come from different backgrounds, most share qualities of leadership.
- Students today will be the leaders of tomorrow.

★ LESSON 2 REVIEW

Check Facts and Main Ideas

1. **Draw Conclusions** On a separate sheet of paper, fill in the spaces to answer the following question:

   What makes a person a good citizen?

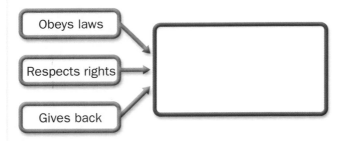

Obeys laws →

Respects rights →

Gives back →

2. What are two ways in which people become citizens?
3. Name some Texas citizens who have become government leaders.
4. What are some responsibilities of citizens?
5. **Critical Thinking:** *Draw Conclusions* Why is it important for citizens to have duties and responsibilities as well as rights?

Link to ⊶ Writing

Write a Speech Think of an important issue in your school or community. Write a speech to persuade others of your point of view. Present your speech to a friend.

Barbara Jordan
1936–1996

Barbara Jordan grew up in a poor neighborhood in Houston, Texas. One important gift Barbara received from her family was the gift of public speaking. Because Barbara and her sisters were not allowed to go to dances, parties, or movies, they spent time at the church where their father preached and their mother often spoke. Barbara learned a lot about public speaking by listening to her parents.

BIOFACT

Barbara Jordan became the first southern African American woman to serve in the U.S. Congress (1973–1979).

In high school, Barbara Jordan became the star of her debate team. She also decided to become a lawyer. This was an unusual goal because, at that time, few African American women were lawyers. Jordan later said,

"I never intended to become a run-of-the-mill person."

As a young lawyer, she worked hard to strengthen rights for African Americans. She then became a member of the Texas legislature and was later elected to the United States Congress.

Learn from Biographies
How do you think Jordan's early life helped her find success in politics later on?

For more information, go online to *Meet the People* at **www.sfsocialstudies.com**.

▶ Girl Scouts can earn badges, such as this Citizenship badge, to symbolize their achievements.

Known for Honesty

Making good decisions is not always easy. Sometimes the best decisions require honesty, or telling the truth to yourself and others. Why is being honest an important part of decision making?

Tameka Grayson, who is a Girl Scout in Austin, says it is important to tell the truth so that people will trust you. Tameka tries to be honest, in part, to follow the Girl Scout Law. This law describes goals, rather than duties or responsibilities.

I will do my best to be:
Honest and fair,
Friendly and
helpful . . .

Girl Scouts in Texas, in other parts of the United States, and throughout the world practice the same Girl Scout Law. That is one reason Girl Scouts are known for their honesty.

BUILDING
CITIZENSHIP
Caring
Respect
Responsibility
Fairness
⭐ Honesty
Courage

Tameka has learned many things about honesty by being a Girl Scout. For example, her troop participates in the annual Girl Scout cookie sale. This is a way Girl Scouts can earn money for troop activities, from trips to volunteer service projects. Before the sales begin, each troop discusses what to do with any money its members might earn. Tameka sold 288 boxes of cookies in 2000 for $3.00 per box. "All the girls turned in the money we earned," she said.

Honesty in Action

What kinds of decisions have you made that you are proud of? Did honesty play an important role in your decision? Explain.

Write Notes and Outlines

What? Notes are bits of information you write in your own words. An **outline** is a framework for organizing information. It helps you see main ideas and details at a glance.

Volunteering the Texas Way

Volunteerism has always been an important part of the Texas culture. Without volunteers, many jobs would be left undone. Even though volunteers aren't paid wages for the good deeds they do, they receive a feeling of satisfaction in helping other people and their communities.

Texana Faulk Conn is a Texas volunteer. She has spent about 65 years helping the deaf and hearing impaired. At only five years old, she became friends with a hearing-impaired girl named Ella. The friendship would later inspire Conn to volunteer her time helping deaf people gain their full rights in society.

Seventy years later, Conn explains,

"For many years, the police would send a car out to my house at three o'clock in the morning to take me to the jail, where a deaf person had been imprisoned. I would interpret for the prisoner. My purpose wasn't to get him out of jail. I simply wanted to help him tell his story and understand the charges placed against him. Those are the rights of any other citizen."

Former Texas governor Ann Richards appointed Conn chair of the Texas Commission for the Deaf and Hard of Hearing. Today all deaf and hearing-impaired Texans are allowed an interpreter by law.

Why? Can you remember everything you read? Holding all that information in your head is next to impossible! Taking notes helps you recall what you read. Suppose you are asked to write a report about outstanding Texas volunteers. How will you keep track of your information? How will you organize it? You could take notes. Then you could use your notes to create an outline. Taking notes and making an outline are also useful ways to study for a test.

How? Follow these steps to take notes and create an outline.

• As you read, look for main ideas and important details. Write these on a sheet of paper or on note cards. Write each main idea as a heading on your card.

• Write important facts and details below the heading. Use your own words. Be sure to write the title of the source, the author's name, the publication date, and the page number in your notes.

• Sort your note cards. Put the cards in an order that makes sense. Then use your cards to create an outline.

• Write the main ideas from your cards next to Roman numerals. Then write important facts about those ideas next to capital letters.

Texas Volunteers

I. Texana Faulk Conn
   A. Had childhood friend who was deaf
   B. Was inspired to help others

II Volunteer Work
   A.
   B. Appointed chair of Texas Commission for the Deaf and Hard of Hearing

▶ **A Roman numeral signals a main idea. A capital letter signals a fact that supports the main idea.**

Think and Apply

❶ Take notes on the article on page 414. Write down the main idea of each paragraph in the article.

❷ In the Texas Volunteers outline, what important fact can go next to *A* under numeral *II*?

❸ How can taking notes and creating an outline help you write a report?

1950   1960   197

1953
Dwight D.
Eisenhower
became
President.

1963
Lyndon B.
Johnson
became
President.

Chapter Summary

Draw Conclusions

On a separate sheet of paper, fill in the "Conclusion" box to answer this question: How do the three branches of state government balance each other?

> The legislative branch makes the laws.

> The executive branch makes sure that laws are enforced.

> The judicial branch makes sure that laws are applied fairly.

Vocabulary

Match each word with the correct definition or description.

1 executive branch (p. 400)

2 legislative branch (p. 401)

3 judicial branch (p. 401)

4 appeal (p. 401)

a. branch that makes sure laws are applied fairly

b. ask for another trial

c. the lawmaking body of a government

d. branch that makes sure that laws are enforced

People

Write a sentence explaining why each of the following people has been important to government in Texas and in the United States.

1 Dwight D. Eisenhower (p. 397)

2 George Herbert Walker Bush (p. 397)

3 George W. Bush (p. 397)

4 Kay Bailey Hutchison (p. 409)

5 Sheila Jackson Lee (p. 409)

6 Henry B. González (p. 409)

7 Henry G. Cisneros (p. 409)

8 John Tower (p. 409)

1980   1990   2000

1972
Barbara Jordan
is elected to the
U.S. Congress.

1981
Henry G. Cisneros
is elected mayor
of San Antonio.

1989
George Herbert
Walker Bush
becomes President.

2001
George W. Bush
becomes President.

Facts and Main Ideas

1. What are two examples of types of local leaders?

2. What is the key to balancing power among the three branches of state and national government?

3. What are two ways to serve your community?

4. **Time Line** How many years after his father became President did George W. Bush begin serving as U.S. President?

5. **Main Idea** What is the main job of local and national government leaders?

6. **Main Idea** What are two duties you have as a citizen of Texas?

7. **Critical Thinking:** *Make Generalizations* What qualities do you think most citizens want in a leader?

Write About History

1. **Write a list** of the three leadership qualities you think are most important in a school board member. Tell why these qualities are important.

2. **Write a letter** to your mayor. Tell about the issues in your city that matter most to you.

3. **Write a paragraph of introduction** for a citizenship handbook. Explain the most important duties of being a citizen.

Apply Skills

Write Notes and Outlines

Read the following part of an outline. Then answer the questions.

> I. Ways to Become a Citizen
>
>   A. Be born in the United States
>
>   B. Be born outside the United States to U.S. citizens
>
>   C. Become a citizen by earning citizenship

1. What is the topic, or main idea, of this section of the outline?

2. How are notes useful in making an outline?

3. How is an outline useful?

Internet Activity

To get help with vocabulary, people, and terms, select the dictionary or encyclopedia from *Social Studies Library* at **www.sfsocialstudies.com.**

417

"Texas, Our Texas"

William J. Marsh

The music for "Texas, Our Texas" was written in 1924 by William J. Marsh of Fort Worth. He wrote the words with Gladys Yoakum Wright. "Texas, Our Texas" became the state song of Texas in 1929 after it won a state song contest. Famous composer John Philip Sousa said that "Texas, Our Texas" was the finest state song he had ever heard.

"Texas, Our Texas"

Words by Gladys Yoakum Wright and William J. Marsh

Music by William J. Marsh

1. Tex - as, our Tex - as! All hail the might - y state!
2. Tex - as, O Tex - as! your free - born sin - gle star
3. Tex - as, dear Tex - as! From ty - rant grip now free.

Tex - as, our Tex - as! So won - der - ful, so great!
Sends out its ra - diance to na - tions near and far.
Shines forth in splen - dor your star of des - ti - ny!

Bold - est and grand - est, With - stand - ing ev - 'ry test;
Em - blem of free - dom! It sets our hearts a - glow
Moth - er of he - roes! We come, your chil - dren true.

O Em - pire wide and glo - rious, You stand su - preme - ly blest.
With thoughts of San Ja - cin - to and glo - rious A - la - mo.
Pro - claim - ing our al - le - giance, Our faith, our love for you.

REFRAIN

God bless you, Tex - as! And keep you brave and strong,

That you may grow in pow'r and worth, Through-out the ag - es long.

God bless you, Tex - as! And keep you brave and strong,

That you may grow in pow'r and worth, Through-out the ag - es long.

Main Ideas and Vocabulary

TEST PREP

Read the passage below and use it to answer the questions that follow.

The story of Texas is the story of change. Industry began to change in Texas during the 1970s. The worldwide demand for oil increased in the 1970s. Prices of oil and gas went up. Money from the sale of oil and gas products brought new wealth to Texas.

People moved to Texas from other parts of the United States and from other countries. Many of them wanted to share in the wealth. Oil prices fell in the 1980s, but Texas remained a major producer of oil and gas.

Other important industries grew during the last part of the 1900s. One was the aerospace industry. Scientists at the Johnson Space Center guided the first <u>astronauts</u> to the moon while the world watched.

In the 1980s, Texas became a center of the <u>high-tech</u> industry. Computers and software businesses opened main offices in Texas cities. Once again, people from other parts of the United States and the world were drawn to the state.

Texas faces many challenges for the future. State and local governments have a duty to Texans. They must find ways to provide needed services. More than ever, Texas citizens and leaders must work together to guide Texas through the twenty-first century.

1 According to the passage, which of these Texas industries boomed in the 1970s?
A manufacturing industry
B automobile industry
C oil industry
D housing industry

2 Why did many people move to Texas during the 1970s?
A to farm
B to share in the wealth
C to train horses
D to join a team

3 In this passage, the word *astronauts* means—
A people who build spaceships
B explorers of outer space
C engineers who study the moon
D people who teach about space travel

4 In this passage, the word *high-tech* means based on—
A computers and other electronic instruments
B the exploration of bodies in space
C games and educational materials
D the production of oil and gas

Vocabulary and People

Match each word or the name of each person with the correct definition or description.

1 **Mae C. Jemison** (p. 373)

2 **Laura Bush** (p. 383)

3 **municipal** (p. 398)

4 **volunteer** (p. 407)

a. the founder of the Texas Book Festival

b. having to do with a city

c. the first African American woman in space

d. a person who gives of his or her time

Write and Share

Prepare a Museum Display Make a list of the most important events and people in Texas from 1950 to the present. Choose one event or person. Write a brief paper on the topic of your choice. Share your topic with other class members.

Apply Skills

Write a Newspaper Article Write a brief newspaper article. Tell about a new candidate for Texas governor. In the article, write about some of the plans the candidate has for the future of Texas. Make sure that the first paragraph of the article answers the questions *Who? What? When? Where? Why?* and *How?*

Read on Your Own

Look for books like these in the library.

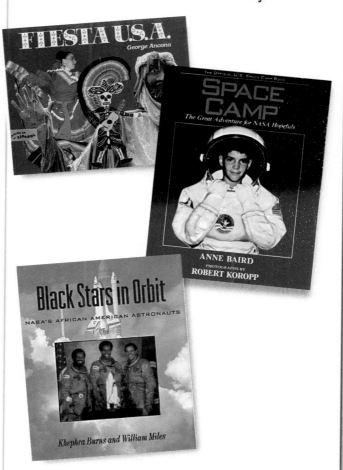

Great State

Create a booklet that shows what's great about Texas today—and what will be great in the future.

1 **Form** a group. Choose a current event in Texas.

2 **Write** a paragraph about the event. Predict what will happen in the future and write several sentences.

3 **Draw** or find pictures that illustrate the event today and what might occur in the future.

4 **Put** your group's paragraphs and pictures together into a booklet. Share it with the class.

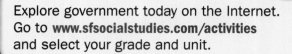

Internet Activity

Explore government today on the Internet. Go to **www.sfsocialstudies.com/activities** and select your grade and unit.

Table of Contents

ATLAS: *World and United States*

Photograph of the Continents	R2
Map of the World: Political	R4
Map of the World: Physical	R6
Map of the Western Hemisphere: Political	R8
Map of the Western Hemisphere: Physical	R9
Map of the United States of America	R10
Map of the United States: Political	R12
Map of the United States: Physical	R14

Geography Terms   **R16**

Facts About Our Fifty States   **R18**

United States Documents: The Declaration of Independence   **R22**

ATLAS: *Texas*

Texas Physical	R26
Texas Road Map	R27
Texas Counties	R28
Texas Temperature and Precipitation	R30

Texas Governors   **R31**

Texas Time Line   **R32**

Texas Missions   **R36**

Flag Etiquette   **R38**

Texas Symbols   **R40**

Gazetteer   **R41**

Biographical Dictionary   **R45**

Glossary   **R51**

Index   **R57**

Credits   **R71**

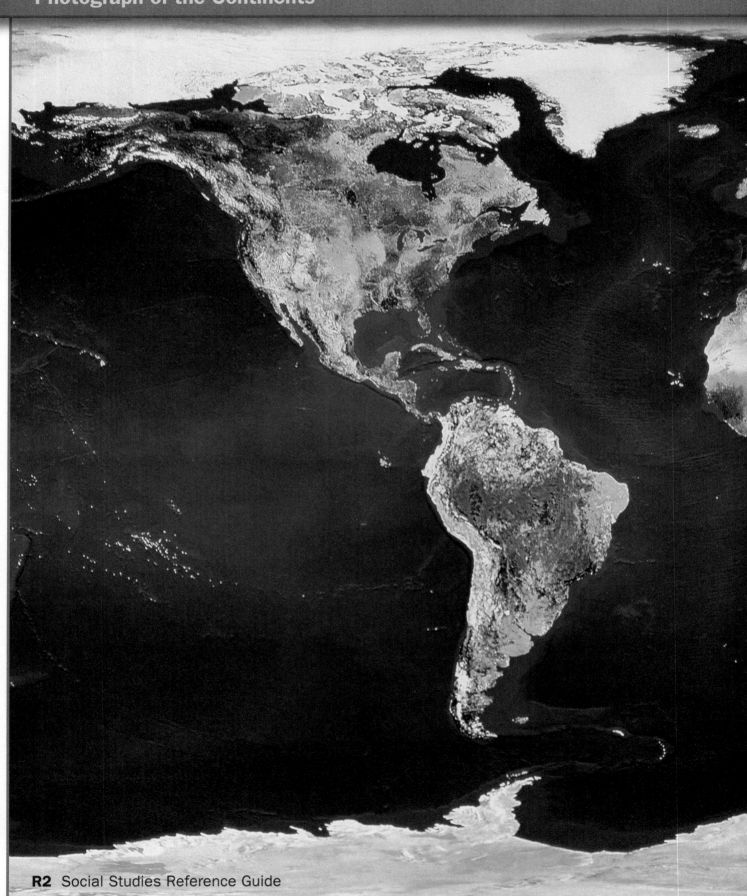

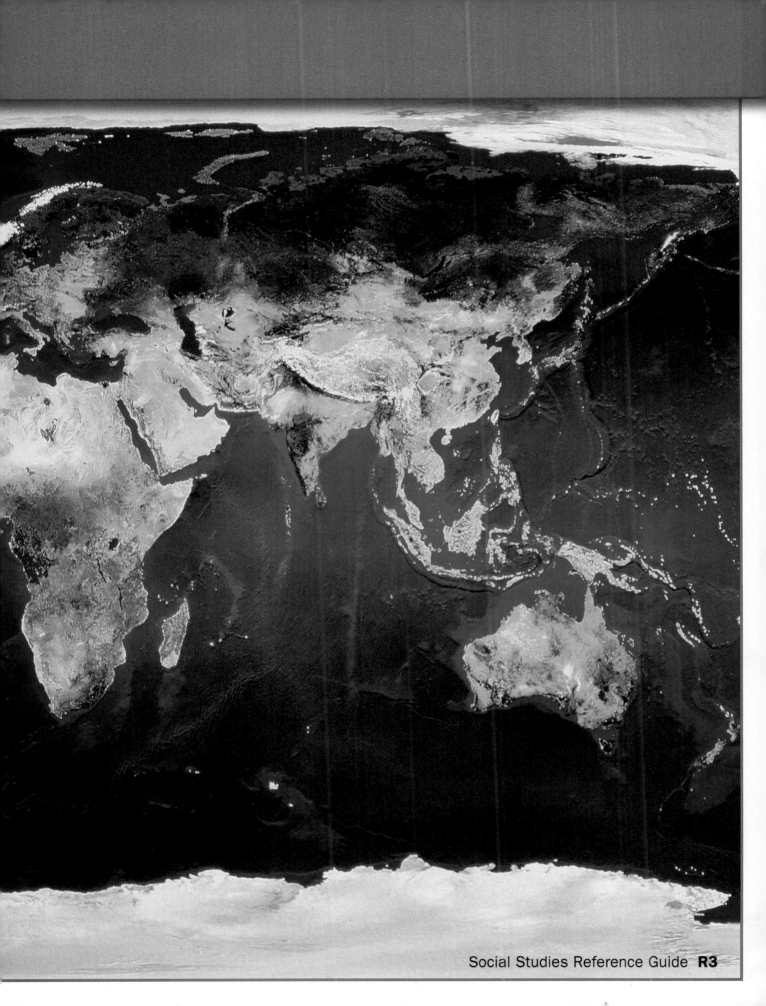

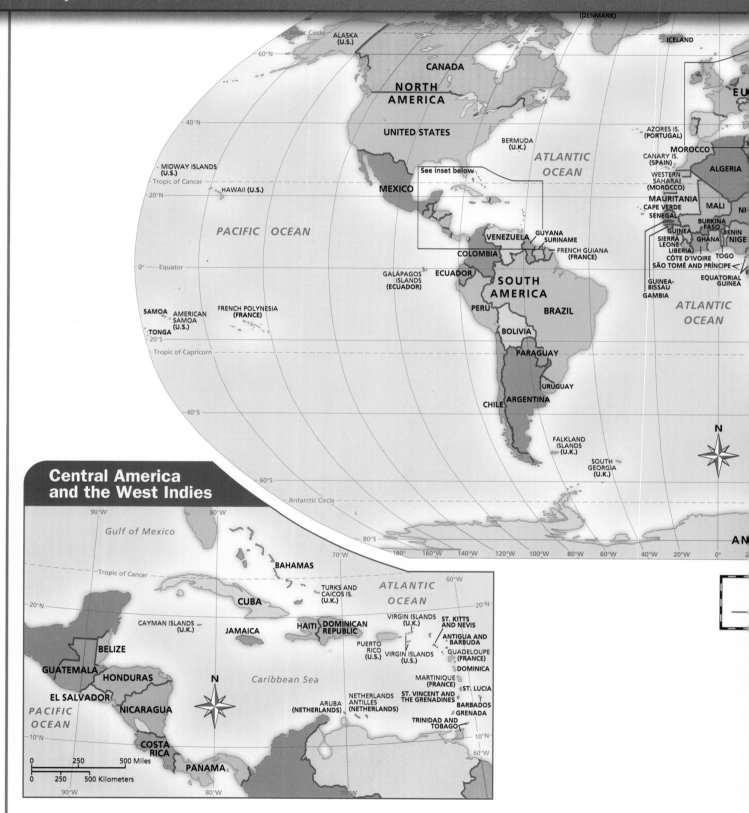

Central America and the West Indies

RUSSIA

ASIA

KAZAKHSTAN

MONGOLIA

UZBEKISTAN

KYRGYZSTAN

GEORGIA
ARMENIA
URKEY

TURKMENISTAN
TAJIKISTAN

NORTH
KOREA

JAPAN

NON SYRIA

AZERBAIJAN

AFGHANISTAN

CHINA

SOUTH
KOREA

PACIFIC OCEAN

EL
IRAQ
JORDAN

IRAN

PAKISTAN

NEPAL

BHUTAN

YPT

KUWAIT
QATAR

BAHRAIN

UNITED
ARAB
EMIRATES

INDIA

MYANMAR
(BURMA)

TAIWAN

Tropic of Cancer

SAUDI
ARABIA

OMAN

BANGLADESH

LAOS

20°N

WAKE ISLAND
(U.S.)

DAN ERITREA

YEMEN

THAILAND

VIETNAM

NORTHERN
MARIANA IS.
(U.S.)

MARSHALL ISLANDS

DJIBOUTI

GUAM (U.S.)

ETHIOPIA

SRI
LANKA

PHILIPPINES

PALAU

FEDERATED STATES
OF MICRONESIA

CAMBODIA

BRUNEI

ANDA

SOMALIA

MALDIVES

MALAYSIA

Equator

KIRIBATI

0°

KENYA

SINGAPORE

NAURU

BURUNDI

INDONESIA

PAPUA
NEW
GUINEA

SOLOMON
ISLANDS

TANZANIA

SEYCHELLES

INDIAN
OCEAN

TUVALU

MALAWI

COMOROS

VANUATU

FIJI

MOZAMBIQUE

MADAGASCAR

MAURITIUS

20°S

ABWE

A

RÉUNION (FR.)

NEW
CALEDONIA
(FRANCE)

AUSTRALIA

SWAZILAND

LESOTHO

NEW
ZEALAND

40°S

| 0 | 1,000 | 2,000 Miles |
| 0 | 1,000 | 2,000 Kilometers |

Scale accurate at Equator

KERGUELEN
ISLANDS
(FRANCE)

60°S

Antarctic Circle

80°S

60°E   80°E   100°E   120°E   140°E   160°E   180°

Arctic Circle

60°N

40°N

border

Europe

N

FINLAND

NORWAY

20°W   10°W   0°

North
Sea

SWEDEN

ESTONIA

50°N

IRELAND

UNITED
KINGDOM

DENMARK

Baltic Sea

LATVIA

RUSSIA

60°N

LITHUANIA
RUSSIA

NETHERLANDS

BELGIUM

GERMANY

POLAND

BELARUS

ATLANTIC

OCEAN

LUXEMBOURG

CZECH
REPUBLIC

UKRAINE

50°N

FRANCE

LIECHTENSTEIN

SLOVAKIA

SWITZERLAND

AUSTRIA

HUNGARY

MOLDOVA

40°N

MONACO

SLOVENIA
CROATIA

ROMANIA

PORTUGAL

ANDORRA

SAN
MARINO

BOSNIA AND
HERZEGOVINA

SERBIA &
MONTENEGRO
(YUGOSLAVIA)

Black Sea

SPAIN

CORSICA
(FR.)

ITALY

BULGARIA

BALEARIC IS.
(SP.)

SARDINIA
(IT.)

MACEDONIA

40°N

10°W

GIBRALTAR (U.K.)

Mediterranean
Sea

ALBANIA

40°E

SICILY
(IT.)

GREECE

| 0 | 250 | 500 Miles |
| 0 | 250 | 500 Kilometers |

MALTA

CRETE
(GR.)

0°   10°E   20°E   30°E

30   40°E   50°E

Northern Polar Region

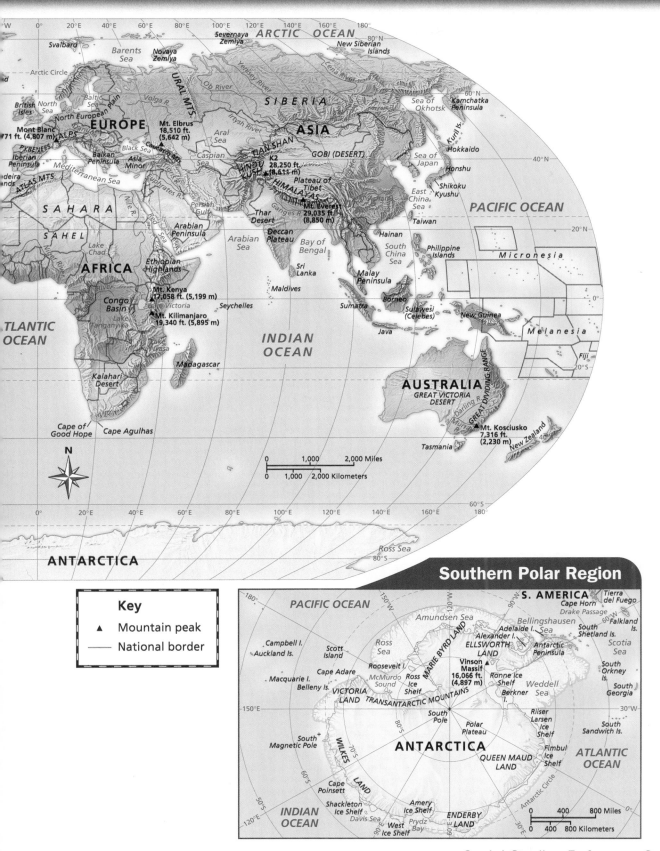

W   0°   20°E   40°E   60°E   80°E   100°E   120°E   140°E   160°E   180°

ARCTIC   OCEAN

Svalbard
Severnaya Zemlya
New Siberian Islands
80°N

Barents Sea
Novaya Zemlya

Arctic Circle

British Isles
North Sea
Baltic Sea
North European Plain
Volga R.
URAL MTS.
Ob River
Yenisey River
Irtysh River
Lena River
SIBERIA
Sea of Okhotsk
Kamchatka Peninsula
60°N

EUROPE
Mont Blanc 71 ft. (4,807 m)
ALPS
PYRENEES
Iberian Peninsula
Balkan Peninsula
Asia Minor
Black Sea
Caspian Sea
Aral Sea
ASIA
TIAN SHAN
GOBI (DESERT)
Kuril Is.
Sea of Japan
Hokkaido
40°N

Mt. Elbrus 18,510 ft. (5,642 m)
Caucasus Mts.
K2 28,250 ft. (8,611 m)
HINDU KUSH
Plateau of Tibet
HIMALAYAS
Mt. Everest 29,035 ft. (8,850 m)
Honshu
Shikoku
Kyushu
East China Sea
Taiwan
20°N

Mediterranean Sea
Madeira Islands
ATLAS MTS.
SAHARA
SAHEL
Nile R.
Red Sea
Euphrates R.
Persian Gulf
Arabian Peninsula
Arabian Sea
Thar Desert
Deccan Plateau
Bay of Bengal
Hainan
South China Sea
Philippine Islands
PACIFIC OCEAN
Micronesia
0°

ATLANTIC OCEAN
Lake Chad
Niger River
AFRICA
Ethiopian Highlands
Congo Basin
CONGO RIVER
Lake Victoria
Mt. Kenya 17,058 ft. (5,199 m)
Mt. Kilimanjaro 19,340 ft. (5,895 m)
Lake Tanganyika
Lake Nyasa
Sri Lanka
Maldives
Seychelles
Sumatra
Malay Peninsula
Borneo
Sulawesi (Celebes)
Java
New Guinea
Melanesia
Fiji
20°S

INDIAN OCEAN
Madagascar
AUSTRALIA
GREAT VICTORIA DESERT
GREAT DIVIDING RANGE
Darling R.
Murray R.

Kalahari Desert
40°S

Cape of Good Hope
Cape Agulhas
Mt. Kosciusko 7,316 ft. (2,230 m)
Tasmania
New Zealand

N

0   1,000   2,000 Miles
0   1,000   2,000 Kilometers

60°S

ANTARCTICA
80°S

Ross Sea

Key

▲ Mountain peak
— National border

Southern Polar Region

PACIFIC OCEAN
180°
150°W
120°W
90°W
60°W
30°W
0°

Amundsen Sea
S. AMERICA
Tierra del Fuego
Cape Horn
Drake Passage
Bellingshausen Sea
Falkland Is.
South Shetland Is.
Scotia Sea

Ross Sea
MARIE BYRD LAND
ELLSWORTH LAND
Adelaide I.
Alexander I.
Antarctic Peninsula
South Orkney Is.
South Georgia

Campbell I.
Auckland Is.
Scott Island
Roosevelt I.
McMurdo Sound
Ross Ice Shelf
Vinson Massif 16,066 ft. (4,897 m)
Ronne Ice Shelf
Berkner I.
Weddell Sea
South Sandwich Is.

Cape Adare
VICTORIA LAND
TRANSANTARCTIC MOUNTAINS
South Pole
Polar Plateau
Riiser Larsen Ice Shelf
30°W

Macquarie I.
Belleny Is.
150°E
80°S
70°S
ANTARCTICA
QUEEN MAUD LAND
Fimbul Ice Shelf
ATLANTIC OCEAN

South Magnetic Pole
WILKES LAND
60°S
50°S

Cape Poinsett
120°E
Shackleton Ice Shelf
Davis Sea
West Ice Shelf
Amery Ice Shelf
Prydz Bay
ENDERBY LAND
Antarctic Circle
60°E

INDIAN OCEAN
30°E
0°

0   400   800 Miles
0   400   800 Kilometers

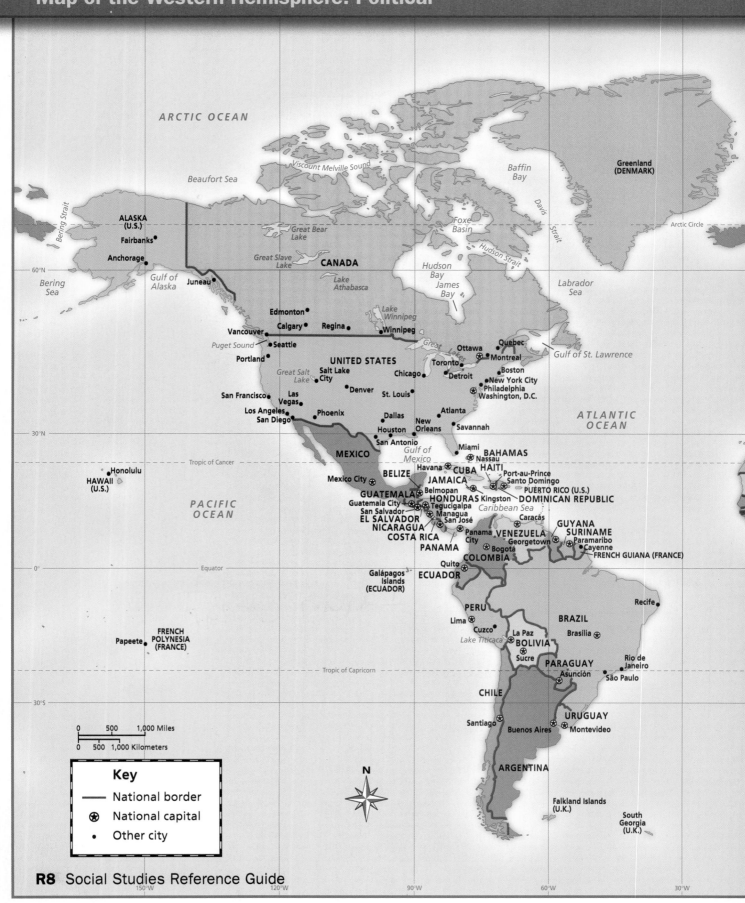

ARCTIC OCEAN

Viscount Melville Sound

Beaufort Sea

Baffin Bay

Greenland (DENMARK)

Davis Strait

ALASKA (U.S.)

Fairbanks •

Great Bear Lake

Foxe Basin

Arctic Circle

Anchorage •

Great Slave Lake

CANADA

Hudson Strait

60°N

Bering Sea

Gulf of Alaska

Juneau •

Hudson Bay

James Bay

Labrador Sea

Bering Strait

Lake Athabasca

Edmonton •

Lake Winnipeg

Calgary • Regina •

Winnipeg •

Quebec

Vancouver •

Puget Sound Seattle •

Great Ottawa ⊛ Montreal

Gulf of St. Lawrence

Portland •

UNITED STATES

Toronto • Boston

Great Salt Lake Salt Lake City

Chicago • Detroit • New York City

Philadelphia

San Francisco •

Denver •

St. Louis •

Washington, D.C.

ATLANTIC OCEAN

Las Vegas •

Atlanta •

Los Angeles •

Phoenix •

Dallas •

San Diego •

Houston •

New Orleans •

Savannah •

30°N

San Antonio •

Miami •

MEXICO

Gulf of Mexico

BAHAMAS

Nassau •

Tropic of Cancer

Honolulu •

HAWAII (U.S.)

Havana ⊛ CUBA HAITI

Mexico City ⊛

BELIZE

Port-au-Prince

Santo Domingo

PACIFIC OCEAN

GUATEMALA

Belmopan ⊛ JAMAICA Kingston PUERTO RICO (U.S.)

Guatemala City ⊛ HONDURAS DOMINICAN REPUBLIC

San Salvador ⊛ Tegucigalpa ⊛

Caribbean Sea

EL SALVADOR Managua ⊛ Caracas •

NICARAGUA San José ⊛ GUYANA

COSTA RICA Panama VENEZUELA SURINAME

PANAMA City ⊛ Georgetown ⊛ Paramaribo ⊛

Quito ⊛ ⊛ Bogotá Cayenne •

COLOMBIA FRENCH GUIANA (FRANCE)

0° Equator

Galápagos Islands (ECUADOR)

ECUADOR

Recife •

PERU BRAZIL

Lima •

FRENCH POLYNESIA (FRANCE)

Cuzco • La Paz ⊛ Brasília ⊛

Lake Titicaca BOLIVIA

Papeete • Sucre ⊛ Rio de Janeiro

PARAGUAY

Tropic of Capricorn

Asunción ⊛ São Paulo •

CHILE

30°S

URUGUAY

Santiago ⊛ Montevideo ⊛

Buenos Aires ⊛

0 500 1,000 Miles

0 500 1,000 Kilometers

ARGENTINA

Falkland Islands (U.K.)

South Georgia (U.K.)

N

Key

— National border

⊛ National capital

• Other city

150°W 120°W 90°W 60°W 30°W

ARCTIC OCEAN

North Magnetic Pole

Queen Elizabeth Islands

Ellesmere Island

Melville Island

Viscount Melville Sound

Devon Island

Banks Island

Victoria Island

Baffin Bay

Greenland

Point Barrow

Beaufort Sea

Brooks Range

Bering Strait

Mt. McKinley 20,320 ft. (6,194 m)

Yukon River

Yukon Plateau

Mackenzie Mts.

Mackenzie River

Liard R.

Great Bear Lake

Great Slave Lake

CANADIAN

Foxe Basin

Baffin Island

Davis Strait

Arctic Circle

Cape Farewell

60°N

Bering Sea

Gulf of Alaska

Alaska Range

Mt. Logan 19,524 ft. (5,951 m)

Coast Mountains

Peace River

Lake Athabasca

Athabasca

Hudson Bay

James Bay

Labrador

Labrador Sea

Kodiak Island

Alaska Peninsula

Aleutian Islands

Queen Charlotte Islands

Vancouver Island

Puget Sound

ROCKY

Snake

Saskatchewan River

GREAT

Lake Winnipeg

SHIELD

St. Lawrence R.

Newfoundland

Gulf of St. Lawrence

Nova Scotia

Cascade Range

Coast Ranges

Sierra Nevada

MOUNTAINS

Black Hills

Missouri

Mississippi

NORTH AMERICA

Great Lakes

Bay of Fundy

Cape Cod

Long Island

Mt. Whitney 14,495 ft. (4,418 m)

Great Salt Lake

GREAT BASIN

PLAINS

Platte

Colorado R.

INTERIOR PLAINS

Arkansas

Ohio R.

Ozark Plateau

APPALACHIAN MTS.

Cape Hatteras

ATLANTIC OCEAN

30°N

Death Valley (lowest point in N.A.) -282 ft. (-86 m)

Sonoran Desert

Baja California

Sierra Madre Occidental

Sierra Madre Oriental

Rio Grande

COASTAL PLAIN

Gulf of Mexico

Bahamas

Tropic of Cancer

Hawaiian Islands

Citlaltépetl 18,701 ft. (5,700 m)

Yucatán Peninsula

Cuba

Greater Antilles

Hispaniola

Puerto Rico

Lesser Antilles

PACIFIC OCEAN

Lake Nicaragua

Caribbean Sea

Line Islands

Isthmus of Panama

Chimborazo 20,561 ft. (6,267 m)

Lake Maracaibo

Orinoco R.

Llanos

Guiana Highlands

Cape São Roque

Marquesas Islands

Galápagos Islands

Equator

Rio Negro

Amazon R.

AMAZON

0°

Huascarán 22,205 ft. (6,768 m)

BASIN

Tapajós R.

Xingu River

Tocantins

São Francisco R.

Cook Islands

Tuamotu Archipelago

Society Islands

Lake Titicaca

Altiplano

ANDES

Mato Grosso Plateau

Brazilian Highlands

SOUTH AMERICA

Tropic of Capricorn

Atacama Desert

Gran Chaco

Paraguay R.

Paraná R.

Iguazú Falls

30°S

Mt. Aconcagua 22,831 ft. (6,959 m)

Uruguay R.

Pampa

Valdés Peninsula (lowest point in S.A.) -131 ft. (-40 m)

Patagonia

Strait of Magellan

Tierra del Fuego

Falkland Islands

South Georgia

Cape Horn

0 500 1,000 Miles

0 500 1,000 Kilometers

N

Key

▲ Mountain peak

▼ Below sea level

— National border

150°W   120°W   90°W   60°W   30°W

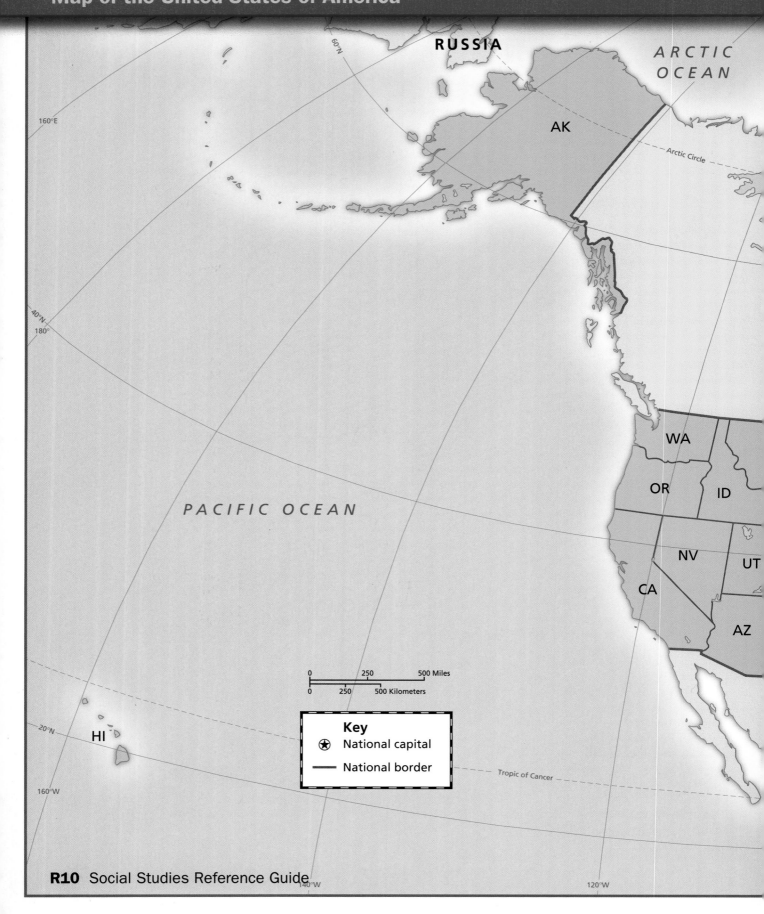

RUSSIA

ARCTIC OCEAN

AK

Arctic Circle

PACIFIC OCEAN

WA

OR

ID

NV

UT

CA

AZ

| 0 | 250 | 500 Miles |
| 0 | 250 | 500 Kilometers |

Key

⊛ National capital

— National border

Tropic of Cancer

HI

20°N

160°W

40°N
180°

160°E

60°N

140°W

120°W

Greenland
(DENMARK)

CANADA

MEXICO

Gulf of Mexico

ATLANTIC
OCEAN

BAHAMAS

CUBA

JAMAICA

HAITI

DOM.
REP.

State or Area	Abbreviation
Alabama	AL
Alaska	AK
Arizona	AZ
Arkansas	AR
California	CA
Colorado	CO
Connecticut	CT
Delaware	DE
District of Columbia	DC
Florida	FL
Georgia	GA
Hawaii	HI
Idaho	ID
Illinois	IL
Indiana	IN
Iowa	IA
Kansas	KS
Kentucky	KY
Louisiana	LA
Maine	ME
Maryland	MD
Massachusetts	MA
Michigan	MI
Minnesota	MN
Mississippi	MS
Missouri	MO
Montana	MT
Nebraska	NE
Nevada	NV
New Hampshire	NH
New Jersey	NJ
New Mexico	NM
New York	NY
North Carolina	NC
North Dakota	ND
Ohio	OH
Oklahoma	OK
Oregon	OR
Pennsylvania	PA
Rhode Island	RI
South Carolina	SC
South Dakota	SD
Tennessee	TN
Texas	TX
Utah	UT
Vermont	VT
Virginia	VA
Washington	WA
West Virginia	WV
Wisconsin	WI
Wyoming	WY

100°W   80°W   60°W

Atlas
Map of the United States: Political

RUSSIA

ARCTIC OCEAN

Arctic Circle

ALASKA (AK)

Nome

Fairbanks

CANADA

Bering Sea

Anchorage

Juneau

PACIFIC OCEAN

0   250   500 Miles
0   250   500 Kilometers

70°N
180°
60°N
170°W
160°W
150°W
140°W

50°N
40°N
30°N

PACIFIC OCEAN

Region Key
Northeast
Southeast
Midwest
Southwest
West

Key
⊛ National capital
★ State capital
• Major city
— National border

130°W

0   250   500 Miles
0   250   500 Kilometers

Olympia ★   • Seattle   River
WASHINGTON (WA)   • Spokane
Portland   Columbia
Salem ★
• Eugene
OREGON (OR)

Great Falls •   Missouri River
Helena ★   MONTANA (MT)
Billings •

Boise ★   IDAHO (ID)
Pocatello •

WYOMING (WY)
Casper •

Great Salt Lake   • Ogden
Reno •   Salt Lake City ★   • Provo
Sacramento ★   ★ Carson City
San Francisco • • Oakland   NEVADA (NV)
• San Jose
UTAH (UT)   Cheyen

Denve
Colorad Spring
COLORADO (CO)   Pue

CALIFORNIA (CA)
Las Vegas •
River
Los Angeles •
• Long Beach
ARIZONA (AZ)   Sant •
• Albuque
San Diego •   NEW MEXICO (NM)
★ Phoenix
Colorado
Tucson •

El Paso •
Rio Grande

160°W   155°W   22°N
HAWAII (HI)   N
Honolulu ★
PACIFIC OCEAN   120°W
20°N
Hilo

MEXICO

110°W

0   75   150 Miles
0   75   150 Kilometers

CANADA

NORTH DAKOTA
(ND)

Grand Forks

★ Bismarck

Fargo

Duluth

MINNESOTA
(MN)

Lake Superior

NEW HAMPSHIRE (NH)

VERMONT (VT)

MAINE
(ME)

Augusta ★

SOUTH DAKOTA
(SD)

★ Pierre

Minneapolis

★ St. Paul

Green
Bay

Lake Michigan

MICHIGAN
(MI)

Lake Huron

Lake Ontario

Burlington

Montpelier ★

Portland

★ Concord

Sioux
Falls

WISCONSIN
(WI)

Madison ★

Milwaukee

Grand
Rapids

Lansing ★

Detroit

Albany ★

Buffalo

NEW YORK
(NY)

Boston ★

MASSACHUSETTS
(MA)

★ Providence

Missouri

IOWA
(IA)

Cedar
Rapids

Rockford

Chicago

Gary

Toledo

Cleveland

Lake Erie

Hartford ★

RHODE ISLAND
(RI)

NEBRASKA
(NE)

Omaha

Des
Moines

Davenport

Fort
Wayne

OHIO
(OH)

PENNSYLVANIA
(PA)

Wheeling

Pittsburgh

Newark

New York

CONNECTICUT
(CT)

Lincoln ★

Peoria

Springfield

Indianapolis ★

Columbus ★

Harrisburg ★

Trenton ★

NEW JERSEY (NJ)

Philadelphia

Baltimore

Dover

DELAWARE (DE)

Kansas
City

Kansas
City

St.
Louis

ILLINOIS
(IL)

INDIANA
(IN)

Cincinnati

Ohio

River

WEST
VIRGINIA
(WV)

Annapolis ✪

MARYLAND (MD)

Topeka ★

Jefferson
City ★

Evansville

Louisville

Frankfort ★

Charleston ★

Richmond ★

Washington, D.C.

KANSAS
(KS)

Mississippi

River

St. Louis

VIRGINIA
(VA)

Norfolk

Wichita

MISSOURI
(MO)

KENTUCKY
(KY)

Nashville

Knoxville

Raleigh

NORTH CAROLINA
(NC)

Tulsa

TENNESSEE
(TN)

Charlotte

Oklahoma
City ★

Fort
Smith

Memphis

Columbia

SOUTH
CAROLINA
(SC)

OKLAHOMA
(OK)

Little
Rock ★

Birmingham

Atlanta ★

Charleston

ARKANSAS
(AR)

MISSISSIPPI
(MS)

ALABAMA
(AL)

GEORGIA
(GA)

Savannah

ATLANTIC
OCEAN

Fort
Worth

Dallas

Shreveport

Jackson ★

Montgomery ★

Columbus

LOUISIANA
(LA)

TEXAS
(TX)

Austin ★

Baton Rouge

Biloxi

Mobile

Tallahassee ★

Jacksonville

San
Antonio

Houston

New Orleans

Laredo

Corpus
Christi

N

Gulf of Mexico

FLORIDA
(FL)

Tampa

Miami

BAHAMAS

50°N

40°N

70°W

30°N

80°W

100°W

90°W

Atlas
Map of the United States: Physical

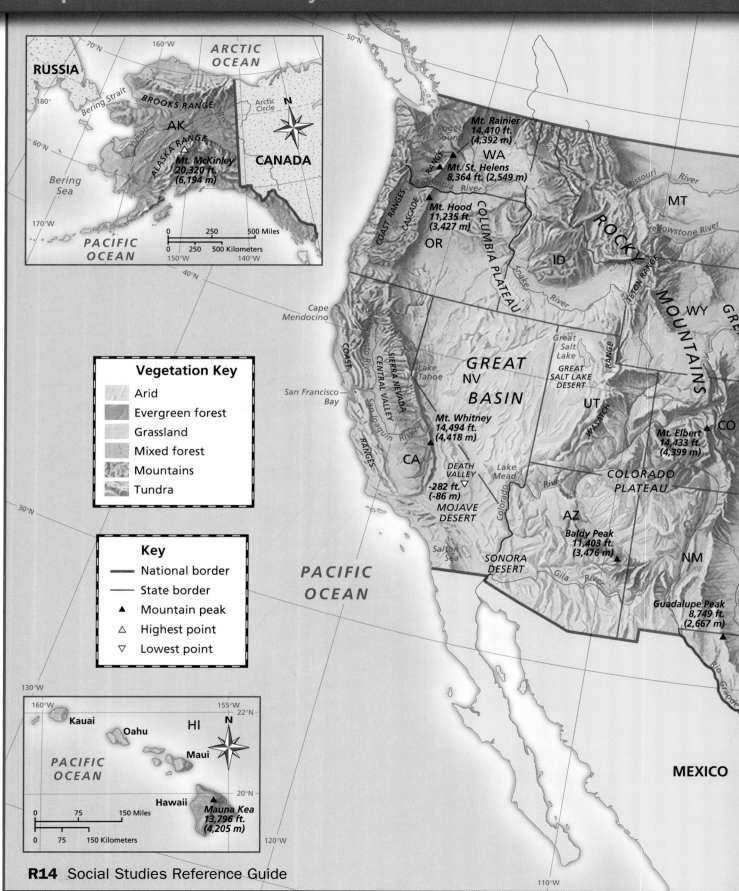

Vegetation Key
- Arid
- Evergreen forest
- Grassland
- Mixed forest
- Mountains
- Tundra

Key
- ▬ National border
- — State border
- ▲ Mountain peak
- △ Highest point
- ▽ Lowest point

RUSSIA

ARCTIC OCEAN

BROOKS RANGE

AK

ALASKA RANGE

Mt. McKinley 20,320 ft. (6,194 m)

CANADA

Bering Strait

Yukon River

Arctic Circle

N

Bering Sea

PACIFIC OCEAN

0   250   500 Miles
0   250   500 Kilometers

Cape Mendocino

COAST RANGES

CASCADE RANGE

Puget Sound

Mt. Rainier 14,410 ft. (4,392 m)

WA

Mt. St. Helens 8,364 ft. (2,549 m)

Columbia River

Mt. Hood 11,235 ft. (3,427 m)

OR

COLUMBIA PLATEAU

ID

Snake River

MT

Missouri River

Yellowstone River

ROCKY MOUNTAINS

TETON RANGE

WY

COAST RANGES

Sacramento River

SIERRA NEVADA

CENTRAL VALLEY

San Joaquin River

Lake Tahoe

San Francisco Bay

GREAT

NV

BASIN

Great Salt Lake

GREAT SALT LAKE DESERT

WASATCH RANGE

UT

Mt. Whitney 14,494 ft. (4,418 m)

CA

DEATH VALLEY -282 ft. (-86 m)

MOJAVE DESERT

Lake Mead

Colorado River

COLORADO PLATEAU

Mt. Elbert 14,433 ft. (4,399 m)

CO

Salton Sea

SONORA DESERT

AZ

Baldy Peak 11,403 ft. (3,476 m)

NM

Gila River

Guadalupe Peak 8,749 ft. (2,667 m)

PACIFIC OCEAN

Rio Grande

MEXICO

Kauai

Oahu

HI

N

Maui

PACIFIC OCEAN

Hawaii

Mauna Kea 13,796 ft. (4,205 m)

0   75   150 Miles
0   75   150 Kilometers

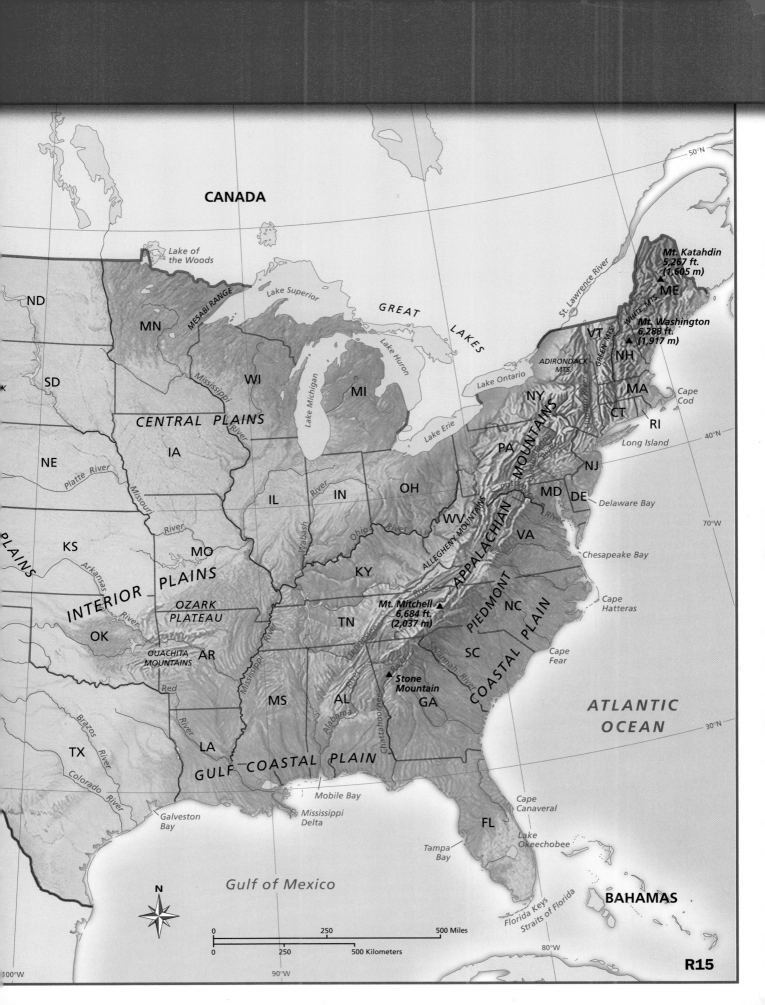

CANADA

Lake of the Woods

ND

MN

MESABI RANGE

Lake Superior

GREAT

LAKES

St. Lawrence River

Mt. Katahdin
5,267 ft.
(1,605 m)
▲

ME

SD

WI

Lake Michigan

MI

Lake Huron

Mississippi River

Mt. Washington
6,288 ft.
(1,917 m)
▲

VT

GREEN MTS.

WHITE MTS.

NH

ADIRONDACK
MTS.

Lake Ontario

NY

MA

Cape Cod

CT

RI

Long Island

CENTRAL PLAINS

IA

NE

Platte River

IL

Missouri River

IN

OH

PA

APPALACHIAN

MOUNTAINS

Hudson River

NJ

MD

DE

Delaware Bay

70°W

PLAINS

KS

Arkansas River

MO

INTERIOR PLAINS

OZARK
PLATEAU

Wabash River

Ohio River

KY

WV

ALLEGHENY MOUNTAINS

VA

Potomac River

Chesapeake Bay

Cape Hatteras

OK

OUACHITA
MOUNTAINS

AR

Red River

Mississippi River

TN

Mt. Mitchell
6,684 ft.
(2,037 m) ▲

APPALACHIAN

PIEDMONT

NC

COASTAL PLAIN

SC

Cape Fear

Tennessee River

TX

Brazos River

Colorado River

LA

MS

Alabama River

AL

▲ Stone
Mountain

Chattahoochee River

GA

Savannah River

GULF COASTAL PLAIN

ATLANTIC
OCEAN

30°N

Galveston Bay

Mobile Bay

Mississippi Delta

FL

Cape Canaveral

Lake Okeechobee

Tampa Bay

Gulf of Mexico

N

Florida Keys

Straits of Florida

BAHAMAS

0   250   500 Miles

0   250   500 Kilometers

100°W

90°W

80°W

50°N

40°N

Geography Terms

basin bowl-shaped area of land surrounded by higher land

bay narrower part of an ocean or lake that cuts into land

canal narrow waterway dug across land mainly for ship travel

canyon steep, narrow valley with high sides

cliff steep wall of rock or earth, sometimes called a bluff

coast land at the edge of a large body of water such as an ocean

coastal plain area of flat land along an ocean or sea

delta triangle-shaped area of land at the mouth of a river

desert very dry land

fall line area along which a river forms waterfalls or rapids as it drops to lower land

forest large area of land where many trees grow

glacier giant sheet of ice that moves very slowly across land

gulf body of water, smaller than a bay, with land around part of it

harbor sheltered body of water where ships safely tie up to land

hill rounded land higher than the land around it

island land with water all around it

lake large body of water with land all or nearly all around it

mesa flat-topped hill, with steep sides

mountain a very high hill; the highest land on Earth

mountain range long row of mountains

mouth place where a river empties into another body of water

ocean any of the four largest bodies of water on Earth

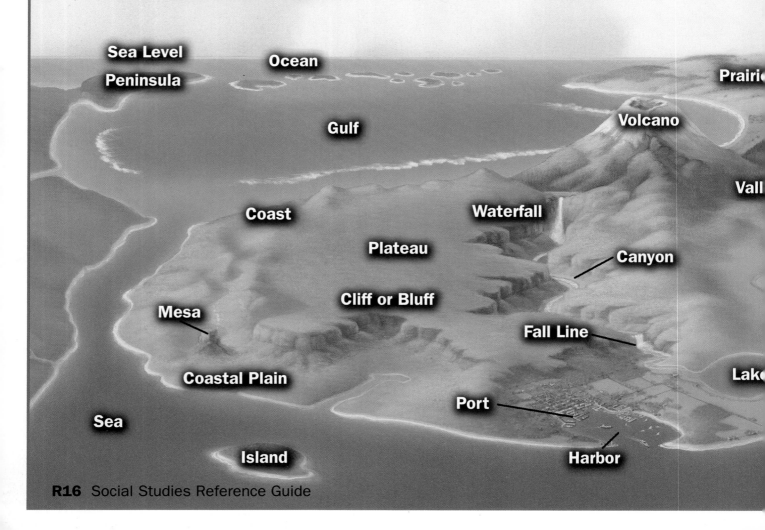

peak pointed top of a mountain

peninsula land with water on three sides

plain very large area of flat land

plateau high, wide area of flat land, with steep sides

port place, usually in a harbor, where ships safely load and unload goods and people

prairie large area of flat land, with few or no trees, similar to a plain

river large stream of water leading to a lake, other river, or ocean

riverbank land at a river's edge

sea large body of water somewhat smaller than an ocean

sea level an ocean's surface, compared to which land can be measured either above or below

slope side of a mountain or hill

source place where a river begins

swamp very shallow water covering low land filled with trees and other plants

timberline imaginary line beyond which trees do not grow

tributary stream or river that runs into a larger river

valley low land between mountains or hills

volcano mountain with an opening at the top, formed by violent bursts of steam and hot rock

waterfall steep falling of water from a higher to a lower place

Facts About Our Fifty States

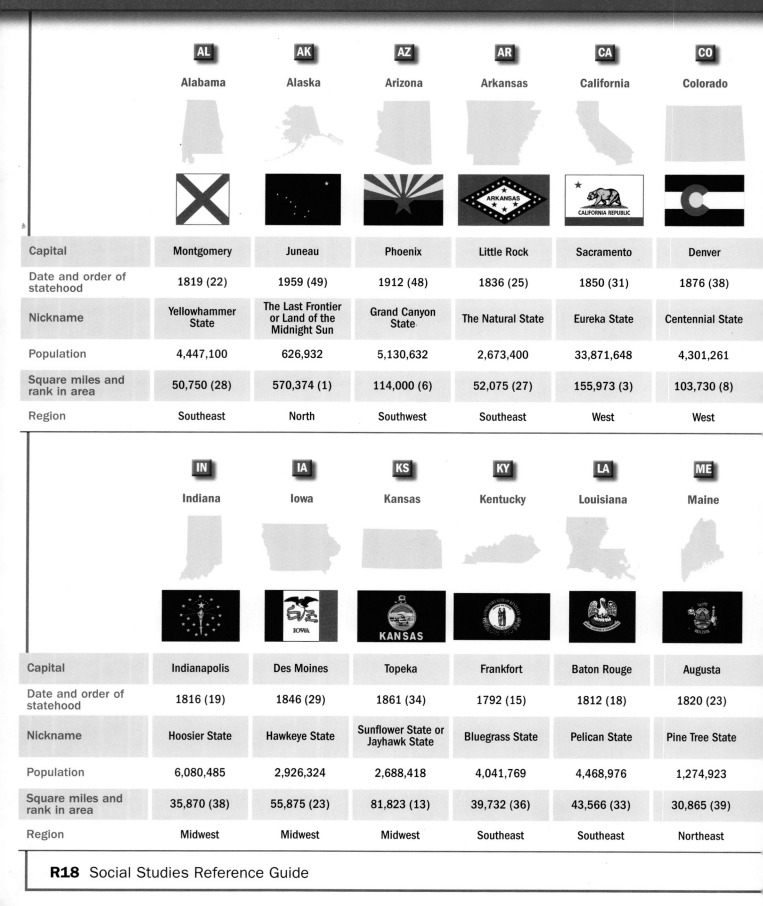

	AL Alabama	**AK** Alaska	**AZ** Arizona	**AR** Arkansas	**CA** California	**CO** Colorado
Capital	Montgomery	Juneau	Phoenix	Little Rock	Sacramento	Denver
Date and order of statehood	1819 (22)	1959 (49)	1912 (48)	1836 (25)	1850 (31)	1876 (38)
Nickname	Yellowhammer State	The Last Frontier or Land of the Midnight Sun	Grand Canyon State	The Natural State	Eureka State	Centennial State
Population	4,447,100	626,932	5,130,632	2,673,400	33,871,648	4,301,261
Square miles and rank in area	50,750 (28)	570,374 (1)	114,000 (6)	52,075 (27)	155,973 (3)	103,730 (8)
Region	Southeast	North	Southwest	Southeast	West	West

	IN Indiana	**IA** Iowa	**KS** Kansas	**KY** Kentucky	**LA** Louisiana	**ME** Maine
Capital	Indianapolis	Des Moines	Topeka	Frankfort	Baton Rouge	Augusta
Date and order of statehood	1816 (19)	1846 (29)	1861 (34)	1792 (15)	1812 (18)	1820 (23)
Nickname	Hoosier State	Hawkeye State	Sunflower State or Jayhawk State	Bluegrass State	Pelican State	Pine Tree State
Population	6,080,485	2,926,324	2,688,418	4,041,769	4,468,976	1,274,923
Square miles and rank in area	35,870 (38)	55,875 (23)	81,823 (13)	39,732 (36)	43,566 (33)	30,865 (39)
Region	Midwest	Midwest	Midwest	Southeast	Southeast	Northeast

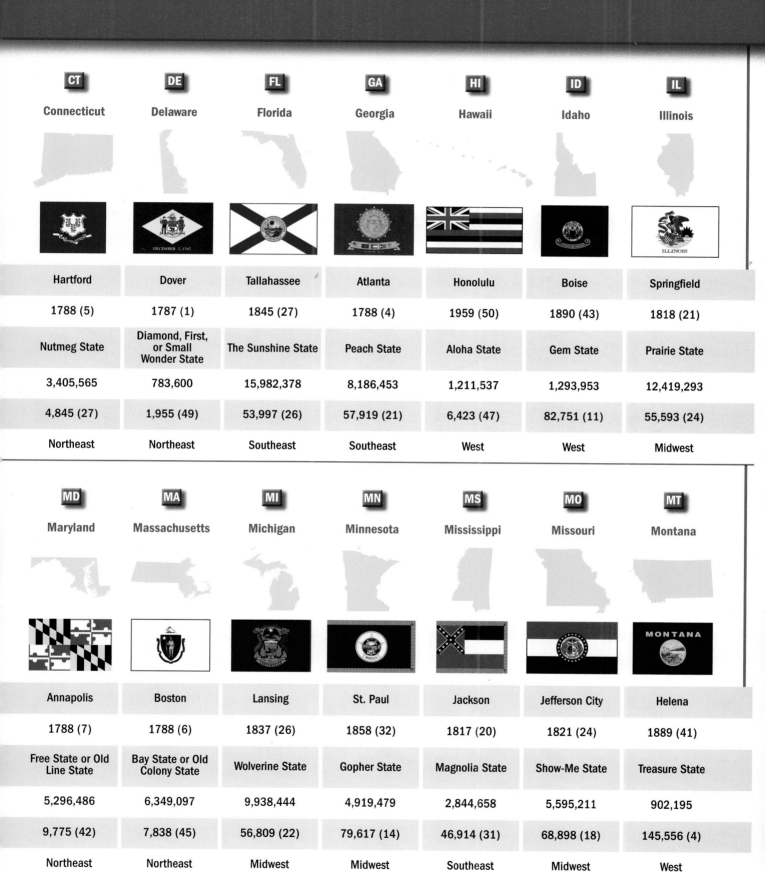

CT	**DE**	**FL**	**GA**	**HI**	**ID**	**IL**
Connecticut	Delaware	Florida	Georgia	Hawaii	Idaho	Illinois
Hartford	Dover	Tallahassee	Atlanta	Honolulu	Boise	Springfield
1788 (5)	1787 (1)	1845 (27)	1788 (4)	1959 (50)	1890 (43)	1818 (21)
Nutmeg State	Diamond, First, or Small Wonder State	The Sunshine State	Peach State	Aloha State	Gem State	Prairie State
3,405,565	783,600	15,982,378	8,186,453	1,211,537	1,293,953	12,419,293
4,845 (27)	1,955 (49)	53,997 (26)	57,919 (21)	6,423 (47)	82,751 (11)	55,593 (24)
Northeast	Northeast	Southeast	Southeast	West	West	Midwest

MD	**MA**	**MI**	**MN**	**MS**	**MO**	**MT**
Maryland	Massachusetts	Michigan	Minnesota	Mississippi	Missouri	Montana
Annapolis	Boston	Lansing	St. Paul	Jackson	Jefferson City	Helena
1788 (7)	1788 (6)	1837 (26)	1858 (32)	1817 (20)	1821 (24)	1889 (41)
Free State or Old Line State	Bay State or Old Colony State	Wolverine State	Gopher State	Magnolia State	Show-Me State	Treasure State
5,296,486	6,349,097	9,938,444	4,919,479	2,844,658	5,595,211	902,195
9,775 (42)	7,838 (45)	56,809 (22)	79,617 (14)	46,914 (31)	68,898 (18)	145,556 (4)
Northeast	Northeast	Midwest	Midwest	Southeast	Midwest	West

Facts About Our Fifty States

	NE	NV	NH	NJ	NM	NY
	Nebraska	Nevada	New Hampshire	New Jersey	New Mexico	New York
Capital	Lincoln	Carson City	Concord	Trenton	Santa Fe	Albany
Date and order of statehood	1867 (37)	1864 (36)	1788 (9)	1787 (3)	1912 (47)	1788 (11)
Nickname	Cornhusker State	Silver State	Granite State	Garden State	Land of Enchantment	Empire State
Population	1,711,263	1,998,257	1,235,786	8,414,350	1,819,046	18,976,457
Square miles and rank in area	76,644 (15)	109,806 (7)	8,969 (44)	7,419 (46)	121,365 (5)	47,224 (30)
Region	Midwest	West	Northeast	Northeast	Southwest	Northeast

	SC	SD	TN	TX	UT	VT
	South Carolina	South Dakota	Tennessee	Texas	Utah	Vermont
Capital	Columbia	Pierre	Nashville	Austin	Salt Lake City	Montpelier
Date and order of statehood	1788 (8)	1889 (40)	1796 (16)	1845 (28)	1896 (45)	1791 (14)
Nickname	Palmetto State	Coyote State or Mount Rushmore State	Volunteer State	Lone Star State	Beehive State	Green Mountain State
Population	4,012,012	754,844	5,689,283	20,851,820	2,233,169	608,827
Square miles and rank in area	30,111 (40)	75,898 (16)	41,220 (34)	261,914 (2)	82,168 (12)	9,249 (43)
Region	Southeast	Midwest	Southeast	Southwest	West	Northeast

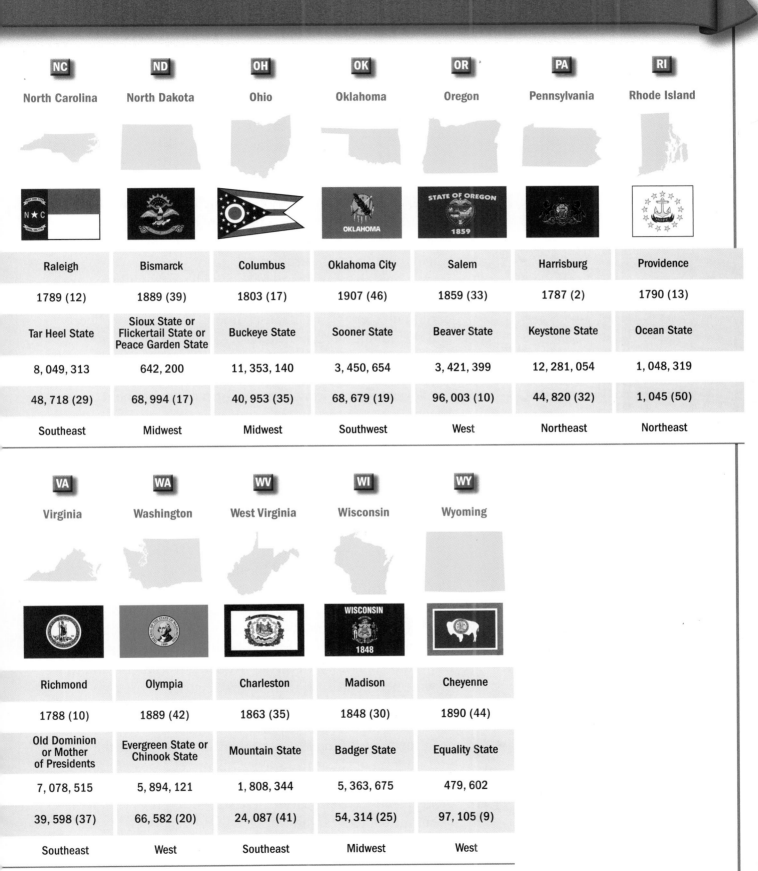

	North Carolina	North Dakota	Ohio	Oklahoma	Oregon	Pennsylvania	Rhode Island
Capital	Raleigh	Bismarck	Columbus	Oklahoma City	Salem	Harrisburg	Providence
Year (order)	1789 (12)	1889 (39)	1803 (17)	1907 (46)	1859 (33)	1787 (2)	1790 (13)
Nickname	Tar Heel State	Sioux State or Flickertail State or Peace Garden State	Buckeye State	Sooner State	Beaver State	Keystone State	Ocean State
Population	8, 049, 313	642, 200	11, 353, 140	3, 450, 654	3, 421, 399	12, 281, 054	1, 048, 319
Area	48, 718 (29)	68, 994 (17)	40, 953 (35)	68, 679 (19)	96, 003 (10)	44, 820 (32)	1, 045 (50)
Region	Southeast	Midwest	Midwest	Southwest	West	Northeast	Northeast

	Virginia	Washington	West Virginia	Wisconsin	Wyoming
Capital	Richmond	Olympia	Charleston	Madison	Cheyenne
Year (order)	1788 (10)	1889 (42)	1863 (35)	1848 (30)	1890 (44)
Nickname	Old Dominion or Mother of Presidents	Evergreen State or Chinook State	Mountain State	Badger State	Equality State
Population	7, 078, 515	5, 894, 121	1, 808, 344	5, 363, 675	479, 602
Area	39, 598 (37)	66, 582 (20)	24, 087 (41)	54, 314 (25)	97, 105 (9)
Region	Southeast	West	Southeast	Midwest	West

In Congress, July 4, 1776

Sometimes in history it becomes necessary for a group of people to break political ties with the country that rules it. When this happens, it is proper to explain the reasons for the need to separate.

When, in the course of human events, it becomes necessary for one people to dissolve the political bands which have connected them with another, and to assume, among the powers of the earth, the separate and equal station to which the laws of nature and nature's God entitle them, a decent respect to the opinions of mankind requires that they should declare the causes which impel them to the separation.

We believe that all men are created equal and given by their Creator certain rights that cannot be taken away. People have the right to live, be free, and seek happiness.

We hold these truths to be self-evident; that all men are created equal, that they are endowed by their Creator with certain unalienable rights, that among these are life, liberty, and the pursuit of happiness.

Governments are established to protect these rights. The government gets its power from the support of the people it governs. If any form of government tries to take away the basic rights, it is the right of the people to change or end the government and to establish a new government that seems most likely to result in their safety and happiness.

That to secure these rights, governments are instituted among men, deriving their just powers from the consent of the governed; that whenever any form of government becomes destructive of these ends, it is the right of the people to alter or to abolish it, and to institute new government, laying its foundation on such principles, and organizing its powers in such form, as to them shall seem most likely to effect their safety and happiness.

Wise judgment will require that long-existing governments should not be changed for unimportant or temporary reasons. History has shown that people are more willing to suffer under a bad government than to get rid of the government they are used to. But when there are so many abuses and misuses of power by the government, it is the right and duty of the people to throw off such government and form a new government to protect their basic rights.

Prudence, indeed, will dictate that governments long established should not be changed for light and transient causes; and accordingly all experience hath shown that mankind are more disposed to suffer, while evils are sufferable, than to right themselves by abolishing the forms to which they are accustomed. But when a long train of abuses and usurpations, pursuing invariably the same object, evinces a design to reduce them under absolute despotism, it is their right, it is their duty, to throw off such government, and to provide new guards for their future security.

The colonies have suffered patiently and now it is necessary for them to change the government. The king of Great Britain has repeatedly abused his power over these states. To prove this, the following facts are given.

Such has been the patient sufferance of these colonies; and such is now the necessity which constrains them to alter their former systems of government. The history of the present king of Great Britain is a history of repeated injuries and usurpations, all having in direct object the establishment of an absolute tyranny over these states. To prove this, let facts be submitted to a candid world.

He has refused his assent to laws the most wholesome and necessary for the public good. He has forbidden his governors to pass laws of immediate and pressing importance, unless suspended in their operation till his assent should be obtained; and when so suspended, he has utterly neglected to attend to them.

He has refused to pass other laws for the accommodation of large districts of people, unless those people would relinquish the right of representation in the legislature, a right inestimable to them, and formidable to tyrants only.

He has called together legislative bodies at places unusual, uncomfortable, and distant from the depository of their public records, for the sole purpose of fatiguing them into compliance with his measures.

He has dissolved representative houses repeatedly, for opposing, with manly firmness, his invasions on the rights of the people.

He has refused, for a long time after such dissolutions, to cause others to be elected; whereby the legislative powers, incapable of annihilation, have returned to the people at large for their exercise; the state remaining, in the meantime, exposed to all the dangers of invasion from without and convulsions within.

He has endeavored to prevent the population of these states; for that purpose obstructing the laws for the naturalization of foreigners, refusing to pass others to encourage their migrations hither, and raising the conditions of new appropriations of lands.

He has obstructed the administration of justice, by refusing his assent to laws for establishing judiciary powers.

He has made judges dependent on his will alone for the tenure of their offices, and the amount and payment of their salaries.

He has erected a multitude of new offices, and sent hither swarms of officers to harass our people and eat out their substance.

He has kept among us, in times of peace, standing armies, without the consent of our legislatures.

He has affected to render the military independent of, and superior to, the civil power.

He has combined with others to subject us to a jurisdiction foreign to our constitution and unacknowledged by our laws, giving his assent to their acts of pretended legislation:

The king has not given his approval to needed laws. He has not allowed his governors to pass laws needed immediately. The king has made the governors delay laws until they can get his permission and then he has ignored the laws.

He has refused to pass other laws for the help of large districts of people, unless those people would give up the right of representation in the legislature, a right priceless to them, and threatening only to tyrants.

He has called together legislative bodies at unusual places, uncomfortable and distant from where they store their public records, and only for the purpose of tiring them into obeying his measures.

He has repeatedly done away with legislative groups that firmly opposed him for taking away the rights of the people.

After he has dissolved these representative meetings, he has refused to allow new elections. Because of this lack of legislative power, the people are exposed to the dangers of invasion from without and violence from within.

He has tried to prevent people from immigrating to these states by blocking the process for foreigners to become citizens, refusing to pass laws to encourage people to travel to America, and making it harder to move to and own new lands.

He has interfered with the administration of justice by refusing to approve laws for establishing courts.

He has made judges do what he wants by controlling how long they serve and how much they are paid.

He has created many new government offices and sent many officials to torment our people and live off of our hard work.

In times of peace, he has kept soldiers among us, without the consent of our legislatures.

He has tried to make the military separate from, and superior to, the civil government.

He and others have made us live under laws that are different from our laws. He has given his approval to these unfair laws that parliament has adopted:

For forcing us to feed and house many British soldiers;

For using pretend trials to protect British soldiers from punishment for murdering people in America;

For cutting off our trade with the world;

For taxing us without our consent;

For taking away, in many cases, the benefits of trial by jury;

For taking us to Britain, to be tried for made-up offenses;

For doing away with the free system of English laws in a neighboring province, and establishing a harsh government there, and enlarging its boundaries, as a way to introduce the same absolute rule into these colonies;

For taking away our governing documents, doing away with our most valuable laws, and changing our governments completely;

For setting aside our own legislatures, and declaring that Great Britain has power to make laws for us in all cases whatsoever.

He has deserted government here by not protecting us and waging war against us.

He has robbed our ships on the seas, destroyed our coasts, burned our towns, and destroyed the lives of our people.

He is at this time sending large armies of foreign hired soldiers to complete the works of death, destruction, and injustice. These deeds are among the cruelest ever seen in history, and are totally unworthy of the head of a civilized nation.

He has forced our fellow citizens, who were captured on the high seas, to fight against America, to kill their friends and family, or to be killed themselves.

He has stirred up civil disorder among us, and has tried to cause the merciless killing of the people living on the frontiers by the Indians, whose rule of warfare includes the deliberate killing of people regardless of age, sex, or conditions.

In every stage of these mistreatments we have asked for a solution in the most humble terms; our repeated requests have been answered only by repeated injury. A prince who is so unfair and acts like a dictator is unfit to be the ruler of a free people.

For quartering large bodies of armed troops among us;

For protecting them, by a mock trial, from punishment for any murders which they should commit on the inhabitants of these states;

For cutting off our trade with all parts of the world;

For imposing taxes on us without our consent;

For depriving us, in many cases, of the benefits of trial by jury;

For transporting us beyond seas, to be tried for pretended offenses;

For abolishing the free system of English laws in a neighboring province, establishing therein an arbitrary government, and enlarging its boundaries, so as to render it at once an example and fit instrument for introducing the same absolute rule into these colonies;

For taking away our charters, abolishing our most valuable laws, and altering fundamentally the forms of our governments;

For suspending our own legislatures, and declaring themselves invested with power to legislate for us in all cases whatsoever.

He has abdicated government here, by declaring us out of his protection and waging war against us.

He has plundered our seas, ravaged our coasts, burned our towns, and destroyed the lives of our people.

He is at this time transporting large armies of foreign mercenaries to complete the works of death, desolation, and tyranny already begun with circumstances of cruelty and perfidy scarcely paralleled in the most barbarous ages, and totally unworthy the head of a civilized nation.

He has constrained our fellow citizens, taken captive on the high seas, to bear arms against their country, to become the executioners of their friends and brethren, or to fall themselves by their hands.

He has excited domestic insurrection among us, and has endeavored to bring on the inhabitants of our frontiers, the merciless Indian savages, whose known rule of warfare is an undistinguished destruction of all ages, sexes, and conditions.

In every stage of these oppressions we have petitioned for redress in the most humble terms; our repeated petitions have been answered only by repeated injury. A prince, whose character is thus marked by every act which may define a tyrant, is unfit to be the ruler of a free people.

Nor have we been wanting in attentions to our British brethren. We have warned them, from time to time, of attempts by their legislature to extend an unwarrantable jurisdiction over us. We have reminded them of the circumstances of our emigration and settlement here. We have appealed to their native justice and magnanimity; and we have conjured them, by the ties of our common kindred, to disavow these usurpations, which would inevitably interrupt our connections and correspondence. They, too, have been deaf to the voice of justice and consanguinity. We must, therefore, acquiesce in the necessity which denounces our separation, and hold them, as we hold the rest of mankind, enemies in war; in peace, friends.

We, therefore, the representatives of the United States of America, in General Congress assembled, appealing to the Supreme Judge of the world for the rectitude of our intentions, do, in the name and by the authority of the good people of these colonies, solemnly publish and declare that these United Colonies are, and of right ought to be, free and independent states; that they are absolved from all allegiance to the British crown, and that all political connection between them and the state of Great Britain is, and ought to be, totally dissolved; and that, as free and independent states, they have full power to levy war, conclude peace, contract alliances, establish commerce, and do all other acts and things which independent states may of right do. And, for the support of this declaration, with a firm reliance on the protection of Divine Providence, we mutually pledge to each other our lives, our fortunes, and our sacred honor.

We have also asked for help from the British people. We have warned them, from time to time, of attempts by their government to extend illegal power over us. We have reminded them of why we came to America. We have appealed to their sense of justice and generosity; and we have begged them, because of all we have in common, to give up these abuses of power. They, like the king, have not listened to the voice of justice and brotherhood. We must, therefore, declare our separation. In war the British are our enemies. In peace, they are our friends.

Therefore, as the representatives of the people of the United States of America, in this General Congress assembled, appealing to God for the honesty of our purpose, we do solemnly publish and declare that these United Colonies are, and rightly should be, free and independent states. The people of the United States are no longer subjects of the British crown. All political connections between the colonies and Great Britain are totally ended. These free and independent states have full power to declare war, make peace, make treaties with other countries, establish trade, and do all other acts and things that independent states have the right to do. To support this declaration, with a firm trust on the protection of Divine Providence, we pledge to each other our lives, our fortunes, and our sacred honor.

Button Gwinnett (GA)	Benjamin Harrison (VA)	Lewis Morris (NY)
Lymann Hall (GA)	Thomas Nelson, Jr. (VA)	Richard Stockton (NJ)
George Walton (GA)	Francis Lightfoot Lee (VA)	John Witherspoon (NJ)
William Hooper (NC)	Carter Braxton (VA)	Francis Hopkinson (NJ)
Joseph Hewes (NC)	Robert Morris (PA)	John Hart (NJ)
John Penn (NC)	Benjamin Rush (PA)	Abraham Clark (NJ)
Edward Rutledge (SC)	Benjamin Franklin (PA)	Josiah Bartlett (NH)
Thomas Heyward, Jr. (SC)	John Morton (PA)	William Whipple (NH)
Thomas Lynch, Jr. (SC)	George Clymer (PA)	Samuel Adams (MA)
Arthur Middleton (SC)	James Smith (PA)	John Adams (MA)
John Hancock (MA)	George Taylor (PA)	Robert Treat Paine (MA)
Samuel Chase (MD)	James Wilson (PA)	Elbridge Gerry (MA)
William Paca (MD)	George Ross (PA)	Stephen Hopkins (RI)
Thomas Stone (MD)	Caesar Rodney (DE)	William Ellery (RI)
Charles Carroll of Carrollton (MD)	George Read (DE)	Roger Sherman (CT)
	Thomas McKean (DE)	Samuel Huntington (CT)
George Wythe (VA)	William Floyd (NY)	William Williams (CT)
Richard Henry Lee (VA)	Philip Livingston (NY)	Oliver Wolcott (CT)
Thomas Jefferson (VA)	Francis Lewis (NY)	Matthew Thornton (NH)

"Among the natural rights of the Colonists are these: First, a right to life; Secondly, to liberty; Thirdly, to property; together with the right to support and defend them in the best manner they can."

Samuel Adams, The report of the Committee of Correspondence to the Boston Town Meeting

"All, too, will bear in mind this sacred principle, that though the will of the majority is in all cases to prevail, that will to be rightful must be reasonable; that the minority possess their equal rights, which equal law must protect, and to violate would be oppression."

Thomas Jefferson, First Inaugural Address

COLORADO

KANSAS

MISSOURI

NEW MEXICO

OKLAHOMA

ARKANSAS

Rita Blanca
National Grassland

Lake Meredith
National Recreation Area

Canadian River

Amarillo

LLANO
ESTACADO

GREAT PLAINS

CAP ROCK ESCARPMENT

Lubbock

Red River

Wichita Falls

Lake Texoma

Lake
Arrowhead

Lake
Ray Roberts

Texarkana

Wright Patman
Lake

NORTH

Brazos River

CENTRAL

Fort
Worth

Dallas

Sabine River

Lake Fork Res.

Cedar
Creek
Res.

Tyler

LOUISIANA

Toledo
Bend
Res.

Abilene

Lake
Palestine

PLAINS

Guadalupe Peak
8,749 ft.
(2,667 m)

Guadalupe
National Park

Midland

GUADALUPE
MTS.

Odessa

El Paso

PERMIAN
BASIN

Colorado River

Waco

Richland
Creek
Res.

Trinity River

Sam Rayburn
Res.

CHIHUAHUAN DESERT

Rio Grande

DAVIS
MTS.

Pecos River

San Angelo

TEXAS

Bryan

Lake
Livingston

Big Thicket
National
Preserve

Beaumont

STOCKTON
PLATEAU

GLASS
MTS.

EDWARDS
PLATEAU

Austin

COASTAL PLAINS

Houston

Port
Arthur

Big Bend Ranch
State Park

CHISOS
MTS.

Big Bend
National
Park

Amistad
National
Recreation Area

Amistad
Res.

BALCONES

ESCARPMENT

Del Rio

San Antonio

Guadalupe River

Galveston

Galveston
Island

Choke
Canyon
Res.

Matagorda
Island

28°N

MEXICO

Nueces River

Corpus Christi

Gulf of
Mexico

Laredo

RIO
GRANDE
PLAIN

Padre Island
National
Seashore

Padre
Island

Falcon
Res.

26°N

Brownsville

0   50   100 Miles
0   50   100 Kilometers

24°N

N

Key

★ State capital

• Other city

▲ Highest point
  in state

■ Place of interest

96°W   94°W

Texas Road Map

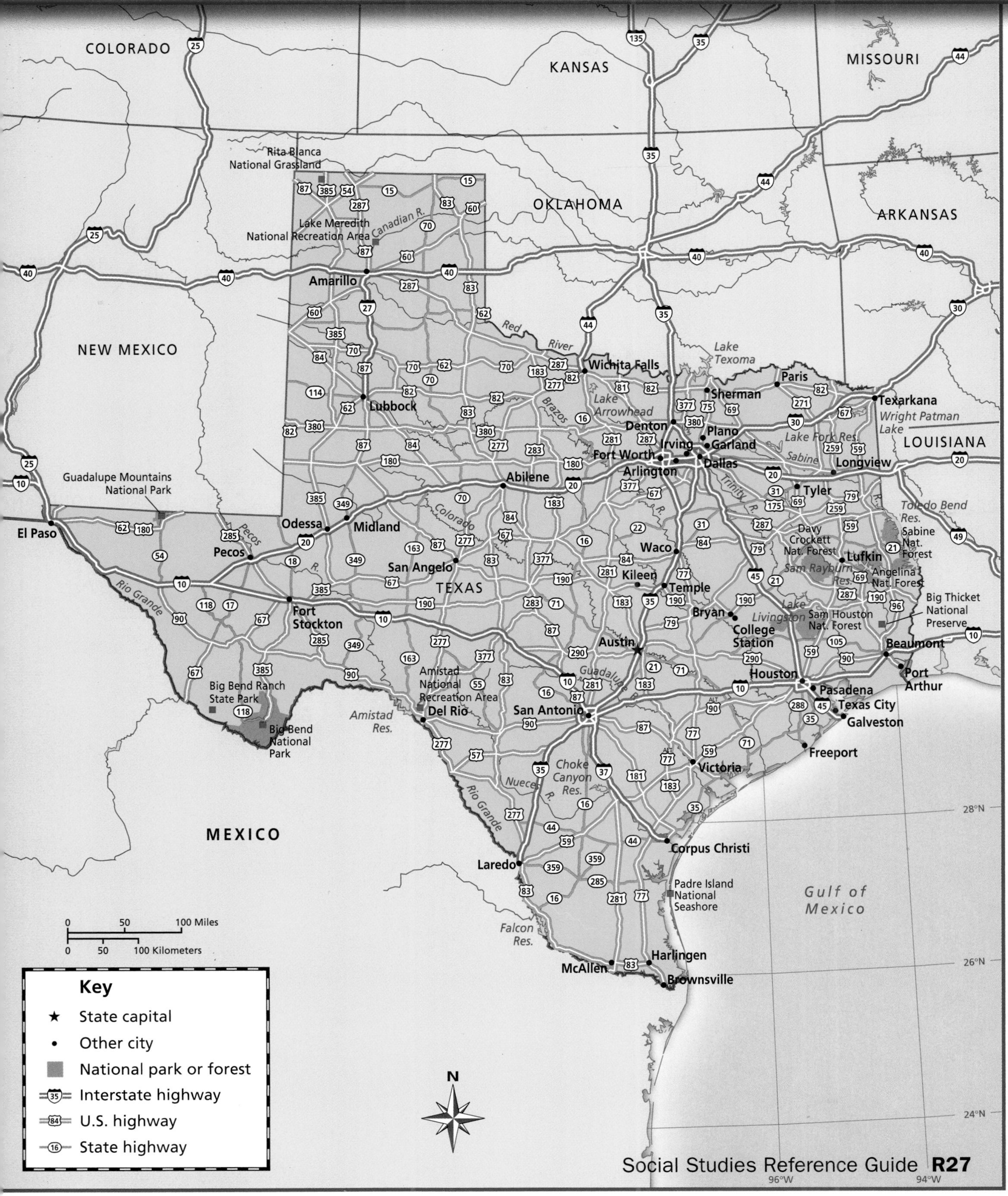

COLORADO
KANSAS
MISSOURI
OKLAHOMA
ARKANSAS
NEW MEXICO
LOUISIANA
MEXICO

Rita Blanca National Grassland
Lake Meredith National Recreation Area
Canadian R.
Red River
Amarillo
Lubbock
Wichita Falls
Lake Texoma
Lake Arrowhead
Denton
Sherman
Paris
Texarkana
Wright Patman Lake
Fort Worth
Irving
Plano
Garland
Dallas
Longview
Arlington
Lake Fork Res.
Sabine
Abilene
Tyler
Toledo Bend Res.
Guadalupe Mountains National Park
El Paso
Odessa
Midland
Pecos
San Angelo
TEXAS
Waco
Kileen
Temple
Bryan
Davy Crockett Nat. Forest
Sam Rayburn Res.
Lufkin
Sabine Nat. Forest
Angelina Nat. Forest
Fort Stockton
College Station
Lake Livingston
Sam Houston Nat. Forest
Big Thicket National Preserve
Beaumont
Big Bend Ranch State Park
Amistad National Recreation Area
Amistad Res.
Del Rio
San Antonio
Austin
Houston
Pasadena
Port Arthur
Texas City
Galveston
Big Bend National Park
Rio Grande
Choke Canyon Res.
Nueces R.
Victoria
Freeport
Laredo
Corpus Christi
Padre Island National Seashore
Gulf of Mexico
Falcon Res.
McAllen
Harlingen
Brownsville
Guadalupe R.
Colorado R.
Pecos R.
Brazos R.
Trinity R.

28°N
26°N
24°N
96°W
94°W

50 100 Miles
50 100 Kilometers

Key

★ State capital
• Other city
▮ National park or forest
🛣 35 Interstate highway
🛣 84 U.S. highway
🛣 16 State highway

Atlas
Texas Counties

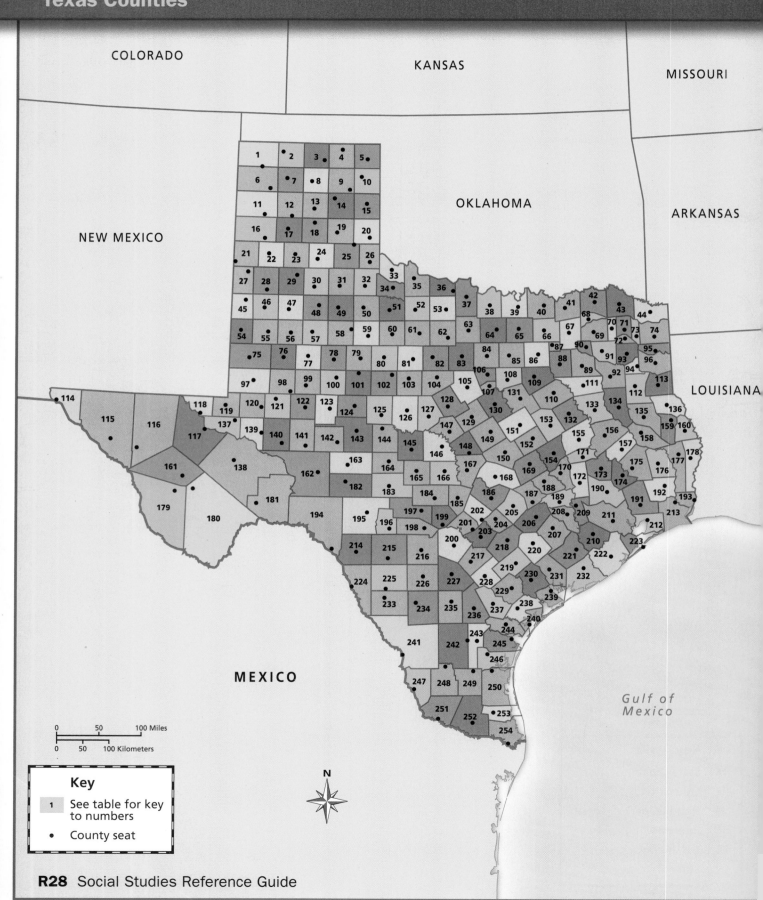

COLORADO

KANSAS

MISSOURI

OKLAHOMA

NEW MEXICO

ARKANSAS

LOUISIANA

MEXICO

Gulf of Mexico

0   50   100 Miles
0   50   100 Kilometers

N

Key

| 1 | See table for key to numbers |

• County seat

TEXAS COUNTIES

County	County Seat	Number
Anderson	Palestine	133
Andrews	Andrews	97
Angelina	Lufkin	158
Aransas	Rockport	240
Archer	Archer City	53
Armstrong	Claude	18
Atascosa	Jourdanton	227
Austin	Bellville	208
Bailey	Muleshoe	27
Bandera	Bandera	198
Bastrop	Bastrop	205
Baylor	Seymour	52
Bee	Beeville	237
Bell	Belton	150
Bexar	San Antonio	200
Blanco	Johnson City	185
Borden	Gail	77
Bosque	Meridian	130
Bowie	New Boston	44
Brazoria	Angleton	222
Brazos	Bryan	170
Brewster	Alpine	180
Briscoe	Silverton	24
Brooks	Falfurrias	249
Brown	Brownwood	127
Burleson	Caldwell	188
Burnet	Burnet	167
Caldwell	Lockhart	204
Calhoun	Port Lavaca	239
Callahan	Baird	103
Cameron	Brownsville	254
Camp	Pittsburg	72
Carson	Panhandle	13
Cass	Linden	74
Castro	Dimmitt	22
Chambers	Anahuac	212
Cherokee	Rusk	134
Childress	Childress	26
Clay	Henrietta	37
Cochran	Morton	45
Coke	Robert Lee	124
Coleman	Coleman	126
Collin	McKinney	66
Collingsworth	Wellington	20
Colorado	Columbus	207
Comal	New Braunfels	201
Comanche	Comanche	128
Concho	Paint Rock	144
Cooke	Gainesville	39
Coryell	Gatesville	149
Cottle	Paducah	32
Crane	Crane	139
Crockett	Ozona	162
Crosby	Crosbyton	48
Culberson	Van Horn	116
Dallam	Dalhart	1
Dallas	Dallas	86
Dawson	Lamesa	76
Deaf Smith	Hereford	16
Delta	Cooper	68
Denton	Denton	65
DeWitt	Cuero	219
Dickens	Dickens	49
Dimmit	Carrizo Springs	33
Donley	Clarendon	19
Duval	San Diego	242
Eastland	Eastland	104
Ector	Odessa	120
Edwards	Rocksprings	195
Ellis	Waxahachie	109
El Paso	El Paso	114
Erath	Stephenville	105
Falls	Marlin	152
Fannin	Bonham	41
Fayette	La Grange	206
Fisher	Roby	79
Floyd	Floydada	30
Foard	Crowell	34
Fort Bend	Richmond	210
Franklin	Mount Vernon	70
Freestone	Fairfield	132
Frio	Pearsall	226
Gaines	Seminole	75
Galveston	Galveston	223
Garza	Post	57
Gillespie	Fredericksburg	184
Glasscock	Garden City	122
Goliad	Goliad	229
Gonzales	Gonzales	218
Gray	Pampa	14
Grayson	Sherman	40
Gregg	Longview	94
Grimes	Anderson	172
Guadalupe	Seguin	203
Hale	Plainview	29
Hall	Memphis	25
Hamilton	Hamilton	129
Hansford	Spearman	3
Hardeman	Quanah	33
Hardin	Kountze	192
Harris	Houston	211
Harrison	Marshall	96
Hartley	Channing	6
Haskell	Haskell	60
Hays	San Marcos	202
Hemphill	Canadian	10
Henderson	Athens	111
Hidalgo	Edinburg	252
Hill	Hillsboro	131
Hockley	Levelland	46
Hood	Granbury	106
Hopkins	Sulphur Springs	69
Houston	Crockett	156
Howard	Big Spring	99
Hudspeth	Sierra Blanca	115
Hunt	Greenville	67
Hutchinson	Stinnett	8
Irion	Mertzon	142
Jack	Jacksboro	63
Jackson	Edna	231
Jasper	Jasper	177
Jeff Davis	Fort Davis	161
Jefferson	Beaumont	213
Jim Hogg	Hebbronville	248
Jim Wells	Alice	243
Johnson	Cleburne	108
Jones	Anson	80
Karnes	Karnes City	228
Kaufman	Kaufman	88
Kendall	Boerne	199
Kenedy	Sarita	250
Kent	Jayton	58
Kerr	Kerrville	197
Kimble	Junction	183
King	Guthrie	50
Kinney	Brackettville	214
Kleberg	Kingsville	246
Knox	Benjamin	51
Lamar	Paris	42
Lamb	Littlefield	28
Lampasas	Lampasas	148
La Salle	Cotulla	234
Lavaca	Hallettsville	220
Lee	Giddings	187
Leon	Centerville	155
Liberty	Liberty	191
Limestone	Groesbeck	153
Lipscomb	Lipscomb	5
Live Oak	George West	236
Llano	Llano	166
Loving	Mentone	118
Lubbock	Lubbock	47
Lynn	Tahoka	56
Madison	Madisonville	171
Marion	Jefferson	95
Martin	Stanton	98
Mason	Mason	165
Matagorda	Bay City	232
Maverick	Eagle Pass	224
McCulloch	Brady	145
McLennan	Waco	151
McMullen	Tilden	235
Medina	Hondo	216
Menard	Menard	164
Midland	Midland	121
Milam	Cameron	169
Mills	Goldthwaite	147
Mitchell	Colorado City	100
Montague	Montague	38
Montgomery	Conroe	190
Moore	Dumas	7
Morris	Daingerfield	73
Motley	Matador	31
Nacogdoches	Nacogdoches	135
Navarro	Corsicana	110
Newton	Newton	178
Nolan	Sweetwater	101
Nueces	Corpus Christi	245
Ochiltree	Perryton	4
Oldham	Vega	11
Orange	Orange	193
Palo Pinto	Palo Pinto	83
Panola	Carthage	113
Parker	Weatherford	84
Parmer	Farwell	21
Pecos	Fort Stockton	138
Polk	Livingston	175
Potter	Amarillo	12
Presidio	Marfa	179
Rains	Emory	90
Randall	Canyon	17
Reagan	Big Lake	141
Real	Leakey	196
Red River	Clarksville	43
Reeves	Pecos	117
Refugio	Refugio	238
Roberts	Miami	9
Robertson	Franklin	154
Rockwall	Rockwall	87
Runnels	Ballinger	125
Rusk	Henderson	112
Sabine	Hemphill	160
San Augustine	San Augustine	159
San Jacinto	Coldspring	174
San Patricio	Sinton	244
San Saba	San Saba	146
Schleicher	Eldorado	163
Scurry	Snyder	78
Shackelford	Albany	81
Shelby	Center	136
Sherman	Stratford	2
Smith	Tyler	92
Somervell	Glen Rose	107
Starr	Rio Grande City	251
Stephens	Breckenridge	82
Sterling	Sterling City	123
Stonewall	Aspermont	59
Sutton	Sonora	182
Swisher	Tulia	23
Tarrant	Fort Worth	85
Taylor	Abilene	102
Terrell	Sanderson	181
Terry	Brownfield	55
Throckmorton	Throckmorton	61
Titus	Mount Pleasant	71
Tom Green	San Angelo	143
Travis	Austin	186
Trinity	Groveton	157
Tyler	Woodville	176
Upshur	Gilmer	93
Upton	Rankin	140
Uvalde	Uvalde	215
Val Verde	Del Rio	194
Van Zandt	Canton	89
Victoria	Victoria	230
Walker	Huntsville	173
Waller	Hempstead	209
Ward	Monahans	137
Washington	Brenham	189
Webb	Laredo	241
Wharton	Wharton	221
Wheeler	Wheeler	15
Wichita	Wichita Falls	36
Wilbarger	Vernon	35
Willacy	Raymondville	253
Williamson	Georgetown	168
Wilson	Floresville	217
Winkler	Kermit	119
Wise	Decatur	64
Wood	Quitman	91
Yoakum	Plains	54
Young	Graham	62
Zapata	Zapata	247
Zavala	Crystal City	225

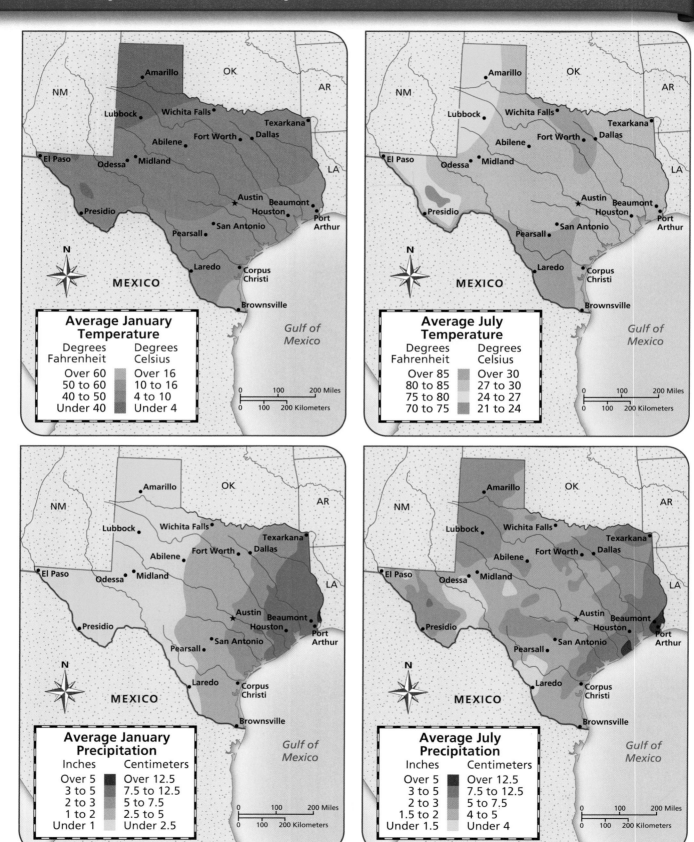

Average January Temperature

Degrees Fahrenheit	Degrees Celsius
Over 60	Over 16
50 to 60	10 to 16
40 to 50	4 to 10
Under 40	Under 4

Average July Temperature

Degrees Fahrenheit	Degrees Celsius
Over 85	Over 30
80 to 85	27 to 30
75 to 80	24 to 27
70 to 75	21 to 24

Average January Precipitation

Inches	Centimeters
Over 5	Over 12.5
3 to 5	7.5 to 12.5
2 to 3	5 to 7.5
1 to 2	2.5 to 5
Under 1	Under 2.5

Average July Precipitation

Inches	Centimeters
Over 5	Over 12.5
3 to 5	7.5 to 12.5
2 to 3	5 to 7.5
1.5 to 2	4 to 5
Under 1.5	Under 4

Texas Governors

J. Pinckney Henderson
1846–1847

George T. Wood
1847–1849

Peter Hansbrough Bell
1849–1853

James W. Henderson
1853

Elisha M. Pease
1853–1857

Hardin R. Runnels
1857–1859

Sam Houston
1859–1861

Edward Clark
1861

Francis R. Lubbock
1861–1863

Pendleton Murrah
1863–1865

Andrew J. Hamilton
1865–1866

James W. Throckmorton
1866–1867

Elisha M. Pease
1867–1869

Edmund J. Davis
1870–1874

Richard Coke (D)
1874–1876

Richard B. Hubbard (D)
1876–1879

Oran M. Roberts (D)
1879–1883

John Ireland (D)
1883–1887

Lawrence Sullivan Ross (D)
1887–1891

James Stephen Hogg (D)
1891–1895

Charles A. Culberson (D)
1895–1899

Joseph D. Sayers (D)
1899–1903

S. W. T. Lanham (D)
1903–1907

Thomas Mitchell Campbell (D)
1907–1911

Oscar Branch Colquitt (D)
1911–1915

James E. Ferguson (D)
1915–1917

William Pettus Hobby (D)
1917–1921

Pat Morris Neff (D)
1921–1925

Miriam A. Ferguson (D)
1925–1927

Dan Moody (D)
1927–1931

Ross S. Sterling (D)
1931–1933

Miriam A. Ferguson (D)
1933–1935

James V. Allred (D)
1935–1939

W. Lee O'Daniel (D)
1939–1941

Coke R. Stevenson (D)
1941–1947

Beauford H. Jester (D)
1947–1949

Allan Shivers (D)
1949–1957

Price Daniel (D)
1957–1963

John Connally (D)
1963–1969

Preston Smith (D)
1969–1973

Dolph Briscoe (D)
1973–1979

William P. Clements (R)
1979–1983

Mark White (D)
1983–1987

William P. Clements (R)
1987–1991

Ann W. Richards (D)
1991–1995

George W. Bush (R)
1995–2000

James Richard Perry (R)
2000–present

(D) Democrat   **(R)** Republican

Texas Time Line

800
Mound Builders (Caddo) farm in Texas.

"Texas" comes from Caddo word for "friend."

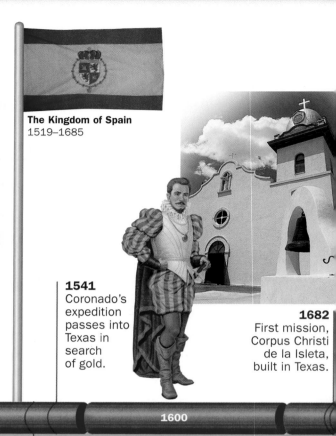

The Kingdom of Spain
1519–1685

1541
Coronado's expedition passes into Texas in search of gold.

1682
First mission, Corpus Christi de la Isleta, built in Texas.

800   1500   1600

About 10,000 years ago
The first people live on Texas plains.

1528
Cabeza de Vaca reaches Texas.

1685
La Salle brings French colonists to Texas.

The Kingdom of France
1685–1690

The Kingdom of Spain
1690–1821

The Mexican Federal Republic
1821–1836

The Republic of Texas
1836–1845

March 1836
Texas declares independence and sets up a new government.

Texas loses the Battle of the Alamo.

1824
Stephen F. Austin founds San Felipe de Austin.

1852
First locomotive comes to Texas.

1700   1800   1810   1820   1830   1840   1850

1700s
Spanish begin ranching in Texas.

1821
Stephen F. Austin brings 300 American colonists to settle Texas.

1835
Texans battle Mexican troops at Gonzales and Goliad.

Texas troops force Mexican Army from San Antonio.

September 1836
Sam Houston elected President of the new Republic of Texas.

1845
Texas becomes the 28th U.S. state.

1846–1848
United States and Mexico go to war.

Texas Time Line

The Confederate States of America
1861–1865
(official flag 1861–1863)

1874
Joseph Glidden develops an improved barbed wire.

1901
Oil is discovered at Spindletop.

The United States of America
1865–Present

1929
Stock Market crashes/Great Depression begins.

1861
Texas secedes from the Union.

1911
Texas has more miles of railroad track than any other state.

1860   1870   1880   1890   1900   1910   1920   19

1870
Texas rejoins the United States.

1865
Last battle of the Civil War is fought and slaves are freed in Texas.

Civil War ends.

1900
Farming becomes an important industry in Texas.

1914–1918
World War I

1925
Miriam A. Ferguson becomes first woman governor of Texas.

1860
Abraham Lincoln elected President of the United States.

1928
Texas becomes the leading oil-producing state.

2001
Lance
Armstrong
wins his third
Tour de France
bicycling
championship.

1969
Neil Armstrong
walks on the
moon.

Mission Control
at what is now
called the
Johnson Space
Center in
Houston directs
this flight.

1941
United States enters
World War II.

1940   1950   1960   1970   1980   1990   2000

1996
First Texas
Book Festival
opens.

1945
World War II ends.

Texas Missions

Mission San Antonio de Valero
(Mission San Antonio)

Founded in 1718, this famous mission was the site of the Battle of the Alamo.

Mission San José y San Miguel de Aguayo
(Mission San José)

Founded in 1720, this mission was once home to more than 300 people.

Mission San Francisco de la Espada
(Mission Espada)

Founded in 1690 near Weches and relocated to San Antonio in 1731, parts of its irrigation system are still in use today.

Mission Nuestra Señora de la Purisima Concepción de Acuña
(Mission Concepción)

Founded in 1716 in eastern Texas and relocated to San Antonio in 1731, this mission was once decorated with colorful paintings. They have faded away with age.

Mission San Juan Capistrano
(Mission San Juan)

Founded in 1716 in eastern Texas and relocated to San Antonio in 1731, this mission was the center of a thriving farming community.

Honoring Our National Flag

The flag of the United States of America is an important symbol for our country. The flag should be shown respect at all times. Rules about how to honor our flag are shown on these two pages.

The Pledge of Allegiance

I pledge allegiance to the flag of the United States of America and to the Republic for which it stands, one Nation under God, indivisible, with liberty and justice for all.

When saying the Pledge of Allegiance, stand, face the flag, and place your right hand over your heart.

Displaying the Flag

Display the flag only from sunrise to sunset, except when bad weather might damage the flag.

No other flag or pennant should be placed above or, if on the same level, to the right of the flag of the United States of America.

When the flag passes in a parade, stand and either put your hand over your heart or give the military salute, if you are in uniform.

When singing the National Anthem, everyone should rise and stand at attention. A man should remove his hat with his right hand and place the palm of his right hand over his heart.

Flag Holidays

The flag of the United States should be flown every day, but especially on these holidays:

New Year's Day . . . . January 1

Inauguration Day . . . . January 20

Lincoln's Birthday . . . . . . February 12

Washington's Birthday . . third Monday in February

Easter Sunday . . . . varies

Mother's Day . . . . second Sunday in May

Armed Forces Day . . . . . third Saturday in May

Memorial Day . . . . last Monday in May (half-staff until noon)

Flag Day . . . . June 14

Independence Day . . . . . . July 4

Labor Day . . . . first Monday in September

Constitution Day . . . . . . September 17

Columbus Day . . . . second Monday in October

Navy Day . . . . October 27

Veterans Day . . . . November 11

Thanksgiving Day . . . . . . fourth Thursday in November

Christmas Day . . . . December 25

By Executive Order, the flag flies 24 hours a day at the following locations:

The Betsy Ross House, Philadelphia, Pennsylvania

The White House, Washington, D.C.

U.S. Capitol, Washington, D.C.

Washington Monument, Washington, D.C.

Iwo Jima Memorial to U.S. Marines, Arlington, Virginia

Battleground in Lexington, Massachusetts (site of first shots in the Revolutionary War)

Winter encampment cabins, Valley Forge, Pennsylvania

Fort McHenry, Baltimore, Maryland (A flag flying over Fort McHenry after a battle during the War of 1812 provided the inspiration for "The Star-Spangled Banner.")

The Star-Spangled Banner Flag House, Baltimore, Maryland (site where the famed flag over Fort McHenry was sewn)

Jenny Wade House in Gettysburg, Pennsylvania (Jenny Wade was the only civilian killed at the battle of Gettysburg.)

U.S.S. *Arizona* Memorial, Pearl Harbor, Hawaii

Pledge of allegiance to the Texas state flag

(a) The pledge of allegiance to the Texas state flag is "Honor the Texas flag; I pledge allegiance to thee, Texas, one and indivisible."

(b) The pledge of allegiance to the Texas state flag should be said by standing at attention facing the flag with the right hand over the heart. Individuals who are not in uniform and who are wearing a hat should remove it with their right hand and hold it at the left shoulder, with the hand over the heart. Individuals in uniform should remain silent, face the flag, and give the military salute.

(c) The pledge of allegiance to the Texas state flag may be recited at all public and private meetings at which the pledge of allegiance to the United States flag is recited and at state historical events and celebrations.

(d) The pledge of allegiance to the Texas state flag should be recited after the pledge of allegiance to the United States flag if both are recited.

Texas Symbols

State Flower

The **Bluebonnet** gets its name from its blossoms, which look like blue sunbonnets.

State Tree

The **Pecan Tree** earned its title of Texas State Tree in 1919. People enjoy pecans in pies, candy, and stuffing.

State Plant

The **prickly pear cactus** displays yellow, red, orange, or purple flowers in spring and summer.

State Bird

Mockingbirds imitate the calls of other birds with songs. They can even imitate the sounds of whistles and sirens!

State Small Mammal

Armadillos are about the size of large cats. They use their keen sense of smell to find food.

State Large Mammal

Longhorns are named for their long horns. In 1927, a herd of official state longhorns was formed to preserve the breed.

State Mineral

Blue Topaz is a common gemstone used in jewelry. It can also be clear, yellow, orange, red, or green.

Gazetteer

This Gazetteer is a geographic dictionary that will help you locate and pronounce the names of places in this book. Latitude and longitude are given for cities. The page numbers tell you where each place appears on a map (m) or in the text (t).

 **A**

Abilene (ab´ ə lēn´) a major city in the Central Plains region of Texas; 32°N, 99°W (m 53, t 55)

Adobe Walls (ə dō´ bē wȯlz) site of a battle between the U.S. and Native Americans in Texas (m 261, t 261)

Alibates Flint Quarries National Monument (al´ ə bāts flint kwȯr´ ēz nash´ ə nəl mon´ yə mənt) an archaeological site in the Texas Panhandle (m 90, t 92)

Amarillo (am´ ə ril´ ō) a major city in the Great Plains region of Texas; 35°N, 101°W (m 57, t 58)

Art (ärt) a small town in central Texas (t 385)

Austin (ȯ´ stən) the capital city of Texas; 30°N, 97°W (m 14, t 67)

 **B**

Beaumont (bō´ mont) an oil boomtown of the early 1900s (m 314, t 315)

Beringia (bir ən gē´ ə) a grassy plain that connected Asia and North America long ago (m 91, t 91)

Bering Strait (bir´ ing strāt´) a waterway separating Asia and North America (m 91, t 91)

Blackland Prairie (blak´ lənd prâr´ ē) an area of dark soil that lies west of the Post Oak Belt of Texas (m 65, t 67)

Brownsville (brouns´ vil) a southern Texas town near the site of the last battle of the U.S. Civil War (m 242, t 247)

 **C**

Caddoan Mounds (kad´ ō ən moundz) mounds in the Piney Woods region that were built by the Caddo more than 1,200 years ago (m 96, t 97)

Canada (kan´ ə də) one of the two countries that border the United States (m 9, t 12)

Canyon (kan´ yən) a town in northwestern Texas (t 344)

Caprock Escarpment (cap´ rok e skärp´ mənt) a line of steep slopes or cliffs that separate the Great Plains and Central Plains regions of Texas (m 57, t 57)

Central Plains region (sen´ trəl plānz rē´ jən) a flat and rolling region that extends from Texas through parts of Canada (m 51, t 53)

Coastal Plains region (kō´ stl plānz rē´ jən) the largest region in Texas (m 64, t 65)

Columbia (kə lum´ bē ə) the first capital city of the Texas Republic (m 188, t 195)

Cross Timbers (krȯs tim´ bərz) an area of land in the Central Plains of Texas with two strips of forest (m 53, t 54)

Cuzco (küz´ ko) the capital of the Inca empire (m 108, t 111)

 **D**

Dallas (dal´ əs) a major Texas city located in the Blackland Prairie of Texas; 32°N, 96°W (m 65, t 67)

Pronunciation Key

a in hat	ȯ in all	sh in she
ā in age	ō in open	th in thin
â in care	ô in order	ᴛʜ in then
ä in far	oi in oil	zh in measure
e in let	ou in out	ə = a in about
ē in equal	u in cup	ə = e in taken
ėr in term	ú in put	ə = i in pencil
i in it	ü in rule	ə = o in lemon
ī in ice	ch in child	ə = u in circus
o in hot	ng in long	

Gazetteer

Deep Ellum (dēp əl lum´) a district in Dallas that was founded by African Americans and was famous for music in the 1920s (t 334)

Dodge City, Kansas (doj sit´ē kan´zəs) a railroad town that was the end of many cattle drives; 37°N, 100°W (m 274, t 275)

Dolores Hidalgo, Mexico (dō lō res hi dal´gō mek´sə kō) the site of the beginning of the Mexican Revolution in 1810 (m 138, t 139)

Eagle Pass a city on the Rio Grande in the western part of the Coastal Plains region (m 102, t 106)

Edwards Plateau (ed´wərdz pla tō´) a high, hilly stretch of land south of the High Plains of Texas (m 57, t 57)

El Capitan (el ca pē tan´) a large mountain in the Mountains and Basins region of Texas (m 61, t 63)

El Paso (el pas´ō) the only major Texas city in the Mountains and Basins region of Texas; 31°N, 106°W (m 61, t 62)

Fort Worth (fôrt wėrth) a city in the Central Plains of Texas; 32°N, 97°W (m 53, t 54)

Galveston (gal´vəs tən) a city in Texas on the Gulf of Mexico that was struck by a violent hurricane in 1900; 29°N, 94°W (m 28, t 29)

Galveston Island (gal´vəs tən ī´lənd) an island in the Gulf of Mexico reached by Cabeza de Vaca in 1528 (m 116, t 119)

Garcitas Creek (gar sē´təs krēk) site of a small fort built by La Salle (m 116, t 122)

Goliad (gō´lē ad) southern Texas town; site of a massacre of Texan troops in 1836; 29°N, 97°W (m 171, t 171, t 189)

Gonzales (gon zahl´əs) southern Texas town; site of a battle between Mexican soldiers and Texan soldiers in 1835; 29°N, 97°W (m 170, t 171)

Grand Prairie (grand prâr´ē) a large, grassy area of land in the Central Plains of Texas (m 53, t 54)

Great Plains region (grāt plānz rē´jən) a high, flat grassland in Texas (m 56, t 57)

Guadalupe Hidalgo (gwä´dl üp´ hi dal´gō) a village near Mexico City, Mexico, in which the treaty ending the war between the U.S. and Mexico was signed (m 216, t 219)

Guadalupe Peak (gwä´dl üp´ā pēk) the highest point in Texas (m 13, 61; t 13, 61)

Gulf Coast Plain (gulf kōst plān) an area in Texas along the Gulf of Mexico (m 65, t 66)

Gulf of Mexico (gulf uv mek´sə kō) a large body of water near Texas (m 9, t 12)

Harlem (här´ləm) a neighborhood in New York City where many African American artists gathered in the 1920s (t 334)

Harrisburg (har´is bėrg´) a town on the San Jacinto River in Texas, later renamed Houston (m 188, t 190)

High Plains (hī plānz) an area of land in the Texas Panhandle (m 57, t 57)

Houston (hyü´stən) a port city in Texas located near the Gulf of Mexico; 29°N, 95°W (m 65, t 67)

Indian Territory (in´dē ən ter´ə tôr´ē) an area of land set aside for Native Americans; today it is the state of Oklahoma (t 260)

Ingleside (ing´gəl sīd) a town in Texas; 27°N, 97°W (m 9, t 26)

★ J ★

Juárez (hwär´ es) a town in Mexico across the Rio Grande from El Paso, Texas; 31°N, 106°W (m 61, t 62)

★ K ★

King Ranch (king ranch) a cattle ranch in South Texas (m 268, t 268)

★ L ★

Laredo (lar ā´ dō) a town on the Rio Grande where Santa Anna crossed into Texas in 1836; 27°N, 99°W (m 180, t 181)

Leander (lē an´ dər) a town in central Texas; 30°N, 97°W (m 28, t 30)

Livingston (liv´ ing ston) a city in Texas near the Alabama-Coushatta Reservation; 30°N, 94°W (m 96, t 100)

Llano Basin (lä´ nō bā´sn) a rocky, bowl-shaped area near the Edwards Plateau in Texas (m 57, t 57)

Lubbock (lub´ ək) a city in Texas known as "the Hub of the Great Plains"; 33°N, 101°W (m 57, t 58)

Lufkin (luf´ kin) a sawmill town in East Texas (m 306, t 308)

★ M ★

Mexico (mek´ sə kō) one of the two countries that border the United States (m 9, t 12)

Mexico City (mek´ sə kō) a city in Mexico where Stephen F. Austin met with Santa Ana (m 148, t 150)

Midland (mid´ lənd) a major city in the Great Plains region of Texas; 32°N, 101°W (m 57, t 58)

Monterrey, Mexico (mon´ tər rā mek´ sə kō) a town in Mexico where monarch butterflies stay through the winter (m 36, t 42)

Mountains and Basins region (moun´ tənz and bā´ snz rē´ jən) a large area of land in western Texas (m 60, t 61)

★ N ★

New Braunfels (nü brôn´ fəlz) a town in central Texas settled by Germans (m 204, t 208)

North America (nôrth ə mer´ ə kə) a continent in the Western Hemisphere where Texas is located (m 11, t 11)

★ O ★

Odessa (ō des´ ə) a major city in the Great Plains region of Texas; 31°N, 102°W (m 57, t 58)

★ P ★

Padre Island (pä´ drā ī´ lənd) a narrow, sandy island that runs along the Texas coast of the Gulf of Mexico (m 65, t 68)

Palo Alto (pa lō al´ tō) a town in Mexico that was the site of the first battle of the Mexican War (m 216, t 217)

Palo Duro Canyon (pə´ lō dur´ ō kan´ yən) the second largest canyon in the United States (m 57, t 59)

Panna Maria (pan´ ə mar´ ē ə) a town in Texas settled by Poles in 1854 (m 204, t 209)

Pearl Harbor, Hawaii (pėrl här´ bər hə wī´ ē) a U.S naval base bombed by Japan on December 7, 1941 (t 342)

Piney Woods (pī´nē wůdz) part of a large forest that stretches from the coast of the Atlantic Ocean to Texas (m 65, t 66)

Pronunciation Key

a in hat	ȯ in all	sh in she
ā in age	ō in open	th in thin
â in care	ô in order	ᴛʜ in then
ä in far	oi in oil	zh in measure
e in let	ou in out	ə = a in about
ē in equal	u in cup	ə = e in taken
ėr in term	ů in put	ə = i in pencil
i in it	ü in rule	ə = o in lemon
ī in ice	ch in child	ə = u in circus
o in hot	ng in long	

Gazetteer

Post Oak Belt (pōst ōk belt) a stretch of rolling hills and prairie in the northeast of Texas (m 65, t 67)

Red River (red riv´ər) a river in the Texas Panhandle (m 261, t 262)

Rio Grande Valley (rē´ ō grand´ val´ ē) a valley in Texas where citrus fruits are grown (m 9, t 38)

Rolling Plains (rōl´ ing plānz) an area of land in the Central Plains of Texas with many ranches and oil fields (m 53, t 54)

Sabine Pass (sā´ bin pas) a battle site of the U.S. Civil War (m 246, t 246)

Saltillo (säl tē´ yō) a town in Mexico where Stephen F. Austin was arrested and jailed (m 148, t 150)

San Angelo (san an´ gəl ō) a town in Texas where some of the first cattle drives began; 31°N, 100°W (m 274, t 275)

San Antonio (san an tō´ nē ō) a major city in southern Texas where the Alamo is located; 29°N, 98°W (m 65, t 67)

San Felipe de Austin (san fəl ē´ pā dā ô´ stən) the first town of the Austin colony in Texas (m 138, 140, t 141)

Sedalia, Missouri (sə da´ lē ə mə zur´ ē) a railroad town that was the end of many cattle drives (m 274, t 275)

South Texas (south tek´ səs) the southern part of Texas, known for longhorn cattle (m 266, t 267)

South Texas Plain (south tek´ səs plān´) a large, dry area in southern Texas (m 65, t 66)

Spindletop (spin´ dl top) the hill near Beaumont where drillers struck an oil gusher in 1901 (m 315, t 315)

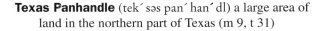

Tenochtitlan (tā nòch´ tē tlän´) an ancient city in Mexico that was once the center of the Aztec empire (m 108, t 110)

Texas Panhandle (tek´ səs pan´ han´ dl) a large area of land in the northern part of Texas (m 9, t 31)

Tikal (tē käl´) a town in Central America that was once the capital of the Mayan Empire (m 108, t 109)

Tyler (tī´ lər) a town in Texas known as the "Rose Capital of America"; 32°N, 95°W (m 36, t 39)

Velasco (vəl ahs´ kō) site of the signing of the treaty ending the fighting between Texas and Mexico (m 188, t 192)

Victoria (vik tôr´ ē ə) a town near the Guadalupe River in Texas (m 138, t 144)

Washington, D.C. (wäsh´ ing tən dē´ sē´) the capital city of the United States; 38°N, 77°W (m 396, t 403)

Washington-on-the-Brazos (wäsh´ ing tən on тнə brä´ zōs) site of the signing of the Texas Declaration of Independence (m 170, t 174)

Western Hemisphere (wes´ tərn hem´ ə sfir) the half of Earth west of the Prime Meridian (m 11, t 11)

Ysleta (yes lə´ tə) an old mission town near El Paso, Texas (m 126, t 127)

Biographical Dictionary

This Biographical Dictionary tells you about the people in this book and how to pronounce their names. The page numbers tell you where the person first appears in the text.

Armstrong, Lance (ärm´ strông´) (1971–) Bicycling champion who won the Tour de France in 1999, 2000, and 2001. (p. 384)

Armstrong, Neil A. (ärm´ strông´) (1930–) United States astronaut who, on July 20, 1969, became the first human to set foot on the moon. (p. 372)

Arnold, Hendrick (är´ nld) (?–1849) Free African American scout who fought in the Texas Revolution. (p. 190)

Austin, Moses (ȯ´ stən) (1767–1821) American businessman who received a grant from the Spanish government to bring 300 families to Texas. (p. 140)

Austin, Stephen F. (ȯ´ stən) (1793–1836) Known as the "Father of Texas." He established a colony of settlers in Texas at the end of 1821. (p. 140)

Bedichek, Roy (bə´ di chək) (1878–1959) Texas naturalist who wrote a book about his experiences with nature in Texas. (p. 38)

Benavides, Santos (bə nah vē´ dās) (1823–1891) Highest ranking Mexican American to serve in the Confederacy. (p. 246)

Biggers, John (big´ gərs) (1924–2001) Artist and teacher who founded the art department at Texas Southern University in Houston. (p. 67)

Blanton, Annie Webb (blan´ tən) (1870–1945) First woman elected to statewide office in Texas. (p. 328)

Bonham, James (bon´ əm) (1807–1836) The last Texan to enter the Alamo before the battle began there. (p. 182)

Borden, Gail (bôr´ dən) (1801–1874) He invented condensed milk in 1853. He also set up a newspaper in 1835 called the *Telegraph and Texas Register*. (p. 142)

Bowie, James (bō´ ē) (1796–1836) Colonel who readied Texas soldiers for the Alamo battle. He was famous for the "bowie" knife that he used. (p. 182)

Buffalo Soldiers (buf´ ə lō sōl´ jərz) African American soldiers who fought against the Plains Indians in Texas. (p. 259)

Burnet, David G. (bùr´ nət) (1788–1870) Texas lawyer and landowner who was chosen as the first president of the Republic of Texas. (p. 176)

Bush, George Herbert Walker (bùsh) (1924–) President of the United States from 1989 to 1993. (p. 397)

Bush, George W. (bùsh) (1946–) Governor of Texas from 1994 to 2000. He began serving as President of the United States in 2001. (p. 397)

Bush, Laura (bùsh) (1946–) First Lady of Texas from 1994 to 2000. She founded the annual Texas Book Festival. She became First Lady of the United States in 2001. (p. 383)

Cabeza de Vaca, Alvar Núñez (kä bā´ zä dä vä´ kä) (c.1490–c.1560) Spanish explorer who traveled through present-day Texas, New Mexico, and Mexico. (p. 118)

Pronunciation Key

a in hat	ȯ in all	sh in she
ā in age	ō in open	th in thin
â in care	ô in order	ᴛʜ in then
ä in far	oi in oil	zh in measure
e in let	ou in out	ə = a in about
ē in equal	u in cup	ə = e in taken
ėr in term	ù in put	ə = i in pencil
i in it	ü in rule	ə = o in lemon
ī in ice	ch in child	ə = u in circus
o in hot	ng in long	

Biographical Dictionary

Cabrillo, Juan Rodríguez (kä brē´ yō, wän rod rē´ gāz) (?–1543) The first European to explore the California coast. (p. 125)

Cazneau, Jane McManus (käz nyō) (1807–1878) Writer sent to Mexico to seek peace. She was the only female newspaper reporter in the Mexican War. (p. 218)

Childress, George C. (chil´ drəs) (1804–1841) Head of the group that wrote the Texas Declaration of Independence in 1836. (p. 174)

Chisholm, Jesse (chiz´ əm) (1805?–1868) Texas trailherder. He blazed a trail between Mexico and Kansas that became known as the Chisholm Trail. (p. 275)

Cisneros, Henry G. (sis nār´ ōs) (1947–) Mayor of San Antonio from 1981 to 1989. He served as U.S. Secretary of Housing and Urban Development under former president William Jefferson Clinton. (p. 409)

Coahuiltecan (kō ə hwē´ tə kən) Native American groups who hunted and gathered all across southern Texas beginning thousands of years ago. (p. 99)

Columbus, Christopher (kə lum´ bəs) (1451?–1506) Sea captain and trader who tried to find a western route to Asia for Spain. He landed instead on an island near modern-day Florida. (p. 117)

Coronado, Francisco Vásquez de (kôr´ ə nä´ do, frän sēs´ kō väs´ kes´ ᴛнa) (c.1510–1554) Spanish explorer who led an expedition to search for the Seven Cities of Cíbola. (p. 120)

Cortés, Hernando (kôr tez´) (1485–1547) Spanish conquistador who defeated the Aztecs and their leader Moctezuma of Tenochtitlan, now Mexico City. (p. 118)

Cós, General de (kōs) (1800–1854) General in the Mexican army during the Texas Revolution. (p. 172)

Crockett, David (Davy) (krok´ it) (1786–1836) Frontiersman and political and military leader. He led a group of volunteers from Tennessee to fight at the Alamo. He died at the battle. (p. 182)

Davis, Edmund (dā´ vis) (1827–1883) Governor of Texas from 1870 to 1874. (p. 253)

Davis, Jefferson (dā´ vis) (1808–1889) President of the Confederacy during the Civil War. (p. 245)

De Soto, Hernando (di sō´ tō) (1500?–1542) Spanish explorer who traveled through present-day southeastern United States. He was the first European to see the Mississippi River in 1540. (p. 122)

Díaz, Porfirio (dē´ äs, por fē´ rē ō) (1830–1915) Mexican president who was removed from office in 1910 at the start of the Mexican Revolution. (p. 325)

Dickinson, Susanna Wilkerson (dik´ ən sən) (c. 1814–1883) Alamo survivor who is said to have helped carry word of the battle outcome to Sam Houston. (p. 183)

Eisenhower, Dwight David (ī´ zn hou´ ər) (1890–1969) Commander in Chief of the Allied forces in western Europe during World War II. He was President of the United States from 1953 to 1961. (p. 397)

Estéban (əs tə´ bän) (1500?–1539) Enslaved African who explored present-day southern Texas with Cabeza de Vaca. (p. 119)

Fannin, James (fan´ nən) (1804–1836) Colonel during the Texas Revolution who was killed at Goliad on March 27, 1836. (p. 182)

Ferguson, Miriam "Ma" (fər´ gu sun) (1875–1961) Elected first female governor of Texas. Her husband, James Edward Ferguson, was removed from office. (p. 331)

Ford, Henry (fôrd) (1863–1947) American automobile manufacturer who, in 1903, built a factory to make cars. He was the first to use an assembly line. (p. 309)

Gaines, Matthew (gānz) (1840–1900) African American elected to the Texas Senate in 1869. (p. 252)

Glidden, Joseph F. (glid´ ən) (1813–1906) Invented the

first commercially successful barbed wire. (p. 277)

González, Henry B. (gon zä´ləz) (1916–2000) First Hispanic from Texas to be elected to a seat in the U.S. Congress. (p. 409)

Goodnight, Charles (güd´ nit) (1836–1929) American cattleman who helped establish the JA Ranch in the Texas Panhandle and blazed a famous cattle trail. (p. 268)

Goodnight, Mary Ann "Aunt Molly" Dyer (güd´ nit) (1839–1926) Known as "Mother of the Panhandle." She opened Goodnight College with husband Charles Goodnight and her brothers. (p. 272)

Granger, Gordon (grān´ jər) (1822–1876) Union general who rode through Texas to announce that all enslaved Texans were free under United States law. (p. 251)

Grant, Ulysses S. (grant) (1822–1885) General who led the Union Army during the Civil War; eighteenth President of the United States. (p. 245)

Gray, William F. (grā) (1787–1841) Lawyer, author, and colonel who kept a diary of events during the Convention of 1836 at Washington-on-the-Brazos. (p. 178)

Idar, Jovita (ē´ där) (1885–1946) Worked for Tejano rights, first as a teacher and then as a writer. (p. 325)

Jemison, Mae C. (jəm´ ə sun) (1956–) First African American woman to fly in space, in 1992. (p. 373)

Jimenez, Flaco (hē mə´ nəz) (1939–) Accordionist and Norteño musician, he is the brother of Santiago Jimenez, Jr. In 2001, he received the first Texas Medal of the Arts in folk arts. (p. 385)

Jimenez, Santiago, Jr. (hē mə´ nəz) (1944–) Accordionist and Norteño musician, he is the brother of Flaco Jimenez. In 2001, he received the first Texas Medal of the Arts in folk arts. (p. 385)

Johnson, Claudia Alta Taylor "Lady Bird" (jon´ sən) (1912–) First Lady of the United States from 1963 to 1969. She founded the National Wildlife Research Center near Austin in 1982. (p. 26)

Johnson, Frank (jon´ sən) (1799–1884) Led an attack, with Ben Milam, on Mexican soldiers in San Antonio on December 5, 1835. (p. 172)

Johnson, Lyndon B. (jon´ sən) (1908–1973) President of the United States from 1963 to 1969. (p. 341)

Jones, Anson (jōnz) (1798–1858) Last president of the Republic of Texas. (p. 206)

Joplin, Scott (jop´ lən) (1868–1917) Ragtime composer and musician. (p. 332)

H

Henderson, James Pinckney (hən´ dər sun) (1808–1858) First governor of Texas. (p. 207)

Hidalgo, Father Miguel (hi dal´ gō) (1753–1811) Mexican priest who called for a government fair to all people. This demand started a fight for independence from Spain. (p. 139)

Higgins, Pattillo (hig´ gənz) (1863–1955) Texas businessman who discovered oil at Spindletop in 1901. (p. 315)

Holley, Mary Austin (hol´ ē) (1784–1846) Cousin of Stephen Austin and author of *Texas,* the first history of Texas written in English. (p. 84)

Houston, Sam (hyü´ stən) (1793–1863) A general during the Texas Revolution. He was the first president of the Republic of Texas and governor of Texas from 1859 to 1861. (p. 173)

Hutchison, Kay Bailey (huch´ ə sun) (1943–) First woman to represent Texas in the United States Senate. (p. 409)

Pronunciation Key

a in hat	ȯ in all	sh in she
ā in age	ō in open	th in thin
â in care	ô in order	ᴛʜ in then
ä in far	oi in oil	zh in measure
e in let	ou in out	ə = a in about
ē in equal	u in cup	ə = e in taken
ėr in term	ù in put	ə = i in pencil
i in it	ü in rule	ə = o in lemon
ī in ice	ch in child	ə = u in circus
o in hot	ng in long	

Biographical Dictionary

Jordan, Barbara (jôrd´n) (1936–1996) She was the first African American woman from the South to be elected to the U.S. Congress. (p. 409)

July, Johanna (jủ li´) (1857?–1945?) Vaquera who broke horses and mules. (p. 275)

King, Henrietta (king) (1832–1925) Co-founder of a large ranch in southern Texas. She ran the ranch after the death of her husband, Richard King. (p. 268)

King, Richard (king) (1825–1885) Co-founder of a large ranch in southern Texas. (p. 268)

King, Martin Luther, Jr., (1929–1968) Georgia minister who led a national movement to give all U.S. citizens equal rights. (p. 369)

La Salle, René-Robert Cavelier, Sieur de (lə sal´) (1643–1687) French explorer who helped set up the Fort St. Louis colony. (p. 122)

Lamar, Mirabeau B. (la mär´) (1798–1859) President of the Republic of Texas from 1838 to 1841. (p. 193)

Lee, Robert E. (lē) (1807–1870) General who led a Confederate army during the Civil War. (p. 245)

Lee, Sheila Jackson (lē) (1950–) Represented a part of Houston in the U.S. House of Representatives. (p. 409)

León, Martin de (dā lā´ōn) (1765–1833) Texas rancher who started a colony of Mexican families in Texas in the 1820s. (p. 144)

León, Patricia de la Garza de (dā lā ōn´) (1775–1849) She and husband Martin de León founded the only colony in Texas that was almost entirely Mexican. She started a school and church. (p. 144)

Lincoln, Abraham (ling´kən) (1809–1865) Sixteenth President of the United States and signer of the Emancipation Proclamation. (p. 244)

Loetscher, Ila (lō´chər) (1904–2000) Founded Sea Turtle, Inc., an organization aimed at protecting turtles. (p. 46)

Logan, Greenbury (lō´gən) (1799–?) African American soldier in the Texas Revolution. (p. 175)

Long, Jane (lông) (1798–1880) Member of the Old Three Hundred who settled the Austin Colony. (p. 141)

Lubbock, Francis (lub´ək) (1815–1905) Governor of Texas from 1861 to 1863. (p. 241)

Lucas, Anthony F. (lü´kəs) (1855–1921) Engineer who drilled the first oil well at Spindletop in 1901. (p. 315)

Mackenzie, Ranald S. (mə ken´zē) (1840–1889) Leader of the United States Army at the Battle of Palo Duro Canyon. (p. 262)

Magruder, John B. (mə grü´dər) (1807–1871) Commander of the Texas forces during the Civil War. (p. 246)

Martínez, Antonio María (mär tē´nəz) (?–1823) Spanish governor of Texas from 1817 to 1822. He granted Moses Austin land to found a colony. (p. 140)

Milam, Ben (mi´ləm) (1788–1835) With Frank Johnson, led an attack on the Mexican army in San Antonio on December 5, 1835. (p. 172)

Miller, Doris "Dorie" (mil´ər) (1919–1943) Crew member aboard a U.S. Navy ship. He showed admirable bravery during the attack on Pearl Harbor. (p. 348)

Moctezuma II (mok təh zü´mä) (1466–1520) Leader of the Aztecs in 1519 when Cortés arrived in what is now Mexico. (p. 118)

Moczygemba, Leopold (mō kzē gām´bə) (1825–1891) Priest who helped found Panna Maria and encouraged Polish immigrants to settle in Texas. (p. 209)

Moscoso de Alvarado, Luis de (mōs kō´sō dā äl vä rä´dō) (1505–1551) Spanish explorer who took over an expedition in the present-day southeastern United States after de Soto died. (p. 122)

Murphy, Audie (mər´fē) (1924–1971) American soldier awarded the most medals for his service during World War II. (p. 342)

Navarro, José Antonio (nä vär´rō) (1795–1871) Mexican leader who signed the Texas Declaration of Independence. (p. 207)

Nelson, Willie (nəl´ sən) (1933–) Famous singer-songwriter and guitar player from Abbott, Texas. (p. 385)

Ney, Elisabet (nā) (1833–1907) Artist who carved life-sized sculptures of Stephen F. Austin and Sam Houston. These now stand in the state Capitol. (p. 308)

Niza, Fray Marcos de (nē´ zə) (1495–1558) Spanish priest and explorer who claimed to have seen the Seven Cities of Gold. (p. 120)

Oñate, Juan de (ō nyä´ tā) (1549–1628) Conquistador who claimed land in present-day Texas for Spain. (p. 122)

Parker, Quanah (pär´ kėr, kwä´ nə) (c. 1845–1911) Comanche leader who worked to settle disputes between Native Americans and the United States government. (p. 261)

Perez, Selena Quintanilla (pə rəz´) (1971–1995) Grammy award–winning Tejano singer. (p. 385)

Piñeda, Alonso Alvarez de (pē nyā´ də) (?–1520) Spanish explorer who was the first European to reach Texas in 1519. (p. 122)

Polk, James K. (pōk) (1795–1849) President of the United States, when Texas became the 28th state in 1845. (p. 217)

Ramsey, Buck (ram´ sē) (1938–1998) Famous cowboy-poet who lived in the Texas Panhandle. (p. 292)

Rayburn, Sam (rā´ bėrn) (1882–1961) Represented Texas in the U.S. House of Representatives from 1912 to 1961. (p. 341)

Ride, Sally (rīd) (1951–) First female U.S. astronaut in space. (p. 11)

Rodriguez, Cleto (rod rē´ gāz) (1923–1990) World War II hero who fought bravely in the Philippines. (p. 342)

Roosevelt, Franklin D. (rō´ zə velt) (1882–1945) President of the United States from 1933 to 1945. (p. 341)

Santa Anna, Antonio López de (sän´ tä ä´ nä) (1794–1876) President of Mexico and general during the Texas Revolution. (p. 150)

Satanta (sä tan´ tə) (1820–1878) Kiowa leader who tried to prevent the United States government from forcing Native Americans to live on reservations. (p. 260)

Scott, Winfield (skot) (1786–1866) General in the United States Army during the Mexican War. (p. 218)

Seguín, Erasmo (sā gēn´) (1782–1857) Tejano rancher who befriended the settlers in Austin's colony. (p. 144)

Seguín, Juan (sā gēn´) (1806–1890) Tejano leader who joined the Texans' fight for independence from Mexico. (p. 172)

Smith, Erastus "Deaf" (1787–1837) Scout for Sam Houston during the Texas Revolution. (p. 190)

Stinson, Katherine (stin´ sun) (1891–1977) Professional aviator who also ran a flying school in San Antonio. (p. 327)

Pronunciation Key

a in hat	ȯ in all	sh in she
ā in age	ō in open	th in thin
â in care	ô in order	ᴛн in then
ä in far	oi in oil	zh in measure
e in let	ou in out	ə = a in about
ē in equal	u in cup	ə = e in taken
ėr in term	u̇ in put	ə = i in pencil
i in it	ü in rule	ə = o in lemon
ī in ice	ch in child	ə = u in circus
o in hot	ng in long	

Biographical Dictionary

Taniguchi, Isamu (tä nē gü´chē) (1897–1992) Planted a Japanese garden in Zilker Park, in Austin. (p. 38)

Taylor, Zachary (tā´lôr) (1784–1850) General in the United States Army during the Mexican War and President of the United States from 1849 to 1850. (p. 217)

Tower, John (tou´ər) (1925–1991) Politician in Texas and U.S. government. At age 36, he was the youngest person to serve in the U.S. Senate. (p. 409)

Travis, William (tra´vəs) (1809–1836) Texan leader at the Alamo. (p. 182)

Urrea, General José de (ər rā´ə) (1797–1849) Mexican general who defeated Fannin at Goliad. (p. 189)

Williams, Elizabeth "Lizzie" Johnson (wil´yəmz) (1840–1924) One of the first women in Texas to own cattle and to drive them on cattle trails. (p. 275)

Wilson, Woodrow (wil´sən) (1856–1924) Twenty-eighth President of the United States, from 1913 to 1921. (p. 326)

Zavala, Lorenzo de (zə vä´lə) (1788–1836) Empresario and first vice-president of the Republic of Texas. (p. 144)

Glossary

This Glossary will help you pronounce and understand the meanings of the vocabulary words in this book. The page numbers tell you where the word first appears.

 **A**

adobe (ə dō´ bē) bricks formed from clay and straw that are dried in the sun (p. 103)

aerospace (âr´ ō spās) an industry that builds and operates spacecrafts (p. 373)

agriculture (ag´ rə kul´ chər) the planting of seeds to grow food (p. 93)

annexation (an´ ek sā´ shən) when territory becomes part of a larger country (p. 205)

appeal (ə pēl´) to ask for another trial (p. 401)

aquifer (ak´ wə fər) an underground layer of spongy rock that holds water (p. 16)

archaeologist (är kē ol´ ə jist) a scientist who finds and studies artifacts (p. 92)

artifact (är´ tə fakt) an object made by people (p. 92)

assembly line (ə sem´ blē lin) a line of workers who put together just one part of each product riding on a moving platform past the workers (p. 309)

astronaut (as´ trə nȯt) a scientist who explores and studies space (p. 373)

atlatl (at´ lətl) a throwing stick used by ancient people in Texas to make spears fly far and fast (p. 92)

 **B**

barbed wire (bärbd wīr) a twisted wire with very sharp points, or barbs (p. 277)

bar mitzvah (bär mits´ və) a Jewish boy accepting religious responsibilities (p. 382)

barrier island (bar´ ē ər ī land) a narrow island between the ocean and the mainland (p. 68)

basin (bā´ sn) a low, bowl-shaped landform (p. 61)

bat mitzvah (bät mits´ və) a Jewish girl accepting religious responsibilities (p. 382)

bayou (bī´ ü) a marshy, slow-moving body of water, such as a stream (p. 66)

Bill of Rights (Texas Constitution) (bil uv rītz) certain rights that belong to all Texans (p. 175)

black gold (blak gōld) another name for oil (p. 316)

blizzard (bliz´ ərd) a storm with high winds, snow, and ice (p. 30)

blockade (blo kād´) to block (p. 246)

bond (bond) a certificate given in exchange for money that a person could cash in at a later date (p. 327)

boom (büm) a time of rapid growth (p. 283)

border (bôr´ dər) a boundary line (p. 62)

boundary (boun´ dər ē) a line that separates one place from another (p. 217)

brand (brand) a design burned into the hide of a cow (p. 268)

Buffalo Soldier (buf´ ə lō sol´ jər) the nickname for an African American soldier who fought against the Plains Indians (p. 259)

 **C**

cash crop (kash krop) a crop that is grown to be sold at a market (p. 143)

Pronunciation Key

a in hat	ȯ in all	sh in she
ā in age	ō in open	th in thin
â in care	ô in order	ᴛʜ in then
ä in far	oi in oil	zh in measure
e in let	ou in out	ə = a in about
ē in equal	u in cup	ə = e in taken
ėr in term	u̇ in put	ə = i in pencil
i in it	ü in rule	ə = o in lemon
ī in ice	ch in child	ə = u in circus
o in hot	ng in long	

Glossary

cavalry (kav´əl rē) a group of soldiers who fight battles on horseback (p. 246)

citizen (sit´ə zen) a member of a nation, state, county, or town (p. 397)

citrus fruit (sit´rəs früt) fruit such as grapefruit and orange that grows on trees in warm climates (p. 39)

city-state (sit´ē stāt) a city with its own separate government and leaders (p. 109)

climate (klī´mit) the weather patterns of an area over a long period of time (p. 31)

colony (kol´ə nē) a settlement of people who have left one country to live in another (p. 122)

confederacy (kən fed´ər ə sē) several groups of people who agree to work together for a common goal (p. 97)

congress (kong´gris) the lawmaking body of a nation or a republic (p. 193)

conquistador (kon kē´stə dôr) a Spanish conqueror (p. 118)

conserve (kən sėrv´) to save something (p. 24)

constitution (kon´stə tü´shən) a plan of government (p. 175)

convention (kən ven´shən) a formal meeting (p. 150)

county (koun´tē) one of the sections into which a state is divided (p. 399)

county seat (koun´tē sēt) a city or town chosen to be the center of government for a county (p. 399)

cultivated vegetation (kul´tə vā´tid vej´ə tā´shən) plants that are grown from seeds or other plant parts (p. 38)

culture (kul´chər) way of life (p. 93)

custom (kus´təm) the way a group of people does something (p. 381)

debt (det) money owed to others (p. 194)

depot (dē´pō) a train station (p. 286)

depression (di presh´ən) a period during which business slows down and prices fall (p. 339)

descendant (di sen´dənt) a person's children, grandchildren, and so on (p. 91)

desert (dez´ərt) a dry area that receives fewer than 10 inches of rain a year (p. 61)

discrimination (dis krim´ə nā´shən) when one group denies rights to another (p. 325)

drought (drout) a long period with little or no rain (p. 24)

dugout canoe (dug´out´kə nü´) a canoe made by scooping out a long log (p. 98)

empire (em´pīr) a group of governments under the control of one ruler (p. 109)

empresario (em prəs är´ē ō) a person who brought settlers into a Texas colony, divided up the land, and enforced the law (p. 141)

endangered (en dān´jərd) when a species is in danger of dying out completely (p. 43)

environment (en vī´rən mənt) the surroundings of living things (p. 21)

escarpment (e skärp´mənt) a line of steep slopes or cliffs (p. 15)

ethnic group (eth´nik grüp) a group of people who may share things in common, such as language, religious beliefs, and other ways of life (p. 381)

executive branch (eg zek´yə tiv branch) the branch of government that makes sure laws passed by the legislative branch are carried out (p. 400)

expand (ek spand´) to spread out (p. 217)

fact (fakt) a statement that can be proved to be true (p. 312)

free enterprise (frē en´tər prīz) a system in which people have freedom in selling and buying (p. 240)

frontier (frun tir´) the farthest part of a settled country, next to lands that are not yet settled (p. 239)

geography (jē og´ rə fē) the study of Earth's land and how people use it (p. 15)

government (guv´ ərn mənt) a system for ruling or running a town or country (p. 103)

helium (hē´ lē əm) a natural gas lighter than air with no color or smell (p. 58)

heritage (her´ ə tij) shared history (p. 381)

high-tech (hī´ tək´) an industry that makes computers, software, and Internet Web sites (p. 373)

hurricane (hėr´ ə kān) a violent storm with high winds and heavy rain (p. 29)

immigrant (im´ ə grənt) a person from one country who comes to live in a new region or country (p. 141)

industry (in´ də strē) a business that makes a product or provides a service (p. 308)

inland (in´ lənd) away from the coast toward land (p. 65)

Internet (in´ tər net) a connection of computers that allows people to share information almost instantly (p. 336)

invention (in ven´ shən) a newly created product (p. 307)

irrigate (ir´ ə gāt) to use a system of ditches, pipes, or streams to transport water to crops (p. 39)

irrigation (ir´ ə gā´ shən) a system of transporting water to crops (p. 39)

jazz (jaz) a type of music that began in the southern United States. It was created by African Americans and became very popular during the 1920s (p. 332)

judicial branch (jü dish´ əl branch) the branch of government made up of courts and judges that make sure that state and national laws are applied fairly (p. 401)

junction (jungk´ shən) a place where two or more rail lines meet (p. 286)

Juneteenth (jün tēnth´) celebration remembering when slaves in Texas learned that they were free on June 19th, 1866 (p. 251)

landform (land´ fôrm´) a feature of Earth's surface (p. 15)

landmark (land´ märk´) an object, such as a mountain, that stands out from the area around it (p. 55)

legislative branch (lej´ ə slā´ tiv branch) the branch of government that makes laws (p. 401)

legislature (lej´ ə slā´ chər) a group of elected people who make new laws (p. 207)

lignite (lig´ nīt) a kind of soft coal (p. 67)

line rider (līn rī´ dər) a cowhand who rides up and down the borders of a ranch to watch the cattle (p. 269)

livestock (liv´ stok´) beef cattle, dairy cattle, sheep, goats, hogs, chickens, and turkeys (p. 54)

locomotive (lō´ kə mō´ tiv) a train engine (p. 284)

mainland (mān´ land´) the main part of a continent (p. 68)

Pronunciation Key

a in hat	ȯ in all	sh in she
ā in age	ō in open	th in thin
â in care	ô in order	ᴛʜ in then
ä in far	oi in oil	zh in measure
e in let	ou in out	ə = a in about
ē in equal	u in cup	ə = e in taken
ėr in term	u̇ in put	ə = i in pencil
i in it	ü in rule	ə = o in lemon
ī in ice	ch in child	ə = u in circus
o in hot	ng in long	

Glossary

manufacture (man´ yə fak´ chər) to make goods by hand or with machinery (p. 308)

migrate (mī´ grāt) to move from one area or country to another (p. 97)

militia (mə lish´ ə) a group of volunteer soldiers (p. 142)

mission (mish´ ən) a religious settlement (p. 127)

mohair (mō´ hâr) the hair of Angora goats (p. 57)

monument (mon´ yə mənt) a memorial (p. 191)

municipal (myü nis´ ə pəl) of a city or town (p. 398)

natural resource (nach´ ər əl ri sôrs´) a resource that comes from the earth (p. 21)

natural vegetation (nach´ ər əl vej´ ə tā´ shən) trees, grasses, flowers, and plants that grow naturally (p. 37)

nomad (nō´ mad) a person who does not have a permanent home, but who moves from place to place within a certain area (p. 98)

nonrenewable resource (non´ ri nü´ ə bəl ri sôrs´) a resource that cannot be replaced (p. 23)

norther (nôr´ ŦHər) a powerful mass of cold air (p. 30)

nullify (nul´ ə fī) cancel (p. 244)

oil refinery (oil´ ri fī´ nər ē) a factory where crude oil straight from the ground is cleaned, processed, and turned into useful oil products (p. 316)

open range (ō´ pən rānj´) grassy plains (p. 267)

opinion (ə pin´ yən) a statement that tells about personal feelings (p. 312)

orator (or´ ə tər) a skillful and powerful public speaker (p. 409)

orchard (ôr´ chərd) a place where fruit and nut trees are grown (p. 39)

petition (pə tish´ ən) to make a request of someone in charge (p. 174)

petroleum (pə trō´ lē əm) oil (p. 317)

plain (plān) a large area of flat land with gently rolling hills and few trees (p. 15)

plantation (plan tā´ shən) a large farm that produced crops to sell (p. 243)

plateau (pla tō´) a high, level stretch of land (p. 15)

political party (pə lit´ ə kəl pär´ tē´) an organized group of people who share similar ideas about how to run a government (p. 397)

pollution (pə lü´ shən) harmful substances that spoil the environment (p. 24)

port (pôrt) a place where ships can dock (p. 67)

precipitation (pri sip´ ə tā´ shən) the moisture that falls to the ground (p. 33)

presidio (pri sid´ ē ō) a fort (p. 128)

primary source (prī´ mer´ ē sôrs´) information that comes from an eyewitness (p. 178)

profit (prof´ it) the money a producer has left over after all the costs of making or selling the goods or services are paid (p. 240)

pueblo (pweb´ lō) a Spanish word that means "village" (p. 103)

quarry (kwôr´ ē) an open pit where people mine, or dig up, rocks (p. 92)

quinceañera (kēn sā änye´ rä) a Hispanic celebration that a girl might have on her fifteenth birthday (p. 382)

recycle (rē sī´ kəl) to use something more than once (p. 25)

region (rē´ jən) a large area whose parts have something in common (p. 53)

renewable resource (ri nü´ ə bəl ri sôrs´) a resource that can be replaced after it is used (p. 22)

republic (ri pub´ lik) a type of government in which people choose leaders to represent them (p. 193)

research (rē´ sərch´) to find out more about a topic (p. 336)

reservation (rez´ ər vā´ shən) an area of land set aside as a place for Native Americans to live (p. 97)

resolution (rez´ ə lü´ shən) a decision (p. 206)

resource (ri sôrs´) a material that helps people meet their needs (p. 21)

responsibility (ri spon´ sə bil´ ə tē) a thing a person is supposed to manage, look after, do, and so on. (p. 407)

retail (rē´ tāl) a sale from a merchant to the public (p. 58)

revolution (rev´ ə lü´ shən) a fight against the government; the overthrow of a government by its citizens (p. 139)

right (rīt) a freedom that belongs to citizens (p. 149)

roundup (round´ up´) when cowhands from different ranches drive all the cattle they find into one area (p. 269)

rural (rùr´ əl) in the countryside (p. 307)

scout (skout) a person who gathers clues about an enemy or a location (p. 190)

search engine (serch´ en´ jin) a special Web site that locates other Web sites that can provide information on a topic (p. 336)

secede (si sēd´) to separate (p. 245)

secondary source (sek´ ən der´ ē sôrs) information that comes from someone who was not present at an event (p. 178)

segregation (seg´ rə gā´ shən) racial separation (p. 369)

sharecropper (shâr´ krop´ ər) a farmer who pays part of what he or she grows to a landowner (p. 252)

siege (sēj) the surrounding of a place by enemy forces trying to capture it (p. 181)

skirmish (skèr´ mish) a minor battle (p. 217)

slave (slāv) a person who is owned by another person (p. 110)

sorghum (sôr´ gəm) grass and grain raised as food for animals (p. 38)

special district (spesh´ əl dis´ trikt) a government district organized for a specific purpose, such as a school district (p. 399)

spring (spring) a place where underground water comes to the surface (p. 16)

stampede (stam pēd´) when a herd of cattle becomes frightened and runs wildly (p. 275)

stock (stok) a share of ownership in a company (p. 339)

suffrage (suf´ rij) the right to vote (p. 328)

tariff (tar´ if) money a government charges to import goods into a country (p. 388)

tax (taks) money paid to a government in exchange for services (p. 193)

technology (tek nol´ ə jē) the use of scientific knowledge, skills, and tools to help people meet their needs (p. 373)

temperature (tem´ pər ə chər) a measurement telling how hot or cold something is (p. 32)

tepee (tē´ pē) a cone-shaped tent made of animal skins that can be put up and taken down quickly (p. 104)

threatened (thret´ nd) when a species is likely to become endangered (p. 43)

time zone (tīm zōn) an area in which all the clocks are set to the same time (p. 62)

Pronunciation Key

a in hat	ȯ in all	sh in she
ā in age	ō in open	th in thin
â in care	ô in order	ŦH in then
ä in far	oi in oil	zh in measure
e in let	ou in out	ə = a in about
ē in equal	u in cup	ə = e in taken
èr in term	ù in put	ə = i in pencil
i in it	ü in rule	ə = o in lemon
ī in ice	ch in child	ə = u in circus
o in hot	ng in long	

Glossary

tornado (tôr nāʹ dō) a fierce and swirling tunnel of wind (p. 30)

trade (trād) the buying and selling of goods (p. 11)

trading post (trādʹ ing pōst) a small frontier store (p. 67)

tradition (trə dishʹ ən) a belief or way of doing something that is handed down from older to younger group members (p. 382)

travois (trə voiʹ) a wooden frame used by Native Americans to carry possessions from place to place (p. 104)

treaty (trēʹ tē) a formal agreement between two countries (p. 192)

tribute (tribʹ yüt) a payment in goods or money made to a ruler (p. 110)

urban (ėrʹ bən) in the city (p. 307)

vaquero (vä kerʹ ō) a cowboy (p. 145)

vegetation (vejʹ ə tāʹ shən) plants and trees (p. 37)

veto (vēʹ tō) to refuse to sign a bill into law (p. 400)

villa (vilʹ ə) a town (p. 129)

volunteer (volʹ ən tirʹ) to give of one's time in the community or state without pay (p. 407)

waterway (wôʹ tər wāʹ) a body of water, such as a river, lake, or gulf (p. 16)

weather (weтнʹ ər) description of the air at a certain time and place (p. 29)

wholesale (hōlʹ sālʹ) a sale from a merchant to another business (p. 58)

Index

Titles appear in *italics*. Page numbers in bold type indicate vocabulary definitions. An *m* following a page number indicates a map. The terms *See* and *See also* direct the reader to alternative entries.

A

Abilene, Texas, 55
Adair, Christia, 369
Adobe, 103
Adobe villages, 120
Adobe Walls, Battle of, 261
Aerospace, 372–373
African Americans
  artists, 334
  Buffalo Soldiers, 259
  discrimination against, 333, 369
  equal rights, 369
  Freedmen's Bureau, 252
  freedom for, 251
  Governor Edmond Davis and, 253
  jazz and, 332
  Gaines, Mathew, 252
  Jemison, Mae C., 373
  Joplin, Scott, 332
  Jordan, Barbara, 368–369, 409, 411
  King, Martin Luther, Jr., 369
  Kwanzaa, 383
  Miller, Doris "Dorie," 342, 348–349
  Reconstruction and, 252
  slaves. *See* Slavery; Slaves
Agencies of government, 401
Agriculture, 93, 97, 371
  crops. *See* Crops
  farmers. *See* Farmers
  ranches. *See* Ranching industry

Airplanes, 327
  pilot training, 327, 329
Alabama-Coushatta Reservation, 100
Alamo, The, 67, 174, 180–187, 224–225
Alamo Chapel, 183
Alibates Flint Quarries National Monument, 92
Allied Powers, World War I, 326–327, 326*m*
Allies, World War II, 342–343
Almanacs, 94–95
Amarillo, Texas, 58
Ames, Jessie Daniel, 328
Anasazi people, 102–103
Andes Mountains, 111
Angel of the Alamo, 224–225
Anglo Americans, 149
Animals, 41–44
  armadillos, 43
  birds, 41, 43
  buffalo, 104, 260–261
  butterflies, 42
  cattle. *See* Cattle
  endangered species, 43–44, 46–47
  in Great Plains region, 57
  horses. *See* Horses
  in Mountains and Basins region, 61
  sea turtles, 46–47
  threatened species, 43–44
  wildlife, 41–44, 46–47
Annexation, 205
Annual Move, The, 339
Anthem, 292–293
Apache people, 105
Appeal, 401

Appointed leaders, 397, 408
Appomattox Court House, Virginia, 250
Aquifers, 16–17, 24
Archaeologists, 92
Archaeology, 90–92
Argentina, 271, 281
Arkansas, 12
Armadillo, 43
Armstrong, Lance, 363, 384, 387
Armstrong, Neil A., 372
Army, U.S., 259, 262–263
Arnold, Hendrick, 175, 190
Arrowheads, 92, 344
Art, 345–346
  paintings. *See* Paintings
Art, Texas (town), 385
Artifacts, 92
Artists, 292–293, 311, 345–346, 385
  authors, 41, 76–77, 345
  Biggers, John, 5, 67, 69
  Huddle, William H., 161–163, 192
  musicians, 332, 334, 345, 385
  Ney, Elisabet, 311
  Onderdonk, Julian, 2–3
Arts, 69, 131, 385
Asian cultures, 383
Assembly line, 309
Astronauts, 372–373
Atakapan people, 99
Athletes, 384, 387
Atlas, 94–95
Atlatls, 92
Austin, Moses, 140

Austin, Stephen Fuller
  biographical sketch of, 4, 85, 151
  city of Austin and, 136, 195
  colony of Austin and, 140–141
  as commander-in-chief, 172
  immigration and, 150
  jailing of, 150
  quote by, 83
  Texas Declaration of Independence and, 167
Austin, Texas, 45, 67, 236
  Barton Springs, 17
  book festival in, 383
  as capital of Republic, 195
  Capitol building of, 394, 400
  filmmaking in, 386
  high-tech industry in, 374
  history museum in, 385
  sister city of, 404–405
  statehood and, 206
  wildflower center in, 27
  Zilker Park in, 45
Austin Colony, 140–143, 140*m*
  colonists' convention, 150
  Consultation meeting, 173
  San Felipe de Austin, 136, 140–143, 150, 173
Authors
  Brewer, J. Mason, 345
  dePaola, Tomie, 76–77
  Parker, Laurie, 41
  Porter, Katherine Anne, 345

Index

Texas Book Festival, 383
Automobiles, 330
  change caused by, 307, 331
  manufacturing of, 309
Axis Powers, World War II, 342–343
Aztec people, 88, 110, 110*m*, 118

Balcones Escarpment, 15, 15*m*
Ballard, Josephine, 355
Bandelier National Monument, 102
Bar graphs, 152–153
Bar mitzvah, 382
Barbed-wire fencing, 277
Barrier islands, 68
Barton Springs, 17
Basins. *See* Mountains and Basins region
Bat mitzvah, 382
Bats, 43
Battles, 217
  Battle of Adobe Walls, 261
  Battle of the Alamo, 180–187, 224–225
  Battle of Palo Duro Canyon, 262–263
  Battle of San Jacinto, 188–191, 191*m*, 344
  Civil War, 245–247, 246*m*
  Goliad, Texas, 170–171, 171*m*, 189
  Gonzales, Texas, 170–171, 171*m*
  for independence, 169*m*
  Indian Wars, 258–264
  San Antonio, Texas, 172
Bayous, 66

Beaumont, Texas, 304, 315
Bedichek, Roy, 4, 38
Benavides, Santo, 246
Bering Strait, 91, 91*m*
Beringia, 88, **91**
Big Bend National Park, 13, 61, 61*m*
Big Dipper in slaves' songs, 243
Big Thicket National Preserve, 12, 13*m*, 65*m*, 66
Biggers, John, 5, 67, 69
Bill of Rights, 175
Biographies
  Armstrong, Lance, 387
  Austin, Stephen Fuller, 151
  Biggers, John, 69
  Coronado, Francisco Vásquez de, 124
  Dickinson, Susanna Wilkerson, 185
  Gonzales, Patrisia, 107
  Goodnight, Charles, 270
  Houston, Sam, 211
  Johnson, "Lady Bird," 27
  Johnson, Lyndon Baines, 375
  Jordan, Barbara, 411
  July, Johanna, 279
  Ney, Elisabet, 311
  Parker, Quanah, 265
  Rayburn, Samuel Taliaferro, 347
  Seguín, Juan, 177
  Stinson, Katherine, 329
  Taniguchi, Isamu, 45
Birds, 41, 43
Birthday traditions, 382
"Black gold." *See* Oil
Blackland Prairie area, 65, 65*m*, 67
Blackshear, Kathleen, 345
Blanton, Annie Webb, 328

Blizzards, 30
Blockade, 246
Blue topaz, 57
Bluebonnet Field, 2–3
Bluebonnet flowers, 2–3, 40, 76–77
"Blues" music, 334–335
Boats
  canoes, 98
  shrimp boats, 66
Bob Bullock Texas State History Museum, 385
Bodies of water. *See* Waterways
Bolivia, 198–199, 199*m*
Bonds, 327
Bonham, James, 182
Books,
  authors. *See* Authors
  Texas Book Festival, 383
Booms
  business boom, 331
  oil booms, 316–317, 331, 370–371
  railroad boom, 283–287
Borden, Gail, 142
Borders, 12, 13*m*, **62,** 217*m*, 239
  Rio Grande as, 13, 62, 217
  troubles on, 325
Borland, Margaret, 280
Boundaries, 217, 217*m*. *See also* Borders
Bowie, James, 172, 182–183, 225
Brackenridge, Mary Eleanor, 328
Branches of government, 400–401, 403
Brands, 268–269
Brazos River, 141
Brewer, J. Mason, 345
Brownsville, Texas, 66
Buffalo, 104, 260–261
Buffalo Bayou, 191, 191*m*

Buffalo Soldiers, 259
Bulldoggers, 276
Burnet, David G., 176, 192, 194
Bush, George Herbert Walker, 397
Bush, George W., 397
Bush, Laura, 383
Businesses. *See also* Industry
  boom in, 331
  changes in, 371
  The Great Depression, 322, 339–341
  railroad companies and, 284–285
Butterflies, 42

Cabeza de Vaca, Alvar Núñez, 84, 118–119
Cabrillo, Juan Rodríguez, 125
Caddo people, 97
Caddoan Mounds, 88, 96–97
Caddoan Mounds State Historical Park, 96
California, 119, 125
Canada, 12
  Vancouver, British Columbia, 70–71, 71*m*
Canned food industry, 142, 285, 308–309
Canoes, 98
Canyon, Texas, 344
Canyons, 58–59, 114, 121, 262–263
Caprock Escarpment, 56–**57,** 59, 121
Caravans, 225
Cars. *See* Automobiles
Cash crops, 143

Catholic Church. *See* Roman Catholic Church

Catlin, George, 104

Cattle. *See also* Ranching industry
branding of, 268–269
as cash crops, 143
introduction of, 267
longhorn cattle, 43, 267
settlers and, 129

Cattle drives, 274–281

Cattle trails, 276*m*

Cause and effect, 166

Cavalry, 246

Cazneau, Jane McManus, 218

Central America, 108–109

Central Plains region, 52–55, **53,** 72
Comanche Indians and, 104
Great Plains region and, 57
Plains Indians in, 76–77, 104–105, 256–265

Central Powers, World War I, 326–327, 326*m*

Chaps, 276

Cherokee people, 99, 211, 262–263

Cheyenne people, 262–263

Chihuahuan Desert, 61

Children
ethnic groups, 381
labor, 308
townball, 354–355

Childress, George C., 174

Childress, Texas, 286

Chinese immigrants, 283

Chisholm, Jesse, 275–276

Chisos Mountains, 61*m*

Christmas, 382

Chrysler, Walter, 286

Chrysler Corporation, 286

Chumash people, 125

Cíbola, Seven Cities of, 119–120, 123–124

Cincinnati, Ohio, 190

Cisneros, Henry G., 363, 409

Cities, 54–55, 58, 62, 67, 72
growth of, 286–287
Seven Cities of Cíbola, 119–120, 123–124
Tenochtitlan, 88, 110, 118
urban life, 307–308, 331

"Cities of gold," 119, 123–124

Citizens, 397, 406–413

Citrus fruits, 8, 39, 40, 67

City-state, 109

Civil rights. *See* Rights

Civil Rights Act, 369

Civil War, 237, 242–253, **245,** 245*m*, 246*m*

Clarendon, Texas, 256, 286

Clear Lake, Texas, 372

Climate, 31

Coahuiltecan people, 99

Coal, 67

Coastal flowering vines, 37

Coastal Plains region, 64–68, **65,** 65*m,* 72, 96–101

Cold weather, 30–31

Colonies, 122, 136–155
Austin Colony. *See* Austin Colony
empresarios in, 85, 140–**141,** 144
English language in, 149
home life in, 143
immigrants to, 149–150
San Felipe de Austin. *See* Austin Colony
slavery in, 149
transportation to, 142

Columbia, Texas, 195

Columbus, Christopher, 117

Comanche Feats of Horsemanship, 104

Comanche people, 104
exit of, 264
legend about, 76–77
warriors, 259, 261, 264
wars with, 259, 261–263

Companies. *See* Businesses

Compare and contrast, 86

Computer industry, 373

Concho people, 105

Conclusions, drawing, 364–365

Condensed milk, 142

Confederacy, 97

Confederacy of Southern States, 237*m*, 245

Congress, 193

Conquistadors, 118

Conservation, 24, 25

Constitution, 175
of Texas. *See* Texas Constitution
of U.S., 328

Consultation, 173

Contrast, 86

Convention, 150

Convention of 1836, 174

Coronado, Francisco Vásquez de, 84, 114, 120–121, 124–125

Corpus Christi, Texas, 66

Corpus Christi de la Isleta, 127

Corrals, 276

Cortés, Hernando, 118

Cós, General, 172, 181

Cotton, 38, 143, 244

County, 399

County seats, 399

Court of Criminal Appeals, 401

Courts, 401

Cowboys, 145, 280

Cowgirls, 280

Cowhands
bulldoggers, 276
cattle drives, 285, 274–281
cowboys, 145
trailherders, 275–276
vaqueros, 145, 181, 256, 276

"Cowtown," 54, 286, 308

Criminal cases, 401

Critical thinking, 248–249

Crockett, David "Davy," 164, 182

Crops, 38–39
cash crops, 143
cotton, 38, 143, 244
in Cross Timbers area, 54
cultivated vegetation, 38
in Grand Prairie area, 54
in Gulf Coastal Plains region, 66, 67
irrigation of, 39, 57, 66, 103
in Piney Woods area, 66
in Rolling Plains area, 54
settlers and, 129
sharecroppers and, 252

Cross Timbers area, 53–55, 53*m*

Cross section diagrams, 318–319

Cultivated vegetation, 38. *See also* Crops

Cultural expressions, 380–386

Culture, 93, 346

Customs, 381

Czech immigrants, 209

Dallas, Texas, 67, 304
car factory in, 309

Index

growth and change in, 307

high-tech industry in, 374

Jazz Age and, 322, 332, 334

Women's Museum in, 385

Davis, Edmund, 253

Davis, Jefferson, 245

DeSoto, Hernando, 122

Debt, 194, 252

Declaration of Independence of Texas, 167, 174, 344

Declaration of War

on Japan, 342

on Mexico, 217–218

Deep Ellum district, 332, 334

"Degüello, El," 183

Depots, 286

Depression, 339

Descendants, 91

Deserts, 61

Details, finding, 6

Diary of Mary Austin Holley, 156–157

Díaz, Bernal, 110

Díaz, Porfirio, 325

Dickinson, Angelina, 183

Dickinson, Susanna Wilkerson, 165, 183, 185

Dictionaries, 94–95

Didrikson, Mildred ("Babe"), 384

Diez y Seis de Septiembre (September Sixteenth), 139

Dinosaur Valley State Park, 54

Discrimination, 325, 333, 369

Distance on maps, 288–289

Dobie, J. Frank, 31, 267

Dodge City, Kansas, 275

Dodson, Sarah, 193

Dog-run/dog-trot cabins, 143

Dolores, Mexico, 138–139

"Don't mess with Texas," 20–26

Dozier, Otis, 339

Drawing conclusions, 364–365

Drilling. *See* Oil wells

Droughts, 24, 340

Dugout canoes, 98

Dust Bowl, 340

Eastern Texas

Native Americans in, 100

precipitation in, 32–33

temperatures in, 32, 32*m*

vegetation in, 37

Ecology, 20–27

Education,

for African Americans, 252

school districts, 399

in Terlingua, Texas, 62

Edwards Plateau, 15, 15*m*, 57, 57*m*

Eisenhower, Dwight D., 342, 397

El Capitan, 63

"El Grito de Dolores," 139

El Paso, Texas, 33, 62, 208

El Turco, 120–121

Elected leaders, 397, 408–409

Elections, 207, 396–397, 407–408

Electricity, 307

Elevation, 18–19, 32, 53

Elevation maps, 18, 18*m*, 19

Emancipation Proclamation, 251

Empire, 109

Empresarios, 85, 140–**141**, 144

Encyclopedias, 94, 95

Endangered species, 43, 44, 46–47

Energy, 23

English language, 149

Environment, 20–27, **21**, 44

Equal rights, 369

Equator, 31–32, **132**

Escarpments, 15, 56–57, 57*m*, 59, 121

Esparza, Enrique, 183

Estancias, 271

Estéban, 119–120

Ethnic groups, 381

Ethnic settlements, 208–209, 209*m*

Europe

World War I, 322, 326–327

World War II, 342

European people

German immigrants, 208–209

Karankawa people and, 98

Texas settlers, 239, 239*m*

Executive branch of government, 400–401, 403

Expansion, 217

Explorers, 114–125

Factories, 308–309, 331, 371

Facts, identifying, 312–313

Fair, Texas State, 240

Fairness, 196–197

Fannin, Colonel James, 172, 187, 189

Farmers,

in cattle. *See* Ranching industry

crops of. *See* Crops

Dust Bowl and, 340

Jumano people as, 103

livestock of, 54

plantations of, 243–244

railroad companies and, 284

ranches of, 54, 145, 268–269, 268*m*

as settlers, 129

as sharecroppers, 252

in World War I, 327

"Father of Texas." *See* Austin, Stephen Fuller

Fences, 277–278

Ferguson, Miriam A. "Ma," 331, 333

Fertilizers, 22

Fiction, historical, 224–225

Fiesta San Antonio, 383

Filmmaking, 386

Fishing industry, 66

Flags, 253

Lone Star Flag, 193

Mexican, 173

Mexican army flag captured at San Jacinto, 191

Flight training, 327

Flint, 92

Florida, 65, 117–118

Flowers, 2–3, 27, 39–40, 76–77

Food shortages, 327, 339, 341

Foote, Horton, 385

Ford, Henry, 309

Forests, 12, 65–66

Fort Sumter, South Carolina, 245
Fort Worth, Texas, 54, 275, 286, 308
Forts, 122–123, 128, 171, 259
Fossil fuels, 23, *See also* Oil
Fossils, 90
Free enterprise, 240
Free range ranching, 267–268, 274–283
Freedmen's Bureau, 252
Freedom
  Battle of the Alamo, 180–187, 224–225
  rights of citizens, 407
  for slaves, 251–252
  Texas Declaration of Independence, 167, 174
French explorers, 122–123
Frontier, 229–295, **239**
Fruit, 8, 39–40, 67
Fuel resources, 67, 317, 331, 343, 370, 370*m*
  in Coastal Plains region, 67
  nonrenewable sources of, 23
  oil. *See* Oil industry

Gaines, Matthew, 252
Galveston, Texas, 28–29, 236, 242
  during Civil War, 246
  railroads and, 285
  Union soldiers in, 251
Galveston Harbor, 246
Galveston Island, 119
Garcitas Creek, 122
Gardens, 38

Garner, John Nance, 341
Gasoline, 317, 331, 343
Geography, 8–19, **15**
  regional. *See* Regions of Texas
German Hill Country, 208
German immigrants, 208, 236, 308
German language in Texas, 208
Germany
  in World War I, 326–327
  in World War II, 342
Girl Scouts, 412–413
Glen Rose, Texas, 54
Glidden, Joseph, 277
Gold, cities of, 119–120, 123–124
Goliad, Texas, 167, 171, 171*m*, 189
Gonzales, Patrisia, 85, 107
Gonzales, Texas, 167, 170–171, 171*m*
González, Henry B., 409
Goodnight, Charles, 270
  Ikard, Bose and, 276
  ranch of, 268
  wife of, 272–273
Goodnight, Mary Ann "Aunt Molly" Dyer, 272–273
Goodnight Buffalo Herd, 273
Government, **103**, 193, 394–417
  agencies of, 401
  government bonds, 327
  individuals and, 407
  lawmaking process of, 402
  leaders of, 397, 408–410, 411
  local level of, 398–399
  national level of, 403
  state level of, 400–401
Government bonds, 327

Governor
  African Americans and, 253
  contact information for, 408
  executive branch of government and, 400–401
  first, 207
  first female as, 331, 333
  responsibilities of, 400
Grammy Awards, 385
Grand Prairie area, 53–54
Granger, Gordon, 251
Grant, Ulysses S., 245, 250–251
Grapefruit, 40
Graphs, 152–153
Gray, William, 178
Grayson, Tameka, 412–413
The Great Depression, 322, **339**, 341
Great Plains region, 56–59, **57**, 57*m*, 72, 104
  Plains Indians in, 76–77, 104–105, 256–265
"Green buildings," 25
"El Grito de Dolores," 139
Groundwater, 16–17, 24
Growth, 306–313
Guadalupe Hidalgo, 219
Guadalupe Mountains National Park, 61, 63
Guadalupe Peak, 13, 61*m*
Guatemala, 108
Gulf Coastal Plains region
  location, 65, 65*m*
  Native Americans of, 96–100
  Padre Island of, 68
  regions and cities of, 66–67, 72
Gulf of Mexico, 12, 65
  blockades of, 246, 246*m*
  Coastal Plains region,

64–68, 72, 96–101
  rivers flowing into, 16
  vegetation near, 37
Gusher (oil well), 315

Harlem, New York, 334–335
Helium, 58
Hempstead, Texas, 190*m*
Henderson, James Pinckney, 207
Heritage, 381
Hidalgo, Father Miguel, 138–139
Higgins, Pattillo, 315
High Plains area, 57
High-tech industry, 372–374, **373**
Highways, 26, 331
Historical fiction, 224–225
History of Texas
  culture and art, 346
  early history, 81–160
  heritage, 381
  museums, 67, 191, 344, 385
  1900s, 297–357, 323*m*
  1920s, 330–337
  Spanish heritage, 131
Hobby, Oveta Culp, 342
Hogue, Alexandre, 345
Holley, Mary Austin, 84–85, 156–157
Home life in colonies, 143
Honesty, 412–413
Horned lizards, 43
Horses, 346
  of cavalry, 246
  Comanche people and, 104

Index

cowboys and, 145

frontier travel of, 240

settlers and, 129

stagecoaches and, 238, 283

training of, 275

vaqueros and, 256, 276

House of Representatives of Texas, 400–402

Houston, Sam

Alamo and, 183

as Army commander, 173, 188, 190–192

biographical sketch of, 164, 211

city of Houston and, 195

at Consultation, 173

as president of Republic, 193, 194, 205

quote from, 163

Houston, Texas

Biggers, John in, 5, 67, 69

as capital of Republic, 195

compared with Vancouver, British Columbia, 70–71

Johnson Space Center in, 67, 366, 372–373

map of, 70*m*

port of, 67, 70–71

Houston Ship Channel, 71

Huddle, William H., 161–163, 192

Hueco Tanks State Historical Park, 62

Hunting, 92–93, 260

Hurricanes, 28–29, 68

Hutchison, Kay Bailey, 409

Idar, Jovita, 325, 385

Identify Facts and Opinion, 312–313

Ikard, Bose, 276

Immigrants, 141, 208

of early 1900s, 308

German immigrants, 208, 236, 308

Mexican immigrants, 208

places of origin of, 308, 371

railroad boom and, 283–284

as settlers. *See* Settlers

Inca people, 110*m*

Independence

battles for, 169*m*

celebration of, 394

Mexican Independence Day, 139

of nations, 198–199

Texas declaration of, 167, 174, 344

Indian Territory, 260

battles over, 259–264, 261*m*

Comanche reservation in, 104

map of, 257*m*

Indian Wars, 258–265, 261*m*

Industry, 308. *See also name of specific industry*

inventions and, 305–309

World War II and, 343

Ingleside, Texas, 8, 26

Inland, 65

Inset maps, 220–221

Institute of Texan Cultures, 67

International business, 371

Internet, 373

as reference source, 94

research on, **336**–337

Inventions, 307, 310, 331

condensed milk, 142

industry and, 305–309

microchips, 373

Irrigation, 39, 57, 66, 103

Islamic culture, 383

Islands, 68

Jalapeño peppers, 40

Japan, 342, 348–349

Jazz Age, 322, 332

Jazz music, 332

Jefferson, Blind Lemon, 334

Jemison, Mae C., 373

Jewish culture, 382

Jimenez, Flaco, 385

Jiminez, Santiago, Jr., 385

Johnson, Elizabeth ("Lizzie") Williams, 275, 280

Johnson, Frank, 172

Johnson, Claudia "Lady Bird," 5, 26–27

Johnson, Lyndon Baines

biography of, 375

Civil Rights Act and, 369

Johnson Space Center and, 366, 372

as national leader, 375, 397

National Youth Administration and, 341

Johnson Space Center, 67, 366, 372

Jones, Anson, 164, 194, 206–207

Jones, Jesse, 341

Joplin, Scott, 332

Jordan, Barbara, 368–369, 409, 411

Juárez, 62

Judges, 401

Judicial branch of government, 401, 403

July, Johanna, 275, 279

Jumano people, 103

Junctions, 286

Juneteenth, 251

Karankawa people, 98, 123, 141–142

Karnack, Texas, 27

Kennedy, John F., 397

Kian, 141

Kickapoo Traditional Tribe of Texas, 106

King, Henrietta, 268

King, Martin Luther, Jr., 369

King, Richard, 268

King Ranch, 66, 268

Kiowa people, 105, 260, 262–263

KKK, 333

Ku Klux Klan, 333

Kwanzaa, 383

La Salle, René-Robert Cavelier, Sieur de, 84, 122–123

Lady Bird Johnson Wildflower Center, 27

Lake Texcoco, 88, 110

Lakes, 16

Lamar, Mirabeau B., 165, 193–194

Land grants, 140

Landforms, 15
  basins, 61
  canyons, 58–59, 114, 121, 262–263
  deserts, 61
  escarpments, 15, 56–57, 59, 121
  islands, 68, 119
  lakes, 16
  mountains, 12–13, 21, 61
  plains, 15
  plateau, 15, 57

Landmarks, 55
  natural. *See* Natural landmarks
  regional, 72

Landscape designers, 38

Languages
  English, 149
  German, 208
  Spanish, 131, 149, 276

Lapinski, Tara, 384

Laredo, Texas, 181, 325

Lariats, 256, **276**

Latitude and longitude, 132–133

Law of April 6, 149

Laws, 401–402

Leaders, 207, 396–397, 406, 408–410

Leadership, 410

League of Women Voters, 328

Leander, Texas, 30, 90–91

Leanderthal Lady, 90–91

Lee, Robert E., 245, 250, 251

Lee, Sheila Jackson, 409

The Legend of the Bluebonnet, 76–77

Legislative branch of government, 400–401, 403

Legislature, 207

de León, Martín, 144

de León, Patricia de la Garza, 144

Lewis, Carl, 384

Lignite, 67

Lincoln, Abraham, 244, 251

Line graphs, 152–153

Line riders, 269

Lipan Apache people, 105

Little Dipper, 243

Livestock, 54. *See also* Cattle; Ranching industry

Livingston, Texas, 100

Lizards, 43

Llano Basin area, 57

Llano Estacado, 121

Local governments, 398–399

Locomotive, 284

Loetscher, Ila, 4, 46–47

Logan, Greenbury, 165, 175

Lone Star Flag, 193

"Lone Star State," 193, 202–223

Long, Jane Herbert Wilkinson, 85, 141

Longhorn cattle, 43, 267

Longitude, 132–133

Louisiana, 12, 122, 153, 207

Lubbock, Texas, 58

Lucas, Anthony F., 315

Lucas Gusher, 315–316

Lufkin, Texas, 308

Lumber industry, 22, 66, 285, 308

Lunar New Year, 383

Mackenzie, Ranald S., 262–264

Magruder, John B., 246

Main idea, 6

Mainland, 68

Mammals, 41, 43–44

Mammoths, 91, 93

Manufacturing, 308, 331, 371

Map keys, 350–351

Map scale, 288–289

Maps
  elevation maps, 18–19
  inset maps, 220–221
  latitude and longitude, 117, 132–133
  legends on, 15, 32, 70–71, 98, 110, 125, 128, 140, 171, 190–191, 205, 209, 239, 245–246, 261, 283, 315, 326, 350–351, 370
  road maps, 350–351, 357
  scale on, 53, 57, 61, 65, 91, 105, 288–289
  shape of Texas, 9–11, 14, 199
  of time zones, 378–379

March on San Antonio, 172

Marsh, William J., 418–419

Marshall, Texas, 286

Martínez, Antonio María, 140

Matagordo Bay, 122

Mayan people, 108–109

McCullough, Sam, 175

Meatpacking industry, 285, 308

Mendoza, Lydia, 345

Meridians, 132

Mescalero Apache people, 105

Mexica people, 110

Mexican free-tailed bats, 43

Mexican immigrants, 208

Mexican Independence Day, 139

Mexican Revolution
  of 1800s, 139, 141
  of 1910, 325

Mexican War, 202–203, 216–221

Mexico, 12
  Aztec people, 88, 110, 110*m*, 118
  Chihuahuan Desert, 61
  Dolores, 138–139
  1824 flag of, 173
  gulf of. *See* Gulf of Mexico
  immigrants from, 208
  independence from Spain, 139
  Mexico City, 118–119, 150, 218
  Monterrey, 42
  Saltillo, 150, 404–405, 405*m*
  San Felipe de Austin, 136, 140–143, 150, 173
  Spanish colonies, 136–155
  Texas as territory and, 217
  Texas border with, 62

Mexico City, Mexico, 118–119, 150, 218

Microchips, 373

Midland, Texas, 58

Migration, 97
  of birds, 41
  of butterflies, 42
  of Mound Builders, 97

Milam, Ben, 172

Militias, 142

Milk, condensed, 142

Miller, Doris ("Dorie"), 342, 348–349

Minerals, 23

Mission Control Center, Johnson Space Center, 372

Index

Mission San José y San Miguel de Aguayo, 126–127

Mission Ysleta, 126–127

Missions, 114, 126–129, **127,** 130m

Mockingbirds, 43

Moctezuma II, 118

Moczygemba, Father Leopold, 209

Mohair, 57

Monarch butterflies, 42

Monterrey, Mexico, 42

Monuments
　Alibates Flint Quarries National Monument, 92
　Bandelier National Monument, 102
　San Jacinto Monument and Museum, **191,** 344

Moon landing, 372

Moran, Thomas, 125

Moscoso, Luis de, 122

"Mother of Texas," 85, 141

Mound Builders, 96
　Caddoan Mounds, 88, 96–97

Mountains, 12–13, 21, 61

Mountains and Basins region, 61, 61m, 72
　land and cities of, 60–63
　Native Americans of, 102–107

Movies, 332, 386

Municipal governments, 398–399

Murphy, Audie, 342

Museums
　Bob Bullock Texas State History Museum, 385
　Institute of Texan Cultures, 67
　Panhandle-Plains Historical Museum, 344
　San Jacinto Monument and Museum, 168, 191, 344
　Women's Museum, 385

Music
　"blues," 334–335
　"El Degüello," 183
　jazz, 332
　ragtime, 332
　of settlers, 129
　Texas, Our Texas, 418–419

Musical play, 58–59

Musicians
　Jefferson, Blind Lemon, 334
　Jimenez, Flaco, 385
　Jimenez, Santiago, Jr., 385
　Joplin, Scott, 332
　Mendoza, Lydia, 345
　Nelson, Willie, 385
　Perez, Selena, Quintanilla, 364, 385
　Wills, Bob, 345

NAFTA (North American Free Trade Agreement), 388–389

Nance, David Carey, 245

National Aeronautics and Space Administration (NASA), 372

National forests, 12, 66

National monuments, 92, 102

National parks, 12, 13, 61, 66, 68

National preserves, 12, 66

Native Americans
　Anasazi, 102
　Apache, 105
　Atakapan, 99
　Aztec, 88, 110, 110m, 118
　Caddo, 96–97
　canoes of, 98
　Cherokee, 99, 211
　Cheyenne, 262–263
　Chumash, 125
　Coahuiltecan, 99
　Coastal Plains region, 96–100
　Comanche, 76–77, 104, 262–264
　Concho, 105
　Inca, 108, 111
　Indian Wars, 258–265, 261m
　Jumano, 103
　Karankawa, 98, 123, 141–142
　Kickapoo, 106
　Kiowa, 105, 260, 262–263
　Kwahadi, 265
　Lipan Apache, 105
　maps, 98m
　Mayan people, 108–109
　Mescalero Apache, 105
　missions and, 126–129
　Plains Indians, 76–77, 104–105, 256–265
　Pueblo peoples, 88, 103
　reservations for, 97, 100, 104, 106, 260
　settlers and, 239, 259
　Tigua, 88, 106
　Tonkawa, 99
　villages of, 97–98, 103, 123
　in West Texas, 102–107
　Wichita, 99
　Zuñi, 120

Natural disasters, 28–30, 68

Natural gas, 370, 370m

Natural landmarks
　Cross Timbers area, 53–55
　El Capitan, 63
　Padre Island, 68
　Palo Duro Canyon, 58–59

Natural regions, 50–75

Natural resources, 20–27, **21,** 23

Natural vegetation, 37

Navarro, José, 164, 196–197, 207

Nelson, Willie, 385

New Braunfels, Texas, 208, 236

New Deal, 341

New Mexico, 102

New Spain, 118, 124

Newspapers, 142, 390–391

Ney, Elisabet, 308, 311

Nimitz, Chester, 342

Nineteenth Amendment, U.S., 328

de Niza, Fray Marcos, 120

Nomads, 98

Nonrenewable resources, 23

North America, 11
　Central Plains region, 53, 53m
　Great Plains region, 57, 57m
　Gulf Coastal Plains region, 65, 65m
　Rocky Mountain range, 61, 61m

North American Free Trade Agreement (NAFTA), 388–389

North Pole, 132

North Star, 243

Norther, 30

Notes and outlines, 414–415

Nullify, 244

Nurses, 247, 327

O

Odessa, Texas, 58
Oil, 314–319
  discoveries of, 304,
    314–315, 315*m*
  in Gulf Coastal Plains
    region, 66
  major oil and natural gas
    fields, 370*m*
  near Abilene, Texas, 55
Oil industry
  booms in, 316–317, 331,
    370–371
  changes in, 370–371
  World War II and, 343
Oil refineries, 316, 331
Oil wells, 315–317, 319
Oklahoma, 12
  cattle trails through, 276*m*
  Comanche people in, 104
  Indian Territory in, 260
The Old Chisholm Trail,
  229–231
Old Three Hundred, 142
Olmsted, Frederick Law,
  238
Oñate, Juan de, 122
Onderdonk, Julian, 2–3
Onions, 40
Open range ranching,
  267–268, 274–281, 285
Opinion, 312–313
Oral history, 354–355
Orators, 409
Orchards, 39
Outlines, 414–415

P

Padre, 127
Padre Island, 68

**Padre Island National
  Seashore,** 12, 68
Paintings, 345
  The Annual Move, 339
  Bluebonnet Field, 2–3
  *Comanche Feats of
    Horsemanship,* 104
  *The Building of the
    Railroad,* 284
  The Old Chisholm Trail,
    229–231
  *Point Lobos, Monterey,
    California,* 125
  Surrender of Santa Anna,
    161–163, 168, 192
  West Side Main Plaza,
    172
Palm trees, 37
Palmito Ranch, 247
Palo Duro Canyon, 114
  battle of, 262–263
  Coronado, Francisco
    Vásquez de and, 121
  as landmark, 59
  location of, 58
**Palo Duro Canyon State
  Park,** 58–59
Panhandle. *See* Texas
  Panhandle
**Panhandle-Plains
  Historical Museum,**
  344
Panna Maria, Texas, 209
dePaola, Tomie, 76–77
Parallels, 132
**Parker, Cynthia Ann
  "Naduah,"** 265
Parker, Laurie, 41
Parker, Quanah, 261, 264,
  265
Parks
  Big Bend National Park,
    13, 61, 61*m*
  Caddoan Mounds State
    Historical Park, 96
  Dinosaur Valley State
    Park, 54
  Guadalupe Mountains

    National Park, 61, 61*m*,
    63
  Hueco Tanks State
    Historical Park, 61*m*,
    62
  national parks, 12–13, 61,
    66, 68
  Palo Duro Canyon State
    Park, 58–59
  state parks, 54, 58–59, 62,
    96
Parties, political, 397
Peaches, 39
Pearl Harbor, 342,
  348–349
Pears, prickly, 40
Pecan trees, 40
People
  African Americans. *See*
    African Americans
  biographies of. *See*
    Biographies
  citizen heroes, 46–47,
    196–197, 272–273,
    348–349, 412–413
  Native Americans. *See*
    Native Americans
Peppers, jalapeño, 40
**Perez, Selena
  Quintanilla,** 363, 385
Petition, 174
Petroleum, 317. *See also*
  Oil; Oil industry
Pettus, J.E., 231
Pickett, Bill, 276
Pilot training, 322, 327,
  329
Piñatas, 382
**Piñeda, Álonso Alvarez
  de,** 122
Piney Woods area, 65–66
Places
  cities. *See name of city*
  maps of. *See name of
    place*
  regional. *See* Regions of
    Texas
Plains, 15

  central. *See* Central Plains
    region
  Coastal Plains region,
    64–68, 65*m*, 72,
    96–101
  Great Plains region,
    56–59, 57*m*, 72, 104
  Gulf Coastal Plains
    region, 65*m*, 66, 68, 72,
    96–101
  High Plains area, 57
  Llano Estacado, 121
  Native Americans in,
    76–77, 104–105,
    256–265
  Rolling Plains area,
    53–54, 53*m*
  South Texas Plain area,
    65–66, 65*m*
Plains Indians
  Comanche people,
    104–105, 262–265
  legend about, 76–77
  wars with, 256–264
Plantations, 243–244
Plants
  as crops. *See* Crops
  as symbols, 40
Plateau, 15, 57
Play, *Texas,* 58–59
Pneumonia, 225
Poem, 292–293
***Point Lobos, Monterey,
  California,*** 125
Point of view, 248–249
Poland, 209, 342
Political parties, 397
Polk, James K., 217
Pollution, 24
Population
  of Beaumont, Texas, 316
  of early 1900s, 307
  of Louisiana, 153
  railroad boom and, 284
  of Texas, 152–153
Port Arthur, Texas, 33, 66
Porter, Katherine Anne,
  345

Index

Ports, 67
  blockades of, 246
  Galveston, 285
  Houston, 67, 70–71
Post Oak Belt area, 65, 67
Prairies, 65, 67
Precipitation, 32, 32m, **33**
  in deserts, 61
  lack of, 24, 340
  in Mountains and Basins region, 61
  natural vegetation and, 37
  rain, 24
  snow, 30
Presidents. *See also last name of presidents*
  of Republic of Texas, 192, 194
  of United States, 397
Presidios, 128
Prickly pears, 40
Primary sources, H16, 3, 11, 27, 38, 45, 47, 69, 83, 103, 107, 110, 118, 129, 147, 151, 163, 171, 177, 178–179, 182, 183, 191, 196, 201, 206, 211, 212–213, 231, 246, 248, 251, 260, 261, 264, 265, 267, 270, 273, 279, 299, 311, 312, 329, 347, 349, 361, 372, 375, 383, 387, 389, 398, 411, 414, R22–R25
Prime meridian, 132
Prince Carl of Germany, 208
Profit, 240
Pueblo, 103
Pueblo people, 88, 103

Quan, Gordon, 398

Quanah, 261, 264, 265
Quarries, 92
Queen of the Missions, 126–127
Quinceañera, 382
Quivira, 120–121

Radio broadcasts, 332
Ragtime music, 332
Railroad boom, 283–287
Railroads, 282–289. *See also* Streetcars
  arrival of, 282
  boom of, 283–287
  cattle industry and, 256, 275, 277
  depots of, 286
  farmers and, 285
  fuel for trains on, 317
  growth of, 283–287
  map of, 283m
Rain, 24, 340
Ramadan, 383
Ramsey, Buck, 292–293
Ranching industry, 256, 266–281, 268m, 276
  cattle drives of, 274–281, 285
  cowboys and, 145
  in Fort Worth, Texas, 54–55
  in Gulf Coastal Plains region, 66
  meatpacking industry and, 285, 308
  in Piney Woods area, 66
  railroads and, 285
  stockyards of, 286
Ranchos. *See* Ranching industry
Rayburn, Samuel Taliaferro, 341, 347

Reconstruction era, 252
Recycling, 25
Red Cross, 327
Red River War, 262–263
Reference sources, 94–95
Region, 53
Regions of Texas
  central. *See* Central Plains
  Coastal Plains, 64–68, 65m, 72, 96–101
  Eastern Texas, 32, 33, 37, 41, 100
  Great Plains, 56–59, 57m, 72, 104
  Gulf Coastal Plains, 65m, 66–68, 72, 96–101
  Mountains and Basins, 60–63, 61m, 72, 102–107
  natural, 50–75
  Panhandle. *See* Texas Panhandle
  South Texas, 65–66, 65m, 256, 266–267
  West Texas, 37, 102–107, 277
Religious settlements, 126–130
"Remember Goliad!", 189, 191
"Remember the Alamo!", 184, 191
Renewable resources, 22
Reptiles, 41, 43–44
Republic, 193
Republic of Texas, 168–201
  capital of, 195
  challenges to, 194
  end of, 205–206
  map of, 205m
  presidents of, 194
Reservations, 97, 260
  Alabama-Coushatta Reservation, 100
  of Caddo people, 97

  of Comanche people, 104
  Indian Territory, 104, 260
  of Kickapoo and Tigua people, 106
Reservoirs, 24
Resolution for statehood, 206
Resources, 21
  of Central Plains region, 54
  of Great Plains region, 57–58
  of Gulf Coastal Plains region, 66–67
  natural, 20–27
  of Piney Woods area, 66
Responsibility, 407
Retail merchants, 58
Revolution, 139, 171
  Battle of San Jacinto, 188–191, 191m, 344
  Battle of the Alamo, 180–187, 224–225
  early battles of, 171–172
  Texas Declaration of Independence and, 167, 174
  Treaty of Velasco, 192
Ride, Sally Kristen, 5, 11
Rights, 149
  of African Americans, 252
  of citizens, 407
  equal rights, 369
  suffrage, 328
Rio Bravo. *See* Rio Grande
Rio Grande, 13, 24
  as border, 13, 13m, 62, 217
  temperature near, 32m
  vegetation near, 37
Rio Grande Valley, 38–39, 66
River Walk in San Antonio, 67
Rivers
  Brazos River, 141
  flowing into Gulf of

Mexico, 16
Red River War, 262–263
Rio Grande. *See* Rio Grande
San Antonio River, 67, 127
San Jacinto River, 191
Road maps, 350–351
Roads, 307, 331
"Roaring Twenties," 330–337, **331**
Rocky Mountains, 61, 61*m*
Rodeos, 276
Rodríguez, Cleto, 342
Rogers, Lisa Waller, 224–225
Rolling Plains area, 53–54, 53*m*
Roman Catholic Church, 117, 127
missions of, 126–130
Roosevelt, Franklin D., 341
Rose, Moses, 183
Roses, 39
Roundups, 268–**269**
Runaway Scrape, 189
Rural life, 307, 331
Ryan, Nolan, 384

Sabine Pass, 246
Saltillo, Mexico, 150, 404–405, 405*m*
San Angelo, Texas, 256, 275
San Antonio, Texas, 66–67, 114
battle at, 172
Battle of the Alamo, 180–187, 224–225
defeat of Mexicans at,

167
Fiesta San Antonio, 383
mission at, 126–127
pilot training in, 322, 327
River Walk in, 67
Texas Folklife Festival in, 366, 380–381
San Antonio River, 67, 127
San Diego Bay, California, 125
San Felipe de Austin. *See* Austin Colony
San Jacinto, Texas, 188–195, 344
San Jacinto Monument and Museum, 191, 344
San Jacinto River, 191
San José Mission, 126–127
Santa Anna, Antonio López de, 150, 173
capture of, 192
Mexican defeats and, 167
San Antonio and, 173–174, 181
The Surrender of Santa Anna, 161–163, 192
Satanta, 260
Sawmills, 308
Sawyer, Frances, 26
Scale on maps, 288–289
School districts, 399
Schools
for African Americans, 252
districts, 399
in Terlingua, Texas, 62
Scott, Winfield, 218
Scouts, 190, 218
Sculpture, 311
Search engine, 336
Sea turtles, 46–47
Sea Turtles, Inc., 47
Secede, 245
Secession from United States, 244–245

Secondary sources, 178–179
Sedalia, Missouri, 275
Segregation, 369
Seguín, Erasmo, 144, 177
Seguín, Juan, 144, 165, 172, 177, 180
Senate of Texas, 400, 402
Sequence, 234–235
Service industries, 371
Settlements
Austin Colony, 136, 140–143, 140*m*, 150, 173
ethnic, 208–209
missions, 126–130, 130*m*
Spanish, 114, 126–131, 140
Settlers, 129, 239. *See also* Colonies
Anglo American, 140
Native Americans and, 239, 258–265, 261*m*
Spanish, 114, 126–131
Seven Cities of Cíbola, 119, 123–124
Severe weather
droughts, 24, 340
storms, 28–30, 68
Sharecroppers, 252
Shipping. *See* Ports; Railroads
Shrimp boats, 66
Sideoats grama, 40
Siege, 181
Skirmish, 217
Slavery
annexation of Texas and, 205
Civil War and, 237, 242–253, 246*m*
in colonies, 149
Emancipation Proclamation, 251
Texas Constitution and, 175
Slaves, 110
immigration of, 239

on plantations, 243–244
Slovak immigrants, 209
Smith, Erastus "Deaf," 190
Smith, Henry, 173
Smithwick, Noah, 189, 206
Snow, 30
Soil, 22
Solar energy, 23
Solis, Father, 129
Sombreros, 145
Songs, state song, 418–419
Sorghum, 54
Sources
primary and secondary, 178–179
reference sources, using, 94–95
South America, 111
Incan people in, 110*m*, 111
South Carolina, 245
South Padre Island, 46–47
South Pole, 132
South Texas, 256, 267
South Texas Plain area, 65–66
Space industry, 372–373
Spain
colonial government of, 138–155
explorers from, 114–125
land grants from, 140
Mexican independence from, 139
settlers from, 114, 126–131
Texan heritage from, 131
Spanish explorers, 114–125
Coronado, Francisco Vásquez de, 120–121, 124–125
routes of, 115*m*, 117*m*, 121*m*

Index

Seven Cities of Cíbola and, 120–121, 124
Spanish heritage, 131
Spanish language, 131, 149, 276
Special district government, 399
Spindletop oil well, 304, 315–316
Sports, 384
Springs, 16–17
Stagecoaches, 238
Stampedes, 275
State constitution. *See* Texas Constitution
State Fair, 240
State government, 400–402, 408. *See also* Governor
State parks
Caddoan Mounds State Historical Park, 96
Dinosaur Valley State Park, 54
Hueco Tanks State Historical Park, 61*m*, 62
Palo Duro Canyon State Park, 58–59
State symbols
animals, 41–43
plants, 40
state song, 418–419
Statehood, 194, 202–223, 203*m*
Steel mills, 343
Stinson, Katherine, 327, 329
Stinson School of Flying, 327, 329
Stock market crash, 339
Stocks, 339
Stockyards, 286
Stories
Angel of the Alamo, 224–225
The Legend of the Bluebonnet, 76–77

Storms, 28–30, 68
Streams, 16
Streetcars, 307
Suffrage, 328
Sugar industry, 285
Summarizing and reading social studies, 302–303
Supreme Court of Texas, 401
The Surrender of Santa Anna, 161–163, 168, 192
Survivors of Battle of the Alamo, 183
Swoopes, Sheryl, 384
Symbols. *See* State symbols

Taniguchi, Isamu, 4, 38, 45
Tariff, 388
Tax, 193
Taylor, Claudia Alta, 5, 26–27
Taylor, Zachary, 217
Technology, 371–374, **373**
Tejanos and Tejanas, 144. *See also* Ranching industry
León, Martin de, 144
León, Patricia de la Garza de, 144
Navarro, José, 164, 196–197
Seguín, Erasmo, 144, 177
Seguín, Juan, 144, 165, 172, 177, 180
Telegraph and Texas Register, 142
Telephones, 307
Temperature, 32, 37
Temporary government,

176
Tenochtitlan, 88, 110, 110*m*, 118
Tepees, 104
Terlingua, Texas, 62
Texas
cities of. *See name of city*
Congress, 193
Constitution. *See* Texas Constitution
Declaration of Independence, 167, 174, 344
future of, 410
government of, 193, 394–417
governor of. *See* Governor
history of. *See* History of Texas
immigrants in. *See* Immigrants
Independence Day, 167, 174, 344, 383
modern times in, 366–393, 367*m*
regions of. *See* Regions of Texas
Republic of, 168–201
statehood of, 194, 202–223, 203*m*
Supreme Court of, 401
Texas (play), 58–59
Texas, Our Texas, 418–419
Texas Alphabet, 41
Texas Book Festival, 383
Texas Constitution
of 1836, 175, 193
of 1845, 207
of 1876, 253
branches of government and, 400–401
Texas (diary of Mary A. Holley), 156–157
Texas Folklife Festival, 366, 380–381
Texas frontier, 229–295, **239**

"Texas Gold." *See* Oil
Texas Hill Country, 39, 57
Texas Independence Day, 167, 174, 344, 383
Texas League of Women Voters, 328
Texas Medal of Arts Awards, 69, 385
Texas Medical Center, 67
Texas Panhandle, 8, 14
archaeology of, 92
climate of, 31
dust storms in, 340
The Great Depression in, 322, 339
High Plains area of, 57
historical museum of, 344
landmark of. *See* Palo Duro Canyon
Texas Rangers, 218
Texas red grapefruit, 40
Texas Southern University, 5
Texas State Fair, 240
Texas sweet onion, 40
Texas Tech University, 58
Thanksgiving Day, 382
Thigpen, Gwen, 224–225
Thinking skills, 248–249, 312–313
Threatened species, 43–44
Tigua people, 88, 106
Tikal, 108–109
Time lines, 186–187
Time zones, 62, **378**–379
Tonkawa people, 99
Tornadoes, 30
Tower, John, 409
Townball, 354–355
Towns and villages, 128–129, 398–399
colonies. *See* Colonies
early settlements. *See* Settlements
local governments of, 398–399

Native American, 97–98, 103, 123
Seven Cities of Cíbola, 119–120, 123–124
villas, 128–129
Trade, 11
by Comanche people, 104
Dallas and, 67
by Jumano people, 103
retail and wholesale, 58
by settlers, 240
Trade goods, 92–93
Trading post, 67
Traditions, 382–383
Trailherders, 275, 276*m*
Train stations, 286
Trains. *See* Railroads
Transportation
by airplane, 371
by automobile, 307, 309, 330, 331
to colonies, 142
frontier and, 238, 240–241
by horse, 240
by rail. *See* Railroads
by road, 307, 331
by stagecoach, 238
by streetcar, 307
by trolley, 307
Transportation industry, 371
Travel. *See* Transportation
Travis, William B., 182
Travois, 104
Treaties, 192, 219, 260
Treaty of Guadalupe Hidalgo, 219
Treaty of Velasco, 192
Trees, 22, 37–40
Trevino, Lee, 384
Tribute, 110
Trolleys, 307
Tropical storms, 28, 68
Troutman, Joanna, 193
"Turtle Lady," 4, 46–47
Turtles, sea, 46–47

Tyler, Texas, 39

Underground water, 16–17, 24
Union states, 237*m*, 245
United States
Army of, 259, 262–263
Civil War between, 237, 242–253, **245,** 245*m,* 246*m*
government of, 403, 409
Mexican War, 202–203, 216–221
Nineteenth Amendment of, 328
Urban life, 307–308, 331
Urrea, General, 189
U.S. Army, 259, 262–263

Vance, W. Silas, 354–355
Vancouver, British Columbia, 70–71, 71*m*
Vaqueros, 145, 181, 256, 276. *See also* Cowboys
Vegetation, 37–40. *See also* Crops
Velasco, Treaty of, 192
Veto, 400
Victoria, Texas, 144
Villages. *See* Towns and villages
Villanueva, Andrea Castañón, 224–225
Villas, 128–129
Vines, 37
Volunteers, 407

Voting
elections, 396–397, 408
Republic of Texas, 207
right and responsibility for, 407
rules governing, 407
suffrage, 328

Wars
Civil War, 237, 242–253, **245,** 245*m,* 246*m*
Indian Wars, 258–265, 261*m*
Mexican War, 202–203, 216–221
World War I, 322, 326–327, 326*m*
World War II, 342–343, 348–349
Washington, D.C., 403, 409
Washington-on-the-Brazos, Texas, 168, 174–176, 206
Water. *See also* Precipitation; Waterways
irrigation, 39, 57, 66, 103
as natural resource, 24
sources of, 16–17, 284
as transportation routes, 16
Water supply
for cattle, 277–278
for steam locomotives, 284
Waterways, 16 *See also name of waterway*
Weather, 8, 24, 28–35, **29,** 68
precipitation. *See* Precipitation
severe weather, 28–30, 68

Wells
natural gas, 370
oil, 315–317, 319
water, 284
West Texas
climate in, 37
Great Plains region, 56–59, 72, 104
Mountains and Basins region, 60–63, 72, 102
Native Americans in, 76–77, 102, 104, 256–265
open range ranching in, 275
Western Hemisphere, 11
early civilizations of, 108–111
Spanish explorers in, 117
Wholesale merchants, 58
Wichita people, 99
Wildflowers
bluebonnets, 2–3, 40, 76–77
Johnson, Lady Bird and, 26–27
Wildlife, 41–44
endangered turtles, 46–47
Goodnight, Molly and, 272–273
Native Americans and, 104, 260–261
Wildlife refuges, 44
Williamson, Clara, 229–231, 284
Wills, Bob, 345
Wilson, Woodrow, 326
Wind, 29–30, 32, 68
Windmills, 277–278
Winter, 30–31
Women
museum honoring, 385
role during wars, 327, 343
suffrage for, 328
Women's Museum, 385
World War I, 322, 326–327, 326*m*

Index

World War II, 342–343, 348–349

Wright, Gladys Yoakum, 418–419

Ysleta, Texas, 88, 106, 127

Yucca, 37

Zavala, Lorenzo de , 85, 144, 176

Zilker Park, 45

Zoos, 44

Zuñi people, 120

Credits

Text Dorling Kindersley (DK) is an international publishing company specializing in the creation of high quality reference content for books, CD-ROMs, online and video. The hallmark of DK content is its unique combination of educational value and strong visual style. This combination allows DK to deliver appealing, accessible and engaging educational content that delights children, parents and teachers around the world. Scott Foresman is delighted to have been able to use selected extracts of DK content within this Social Studies program.

34–35 from *Hurricane & Tornado* by Jack Challoner. Copyright ©2000 by Dorling Kindersley Limited.
280–281 from *Cowboy* by David H. Murdoch. Copyright ©1993 by Dorling Kindersley Limited.
310 from *Invention* by Lionel Bender. Copyright ©1991 by Dorling Kindersley Limited.
41 From *Texas Alphabet* by Laurie Parker. Copyright ©2000 by Quail Ridge Press. Reprinted by permission of Quail Ridge Press.
76–77 From *The Legend of the Bluebonnet* by Tomie dePaola. Copyright ©1983 by Tomie dePaola. Used by permission of G. P. Putnam's Sons, an imprint of Penguin Putnam Books for Young Readers, a division of Penguin Putnam, Inc.
224–225 From *Angel of the Alamo* by Lisa Waller Rogers. Copyright ©2000 Lisa Waller Rogers. Reprinted by permission of W. B. Benson & Company, Inc.
414 "A Cowboy Poet" and "Volunteering the Texas Way" from *Texas Traditions* by Robyn Montana Turner. Reprinted by permission of the author.
293 "Anthem" and "Seven" from *And As I Rode Out in the Morning* by Buck Ramsey. Copyright ©1993 Texas Tech University Press. Reprinted with permission.
156–157 From *Diary of Mary Austin Holly: 1835–1838* by Mary Austin Holly. Reprinted by permission of The Center for American History.
390 Bob Bullock Texas State History Museum "Making History" by Dick Stanley from *Austin American Statesman.* Reprinted by permission.
From *Texas Boys in Gray* by Evault Boswell. Copyright ©2000 Evault Boswell. Reprinted by permission.
340 Lyrics from *Dust Bowl Refugee,* words and music by Woody Guthrie, TRO– Copyright ©1960 (Renewed), 1963 (Renewed) Ludlow Music, Inc., New York, NY. Used by permission.
178 From "The Diary of Col. William Fairfax Gray" from *Virginia to Texas, 1835–36* by Col. William Fairfax Gray. Reprinted with permission.
419 Song "Texas, Our Texas," music by William J. Marsh, lyrics by Gladys Yoakum Wright & William J. Marsh. Reprinted by permission.
315 From "Pattillo Higgins Suffered Years of Disappointments Before Spindle Top Strike" by Pattillo Higgins. *Beaumont Enterprise,* 1941. Reprinted by permission.

Maps Mapquest.com, Inc.

Illustrations 14 Mike Krone; 15 David Griffin; 16 Carla Kiwior; 22 John Sandford; 42, 80 Holly Cooper; 70, 71 Gary Antonelli; 84, 124, 325 Robert Gunn; 85, 146, 348 John Wilson; 88, 89, 114, 115, 136, 137, 168, 169, 194, 202, 203, 206, 366, 367, 394, 395 Neal Armstrong; 121 Derek Grinnell; 165, 175 Charles Pyle; 176, 222 Jeff Grunewald; 177 Ralph Canaday; 183 Dan Bridy; 193 Richard Stergulz; 196 Guy Porfirio; 212, 213 Troy Howell; 213 Yoshi Miyake; 222 Bruce Marshall 233, 277 Domenick D'Andrea; 243 Roberta Polfus; 274 Peter Siu; 285, 382 Elizabeth Wolf; 311, 329 Linda Holt Ayriss; 312 Maryjo Koch; 319 Susan J. Carlson; 345 Carlotta A. Tormey; 398 Kevin Sprouls; 408 Paul Perreault

Photographs Every effort has been made to secure permission and provide appropriate credit for photographic material. The publisher deeply regrets any omission and pledges to correct errors called to their attention in subsequent editions.

Unless otherwise acknowledged, all photographs are the property of Scott Foresman, a division of Pearson Education.

Front Matter: iii Courtesy of the Witte Museum, San Antonio, Texas; iv David Muench/Corbis; vi Texas State Library & Archives Commission/Texas State Library, Austin; vii The Roland P. Murdock Collection, Wichita Art Museum, Wichita, KS; ix D. Boone/Corbis; x (T)

Credits

Earth Imaging/Stone, (B) John Boykin/Corbis; xi Bob Daemmrich/Daemmrich Photography; xiii David Muench/David Muench Photography, Inc; H4 (TC) Jeff Cadge/Image Bank, (BL) Jeff Greenberg/Index Stock Imagery, (TL) Chris Sheridan, (TR) David Young-Wolff/PhotoEdit, (BC) Jeff Greenberg/Unicorn Stock Photos, (BR) Peter Cade/Stone; H5 (L) Bill Aron/PhotoEdit, (R) Stephen Wilkes/Image Bank; H6 (R, L, Bkgd) David Muench/David Muench Photography, Inc; H7 (L) F.W. Biddenstadt/F.W. Biddenstadt, (R) David Muench/Stone ; H8 Earth Imaging/Stone; H17 ©David Young-Wolff/Stone. **Unit 1:** 1 Courtesy of the Witte Museum, San Antonio, Texas; 2 Courtesy of the Witte Museum, San Antonio, Texas; 4 (R) Texas Department of Transportation, (L) The Granger Collection, New York, (CL) PPC, CN02496 The University of Texas at Austin/Center for American History, (CR) The UT Institute of Texan Cultures at San Antonio, No. 85-915; 5 (C) Earlie Hudnall, (R) NASA, (L) Frank Wolfe; 7 Photo courtesy Texas Parks and Wildlife © 2002; 8 (TC) J. Griffis Smith, (T) Will van Overbeek, (BC) Laurence Parent, (B) Texas Department of Transportation; 10 Corbis; 11 NASA; 12 (BL, L) Texas Department of Transportation/RMT, (C) Laurence Parent; 13 Laurence Parent; 17 Will van Overbeek; 21 Texas Department of Transportation; 22 (Bkgd) Laurence Parent, (Inset) PhotoDisc; 23 Laurence Parent; 24 TDOT; 25 (CR) Michael Newman/PhotoEdit, (B) PhotoDisc; 27 (Inset, CL) Frank Wolfe, (Bkgd) David Muench Photography, Inc, ; 28 Reuters NewMedia Inc/Corbis; 29 Corbis-Bettmann; 30 Warren Faidley/Weatherstock; 31 Laurence Parent; 33 PhotoDisc; 34 (BL) J. C. Allen and Son/FLPA-Images of Nature, (CR) NRC/FLPA-Images of Nature; 35 © Gene E. Moore; 36 Jeanne Payne; 37 (B) Laurence Parent, (T) Texas Department of Transportation; 38 (TR) Texas Department of Transportation, (BR) PhotoDisc, (BL) NioGraphics/Pun Nio; 39 (TL) Texas Department of Transportation, (BR) Bill Ross/Corbis, (CR) NioGraphics/Pun Nio; 40 (TL) Texas Department of Transportation, (TCR) Texas Pecan Growers Association, (BL) NioGraphics/Pun Nio; 40 (TCR) Texas Department of Transportation, (C, BR) NioGraphics/Pun Nio, (CL) Burke/Triolo Productions/FoodPix, (TR) David Muench Photography, Inc; 42 PhotoDisc; 43 (BL) Merlin D. Tuttle/Bat Conservation International, (CL) John Boykin/Corbis, (T, C, BR) Texas Department of Transportation; 44 PhotoDisc; 45 (BR) The UT Institute of Texan Cultures at San Antonio, No. 85-915, (Bkgd) NioGraphics/Pun Nio, (L) Peter Hampton; 46 (T) Texas Department of Transportation, (B) Victoria McCormick/Animals Animals/Earth Scenes; 47 K. Neely/U.S. Geological Survey; 48 Texas Department of Transportation/RMT; 50 (T) Texas Department of Transportation, (BC) Joel Salcido 52 PhotoDisc; 54 (BL) Laurence Parent, (C) Texas Department of Transportation (BR, R) Photo courtesy Texas Parks and Wildlife © 2002; 55 Texas Department of Transportation; 56 Laurence Parent; 57 Robert De Gugliemo/Photo Researchers, Inc.; 58 Texas Department of Transportation; 59 Laurence Parent; 60 David Muench Photography, Inc; 62 (B) Joel Salcido, (T) Laurence Parent; 63 David Muench Photography, Inc; 64 David Muench Photography, Inc; 66 Texas Department of Transportation; 67 Texas Department of Transportation; 69 (CL) Photograph by Bob Straus/Medal designed by Brian Mikeska/Texas Cultural Trust, (R) Earlie Hudnall, (Bkgd) Randy Faris/Corbis; 70 David R. Frazier/Photo Researchers, Inc.; 71 Phylis Picardi/Index Stock Imagery; 74 Earlie Hudnall. **Unit 2:** 81 David Muench/Corbis; 82 David Muench/Corbis; 83 Panhandle-Plains Historical Museum, Research Center, Canyon, Texas; 84 The Granger Collection, New York; 85 (R) The Granger Collection, New York, (CR) From the Collections of the Fort Bend Museum Association, Richmond, Texas; 87 David Muench/Corbis; 88 (BC) Bill Wright Photography, (TC) Randy Mallory, (B) The Granger Collection, New York; 90 (B) Chuck Place/Chuck Place Photography; 92 (T) Alibates National Monument, (B, T) Danny Lehman/Corbis; 97 Randy Mallory; 99 (T) Marilyn "Angel" Wynn/Nativestock, (B) Richard A. Cooke/Corbis; 100 Randy Mallory; 101 Smithsonian Institution; 102 The Lone Art Museum, The University of Miami/Superstock/SuperStock; 103 © John Running; 104 "Comanche Feats of Horsemanship" by George Catlin, painted 1834–1835, Accession Number: 1985.66.487 _za4749a8d0, Oil on fabric Dimensions 24 x 29 in. (cm. 61.0 x 73.7), Gift of Mrs. Joseph Harrison, Jr./Smithsonian Institution; 105 (T) The Lone Art Museum, The University of Miami/Superstock/SuperStock, (B) Marilyn "Angel" Wynn/Nativestock; 106 Bill Wright Photography; 107 Tom Bean; 109 David Hiser/Stone; 111 SuperStock; 112 (B) David Hiser/Stone, (C) Marilyn "Angel" Wynn/Nativestock; 114 (TC) Buddy Mays/Corbis, (B) SuperStock, (T) Laurence Parent/Laurence Parent; 116 The Granger Collection, New York; 119 Texas State Library, Austin; 120

Buddy Mays/Corbis; 123 © Photo, Texas Historical Commission; 124 (Bkgd) Laurence Parent, (CL) Archivo Iconographico/Corbis; 125 (L) White House, Washington DC, USA//Bridgeman Art Library International Ltd., (R) Chuck Place Photography; 127 (BL) SuperStock, (TR) Robert & Linda Mitchell; 129 © John Running; 131 SuperStock; 134 (BL) The Granger Collection, New York, (TL) Texas State Library, Austin; 136 (T) San Felipe de Austin Historical Association, (B) Phillip de Bay/Corbis; 138 (L) The Granger Collection, New York, (R) PhotoDisc; 139 Bob Daemmrich/Daemmrich Photography; 140 The Granger Collection, New York; 141 (TR) From the Collections of the Fort Bend Museum Association, Richmond, Texas, (TCR) PhotoDisc; 142 (T, C) Daughters of the Republic of Texas at the Alamo, CN95.83, (B) Bettman/Corbis; 143 San Felipe de Austin Historical Association; 145 Witte Museum/Courtesy of the Witte Museum, San Antonio, Texas; 147 AP/Wide World; 149 (BR) Austin papers, 1676, Certificate of Citizenship, CN 07162, The University of Texas at Austin/Center for American History; 151 (Bkgd) Bob Daemmrich/Daemmrich Photography, (R) E. Beggs/Texas State Preservation Board, Austin Texas, (L) Richard Cummings/Corbis; 155 E. Beggs/Texas State Preservation Board, Austin Texas. **Unit 3:** 161 Texas State Library & Archives Commission/Texas State Library, Austin; 162 Texas State Library & Archives Commission/Texas State Library, Austin; 164 (L, CL, R) The Granger Collection, New York, (CR) The UT Institute of Texan Cultures at San Antonio, No. 68-465. Courtesy of Navarro Elementary School, San Antonio, Texas; 165 (L) The Granger Collection, New York, (CR) Seguin Family Historical Society, (R) The UT Institute of Texan Cultures at San Antonio, No. 74-266. Courtesy of Dudley G. Wooten, A Comprehensive History of Texas. Dallas, Wm. G. Scarff; 167 "First Shot"mural / Gonzales City Hall/The Mosaic Mural commemorates the firing of the "First Shot of the Texas Revolution,"Texas, Oct. 2nd 1835 Bert Rees, Austin, Texas; 168 (T) The UT Institute of Texan Cultures at San Antonio, No. 72-3492. Courtesy of Texas State Library, Archives Division, (B) Texas State Library & Archives Commission/Texas State Library, Austin, Sandy Felsenthal/Corbis; 170 Bruce Marshall; 172 The UT Institute of Texan Cultures at San Antonio, No. 73-94. Courtesy of Mrs. William Ochse; 173 (L) North Wind Pictures/North Wind Picture Archives, (R) Courtesy Texas Military Forces Museum; 174 (B) The UT Institute of Texan Cultures at San Antonio, No. 68-218. Courtesy of Texas State Library, Archives, (TR) The UT Institute of Texan Cultures at San Antonio, No. 72-3492. Courtesy of Texas State Library, Archives Division; 177 © Dorling Kindersley; 181 (T) The Granger Collection, New York, (C) Sandy Felsenthal/Corbis, (B) SuperStock; 184 Sandy Felsenthal/Corbis; 185 Deborah Cannon/Austin American-Statesman; 186 The Granger Collection, New York; 187 (B) The UT Institute of Texan Cultures at San Antonio, No. 68-216. Courtesy of Texas State Library, Austin, (C) The UT Institute of Texan Cultures at San Antonio, No. 68-217. Courtesy of Texas State Library, Austin, (T) The UT Institute of Texan Cultures at San Antonio, No. 68-2558. Courtesy of Texas State Library, Austin; 188 Craig Aurness/Corbis; 190 Texas State Library, Austin; 191 Texas State Library, Austin; 192 Texas State Library & Archives Commission/Texas State Library, Austin; 195 The Granger Collection, New York; 197 Jeff Cadge/Image Bank; 198 (L) Hulton Archive/Hulton/Archive, (R) The Granger Collection, New York; 199 (L) Caroline Penn/Corbis, (BR) Tiziana and Gianni Baldizzone/Corbis, (Bkgd) A. Littlejohn/H. Armstrong Roberts, (CR) A. Littlejohn/H. Armstrong Roberts; 200 The Granger Collection, New York; 202 Hulton/Archive; 204 The Granger Collection, New York; 205 W. Crutchfield Williams/Crutchfield's Currency; 207 The UT Institute of Texan Cultures at San Antonio, No. 74-508. Courtesy of Texas State Library, Archives Division; 208 (R) The UT Institute of Texan Cultures at San Antonio, No. 85-376. Courtesy of Mr. and Mrs. E.W. Ahlrich, Lake Jackson, Texas, (BL) The UT Institute of Texan Cultures at San Antonio, No. 68-421. Courtesy of Barker History Center, Sid Richardson Hall; 210 Corbis-Bettmann; 211 (R) The Granger Collection, New York, (L) Joe McDonald/Corbis, (Bkgd) Sam Houston Memorial Museum/Sam Houston Memorial Museum; 213 Corbis; 214 Smithsonian Institution; 215 Smithsonian Institution; 218 (T) Hulton/Archive, (B) Bettmann/Corbis-Bettmann; 222 Corbis-Bettmann. **Unit 4:** 229 The Roland P. Murdock Collection, Wichita Art Museum, Wichita, KS; 230 The Roland P. Murdock Collection, Wichita Art Museum, Wichita, KS; 232 (CR) Western History Collections, University of Oklahoma Library, (R, L) The Granger Collection, New York; 233 (L) Western History Collections, University of Oklahoma Library, (CL) The Granger Collection, New York, (R) The Granger Collection, New York; 235 The Roland P. Murdock Collection, Wichita Art Museum, Wichita, KS; 236 Bettmann/Corbis; 238 Grabill; J.C.H./Corbis; 239

Credits